SUFFERING
AND EVIL IN EARLY
CHRISTIAN THOUGHT

HOLY CROSS STUDIES
IN PATRISTIC THEOLOGY AND HISTORY

Previously published in the series

Wealth and Poverty in Early Church and Society
edited by Susan R. Holman

Apocalyptic Thought in Early Christianity
edited by Robert J. Daly, SJ

The Holy Trinity in the Life of the Church
edited by Khaled Anatolios

SUFFERING
AND EVIL IN EARLY
CHRISTIAN THOUGHT

EDITED BY

NONNA VERNA HARRISON
AND DAVID G. HUNTER

Baker Academic
a division of Baker Publishing Group
Grand Rapids, Michigan

ORTHODOX
PRESS

© 2016 by The Stephen and Catherine Pappas Patristic Institute of Holy Cross Greek Orthodox
School of Theology

Published by Baker Academic
a division of Baker Publishing Group
P.O. Box 6287, Grand Rapids, MI 49516-6287
www.bakeracademic.com

Printed in the United States of America

Library of Congress Cataloging-in-Publication Data
Names: Harrison, Verna E. F., editor.
Title: Suffering and evil in early Christian thought / edited by Nonna Verna Harrison and David G.
    Hunter.
Description: Grand Rapids : Baker Academic, 2016. | Series: Holy Cross studies in patristic
    theology and history | Includes bibliographical references and index.
Identifiers: LCCN 2016011173 | ISBN 9780801030789 (pbk.)
Subjects: LCSH: Suffering—Religious aspects—Christianity—History of doctrines—Early church,
    ca. 30–600. | Good and evil—Religious Aspects—Christianity—History of doctrines—Early
    church, ca. 30–600.
Classification: LCC BR195.S93 S84 2016 | DDC 231/.809—dc23
LC record available at https://lccn.loc.gov/2016011173

In keeping with biblical principles of
creation stewardship, Baker Publishing Group advocates the responsible
use of our natural resources. As a
member of the Green Press Initiative, our company uses recycled
paper when possible. The text paper
of this book is composed in part of
post-consumer waste.

16 17 18 19 20 21 22   7 6 5 4 3 2 1

CONTENTS

PREFACE

DAVID G. HUNTER

This volume of essays has its distant origins in the Third Annual Conference of the Pappas Patristic Institute, "Evil and Suffering in the Patristic Period," held at Holy Cross Greek Orthodox School of Theology, October 12–14, 2006. Owing to a variety of factors, its publication has been delayed, but this delay has enabled the editors to produce a collection that differs in many respects from the original conference presentations. All of the original six plenary lectures have been included (Anderson, Behr, Harrison, Hunter, Skedros, and Ware), although most in a considerably revised form. Of the original twenty-four shorter communications delivered at the 2006 conference, only six are present here (Finn, Gavrilyuk, Martens, Phillips, Quinn, and Walton). An effort was made to include chapters that addressed a range of patristic writers, Eastern and Western, and that would be accessible to a wide audience. Because this topic deserves a theologically nuanced treatment, the editors decided to solicit additional essays, including two that highlighted the christological contribution of patristic thought to the problem of evil and suffering (Daley, Smith).

The editors express their thanks to a number of people who have supported this project. First, thanks are owed to Dr. Bruce Beck, director of the Pappas Patristic Institute, for organizing the original conference and facilitating the participation of the contributors. We also acknowledge the assistance of the Editorial Board of the series Holy Cross Studies in Patristic Theology and History, which conducted an initial screening of the papers presented at the conference. We also thank Professor Brian Daley of the University of Notre

Dame and Professor J. Warren Smith of Duke University Divinity School for agreeing to contribute their essays to the collection. Let me also thank Nonna Verna Harrison for her essay about John Chrysostom on the man born blind, written for this volume.

We appreciate Mr. James Kinney of Baker Academic, who saw the project through the final stages of production. Most of all we express our deep gratitude to Dr. James Ernest, who departed Baker Academic for William B. Eerdmans Publishing just as this volume was going to press. James has been a stalwart supporter of the Pappas Patristic Institute conferences and has enabled the Holy Cross Studies in Patristic Theology and History to prosper. We wish him the very best in his new position.

Finally, we acknowledge the publishers who have granted permission to reprint material that has been published elsewhere: Yale University Press, for allowing us to use material from Gary Anderson's book *Sin: A History* (Yale University Press, 2009) in his chapter "*Christus Victor* in the Work of Ephrem, Narsai, and Jacob of Serug"; Eerdmans, for letting us reprint Brian Daley's chapter, "The Word and His Flesh: Human Weakness and the Identity of Jesus in Patristic Christology," which originally appeared in *Seeking the Identity of Jesus*, edited by Beverly Gaventa and Richard Hays (Eerdmans, 2008), 251–69; and *Pro Ecclesia*, which originally published J. Warren Smith's essay, "Suffering Impassibly: Christ's Passion in Cyril of Alexandria's Soteriology," *Pro Ecclesia* 11, no. 4 (Fall 2002): 463–83.

Introduction

Nonna Verna Harrison

What do we think of when we consider the end of the world? Nuclear war, robots or computers taking over the earth with humans as their slaves, a meteor strike blocking the earth's sunlight and causing living things to die, climate change gone awry, exhaustion of the earth's resources? Or perhaps the devil attacking everyone, pitting brother against brother, inspiring a ruthless dictator, and finally eradicating all human life? Whatever it is, it is probably a mega-nightmare scenario. One imagines oneself, as a mere human being alone, or even in a large family, completely overwhelmed and unable to begin to cope with the life-threatening challenges.

John W. Martens writes that Hollywood movies have repeatedly shown such scenarios on the silver screen, and they attract large audiences. I wonder what attracts people to such movies. They portray the apocalypse, but God is either absent or inactive. A few people fight against it, but evil is well organized, powerful, and relentless. Could it be that many people today can identify with the protagonists in these movies, though perhaps not consciously? Do not many experience life as an ongoing series of unjust and hurtful challenges, threats to their well-being or even their survival? They struggle to get by, and maybe they beg God for help over and over, but it seems there is no response. The struggles of our small lives are certainly not the apocalypse, but like the people in the films, we are often beset by suffering and evil and cannot find a way out of it.

If struggling people are theologically minded, they find themselves racking their brains about why it happens, why God does not help, what they might be doing wrong in their relationship with God. Or they may wonder why God allows suffering. Why doesn't God do something to stop evil actions that are hurting people? These are questions about the area of theology called theodicy. And they may be the toughest theological questions of all. To be sure, questions about the Trinity, or about how Christ can be both fully divine and fully human, encounter profound mysteries and lead us to a contemplative silence; they can be answered only a little at a time, and only in part. But the questions about God, suffering, and evil arise from a heart full of anguish. They tear at our faith in an age when faith seems weak anyway. We may wonder: What did Christians say about these questions in the early days of the church, a time of persecution and missionary expansion when faith was strong? Can the church fathers and mothers offer us any convincing answers?

The purpose of this book is to show some of the different answers that church fathers and mothers found to these kinds of questions. The chapters are written by authors with different perspectives, and they discuss different perspectives among the early Christians. So by reading them, we can approach the questions of theodicy from a variety of angles. Perhaps each one of us can find at least the beginning of an answer that will satisfy our own questioning heart.

The first two chapters are introductions to the book. Paul Gavrilyuk's essay provides a road map of the theological framework on which early orthodox Christians agreed: God did not create evil, it arose from free choices by people and fallen angels, and God will destroy evil in the end. John Martens then discusses the book of Revelation and other ancient apocalypses. Unlike cinematic nightmares, they end not with Satan destroying humankind but with God destroying evil and restoring paradise.

The rest of the book is about that long period between the beginning and the end, the time in which we presently live, beset by suffering and evil. The chapters are arranged historically. A number of them are about how Christian people responded to suffering, while others discuss how God responds to suffering in the human world he created. James Skedros examines the early martyrs and describes how the church in later generations learned from their examples. John Behr explores Irenaeus's teaching that people can learn from their own wrong choices, sufferings, and mortality so that they turn to God. Here we also see how God oversees people's educational process as they learn to serve him, so that finally death brings their sinfulness to an end: they share in the resurrection and become God's likeness. Dennis Quinn discusses Lactantius's writing to show how some in the early church saw persecutions in the "pagan" Roman Empire as caused by demons and saw Constantine as called by God to defeat those evil spirits. In Gary Anderson's essay, we see three Syrian theologians offering different explanations of how Christ gets rid of the debt people owe because of their sins. Nonna Verna Harrison then discusses how three Greek theologians had differing analyses of the causes of social injustice.

The next two chapters focus on John Chrysostom's use of Scripture to address the problem of suffering. Douglas Finn examines on how Chrysostom found strengths in Job that enabled him to endure great suffering with integrity and made him an example that others can follow, while Nonna Verna Harrison discusses the strengths Chrysostom saw in the man born blind (John 9) and commends his critique of discrimination against people with disabilities. The following two chapters turn their attention to Augustine. Regina Walton describes how two exemplary women, Gregory of Nyssa's sister Macrina and Augustine's mother Monica, each faced death and counseled their loved ones on how to handle their grief. David Hunter then examines Augustine's changing ideas about the root of sin, earlier as sensuality and later as self-centeredness that fractures human community.

The final four chapters address specific theological and christological questions related to human suffering. Eric Phillips draws on the writing of Theodore of Mopsuestia to discuss how God guides people to let go of bitterness toward those who caused their sufferings and to learn how to wish them good. According to Theodore, God trains people to let go of bitterness and choose good even when they are in hell, with the result that in the end everybody will be saved. Brian Daley's essay on the christological reflections of four Greek theologians and J. Warren Smith's essay on the soteriology of Cyril of Alexandria show how the divine Word incarnate as Jesus Christ experienced human sufferings so as to overcome them within himself through divine life and human strength; then he could share his divine life and human strength with other sufferers, enabling them to overcome along with him. In the concluding essay, Bishop Kallistos Ware offers his own perspective on how God suffers, drawing on early Christian and contemporary theologians. He says that God suffers in his love for humankind, yet he overcomes human suffering because his suffering love is active, powerful, and creative.

1

An Overview of Patristic Theodicies

Paul L. Gavrilyuk

The Problem of Evil in Antiquity

There was no shortage of solutions to the problem of evil in antiquity. Consider, for example, the wealth of insight afforded by Greek tragedy. The tragic poets locate evils variously in the will of the gods, in the ignorance of humans and their tendency to be carried away by passions, and, more frequently, in the mysterious workings of fate (*tychē*, *moira*, *atē*) and necessity (*anankē*). Even if the specific cause of one's misfortunes is obscure, it is a divine law, first announced by the father of Greek tragedy, Aeschylus, "that man must learn by suffering [*pathei mathos*]."[1] According to Aristotle, the pretended *pathos* of the tragic actors was intended to evoke an empathic *catharsis* in the spectators.[2]

The Stoics agreed with the tragic poets that bearable suffering could become a learning experience. They argued that it was pointless to regard unavoidable misfortunes as evil. They proposed that the best solution was to see all seemingly unfortunate events in the larger context of one's life. They located

---

1. Aeschylus, *Agamemnon* 177, trans. Peter Meineck, in *Oresteia* (Indianapolis: Hackett, 1998), 9. See William Chase Greene, *Moira: Fate, Good, and Evil in Greek Thought* (Cambridge, MA: Harvard University Press, 1944), 99–100.
2. Aristotle, *Poetics* 6 (1449b27).

evil in intentions that were not in accordance with reason: it was evil to inflict pain, but not to endure it.[3] The Stoic moral theory taught one how to endure ills with dignity by taking into account the bigger picture.

Plato was the first Greek philosopher to insist that evil, unless it served the purpose of remedial punishment for sin, could not be attributed to the gods. In the *Republic* he formulates the problem in the following way: "For the good things we must assume no other cause than God, but the cause of evil we must look for in other things and not in God."[4] However, Plato's answer to the question of evil's origin was far from consistent. In *Timaeus* he attributed imperfections of embodied beings to the creative agency of the lesser gods and to the intransigence of the receptacle (*hypodochē*), the world's chaotic substratum, which would come to acquire the more technical designation of matter (*hylē*).[5] In *Theaetetus* 176a, Plato hinted at the necessity of ontological dualism; he observed that it is impossible for evil to cease to exist, "for there must always be something opposed to the good."[6] He did not develop this idea but rather emphasized that the material world was beautiful, good, and ordered to the degree to which it reflected the realm of the eternal forms. For Plato, the forms imprint structure, beauty, and order into the world's matter.

Building upon Plato's vision, Plotinus placed matter at the very bottom of the hierarchy of forms, as that which was completely unbounded, measureless, and formless (*apeiron, ametron, aneideon*). It followed that matter was a "privation of the good" (*sterēsis tou agathou*) and therefore "evil in itself" (*to kakon to auto*) or "the primary evil" (*prōton kakon*).[7] However,

---

3. Anthony A. Long, "The Stoic Concept of Evil," *Philosophical Quarterly* 18 (1968): 329.

4. Plato, *Republic* 379C, in *The Collected Dialogues of Plato, Including the Letters*, ed. Edith Hamilton and Huntington Cairns (Princeton: Princeton University Press, 1982), 626; Greene, *Moira*, 298. Cf. Plato, *Timaeus* 30A.

5. Plato, *Timaeus* 40–42, 50–51. For patristic critique of the Platonic idea that some things were created by lesser gods, see Augustine, *City of God* 12.25, who also denies that angels had any part in creation. According to Philo, *De confusione linguarum* 35.179, some imperfections in creation are precisely attributable to angelic participation in the original creation. See Harry A. Wolfson, *Philo*, LCL (Cambridge, MA: Harvard University Press, 1948), 1:273. For an illuminating discussion of Platonic theodicy, see Peter Harrison, "Laws of Nature, Moral Order, and the Intelligibility of the Cosmos," in *The Astronomy Revolution: 400 Years of Exploring the Cosmos*, edited by Donald G. York, Owen Gingerich, and Shuang-Nan Zhang (Boca Raton, FL: CRC, 2011), 375–386. For a review of different competing theories of Plato's theodicy, see Harold Cherniss, "The Sources of Evil according to Plato," *Proceedings of the American Philosophical Society* 98 (1954): 23–30.

6. *Plato: Complete Works*, ed. John M. Cooper and D. S. Hutchinson (Indianapolis: Hackett, 1997), 195. This passage is discussed in Plotinus, *Enneads* 1.8.6. On matter's preexistence, see *Enneads* 2.4.5.

7. Plotinus, *Enneads* 1.8.4; cf. a similar point attributed to the Platonizing Celsus in Origen, *Against Celsus* 4.66.

against the gnostics, Plotinus argued that the material world was a beautiful, good, yet imperfect reflection of the intellectual universe of the forms.[8]
Some critics observe that Plotinus was not able to fully account for the tension in his system between the evil of matter and the beauty of the material
cosmos.[9]

Early Christian Theodicies

In early Christianity, no one theodicy was ever adopted as binding upon
the church as a whole. In the history of Christian doctrine, more generally,
theodicy has never reached the level of dogmatic precision attained by the
doctrines of the Trinity and the incarnation. Nevertheless, a tangible degree
of unity has been achieved, in part by holding to theistic ontology, and in
part by excluding the rival proposals of Marcion, the gnostic teachers, Mani,
and most philosophers. For example, the shared commitment to monotheism
ruled out all forms of strong ontological dualism. The benevolent and almighty
Creator tolerated no eternal opposite, be it another divine agent, or matter, or
the realm of darkness and chaos. God's goodness and power were not limited
by matter but rather worked through it. The cosmological speculations of
the gnostics received no less vigorous criticism, conveyed by declarations that
the world was not an afterthought of an incompetent committee of gods or a
result of Sophia's fall from the divine realm. Irenaeus, Tertullian, and Origen,
among others, concurred with Neoplatonists such as Plotinus that God was
not the author of evil.[10] However, unlike the Neoplatonists, the church fathers
refused to locate the origin of evil in matter.[11]

Nourished by the biblical account of creation, the orthodox Christians
rejected ontological dualism and held that the omnipotent and benevolent God
created everything good. It followed that evil could not be among the things
originally created; in this sense, it was nonbeing. Following the Neoplatonists,
Christian theologians explained that evil was a privation (*sterēsis*) of the good

8. Plotinus, *Enneads* 1.8.3–5. See Denis O'Brien, *Théodicée plotinienne, théodicée gnostique* (Leiden: Brill, 1993).

9. See Edward B. Costello, "Is Plotinus Inconsistent on the Nature of Evil?," *International Philosophical Quarterly* 7 (1967): 483–97; John M. Rist, "Plotinus on Matter and Evil," *Phronesis* 6 (1961): 154–66.

10. Origen, *Against Celsus* 6.53–55; Tertullian, *Against Marcion* 2.9; Augustine, *Free Will* 1.2; 4.10. Only a fragment of Irenaeus's letter to Florinus, titled *On the Sole Sovereignty* or *That God Is Not the Author of Evil*, survives in Eusebius, *Ecclesiastical History* 5.20.

11. Tertullian, *Against Hermogenes* 9–11; Athanasius, *Against the Pagans* 6; *The Incarnation* 2; Augustine, *Confessions* 7.5.7, trans. Henry Chadwick (Oxford: Oxford University Press, 1998), 116.

in a way similar to how darkness was the absence of light.[12] Evil was not a substance since it was parasitic upon the good and thus depended upon the good for its existence.[13] Pseudo-Dionysius, following the Neoplatonist Proclus, proposed that evil was beyond nonbeing, since evil was more than mere lack of the good, mere absence of being, in that evil was destructive of that which is good.[14] Yet without introducing this technical and potentially misleading distinction between nonbeing and "beyond nonbeing," most patristic theologians taught that evil was nonbeing in the sense of being the corruption, perversion, and destruction of the good.[15]

Within the framework of Christian theism, the belief that evil was nonbeing did not lead to the conclusion that evil was a grand illusion. On the contrary, from its very beginning Christianity was characterized by a keen sense that evil was real, powerful, and all-pervasive. Hence, the insight that evil was nonbeing was bound to provide only a partial answer. If God is not the author of evil, then who or what is? What feature of creation could be causally connected to evil without at the same time implicating God? Relatively early among patristic theologians, a broad agreement emerged that the free will of some rational creatures accounted for the actualization of evil. The Creator could not be held responsible for the free evil choices that rational creatures made, since God did not causally determine these choices.[16] However, when God chooses to permit evil, he always draws greater good out of that evil.[17] Thus God could be said to cause "external evil" in the form of physical suffering, when it serves the divine purpose of admonishing, converting, chastising, punishing, teaching, and curing those who are turned away from God.[18]

12. Plotinus, *Enneads* 2.4.5, 10; cf. Athanasius, *Against the Pagans* 7.4–5.

13. Augustine writes in *Enchiridion* 8.27: "He judged it better to bring good out of evil than not to permit any evil to exist," trans. J. F. Shaw, *The Enchiridion on Faith, Hope and Love* (Washington, DC: Regnery, 1996), 33; cf. ibid., 24.96; *Confessions* 7.12.18; Athanasius, *Against the Pagans* 4.4; 7.3; *The Incarnation* 4.5; this point is emphasized by Gillian R. Evans, *Augustine on Evil* (New York: Cambridge University Press, 2000).

14. Pseudo-Dionysius, *Divine Names* 4; Proclus, *On the Subsistence of Evils* 38.7–11, discussed in Carlos Steel, "Proclus on the Existence of Evil," *Proceedings of the Boston Area Colloquium in Ancient Philosophy* (Lanham, MD: University Press of America, 1986), 95.

15. Augustine, *The Nature of the Good* 4.

16. Augustine problematized this claim in *Free Will* 1.2.4: "We believe that everything which exists is created by one God, and yet that God is not the cause of sin. The difficulty is: if sin goes back to souls created by God, and souls go back to God, how can we avoid before long tracing sin back to God?"; trans. Dom Mark Pontifex, *St. Augustine: The Problem of Free Choice*, ACW 22 (Westminster, MD: Newman, 1955), 38.

17. Origen, *Against Celsus* 7.68, points out that God permits evil but does not order evil by his will. Cf. Lactantius, *On the Anger of God* 13; Augustine, *City of God* 1.8–29; 11.18.

18. Tertullian, *Against Marcion* 2.13–15; Origen, *Against Celsus* 6.56. See Hans Schwartz, *Evil: A Historical and Theological Perspective* (Minneapolis: Fortress, 1995), 103.

In addition to these philosophical considerations, the biblical narrative framework was indispensable for addressing the problem of evil. Salvation history, from creation to eschaton, offered the most comprehensive theodicy. Christians relied upon the creation account to support their claim that God was not the author of evil. For example, the fathers drew in part upon Genesis 3 and the story of the watchers in Genesis 6 to construct their theories of the human and angelic falls, respectively.[19] All patristic authors agreed that evil was causally connected to the misuse of free will, although their accounts of the fall differed considerably.[20] Evil resides in the inclination of the free rational agent who prefers the finite good of creatures to the infinite good of the Creator.[21]

It may be objected that while free choice could account for the existence of moral evil, the cause of natural evil was left unexplained. This challenge was met in different ways. Some fathers replied that the human choice of evil had tragic and far-reaching consequences for the rest of creation. Others argued that "natural evil" was a misnomer: strictly speaking, all evils were unnatural. Augustine proposed that such disasters as fires and hurricanes represent the working of natural forces that are inherently good but can be misdirected so as to harm humans.[22] Others speculated, drawing upon Stoic views, that natural disasters are not evil at all, because no evil intention is involved.[23] Still others deferred to the universal religious insight that natural disasters are a form of divine punishment for human disobedience. God sent natural disasters to admonish, correct, or restrain, and to mete out retribution for sin.[24] Origen more imaginatively hinted that natural disasters were a part of the demonic revolt against God.[25] On this analysis, natural evil is reducible to moral evil in its demonic form. Despite their considerable differences, these accounts of natural evil share one general point in common: the ethical categories of

19. Annette Yoshiko Reed, *Fallen Angels and the History of Judaism and Christianity: The Reception of Enochic Literature* (New York: Cambridge University Press, 2005).

20. Tertullian, *Exhortation to Chastity* 2.4–5; Augustine, *Free Will* 3.17, 48; *On True Religion* 12.23; cf. *City of God* 13.14: "Hence from the misuse of free will there started a chain of disasters: mankind is led from that original perversion, a kind of corruption at the root, right up to the disaster of the second death, which has no end," trans. Henry Bettenson, *Augustine: Concerning the City of God* (London: Penguin Books, 1984). See David Ray Griffin, "Augustine and the Denial of Genuine Evil," in *The Problem of Evil: Select Readings*, ed. Michael L. Peterson (Notre Dame, IN: University of Notre Dame Press, 1992), 197.

21. Athanasius, *Against the Pagans* 7.3–5; *The Incarnation* 15; Augustine, *Confessions* 7.18.

22. Augustine, *City of God* 11.22.

23. Plotinus, *Enneads* 1.4.4–13; 1.8; 4.4–44.

24. Lactantius, *On the Anger of God* 17.

25. Origen, *Against Celsus* 4.65. See John M. Rist, "Beyond Stoic and Platonist: A Sample of Origen's Treatment of Philosophy (*Contra Celsum* 4.62–70)," in *Platonismus und Christentum* (Münster: Aschendorff, 1983), 233–34.

moral corruption and sinfulness blend with the ontological categories of physical corruptibility, disorder, and death.

The narrative framework of salvation history offered the fathers more than just an explanation of evil's origin. Human history was presented as a series of God's redemptive acts, the climax of which was the divine incarnation. Incarnation was seen as a new creation, as God's restoration of his image and likeness in human beings, as the God-Man's victory over the powers of sin, corruption, death, and the sphere of the demonic. The fruits of this victory, abundantly available in the sacramental life of the church, would be most fully manifest in the eschaton. The hope for the resurrection of the dead and the orientation of life toward the final judgment expanded the horizon for a bigger-picture theodicy. Many ancient Christians endured persecution, torture, and martyrdom with the hope of attesting by their death to the power of Christ's resurrection. Apocalypse, despite its sobering features, also functioned as a theodicy: in the end God's justice will triumph by destroying all evil and rewarding all those who are obedient to God.

Conclusion

The common core of patristic theodicy may be somewhat schematically reduced to the following five points:

1. God is not the author of evil.
2. God prevents or permits evil and draws good out of it.
3. Ontologically evil is nonbeing: a privation, corruption, and perversion of the good.
4. The misuse of angelic and human free will is the cause of evil.
5. Salvation history provides a narrative framework that accounts for the origin, spread, and ultimate destruction of evil.

The task of contemporary theology is to combine the penetrating patristic analysis of the dynamics of moral evil with modern sensitivity to cases of horrendous evil and undeserved suffering. Such a synthesis has the potential of being deeper and more existentially compelling than any version of protest atheism. Still, even if all objections to the traditional theistic account of evil were tested and found inadequate, there is much about this problem that is bound to remain shrouded in mystery, at least on this side of the eschaton.

2

THEODICY IN APOCALYPTIC THOUGHT

From Ancient Visions to (Post)Modern Nightmares

JOHN W. MARTENS

Ancient Apocalypses

The reality of evil is assumed by ancient apocalypses, though it might come in many guises (personal, corporate, or demonic) and under many names (the devil, Satan, Mastema, Belial, or Azazel, to name some of the most common appellations). But although the reality of evil suffuses ancient apocalypses, it is not always clear that the origin of evil, or understanding the origin of evil, is essential to the prophets' understanding of God's nature or the destiny of humanity. With some notable exceptions, reflection upon the nature and purpose of evil is missing from most apocalypses. What each apocalypse stresses in a variety of ways is the limited power of evil and, in light of God's intended and coming end, evil's now-limited lifespan. Implicit in this is the great power of God to deal with evil and the goodness that defines God's nature. I want to return to this key point, but first let us explore some of the ways in which the apocalypses do discuss the origin of evil, when and if they do, and why this might not be a key consideration for apocalyptic thought.

Certainly, questions about why suffering and evil must exist were present in apocalyptic thought. *First Enoch*, cited by the canonical Letter of Jude and generally considered the earliest of all apocalypses, explains the origin of evil as arising from the improper mingling of angels, known as "the watchers," who gazed upon human women and found them delightful and desirable. These fallen angels then came to earth to take these women as their wives and in so doing revealed information about many sorts of sinful activities. Adam and Eve are mentioned in the text, as Raphael explains to Enoch: "This very thing is the tree of wisdom from which your old father and aged mother, they who are your precursors, ate and came to know wisdom; and (consequently) their eyes were opened and they realized that they were naked and (so) they were expelled from the garden" (*1 En.* 32:6). Yet this fall account is not discussed again. Attention to the spread of evil throughout humanity focuses on the discussion and the expansion of the Genesis 6:1–4 account of the sons of God who looked upon the daughters of men. *First Enoch* sees the starting point of human evil in both human action turned away from God and the acts of fallen angels who reject God's order, but the author concentrates most fully on the angelic source of sin. In both cases, however, the fallen angels and the fallen humans breach the boundaries set by God.

The human or angelic origins of sin are the two options most apocalypses consider and are largely implicit in most texts. The book of Daniel focuses largely on the human and corporate nature of evil, describing the human kingdoms that war against the righteous and the kingdom of God. Yet the origin of human sin is not discussed. Perhaps one can work backward through the text from the later apocalyptic chapters to the first six chapters and see that Daniel and his faithful friends in Babylon are living lives in tune with God when they adhere to the limits of the covenant and the law, but beyond that there is little speculation. When Israel is punished, Daniel states that it is because Israel "transgressed your law and turned aside, . . . so the curse and the oath written in the law of Moses, the servant of God, have been poured out upon us, because we have sinned against you" (Dan. 9:11). This basic Deuteronomic evaluation of sin and punishment does not take us to the origin of sin, only to its current breaches of divine law and God's response. But while this might explain Israel's situation of woe, Daniel also sees that the nations are not just acting as God's righteous arm of judgment but in addition are breaching the limits set for them. The nations will fall with the advent of God's kingdom. There is, however, little particular speculation about the nature of human sin among the nations, the gentiles, except that they war against God's righteousness. Arrogance is named as a particular sin of kings (Dan. 7:8, 11), which speaks of the presumption of usurping God's place in human affairs; yet the limits of gentile behavior are not defined, except perhaps in terms of emperor worship or emperors demanding that their subjects worship the gods. This is a strong possibility if we associate the "horn" in Daniel 7 with Antiochus IV Epiphanes. Daniel does not describe the angelic fall. The name of Satan does not appear in the text, nor does any other name of a chief demon or fallen angel. However, we might assume an angelic fall for one specific reason. In Daniel 10:13, 21 and 12:1, Michael is described as the prince of Israel, who contends against the princes of other nations—the prince of Persia is mentioned specifically—and who fights on behalf of Israel in the battle at the end of time. This points to an angelic battle and thus to an angelic fall. Yet what is theologically troubling, at least for those seeking to understand the universal nature of the fall and the origin of sin, is that Michael is basically a geopolitical warrior who fights on behalf of Israel and indeed on behalf of God, but these passages seem to suggest salvation only in a Jewish context. Yet it might not be universal salvation even in a Jewish context: "At that time *your* people shall be delivered, *everyone* who is found written in the book" (Dan. 12:1, emphasis added).

Daniel does not describe how someone outside the bounds of Israel might be saved. It is confusing, then, to speculate on the nature of the fall and how it impacts Israel on the one hand and the nations on the other. *Fourth Ezra*, a text that emerges from the same historical period as the Apocalypse of John, wrestles with the same problems but in a more acute manner. *Fourth Ezra* considers the nature of sin as it affects all humanity both in an individual and in a corporate manner. The angelic messenger explains to Ezra that God gave instruction to all people: "God strictly commanded those who came into the world, when they came, what they should do to live, and what they should do to avoid punishment. Nevertheless they were not obedient and spoke against him" (4 *Ezra* 7:21–22; cf. 5:27–28). These people rejected God and God's ways (7:23–24). The book does trace this sin back to Adam and his fall, which affected all his descendants (7:116–18). But Ezra challenges God to answer for the way in which humanity was created and to explain why only a few should be saved (8:1–3). Indeed, Ezra seems angered that God made human beings with a propensity to sin and blames God for this state of affairs (4:20–27). In this text, fallen angels are not blamed for humanity's descent into sin; God is blamed.

At one point, Ezra is told that humanity's situation is a test, a trial, to choose the righteous, however few they are, from among humankind (4 *Ezra* 7:127–31). In fact, Ezra is told that the world to come has been made for the sake of the few (8:1). Ezra is not satisfied with this answer, at least not initially, but his chagrin is particularly focused on why Israel, chosen from among the nations, faces such pain and sorrow (6:55–59). Sin is, after all, unfaithfulness to the law (9:36), but this seems to be the case for all people, not just the Jews (7:37–39). Sin results in alienation and estrangement from God (7:48). So perhaps the nations turned from God by rejecting either God's covenant or some sort of natural revelation or law. Free will is affirmed in a few passages: it is said that all have turned from God (3:8; 8:56–58). In some ways this sin is due to Adam (7:118), who possessed an evil heart (3:20), in which a grain of evil seed had been planted (4:30); all Adam's descendants have followed him (3:26). The seer asks pointed questions as to why the holy ones must suffer and why God has created humanity with a propensity to sin: "It would have been better for us not to be here than to come here and live in ungodliness, and to suffer and not understand why" (4:12). But ultimately Ezra accepts the ways of God and understands that some number will indeed be saved. Yet how the gentiles ought to be judged remains a peculiar issue that is not solved in *4 Ezra*.

In my view, the Apocalypse of John solves the basic issue: the universality of evil, and thus the universality of salvation. The origin of evil is assumed to be the fall of the angels and Satan in particular (Rev. 12:9; 20:2). Human beings clearly engage in evil also, as seen in the behavior of Babylon, which opposes the holy ones of God. This is no different from the Jewish canonical or noncanonical apocalypses. Again, there is no difference in that evil is in some limited way a test that the righteous must overcome (3:10). The inscrutability of evil and suffering are apparent in the Apocalypse of John when it says that the devil "must be let out for a little while" (20:3). Endurance and faithfulness are essential for the righteous to overcome evil. What sets the Apocalypse of John apart, in my view, is not that the origin of evil is explained much differently than in the Jewish apocalypses, nor that there is much deeper reflection on the origin of evil. *Fourth Ezra* must be seen as the apocalypse that wrestles with this question most fully. Rather, in the Apocalypse of John the answer to sin and suffering is universal. It settles the problem of *4 Ezra* and *1 Enoch* and clarifies the meaning of the holy ones in Daniel: the holy ones are all those who follow Jesus Christ (Rev. 4–10). A universal reality demands a universal response.

Sin and suffering are universal realities, and the Apocalypse of John, like most apocalypses, accepts that reality, accepts the nature of the human condition, and then proposes the answer. The ancient apocalypses, canonical and noncanonical, deal with the reality of suffering and the presence of evil in our midst and mince no words in their presentation of the current suffering of the elect and the fortitude necessary to withstand it: "Do not fear what you are about to suffer. Beware, the devil is about to throw some of you into prison so that you may be tested" (Rev. 2:10). But the reward for perseverance is also clear: "Be faithful until death, and I will give you the crown of life" (2:10). There is redemption, gained by the Lamb who was slain (cf. Rev. 5:6–14), and those who persevere regardless of the terror and persecution they experience in this life will have "every tear" wiped from their eyes and see "all things new" (21:4–5).

The apocalyptic imagination is concerned more with how to conquer sin, and with its inevitable destruction, than with why there is sin. The origin is located in the fall, first of angels and subsequently of human beings; of this there is no question. But the focus is on God's response to the inevitable human question: Given that this is the reality of all our lives, what, God, have you done about sin, and how are you going to resolve this problem? In each case, however, regardless of the number chosen—few in *4 Ezra*, multitudes in the Apocalypse of John (Rev. 7:9)—God acts to eliminate evil and suffering and to reward the righteous.

The apocalypses are guidebooks both to the solution of the problem and to how one shares in the solution. This is especially apparent in the Apocalypse of John. Most apocalypses, it is true, focus little attention on specific sins, or on what precisely constitutes the good life. For instance, there are no lists of commandments. There is indeed a clear sense that these texts are written for those who have already come to share in the communal life of either Israel or the church. One is told, broadly, to remain within the covenant life of the community, to remain faithful, and to avoid idolatry. The issue of idolatry is a key. The life in tune with God is a life in proper order. It is a life constituted by proper worship of the one, true God, not of lusts, material goods, power, or empires. In the midst of suffering, pain cannot be eased by greater wealth or power. In the seeming triumph of sin, victory is not found through participation in its fruits. The hope that apocalypses offer, especially the Apocalypse of John, is the hope to be found in a life shaped in obedience to the Lamb who was slain. Not only will God conquer all evil; God has already conquered. It is evil that is transient. The origin of sin is so little considered, I believe, because ultimately God did not intend a sinful life for us. The reality is paradise. God is good and intends for us only goodness.

Hollywood Nightmares

This is a short and perhaps unsatisfying expression of the heart of apocalyptic thought, but it places the major questions before us in conversation with a number of the products of modern cinema. Movies that take as their basis these ancient apocalyptic scenarios are so numerous as to give pause. Why would these most strange of visions find a home in the movies? Part of the answer may be that the strange visual, symbolic, and mythic images of these texts appeal to the imagination. But this is not the whole answer. One can certainly create a movie dealing with a battle between good and evil without dipping into Jewish and Christian prophecy. In a culture that has jettisoned so much of its Christian cultural heritage, these films point to a deep resonance with the themes of Christian apocalyptic thought in particular.

These movies rely on the acceptance of a couple of basic Christian truths, even if they are sometimes implicit. First, the reality of Christian prophetic literature is assumed; at least we can say that the reality of prophecy in general is assumed. This suggests the acceptance of a spiritual world, however ill defined it is. The content of this spiritual world as a battle between good and evil is also accepted, though the focus rests on Satan, the evil one, or some of his minions. However, God is often left out of the picture, quite literally. A coming end to the world is also understood, and the movies express this in several ways. Given, however, that God is absent from the picture, this coming end becomes the heart of the problem as presented in these movies. The coming end in apocalyptic texts, and in particular in the Apocalypse of John, is about God bringing sin, suffering, and evil to an end; in the case of Christian apocalypses, this is done through his Son Jesus Christ, and in the case of Jewish apocalypses, through the coming Messiah. But if God is absent, what do these films imagine is the fate of sin, evil, and suffering, and who will battle against them?

I explored a number of these films in my study *The End of the World: The Apocalyptic Imagination in Film and Television*.[1] Here I will speak of these films in general terms. Some of them are excellent, some are poor, but Hollywood never ceases to release them and has been doing so since at least the late 1960s, starting with *Rosemary's Baby* and continuing with the release of *Constantine* and beyond. It can be established that these films, with one or two exceptions, share a particular worldview regarding sin, suffering, and evil in much the same way as the ancient apocalypses do. This cinematic worldview, however, does not express the theodicy of Jews and Christians. Rather, the Hollywood worldview reflects modern (or postmodern) disquiet with the nature of evil and the power of the good and unease primarily with human salvation and redemption.

---

1. John W. Martens, *The End of the World: The Apocalyptic Imagination in Film and Television* (Winnipeg: Shillingford, 2003).

The unease runs through the center of these films. In film after film, evil is seen as the power of the apocalypse. The apocalypse is not the act of God to destroy evil, suffering, and sin and to return humanity to its intended state in paradise, but it is the power of Satan come to earth. In one film, *End of Days* (1999), the priest, Father Kovak, challenges the character Cane, a former policeman who has been drawn into the apocalyptic scenario against his will, to accept the reality of God. He states, "If you don't believe in God, how can you understand his Adversary?" Cane is now given support by Father Kovak, and he realizes that Kovak is well aware of what is soon to take place, as he has a book called *The Return of Satan*. Later we find Cane praying for strength to defeat evil and for help as he meditates on Christ crucified. On the other hand, Kovak offers perhaps the most theologically dubious statement ever attributed to a practicing priest: "Our God, he doesn't say that he will save us, he says that we will save ourselves." This is the dilemma these films create, for themselves and for filmgoers: God's existence is accepted, to some degree, but God has become an ineffectual bystander, powerless to stop the march of evil. The fate of the earth rests not in God's hands but in human hands. The character Cane in *End of Days* must act to save a world abandoned by an ineffectual God, a No-God.

Although these films do not define evil well, they accept the reality of malevolence in this world and the spiritual reality of the evil one. Part of the reason is that goodness is either absent or corrupted. God does not take an active role in the defeat of evil; human beings are left to do this on their own, while God perhaps smiles benignly on their efforts. In the 2005 film *Constantine*, God seems to have made a pact with the devil, called in the film "the balance," in which a certain number of souls seems to be set aside for each. In this case God and the devil are equals playing on the field of our souls; God is not the omnipotent God of Christianity but perhaps the good god of Zoroastrianism locked in fearful battle with evil but unable to conquer evil alone. Those who are supposed to represent God on earth—priests, the church—are cast either as incompetent, fearful, and theologically inept or as actually in league with the devil. In the films *The Omen* (1976, remade in 2006) and *Lost Souls* (2000), for example, priests play an active role in bringing Satan or his spawn, an antichrist figure, to earth.

Those who oppose evil, then, are defined not by their moral goodness but by fate or happenstance: they happen to be in the wrong place at the wrong time. If this was meant to show that God can use the basest of human material, all is well: Abraham, Jacob, Moses, David, and Peter all showed themselves as weak human material whom God could mold to procure his providential end.

Instead, these cinematic human opponents of the devil work alone, without God, to outwit the devil and his schemes. There is often nothing good about them, their lives, or the way they live except that they accept responsibility for battling evil. This is not insignificant, of course, except that evil itself seems often to be presented as bringing about the end of human life here on earth. The cinematic apocalypse is not the redemption of the world but simply the devil's attempt to end human life. Sin, suffering, and evil are a part of human life, but God does not present an answer to them, and human attempts to stop Satan in these films do not propose an answer to them either. If Satan is stopped, it is for a short time only; we do not know when Satan might return. And when Satan is stopped, life continues as it had before. If the good is absent or ineffectual, evil is a constant presence that can be held at bay for a while, but its defeat has no notable impact on people or how they lead their lives. Both good and evil are contentless. The apocalypse as nihilism is now being screened at the local Cineplex.

At root in many films, too, is the use of the Apocalypse of John, which stands as a monument behind *The Omen*. Though the Apocalypse is a book of the church, predicting the ultimate overthrow of evil, *The Omen*, by creating its own scriptural text, sees it at root as a story of evil's triumph: "turning man against his brother, 'til man exists no more."[2] That this passage is not in the Apocalypse ought to alert us that the film has a purpose beyond that of the ancient Apocalypse. Of course, the ancient apocalypses do see the end time as fraught with terror and destruction, but this is not the end of the story. The end is paradise; the end is a new Eden. Travail will occur as a preface to the triumph of good. *The Omen* sees the Apocalypse basically as a guidebook for the devil, not for the church. This clearly speaks to modern anxieties about the weakness of organized religion and its supposed meaninglessness, and evil has only gained in stature. The real anxiety is about the absence of good and the overwhelming reality of evil. Although the Christian texts are found to have prophetic significance, the message of hope does not. Who will save us from death and destruction? The church? God? The Messiah? No one will save us. This is the message in a nutshell. Evil desires humanity's demise, even if human life is seen as only chaos, torment, and meaninglessness.

Ben F. Meyer explains that at the heart of the crisis of our culture today is our absence of the sense of a God who cares for his people or who loves them without fail:

2. This is a line from a "biblical" poem about the Antichrist by character Father Brennan in *The Omen* (1976) and used as a tagline in the 2006 remake.

We have reverted to the Greeks; the dull Greek dread of the far side of the divine, an "ultimate" that was impersonal, implacable, and oppressive, has resurfaced in our world, diminishing and poisoning the imagination. We are not alone, says science fiction, so long as there are others—as good as us or maybe even better—somewhere out in space. Otherwise, it is implied, we are indeed alone. In this version the ultimate is neither benevolent nor malevolent, just empty. The near side of the Greek conception of the divine, that of the Olympians, has become one more affirmation of ourselves and our choices. Whether this near side of the divine is harmful or harmless is unsettled.[3]

Because of this reality, our place in the world is unsettled, and we are in an age of anxiety. How do we know whether what is "out there" is benign? We have no way of knowing. If we use ourselves as a model, the results are frightening or at best mixed. Without the sense of a God who cares, without the sense of a God who loves—the end of our world, its destruction, and our chaos or enslavement are beyond response. Like the gods of old, the new gods are inscrutable and unreliable. We, like the people of old, have no idea what to do. Our end might be justified or it might not be justified, but the necessary order for how to respond is missing. We look to our technology and science as our salvation, but we fear it is not good enough. We live at the edge of the precipice, and there is no clear map for how to walk back from it. The apocalypse is upon us, but the divine order is simply chaos. We are not certain what evil is or how to define sin, but we know we are suffering.

In sum, when we examine the (post)modern, (post)apocalyptic movies, we find a genre that retains the theological scaffolding of ancient Christian apocalyptic scenarios while jettisoning the hope of redemption, the resolution of suffering, and the conquest of evil. In many cases, apocalyptic films take seriously the notion of Christian prophecy, but they see this as the power of evil come to earth, which humans must act to stop. Where is God? God has become No-God—distant, silent, and implacable. The postmodern apocalypse is about humanity alienated, frightened, and alone. Yet these films admit the reality of evil and the need to stand against it. How do these films propose human redemption? How do they propose human transformation? Who will save us? The postmodern cinema offers not hope but the dread of the divine found in ancient polytheism: how do we placate and propitiate those whose ways we cannot understand?

The ancient Christians offered a response: God will not stand for evil, for whatever its origin, it offends God and his creation. God is good and will act

3. Ben F. Meyer, "Election-Historical Thinking in Romans 9–11, and Ourselves," *Logos* 7, no. 4 (2004): 171–81.

to "wipe away every tear from their eyes. Death will be no more; mourning and crying and pain will be no more" (Rev. 21:4). Unable to define either good or evil, unable to imagine a God who cares for humanity, apocalyptic films offer a vision of the end that senses the reality of evil but does not have an answer regarding its true source or the power before which it cannot stand. The apostle Paul asks, "Who will rescue me from this body of death?" (Rom. 7:24). His answer: Jesus Christ. The Messiah. The answer of the films? No-God.

3

THE SUFFERING OF MARTYRDOM

Greek Perspectives in the Fourth and Fifth Centuries

JAMES C. SKEDROS

Sometime during the latter half of the ninth century, the monk Euodios wrote a lengthy account entitled *The Forty-Two Martyrs of Amorion*.[1] Though the tale is considered to be legendary, Euodios describes the capture and seven-year ordeal of forty-two Byzantine military commanders and civic leaders seized by the Arabs during the siege and destruction of the Byzantine city Amorion in 838. Amorion was perhaps the largest city in Asia Minor at that time and served as the capital of the Anatolikon region of the Byzantine Empire. The capture and destruction of Amorion was led by the Abbasid caliph al-Mu'tasim; of the nearly seventy thousand soldiers, inhabitants, and refugees crowding the city, more than half were slaughtered. Euodios's martyrdom story is of interest not because of its historical value, which is small,

---

1. Several versions of the martyrdom account survive; see Vatroslav G. Vasilievskij and P. Ni-kitin, *Skazanija o 42 amorijskich mucenikack* (St. Petersburg, 1905). I have used the text written by the monk Euodios, which is dated as after 855/856 by S. Kotzampassi—in "To martyrio tōn saranta dyo martyrōn tou Amoriou: Hagiologika kai hymnologika keimena," *Epistēmonikē Epetēris tēs Philosophikēs Scholēs Aristotēleiou Panepistēmiou Thessalonikēs* 2 (1992): 127—and dated in the second half of the ninth century to the first half of the tenth century by Alexander P. Kazhdan, "Hagiographical Notes," *Byzantion* 56 (1986): 152.

but because of the ideological and theological motifs used to tell the story. The majority of the martyrdom account comprises the lengthy captivity of the forty-two martyrs and numerous discussions between the martyrs and individuals sent by their Arab captors to persuade them to convert to Islam. The martyrs remain firm in their Christian faith only to be eventually murdered by Ethiopian executioners along the bank of the Tigris.[2]

Replete with traditional hagiographic motifs, Euodios's martyrdom account ends in a sermonic, adulatory fashion. I quote his closing words at length since they contain the main themes of this essay:

> O pure and perfect sacrifice, O self-immolated sacrifices and victims pleasing to God, a rational offering, a most fragrant whole-burnt offering and a sacrifice of praise, to Christ a glory truly worthy of its name. Through you, barbarian arrogance was cast down and a throng of unbelievers was clearly overcome by a few soldiers of Christ who were given boldness of speech. Even though only a few God-pleasing individuals, you were easily capable of defeating [the barbarians] and winning that victory which is greater than the victory of generals over physical bodies. They made every effort to turn you away, but they were not strong enough. The heavenly city takes pride in you. Men in authority and of high rank pride themselves in you and use the power of your prayers in times of war. Those who are believers find you as allies. You share in communion with our sufferings. As ones who are acquainted with our wretched and slippery life and with its tumultuous and harsh reality, may you be mediators on behalf of us for the salvation we seek from Christ himself our Lord.[3]

Clouded in praise and admiration, Euodios affirms three significant aspects of martyrdom that have a long tradition in the Greek East: patient endurance as a means of strengthening the faithful, the benefits accrued through suffering even to the point of assisting others toward the goal of salvation, and the gift of *parrēsia* (speaking out boldly in the face of danger or in the presence of God). As I hope this study will show, these three interconnected notions are key aspects in the Greek East's understanding of the suffering of martyrdom.

Theodore the Studite, active one generation before Euodios, lived and wrote during a period of ecclesiastical and imperial struggles that pitted this famous middle Byzantine monastic reformer and Orthodox spokesman against the religious and civic leaders of his day. Embroiled as he was in the Iconoclast, Moechian, and Josephite controversies, Theodore wrote

---

2. Euodios wrongly places Samarra on the banks of the Euphrates (Euodios, *Forty-Two Martyrs of Amorion*, 36, in Vasilievskij and Nikitin, *Skazanija*, 75).

3. Euodios, *Forty-Two Martyrs of Amorion*, 43–44, in Vasilievskij and Nikitin, *Skazanija*, 77–78.

hundreds of letters and produced several treatises in which he articulated his views. At the beginning of the second phase of iconoclasm in 815, Theodore wrote to John, bishop of Sardis, encouraging him: "Bring your holy struggles to the fore, oh crown of fathers, and embrace whatever else will come as well: for people in the church of Christ still live in a time of martyrdom. May you not be diverted from your beautiful confession." Though Bishop John had not paid the ultimate sacrifice, he nonetheless had been abused at the hands of the Iconoclasts. Noting this, Theodore continues, "You were not placed on the cross, because these are not the times. Yet you are a cross-bearer, since you were taken away and abused and ridiculed by the evil-doers."[4]

Renewed iconoclasm, the adulterous scandal known as the Moechian controversy, and the lingering issue of support for the patriarch Joseph led to very few martyrdoms. This, however, did not deter Theodore from using the rhetoric of martyrdom to offer encouragement to those who were suffering at the hands of his opponents and to provide an interpretive framework for their suffering. The patrician Irene was a supporter of icons during the reign of the emperor Leo V (813–20). Theodore wrote eight letters to her, which suggested she was a prominent supporter who associated with the persecuted, helped them, and placed herself in danger. Accordingly, Theodore called Irene "a senator's wife walking among martyrs" and a new martyr.[5] To the monk Arkadios, who had been assigned to work as a weaver in the imperial palace for his iconophile views, Theodore wrote: "[Your sufferings] are the things of saints. But then it is also true that they [the Iconoclasts], though not wanting to, exhibit you to the world as a true servant of the emperor of the universe, a proof of the testimony of God, a refutation of impiety."[6]

The current political and ecclesiastical crises afforded Theodore the opportunity to strengthen his rank-and-file supporters by equating their current state of suffering to that of martyrdom. Theodore links the contemporary struggles confronting his followers with the paradigmatic struggles of the martyrs of the early church. For Theodore, the suffering of his fellow monks is a sign of victory in the struggle over evil. Suffering for the sake of truth encourages those who are on the margin looking in while affirming the truth for which one suffers. In his letter to Irene the patrician, Theodore encourages her in her struggles against iconoclasm and the sufferings she has endured,

---

4. Theodore the Studite, *Letters* 157, quoted in Peter Hatlie, "The Politics of Salvation: Theodore of Stoudios on Martyrdom (*Martyrion*) and on Speaking Out (*Parrhesia*)," *Dumbarton Oaks Papers* 50 (1996): 275.

5. Theodore the Studite, *Letters* 156, in Hatlie, "Politics of Salvation," 269.

6. Theodore the Studite, *Letters* 390, in Hatlie, "Politics of Salvation," 271.

"so that you might strengthen and save many others by your own example."[7] Here we see two key elements of Theodore's views of martyrdom. First, Irene's perseverance strengthens the faithful in their own struggles, perhaps spiritual in general, or more specifically related to iconoclasm. Second, and equally important for Theodore, is that the suffering she endures confirms the truth of her (and Theodore's) convictions. Her acceptance of suffering is proof of the validity of her iconophile beliefs.

Another important rhetorical element in Theodore's view of martyrdom is the notion of *parrēsia*, boldness of speech. For Theodore, *parrēsia* most often means the ability and courage to speak out against the abuses and ills of the day. As Peter Hatlie has observed, "*Parrēsia* represented a bid to keep the message of Theodore and his supporters alive and well."[8] *Parrēsia*, boldness of speech as a form of protest, was not disconnected from martyrdom. Theodore urges his supporters to demonstrate their association with the martyrs through an expression of *parrēsia*.[9] For Theodore, the ancient martyrs shared a witness, their martyrdom, and the ability to speak out with *parrēsia*. In his many letters to his supporters who are currently suffering at the hands of the authorities, Theodore uses the martyrs of old as models of those who spoke out in the face of wrongs, exhibiting their *parrēsia* even though it brought them the ultimate cost of death.

Theodore's frequent use of the model and image of martyrdom coupled with the fact that martyrdom was taking place during his lifetime does not lead, however, to the adoption of the idea that the suffering of the martyr has some kind of redemptive effect upon the Christian faithful. Certainly, for Theodore, martyrdom provided a means of salvation for the one undergoing martyrdom, but the thought that the blood being shed by a martyr has salvific force for the life of the church does not figure into Theodore's understanding of martyrdom. The redemptive quality of martyrdom beyond the individual martyr was, however, part of the apologetic for martyrdom in the early church. Origen, in his *Exhortation to Martyrdom*, one of the most compelling texts of the first three centuries of the Christian faith, hints at the possible efficacious effects of the blood of the martyrs:

> Consider, as well, whether baptism by martyrdom, just as the Savior's [baptism] brought cleansing to the world, may not also serve to cleanse many. For just as those who served the altar according to the Law of Moses thought they were ministering forgiveness of sins to the people by the blood of goats and

7. Theodore the Studite, *Letters* 156, in Hatlie, "Politics of Salvation," 271.
8. Hatlie, "Politics of Salvation," 275.
9. Ibid.

bulls, so also the souls of those who have been beheaded for their witness to Jesus do not serve the heavenly altar in vain but minister forgiveness of sins to those who pray.[10]

Here Origen suggests that martyrs who now "serve the heavenly altar" are capable of offering forgiveness of sins to those who seek such redemption through prayer. Yet can the blood of the martyr atone for the sins of Christians? Origen seems to reply in the affirmative by comparing the blood that was shed by the martyrs to the blood spilled in the murder of Abel: their blood cries to God from the ground (cf. Gen. 4:10). More specifically, Origen argues, "And perhaps just as we have been redeemed by the precious blood of Jesus, . . . so some will be redeemed by the precious blood of the martyrs, since they too have been exalted beyond the exaltations of those who were righteous but did not become martyrs."[11] It is not entirely clear whom Origen has in mind when speaking of the "righteous," but he does seem to suggest that the blood of the martyrs is redemptive as Christ's is.

Origen sees martyrdom as a means of strengthening the faithful and the gift of *parrēsia*. Martyrdom produces "confidence" (*parrēsian*) toward God, the ability to be boldly present before God.[12] Origen does not specifically link this *parrēsia* with a martyr's ability to intercede with God on behalf of others; yet it is clear that the martyr's courage and faith result in a state of *parrēsia*. Likewise, Origen encourages his fellow Christians Ambrose and Protoctetus, to whom his treatise is addressed, to undergo their upcoming suffering "for those who will be built up by our martyrdom."[13] For Origen, the endurance of the martyrs, their confession of faith, and their steadfastness in the face of suffering and pain provide motivation for current and future Christians.

When the imperial reign of Constantine was firmly established over the Greco-Roman world by 324, the period of persecution was brought to an end. The church now had its core of martyrs, from which it would draw strength for centuries to come. Eusebius is one of our earliest Constantinian and post-Constantinian examples of a Christian leader co-opting the suffering, endurance, courage, and faithfulness of the martyrs for the spiritual strengthening of the Christian faithful. For several more generations after Eusebius, some of the great fathers of the so-called golden age of patristics would follow suit and, to use a modern idiom, "preach the martyrs." John Chrysostom

10. Origen, *An Exhortation to Martyrdom* 30, trans. Rowan A. Greer, *Origen*, CWS (New York: Paulist Press, 1979), 62.

11. Origen, *Martyrdom* 50, trans. Greer, 79.

12. Origen, *Martyrdom* 28.

13. Origen, *Martyrdom* 41, trans. Greer, 72.

delivered at least twenty sermons that dealt directly with a particular martyr or the martyrs in general. All three Cappadocian Fathers preached homilies on individual martyrs.[14] Hesychius, a priest in Jerusalem during the fifth century, delivered several sermons on local martyrs. Most of these sermons just mentioned were delivered within the context of a *panegyris*, the annual assembly at a martyr's shrine, a commemoration that included the delivery of a sermon. Basil of Caesarea is our earliest witness to this genre of the martyr homily. Basil is more than one generation removed from the actual events of the martyrdoms about which he preaches. Yet his sermons, along with those of his contemporary bishops and the homilists who followed, contributed to the well-documented phenomenon of the cult of the martyrs during the fourth and fifth centuries. The development of the cult of the martyrs and its explosive growth need not detain us here. Yet the ideology of martyrdom and particularly the role of suffering in martyrdom receive their definitive form in the homilies delivered within this formative stage of the cult of the martyrs. The impact of these homilies is reflected in the manuscript tradition: by the ninth century many of these sermons had been gathered into sermon collections and were being distributed in this way. In what follows, I examine the martyr homilies of the fourth and fifth centuries, considering more closely the three aspects of the suffering of martyrdom already identified in my perhaps too long introduction. The suffering of the martyrs (1) offers encouragement to those who suffer, (2) provides a salvific element to the martyr and the Christian believer, and (3) earns the martyr *parrēsia* before God and on behalf of others.

Suffering as Encouragement

Early in the year 373, at a martyrium outside the city of Caesarea, Basil delivered a sermon at the feast of the martyr Gordios, a citizen of Caesarea who had been martyred during the reign of Licinius.[15] Noticing the large crowd, Basil opens his sermon with a simile by equating the crowd with a swarm of bees buzzing around the hive of the tomb of the martyrs. In good exhortative fashion, early in the homily Basil encourages his audience to "rejoice at the

14. The Cappadocian Fathers contributed greatly to the development of the cult of the martyrs in fourth-century Cappadocia and Pontus; see Vasiliki Limberis, *Architects of Piety: The Cappadocian Fathers and the Cult of the Martyrs* (Oxford: Oxford University Press, 2011). See also James C. Skedros, "The Cappadocian Fathers on the Veneration of the Martyrs," StPatr 37 (2001): 294–300.

15. Four martyr homilies of Basil's have survived: *Gordios, Julitta, The Forty Martyrs,* and *Mamas.*

very remembrance of the exploits of the just, urged on," as he continues, "by what they hear to energetic imitation of good persons."[16] Remembrance of the martyrs is a key element in the cult of the saints. For Basil, remembrance of Gordios's exploits—whether his faithfulness, his agonistic struggles, his suffering, or his death—is sufficient for profiting the Christian.[17] Basil justifies his emphasis on the memory of the martyr's deeds by quoting the Psalms: "The just man will always be remembered" (111:6 LXX).[18]

Memory is a powerful tool. In his homily on Gordios, Basil relates few details about the martyr's life and even fewer about the nature of the martyr's execution. Yet the veracity of his words must ring true since there are, we are told, some in Basil's audience who remember the events. We can assume, though, that for the vast majority of those present there was very little firsthand knowledge or experience of Gordios's martyrdom or martyrdom in general. Basil himself was born in 330, well after the close of persecution. He may, however, have been acquainted with the handful of martyrdoms under the emperor Julian. Nevertheless, what was it that Basil wanted his audience to remember about the martyrs? What was important for Basil?

If memory is a powerful tool, selective memory is perhaps even more powerful. In book 8 of his *Ecclesiastical History*, Eusebius records a first-hand account of persecution in Palestine and its environs from 303 onward. In the opening sections Eusebius is quite explicit about the moral and didactic purposes of retelling the plight of those martyred Christians of Palestine: "We decided to make no mention of those who have been tempted by the persecution or have made utter shipwreck of their salvation (1 Tim. 1:19) and by their own decision were plunged in the depths of the sea; we shall add to the general history only those things which may be profitable, first to ourselves, and then to those who come after us."[19] In other words, Eusebius has chosen to relate only the examples of Christians who withstood to the end—to their deaths—the sufferings undergone for their Christian faith in order to build up the faithful.

Returning to Basil, the bishop of Caesarea most likely did not have the choice of preaching about Christians who failed the test. The church had already begun the process of selective memory for a particular purpose. For

---

16. Basil, *A Homily on the Martyr Gordios* 1, trans. Johan Leemans, *"Let Us Die That We May Live": Greek Homilies on Christian Martyrs from Asia Minor, Palestine and Syria (c. A.D. 350–A.D. 450)*, ed. Johan Leemans et al. (London: Routledge, 2003), 58.

17. Basil, *On Gordios* 2, in *"Let Us Die,"* 59.

18. Basil, *On Gordios* 8, in *"Let Us Die,"* 67; cf. Ps. 111:6–7 LXX, Vulgate (112:6 English).

19. Eusebius, *Ecclesiastical History* 8.2.3, quoted in Timothy D. Barnes, *Constantine and Eusebius* (Cambridge, MA: Harvard University Press, 1981), 157.

Basil, remembrance leads to imitation. Keeping company with noble persons will lead one to imitate the actions of these persons. The same is true for the faithful Christian who remembers the martyrs. In a sermon delivered also in 373 during the feast of the Forty Martyrs of Sebaste, commemorating their martyrium in Caesarea, Basil opens his homily with the following exhortation: "Bless the martyred sincerely, so that you become a martyr by choice, and end up being worthy of the same rewards as theirs, without persecution, without fire, without blows."[20] The message of the martyrs, their "encomium," is nothing less than "the exhortation of the congregation to virtue" (*hē pros aretēn paraklēsis tōn syneilegmenōn*).[21]

One aspect of virtue for Basil, as indicated by the action of the Forty Martyrs, is confessing one's Christian identity publicly. Full disclosure of the martyrs' Christian identity is part of the story line, since the forty were Roman soldiers who stood out among their peers as Christians. The virtue of the forty is found not simply in the confession of their faith but also in their steadfastness in maintaining their faith during extreme torture. Their torture was to stand naked on the ice of a pond throughout the night until they expired. In a vivid, great description, Basil illustrates the forty's suffering by describing what happens to a body exposed to extreme cold temperatures:

> For when a body is exposed to frost it first becomes livid all over, once the blood has frozen. Next it becomes agitated and jumps, teeth chatter, nerves become taut, and the bulk of the body involuntarily becomes contracted. Piercing pain, and unspeakable suffering pervading the very marrow, produces an intolerable feeling for those who are freezing. After that it becomes mutilated, the extremities being burnt as if by fire. . . . Death occurs shortly after as a result of freezing.[22]

The culmination of the story of the Forty Martyrs comes when one of the forty can no longer endure the cold and runs to the baths, denying Christ. Just then, the executioner, seeing what has transpired and being touched by the display of Christian zeal, throws off his clothes and joins the other thirty-nine soldiers, thus completing the sacred number of forty. As he occupies his place among the dying and frozen, this new soldier for Christ exclaims, "I am a Christian," offering the public confession of faith that manifests Christian virtue. Bringing to a close his homily, Basil reiterates the power of remembering these particular martyrs: "Becoming a spectacle for the world and for angels

20. Basil, *A Homily on the Forty Martyrs of Sebaste* 1, in *"Let Us Die,"* 68.
21. Basil, *Forty Martyrs* 2, in *"Let Us Die,"* 69. Just what Basil means by "virtue" (*aretē*) is not necessarily spelled out in this context.
22. Basil, *Forty Martyrs* 5, in *"Let Us Die,"* 72.

and human beings (1 Cor. 4:9), they raised the fallen, they strengthened the ambivalent, they doubled the desire of the pious."[23]

If, for Basil, remembrance of the martyrs leads to virtue among Christians, he does not mean that all Christians are to somehow seek out opportunities for suffering for the faith. Rather, as one might expect, Basil, much like many of his contemporaries, sees the opportunity for Christians to imitate the martyrs in the ascetic movements of his day. The martyrdom of conscience is a well-known commonplace in Christian ascetical literature from the fourth century onward and need not detain us here.[24]

The suffering or patient endurance of the martyr that leads those who take notice to the practice of virtue is a theme found in the martyr homilies of John Chrysostom as well. Yet Chrysostom often identifies the ability of the martyrs to withstand the suffering inflicted upon them with that of the philosophers who are capable of enduring hardships based on the steadiness of their internal disposition. In his homily on the martyr Ignatius, the famous early second-century bishop of Antioch, Chrysostom concludes that God kept Ignatius from death until he reached Rome so that he might teach Rome to practice philosophy. "Truly," says Chrysostom, "it is for this reason that God agreed that he [Ignatius] lose his life there: so that his death would be an instruction in piety for all who inhabit Rome."[25] In his homily on the martyr Barlaam, another Antiochene martyr, Chrysostom is quite emphatic about the exhortative role of the suffering and death of the martyrs:

> Even if a person had achieved great things, they would consider that they had done nothing great, when [they compared] their virtue with [the martyrs'] wrestling matches. . . . For a martyrs' death is an encouragement to believers, churches' bold speech, Christianity's confirmation, death's dissolution, a proof

23. Basil, *Forty Martyrs* 8, in *"Let Us Die,"* 76.

24. This idea is found throughout the later Byzantine period as reflected in the following quote from Symeon the New Theologian: "If some should say: 'Those men were martyrs. They suffered for Christ, and how is it possible for us to become their equals?' We might say in reply to them: You yourselves, too, if indeed you want to, can suffer and be tormented for Christ's sake, and be a martyr every day just like those men were. . . . And how might this be? If you, too, rank yourselves in battle against the vicious demons; if you take your stand by continually opposing sin and your own will. While these stood up against tyrants, we hold against demons and the destructive passions of the flesh which day and night and at every hour tyrannically attack our soul and force us to do things which do not belong to piety and which anger God," *Tenth Ethical Discourse*, in Symeon the New Theologian, *On the Mystical Life: The Ethical Discourses*, trans. Alexander Golitzin, 3 vols. (Crestwood, NY: St. Vladimir's Seminary Press, 1995–97), 1:160.

25. John Chrysostom, *On the Holy Martyr Ignatius* 14, in John Chrysostom, *The Cult of the Saints*, trans. Wendy Mayer (Crestwood, NY: St. Vladimir's Seminary Press, 2006), 113; cited below as Mayer.

of resurrection, ridicule of demons, the Devil's condemnation, an instruction in philosophy, . . . mother of all blessings.[26]

The courage of the martyr in the midst of debilitating pain and suffering is lifted up, retold, and exalted by our fourth- and fifth-century Christian leaders as exemplary of Christian commitment, fortitude, virtue, and piety. Chrysostom could not be more explicit about this when he states, "If [the martyrs] remain steadfast in their tortures and groan over what they suffer, but do not betray their piety, no one holds them responsible for their groans; instead we accept and admire them all the more, for the reason that even though they were in pain they endured it and did not recant."[27] For Chrysostom, a great moralist, the martyr's endurance of suffering is illustrative of the endurance a Christian must demonstrate in the face of the temptations of the worldly life.

Sacrificial Suffering

The suffering procured in martyrdom provided didactic material for Christian leaders of the fourth and later centuries. This moralistic use of the savage and brutal murder of Christians was not the only response Christians would offer. The Christian blood spilled through martyrdom was seen as blood that was capable of sanctifying the earth.[28] Is it possible that the suffering and death of martyrs has a redemptive or salvific effect on the church? If so, in what manner?

To be sure, there is the notion that the death of the martyr is often equated with baptism. In his sermon on the Forty Martyrs of Sebaste, Basil makes this point quite explicit. When the executioner takes the place of the apostate Christian soldier, the executioner exclaims, "I am a Christian" even though he has not received a baptism of water. Rather, Basil extols the courage of the executioner: "He believed in the name of our Lord Jesus Christ; he was baptized into him, not by another, but by his own faith, not in water, but in his own blood."[29] In dramatic fashion, Chrysostom speaks of the martyrdom of Lucian, celebrated in Antioch the day after Epiphany: "Yesterday our Master was baptized with water, today his servant is baptized with blood." Chrysostom does not stop here but continues to explain the impact of the blood of Lucian: "Indeed, don't be astonished if I called his martyrdom a baptism. For in fact here too the Spirit flits around with abundant generosity,

26. Chrysostom, *On Saint Drosis* 4, in Mayer, 195; cf. Chrysostom, *On Saint Barlaam* 12, in Mayer, 188.
27. Chrysostom, *On Saint Barlaam* 7, in Mayer, 184–85.
28. Asterius of Amasea, *A Homily on Stephen the First Martyr* 2.2, in *"Let Us Die,"* 178.
29. Basil, *Forty Martyrs* 7, in *"Let Us Die,"* 74.

and obliteration of sin takes place and a certain wonderful and incredible purification of the soul. And just as those who are being baptized wash in water, so those being martyred wash in their own blood."[30]

Lucian was already a Christian and was not in need of baptism. Yet, if we consider the possibility that the early Christian understanding of baptism still retained a strong component of the notion of the cleansing of sins, then the martyr receives a blessing in which other baptized Christians who are not martyrs cannot partake, that is, a second baptism and the opportunity for the cleansing of all sins on the threshold of death.

The blood of the martyrs therefore functions in a personal redemptive manner, providing a second regeneration and cleansing of sins. Some of our authors do not stop here in their understanding of the power of the martyrs' deaths. Chrysostom relates, for example, how the martyr Barlaam was led to a pagan altar, his hand was outstretched over the altar, and a burning coal with incense was placed in his palm—in anticipation that he would turn his hand over and the incense would fall on the altar, thus allowing his captors to claim that he had sacrificed to the gods. Yet Barlaam remained strong and endured the pain as the coal burned through his hand. Commenting on this torture, Chrysostom states, "The same person becomes altar, victim, and priest."[31]

The sacrifice of the martyr who is at once the one who offers, the offering, and the sacred spot upon which the offering is made—this is a sacrifice that brings redemption through the cleansing of the martyr's sins. Chrysostom graphically expresses this in his homily on the female martyr Drosis. Speaking about her death by fire, Chrysostom relates,

> For although her flesh melted away, and her bones were charred to a crisp, and her nerves were burnt away, and the lymphatic fluid in her body flowed out in every direction, her soul's faith became firmer and more dazzling. And while the people who were watching these events thought that she had died, she was purified all the more. . . . The Christians understood very precisely that in liquefying she shed every stain.[32]

Basil expresses a similar idea by placing the following words in the mouth of the martyr Gordios as he undergoes his torture: "The more you increase my punishments, the more you procure for me greater recompense."[33] The belief

---

30. Chrysostom, *On Saint Lucian* 5, in Mayer, 68.
31. Chrysostom, *On Saint Barlaam* 8, in Mayer, 184.
32. Chrysostom, *On Saint Drosis* 9, in Mayer, 200–201.
33. Basil, *On Gordios* 5, in *"Let Us Die,"* 63.

that the suffering of a martyr offers a redemptive effect to the martyr is commonplace within the patristic literature I have examined.

Yet can we say more about the benefits of suffering? Does the suffering, pain, torture, and eventual death of the martyrs provide help for individuals other than the martyrs themselves? The answer depends, in part, on how one understands the sacrifice that accrues in martyrdom. The Greek patristic tradition is quite unanimous in affirming the intercessory role of the martyrs. This role is "earned" through the "witness" of the martyrs both in their public confession of faith and in the suffering they endure, unto death, for their love for God.[34] One of the most striking examples of this comes from Basil's homily on the Forty Martyrs of Sebaste, where Basil singles out a woman in the crowd gathered for the *panegyris*: "Here a pious woman is found praying for her children, begging for the return of her husband who is away, for his safety because he is sick. Let your [plural] petitions," encourages Basil, "be with the martyrs."[35] The intercessory role of the martyr remains a key interpretive principle of martyrdom throughout the patristic period.

Curiously, though, one searches hard to find a reference to the suffering of martyrs as suffering endured for someone else. Earlier I reported Origen's understanding of this. The martyrs suffer for Christ, for their own forgiveness of sins, and, as we shall see, for eternal life. Yet there is an absence of a notion that the martyr suffers for other Christians in some type of redemptive manner as Christ suffered on the cross. The closest reference I am able to find comes from the pen of the seventh-century monastic Isaac the Syrian:

> On the day when you are pained in some way, either physically or mentally, for the sake of any man, be he good or evil, reckon yourself as a martyr on that day, and as one who suffers for Christ's sake and is deemed worthy of confession. For remember that Christ died for sinners, not for the just. So how great a thing it is to grieve for wicked men and to benefit sinners even more than the righteous.[36]

In his voluminous commentaries on the Letters of Paul, John Chrysostom fails to take the opportunity to equate Paul's suffering, to which the apostle frequently refers in his correspondence, with the suffering of the martyrs. In his commentary on Colossians 1:24, where Paul writes, "I am now rejoicing in my sufferings for your sake, and in my flesh I am completing what is still

---

34. "Moved by love, the martyrs shed their blood that they might not lose Christ," declares Symeon the New Theologian, *The Discourses*, trans. C. J. deCatanzaro, CWS (New York: Paulist Press, 1980), 45.

35. Basil, *Forty Martyrs* 8, in *"Let Us Die,"* 75; see John of Damascus, *Orthodox Faith* 4.15.

36. Isaac the Syrian, *Homily 51*, in *Ascetical Discourses* (Boston: Holy Transfiguration Monastery, 1984), 246.

lacking in Christ's afflictions for the sake of his body, that is, the church," Chrysostom acknowledges that Paul suffers for others only through his suffering for Christ. Here, more than any other place, one might expect to find a reference to the martyrs and their suffering, but Chrysostom does not provide one. In fact, elsewhere Chrysostom is quite explicit about this: "The martyrs were not butchered for our sake and yet we rush together to honor them."[37] We are left, therefore, to understand the suffering of the martyrs as imparting redemption to the martyrs themselves, but not (perhaps with the exception of Origen) providing redemption for others.

The Rewards of Suffering

In a powerful homily on the martyr Julian, Chrysostom begins with a repetition of rhetorical questions centered on the theme that the earthly honors given to the martyrs, as seen in the current gathering of the faithful on the feast of Julian, pale in comparison to the rewards awaiting the martyrs who endure to the end. "If [Christ]," Chrysostom asks, "was crucified and shed his blood for those who hate him, what won't he do for those who shed their blood as a result of their confession for him?"[38] In gratitude for their suffering, Christ offers the martyrs blessings that come from heaven, and it is these blessings, according to Chrysostom, that the martyrs focus on to divert themselves from their pain and torture as they glue "their eyes to heaven and the blessings that come from there."[39] The "blessings that come from heaven" are three: a special grace to endure their suffering, boldness of speech before God, and eternal life.

Christian writers, beginning as early as the second century, have noticed the presence of a distinctive grace received by the martyrs that aids them in enduring the utter distresses of their torture. It is not necessary to question the authenticity of this grace or to explain it away with psychological theories of psychosis or masochism. For my purposes here, I am interested only in how Christian authors, when looking back at the suffering of the martyrs, understand this grace in the context of a suffering human being. Commenting on the Maccabean martyrs, Chrysostom observes that "their constitution is weak, but the grace that sustains them is powerful."[40] The martyr Gordios, upon entering the hippodrome, is described by Basil as having "a certain grace

37. Chrysostom, *A Homily on Julian the Martyr* 1, in *"Let Us Die,"* 129.
38. Ibid.
39. Chrysostom, *Julian the Martyr* 1, in *"Let Us Die,"* 131.
40. Chrysostom, *Homily 1 on the Maccabees* 3, in Mayer, 138–39.

[that] became conspicuous to all as it shown around him from the inside."[41] The grace accompanying the martyrs is never specifically defined, though it is used by our authors to explain how a martyr is able to withstand the tortures and sufferings on their road to death.[42]

Coinciding with this special grace is a further charism, that of *parrēsia*, or boldness of speech. The term *parrēsia* has a long history in Hellenistic, early Christian, and patristic literature. In reference to martyrdom, it has two meanings. It can refer to the boldness of speech that martyrs exhibit in the declaration of their Christian identity. As seen in the word *martyr* itself, a martyr is a witness or a testimony to the Christian confession, to the person of Jesus Christ. Boldness of speech therefore refers to the confidence, courage, and determination of the martyr to confess one's faith in the face of danger and then to maintain this confession. At times our authors understand this type of *parrēsia* as coming from God, and at other times as a result of the conviction of the martyr. The second kind of *parrēsia* is that of bold speech in the presence of God and is a result of the suffering and endurance of the martyrs. In this use, *parrēsia* refers to the communicative and intercessory capability of the martyr after death. That is, the martyr is capable of interceding, or mediating, on behalf of those who pray to the martyr, because of the gift of *parrēsia*—because of the gift of boldness of speech before the throne of God.

In his homily on the martyr Theodore the Recruit, Gregory of Nyssa is quite clear about the intercessory role of the soldier martyr: "To us he left the instructive memory of his contest, he who brings people together, who teaches the Church, who chases demons, . . . [who] looks out for our interests in the presence of God."[43] It is in the presence of God that the martyr exhibits *parrēsia*. According to Chrysostom, the martyr Drosis, after undergoing death by fire, is "dispatched to the emperor in heaven, entering the vaults of heaven with considerable boldness of speech."[44] Just as Christians are called to imitate the virtues of the martyrs by calling to remembrance their endurance and love for Christ, the reward for the faithful Christian can be similar to that of the martyr. If those of us who are alive are able to calm our passions—our anger, desire for money, the flesh, and vainglory—just as the

---

41. Basil, *On Gordios* 4, in *"Let Us Die,"* 62.

42. "Endurance of hardship is a kind of perception or habit. The man who has it will never be afraid of pain, or toil or hardship, nor will he run from them. It was this marvelous grace that enabled the souls of the martyrs to rise superior to their torments," Step 26, in John Climacus, *The Ladder of Divine Ascent*, trans. Colm Luibheid and Norman Russell, CWS (New York: Paulist Press, 1982), 239.

43. Gregory of Nyssa, *A Homily on Theodore the Recruit* 69.3, in *"Let Us Die,"* 90.

44. Chrysostom, *On Saint Drosis* 10, in Mayer, 201.

martyrs demonstrated their virtue by enduring suffering, we can share in the same *parrēsia* that the martyrs have.[45]

Rodney Stark, in his provocative sociological study of martyrdom in early Christianity, argues that Christians endured martyrdom precisely because the reward gained sufficiently compensated for the suffering and inevitable death awaiting the publicly professing Christian.[46] The reward gained through martyrdom is nothing short of immortality or life after death. Regardless of the accuracy of Stark's claims, there is no doubt that as Greek patristic literature of the fourth and later centuries comments on the martyrs of the early church, the most significant and frequently mentioned reward for the suffering and death of the martyrs is life after death. Chrysostom, Basil, and the two Gregorys are all emphatic on this point. Martyrdom leads to eternal life.

Life after death is the most frequent justification offered for enduring the utter brutality, unbearable pain, and eventual death of martyrdom. In fact, Chrysostom suggests that the female martyrs Bernike, Prosdoke, and Domina would not have so readily ventured into their voluntary death had the gates of paradise not been available to them.[47] Into the mouth of the martyr Gordios, Basil puts the following exhortation: "Since, then, one has to die in any case, let us bring life on ourselves by means of death."[48] In his homily on the Forty Martyrs, Basil is even more dramatic when he has the martyrs utter the following words of encouragement to one another: "Since it is of course necessary to die, let us die that we may live."[49] The promise of life eternal, a promise that undergirds the kerygma of the early church, is at the center of the martyr homilies of the fourth and fifth centuries.

Conclusion

This essay has been more of a descriptive enterprise than interpretive. The patristic literature I have examined is quite unanimous in its exaltation of the suffering of the martyrs. Yet it is an exaltation with a purpose. This intention does not exonerate this literature, nor those who produced it, from the charge of sensationalism; the stories told of the suffering of the martyrs are brutal, gory, and from our sanitized twenty-first-century Western culture often downright revolting. This is not to say that the world of the fourth century

45. Chrysostom, *Homily 1 on the Maccabees* 11, in Mayer, 145.
46. Rodney Stark, *The Rise of Christianity* (San Francisco: HarperSanFrancisco, 1997), 163–89.
47. Chrysostom, *On Saints Bernike, Prosdoke, and Domina* 1, in Mayer, 158.
48. Basil, *On Gordios* 8, in "*Let Us Die*," 66.
49. Basil, *Forty Martyrs* 6, in "*Let Us Die*," 73.

was any more violent than ours is today. Rather, as fourth-century Christians looked back on and pondered the atrocious suffering and death that many of their earlier fellow Christians endured for the faith, they not only celebrated the memory of these Christian heroes but also found ways to explain, understand, and profit from their sufferings.

First and foremost, the suffering of martyrdom provided didactic and moralistic examples of individuals who were able to remain faithful to their Christian calling in the face of great physical and emotional pain. Their suffering served as an example of Christian fortitude and love for God. Second, suffering has a redemptive quality. For martyrs, the spilling of their blood was equated with a second baptism and provided an opportunity for the cleansing of sins prior to death. Their suffering was not in vain, at least not for the martyrs. There is also some indication that some of our authors came close to viewing the suffering of the martyrs as having redemptive impact upon nonmartyred Christians. Finally, the martyr who suffers is rewarded with certain charisms or gifts. The boldness that the martyrs exhibit in proclaiming and maintaining their Christian identity is rewarded with a boldness or *parrēsia* in the presence of God. The *parrēsia* that the martyr acquires can be used by the martyr and can be tapped into by the faithful Christian as a means through which prayers can be offered and answered. The martyr, who has received a special grace during the course of the martyrdom, now stands before God, interceding on behalf of those who believe. Finally, it is the end that provides the greatest gift for the martyr: the gift of living in the eternal presence of God.

4

LEARNING THROUGH EXPERIENCE

The Pedagogy of Suffering and Death in Irenaeus

JOHN BEHR

H uman beings are earth that suffers," according to the *Letter of Barnabas*.[1] What he had in mind is clearly the biblical imagery of God taking clay from the earth and fashioning a human being (cf. Gen. 2:7), pummeling, stretching, forming the clay into a particular figure. The clay is passive in the hands of God; it "suffers" as it is being formed. Yet he clearly also has in mind the "sufferings" that we all undergo throughout our lives. This is indeed the common lot of humankind, though experienced in as many different ways as there are human beings. That this is indeed so is also a perennial subject for human reflection and questioning.

It is an even more poignant question for a Christian, for one struggling to affirm faith in a good God who has created everything such that it is "very good" (Gen. 1:31), in the face of the overwhelming suffering and tragedy in the world around us. Theologians have become accustomed to referring all this suffering back to "the fall," the sinful act of human defiance against

---

1. *Barnabas* 6.9, trans. and ed. Kirsopp Lake, *Apostolic Fathers*, vol. 1, LCL (1913; reprint, Cambridge, MA: Harvard University Press, 1976).

God that resulted in the world as we currently experience it—the fallen world and the human beings that God has come to redeem and re-create in Christ. Yet why did he wait so long, and why has his action not been more decisive? Why leave the world, as the apostle Paul put it, "groaning in travail" (Rom. 8:22 RSV)?

However, when we look at the full scope of Paul's words, it seems that there is something more going on. "We know that the whole creation has been groaning in travail until now," that is, creation as a whole has been in labor, giving birth to children of God, and it is to this end that God himself has subjected creation: "For the creation waits with eager longing for the revealing of the children of God; for the creation was subjected to futility, not of its own will but by the will of the one who subjected it, in hope that the creation itself will be set free from its bondage to decay and will obtain the freedom of the glory of the children of God" (Rom. 8:19–21). Thus it is God himself who has subjected creation to decay, to labor pains, but has done so "in hope," looking forward (not backward) to the manifestation of the children of God in the liberty of their glory.

To see this perspective fleshed out more fully, we can do no better than to turn to the writings of Irenaeus of Lyons, near the end of the second century.[2] Irenaeus really is the first great theologian of the church. It is in his writings that we can see coming together, for the first time, all the elements that form the structure and framework of theological reflection thereafter: the writings of the apostles and evangelists, now used as Scripture alongside the Scriptures we now call the "Old Testament"; an appeal to the canon or rule of truth, a creedlike statement of faith acting as a norm in theological reflection, alongside a developed understanding of tradition and episcopal succession; and especially important for this essay, a fully worked out understanding of the "economy" of God, the overarching arc of God's work leading from Adam to Christ. In a striking manner, this economy incorporates creation and salvation together into the unitary work of God, which is that of making human beings in his own image and likeness. For Irenaeus, "the work of God" consists specifically in creating human beings (*Haer.* 5.15.1),[3] that is, taking clay from the earth and fashioning

2. Many of the themes in this essay have been developed more fully, and in a broader context, in my *The Mystery of Christ: Life in Death* (Crestwood, NY: St. Vladimir's Seminary Press, 2006); *Irenaeus of Lyons: Identifying Christianity*, Christian Theology in Context (Oxford: Oxford University Press, 2013); and *Becoming Human: Meditations on Christian Anthropology in Word and Image* (Crestwood, NY: St. Vladimir's Seminary Press, 2013).

3. Irenaeus of Lyons, *Against Heresies* (= *Haer.*) 5.15.2. I am using the SC edition of A. Rousseau (SC 263–64 [*Haer.* 1], 293–94 [*Haer.* 2], 210–11 [*Haer.* 3], 100 [*Haer.* 4], 152–53 [*Haer.* 5] [Paris: Cerf, 1979, 1982, 1974, 1965, 1969]); and the translations in *ANF*, vol. 1 (Edinburgh,

it into his image, molding it with his hands so that humans might reflect his glory, or indeed that they might share in his glory and incorruptibility, becoming not only vessels of his power and operations but also themselves the glory of God. For as Irenaeus puts it, "The glory of God is the living human being" (*Haer.* 4.20.7). Yet what he means by this, as we will see, is somewhat surprising.

It is important to notice the particular character of Irenaeus's theological methodology, which might best be described as phenomenological. That is, he repeatedly emphasizes that our goal is to see things as they *are*, the truth about God and the human being.[4] For Irenaeus, the basis for seeing things in this way is articulated in the canon of truth, which he lays out for the first time near the beginning of his magnum opus, *Against Heresies* (1.10.1). By appealing to a canon, Irenaeus does not mean to curtail all thought but rather means to make reflection possible, for only if we have a canon or criterion (in the sense of a "yardstick") are we able to reflect meaningfully, at all. When he continues by suggesting fruitful avenues for exploration (*Haer.* 1.10.3), he urges that in such theological reflection, we should never substitute something else for the fundamental hypothesis of the Christian faith. This happens when we ask counterfactual questions, as we are prone to do. For instance, if we were to ask, could it have been otherwise, or what would have happened if, say, Adam had not fallen, we would necessarily be grounding our theological reflection on something other than the way in which God has in fact revealed himself in Christ. Instead, we should search out the wisdom and the power that God has revealed in Christ, the crucified and exalted Lord, as preached by the apostles in accordance with the Scriptures.[5] One avenue he suggests, however, is precisely our question: Why was God "patient in regard to the apostasy of the angels who transgressed and in regard to the disobedience of the human being?" And how is it, as Paul says, that "he imprisoned all in disobedience so that he may be merciful to all" (cf. Rom. 11:32; *Haer.* 1.10.3)?

1887; reprint, Grand Rapids: Eerdmans, 1987), adjusting them as needed. Translations of *Haer.* 1–3 by D. J. Unger as revised by J. J. Dillon and M. C. Steenberg have also appeared in the series ACW 55, 64, 65 (New York: Paulist Press, 1992, 2012, 2012). For his *Demonstration of the Apostolic Preaching* (= *Dem.*), I have used my translation in the Popular Patristics Series (Crestwood, NY: St. Vladimir's Seminary Press, 1997).

4. Cf. esp. *Haer.* 5.2.3; and *Dem.* 3. As Hans Urs von Balthasar observes, for Irenaeus "the primary aim is not to think, to impose Platonic intellectual or even mythical categories on things, but simply to *see* what *is*." See his *The Glory of the Lord: A Theological Aesthetics*, vol. 2 (Edinburgh: T&T Clark, 1984), 45.

5. Cf. *Haer.* 1.10.3; 2.25–28; Behr, *Irenaeus of Lyons*, 103–20.

Against Heresies 4.37–39: Learning by Experience

There are two sections of *Against Heresies* in which Irenaeus provides a sustained analysis of these questions: 4.37–39 and 3.20.1–2. These two extended passages offer us much fruit for reflection and deserve to be studied closely before we go on to comment on what he says, and perhaps more important, how he can say what he says.

He describes *Against Heresies* 4.37–39 as an exposition, from Scripture, of "the ancient law of human liberty," the fact that "God created man free, having, from the beginning, power over himself" (*Haer*. 4.37.1).[6] Only such creatures are capable of initiative and response, and this is of fundamental importance, for only such creatures are capable of changing their mode of existence, of growing into the immortality of God. Irenaeus draws out the presuppositions in his opponents' question by rephrasing it rather bluntly:

> "But," they say, "he should not have created angels such that they were able to transgress, nor human beings such that they immediately [*statim*] became ungrateful towards him, because they were created rational and capable of examining and judging. And they are not like irrational or inanimate creatures which are unable to do anything of their own will but are drawn by necessity and force towards the good, with one inclination and one bearing, unable to deviate and without the power of judging, and unable to be anything other than what they were created." (*Haer*. 4.37.6)

His answer is that it would not have benefited either God or human beings for this to have been the case. Communion with God would have been something neither desired nor sought after; it would occur by nature and not by choice (*Haer*. 4.37.6). Freedom, for Irenaeus, is a precondition for creatures to grow into what they are called to become, for creatures to enter into communion with God, and so be transfigured.[7] Irenaeus continues, in 4.37.7, by citing Matthew 11:12 and 1 Corinthians 9:24–27 to emphasize the need for struggle, and this on the grounds that endeavor heightens the appreciation of the gift. Moreover, he continues, as the faculty of seeing is desired more by those who know what it is like to be without sight, so also is health prized more by those who know disease, light by contrast with darkness, and life by contrast with death.

---

6. On this section, see Philippe Bacq, *De l'ancienne à la nouvelle alliance selon S. Irénée: Unité du livre IV de l'Adversus haereses* (Paris: Lethielleux, Presses Universitaires de Namur, 1978), 363–88.

7. Cf. John Behr, *Asceticism and Anthropology in Irenaeus and Clement*, Oxford Early Christian Studies (Oxford: Oxford University Press, 2000), 35–43.

In *Against Heresies* 4.39.1, Irenaeus develops this analysis by contrasting two types of knowledge: that gained through experience and that arrived at by opinion. He points out that the tongue learns of bitterness and sweetness only through experience, and he argues that, in the same way, the human mind receives the knowledge (*disciplina*) of the good (obedience to God, which is life for human beings), through the experience of both good and evil (disobedience, which is death), and so is in a position to reject the evil. In this way, through experience of both, human beings come to cast away disobedience through repentance and become ever more tenacious in their obedience to God. But if someone tries to avoid the knowledge of both good and evil, he will, in Irenaeus's striking language, both forget himself and kill his humanity (*Haer.* 4.39.1).

In 4.37.3, Irenaeus claims that the heavenly kingdom is more precious to those who have known the earthly kingdom, and if they value it more, they will also love it more: and loving it the more, they will be more glorified by God. Irenaeus then concludes:

> God therefore has borne[8] all these things for our sake, in order that, having been instructed through all things, henceforth we may be scrupulous in all things, and, having been taught how to love God in accordance with reason, we may remain in his love. God exhibits patience [*magnanimitatem*] in regard to the apostasy of human beings, and human beings are taught by it, as the prophet says: "Your own apostasy shall heal you." (*Haer.* 4.37.7, quoting Jer. 2:19)

He then immediately continues by placing this particular action of God within the economy as a whole: God thus has determined all things beforehand for the perfection of the human being, and toward the realization and manifestation of his saving plans. Thus goodness may be displayed and righteousness accomplished, and thus the church may be "conformed to the image of his Son" (Rom. 8:29). Thereby finally, the human being may be brought to such maturity as to see and comprehend God (*Haer.* 4.37.7).

8. Rousseau translates *sustinuit* by "*a permis*"; however, as Roger Berthouzoz observes, such a translation characterizes a later theological perspective, and so he proposes instead "*a supporté*," in *Liberté et grace suivant la théologie d'Irénée de Lyon: Le debat avec la gnose aux origines de la theologie chretienne* (Fribourg, Switzerland: Éditions Universitaires; Paris: Cerf, 1980), 216n79. Irenaeus in *Haer.* 5.2.3 employs ἀνέχω in a similar context, a verb that in its New Testament usage (the background for much of Irenaeus's vocabulary) always appears in the middle voice, generally with the sense of "to bear, to endure," as in Matt. 17:17, etc. The Armenian of *Haer.* 4.37.7 seems to be an attempt to explain the middle voice, "He took to Himself" (cf. *Haer.* 35.2 in Texte und Untersuchungen, 137 line 23; for *Haer.* 5.2.3, see 157 line 5). The idea mentioned in *Haer.* 5.2.3, that God has borne our death that we might not be ignorant either of God or of ourselves, echoes Irenaeus's startling words at the end of *Haer.* 4.39.1, cited above.

That Irenaeus can inscribe human apostasy into the unfolding of the divine economy is very striking. It indicates various points. First, it indicates that Irenaeus did not consider the economy simply as a plan that progresses automatically. Rather, as we have seen, God created beings capable of initiative, since only such beings would be able to respond freely to God and to love him. Second, it clearly indicates that Irenaeus does not think, as we are inclined to do, in terms of God having to substitute a "Plan B" when human beings ruin "Plan A" (but more on this later).

So, for Irenaeus, the aim of the whole divine economy is twofold: first, the perfection of humans by, second, the realization and manifestation of the saving plans of God, a perfection that, at the same time, displays his goodness and realizes his justice.

Finally, in this passage, when discussing the question of human freedom, Irenaeus appears to isolate each person's relationship to God by emphasizing the need for each to gain personal experience and to endeavor to love God more. The section nevertheless ends with the assertion that through this process the church, a community, is conformed to the image of the Son, and in this way each is brought to such perfection as to see and comprehend God.

So far we have been looking at *Against Heresies* 4.37 and 39. In 4.38 Irenaeus approaches the same problem from a different angle. He argues that God could have created the human as perfect or as a "god" from the beginning, for all things are possible to God. However, created things, by virtue of being created, are necessarily inferior to the One who created them and hence fall short of the perfect. They are of a later date, infantile, and thus unaccustomed to, and unexercised in, perfect conduct (4.38.1). Yet, as it is possible for a mother to give an infant solid food, so also God could have made humans "perfect" from the beginning, but they, being still in their infancy, could not have received this perfection (4.38.1).[9]

As a creature, the human can never be uncreated, can never cease existing in the mode proper to a creature, that is, being created. But the aim of this creating or fashioning of humans is that they should come to be ever more fully in the image and likeness of the uncreated God. There can be, for humans, no

9. Denis Minns asserts that in arguing this way, Irenaeus is not claiming that the omnipotence of God is restricted by the nature of that on which he is working. See Minns, *Irenaeus* (London: Geoffrey Chapman, 1994), 73–74. Gustaf Wingren earlier pointed out that the infantile state is not itself imperfect, despite only beginning to grow toward its full perfection. See Wingren, *Man and the Incarnation: A Study in the Biblical Theology of Irenaeus* (London: Oliver & Boyd, 1959), 20, 26–35: a newborn child may well have "perfect" limbs yet is unable to walk or run until these limbs are exercised (which includes much falling down).

end to this process, for they can never become uncreated. Human perfection instead lies, according to Irenaeus, in continual submission to the creative activity of God, through which the human is brought to share in the glory of the Uncreated (*Haer.* 4.38.3).

Finally, Irenaeus concludes 4.38 by outlining the preceding discussion in a few brief strokes: "It was necessary, first, for nature to be manifest; after which, for what was mortal to be conquered and swallowed up by immortality, and the corruptible by incorruptibility, and for the human being to be made in the image and likeness of God, having received the knowledge of good and evil" (*Haer.* 4.38.4; cf. Gen. 1:26; 3:5; 3:22; 1 Cor. 15:53; 2 Cor. 5:4).

Thus creation and salvation, the appearance of human nature and the conquering of mortality by immortality, both belong to the same economy, the purposeful arrangement of history. In this economy the acquisition of the knowledge of good and evil has its place, contributing to the realization, in the end, of the original divine intention: making the human in the image and likeness of God.

As we have seen in *Against Heresies* 4.37–39, Irenaeus speaks of God's patience in the face of human apostasy and explains apostasy, within the framework of God's overall economy, by the general principle of the need for newly created humans to acquire experience of both good and evil, in order to hold ever more firmly to the good and to continue indefinitely progressing toward God, thus becoming ever more fully in his image and likeness.

Against Heresies 3.20: The Sign of Jonah

Irenaeus treats the same question of God's great patience in the face of human apostasy in *Against Heresies* 3.20.1–2. Yet this time he brings out certain other aspects, in particular how the role of Christ fits into this divine economy. He begins 3.20 by explaining that God was patient with human apostasy, both because he already foresaw the victory that would be granted to the human through the Word and, following the words of Christ to Paul, because his "power is made perfect in weakness" (2 Cor. 12:9). Irenaeus suggests that it is in this way, through our own weakness and mortality, that God reveals his goodness and magnificent power (*Haer.* 3.20.1).

As an example of this, Irenaeus gives the case of Jonah. By God's arrangement, Jonah was swallowed by the whale, not so he would perish, but so that once he was cast out, he would be more obedient to God and give more glory to the One who had unexpectedly saved him. Irenaeus then continues:

So also, from the beginning, God did bear[10] human beings to be swallowed up by the great whale, who was the author of transgression, not that they should perish altogether when so engulfed, but arranging in advance the finding of salvation. This was accomplished by the Word through the "sign of Jonah" [Matt. 12:39–40] for those who held the same opinion as Jonah regarding the Lord, and who confessed and said, "I am a servant of the LORD, and I worship the Lord God of heaven, who made the sea and the dry land" [Jon. 1:9]. So human beings, receiving an unhoped-for salvation from God, might rise from the dead, and glorify God, and repeat, "I cried to the LORD my God in my affliction, and he heard me from the belly of Hades" [Jon. 2:2]. And they might always continue glorifying God, and giving thanks without ceasing for that salvation which they had obtained from him, "that no flesh should glory in the Lord's presence" [1 Cor. 1:29]. And that human beings should never adopt an opposite opinion with regard to God, supposing that the incorruptibility which surrounds them is their own by nature, nor, by not holding the truth, should boast with empty superciliousness, as if they were by nature like God. (*Haer.* 3.20.1)

For Irenaeus, then, God has borne the human race from the beginning, while it was swallowed up by the whale. For Irenaeus, there is no lost golden age of primordial perfection, no time when, hypothetically (and counterfactually), we might not have needed Christ.[11]

Such language, which one can find in other fathers,[12] sounds strange to us, largely, I suspect, because we are used to thinking of God "before" the creation—deciding, in an all-too-human manner, what he is going to do and

10. Although the Latin is *fuit patiens*, Rousseau suggests that the Greek was ἠνέσχετο and translates this again by "*a permis*"; I have preferred "bear"; see my comments above on *Haer.* 4.37.7. If the parallel with Jonah is indeed to hold, God was more actively involved in this event than is suggested by "*a permis*"; in Jon. 2:1, it is said that the Lord appointed (προσέταξεν) a great whale to swallow up Jonah.

11. Irenaeus does nevertheless write of the "prelapsarian" existence of Adam in occasional comments and discussion in *Against Heresies*, as in 3.22–23; the comments here, however, are made within the Pauline Adam-Christ framework. In *Dem.* 11–16, Irenaeus provides a sustained commentary on the creation and paradisiacal life of Adam and Eve; here, it is to be noticed, the theology that Irenaeus develops out of the opening chapters of Genesis is that of the dependency of the human race on God and the need for grateful obedience, human infancy and their need for growth: that is, Genesis *functions*, within the *Demonstration*, to establish the framework within which salvation history unfolds. See further, Thomas Holsinger-Friesen, *Irenaeus and Genesis: A Study of Competition in Early Christian Hermeneutics*, Journal of Theological Interpretation Supplements 1 (Winona Lake, IN: Eisenbrauns, 2009); and Behr, *Irenaeus of Lyons*, 144–62.

12. See esp. Maximus the Confessor, *Ad Thalassium* 61, where he asserts that the first human squandered his capacity for spiritual pleasure, turning it instead toward the physical senses, ἅμα τῷ γενέσθαι, "together with coming into being."

accomplishing it—as Plan A, but then having to respond to the fall with Plan B. As I pointed out at the beginning, Irenaeus (*Haer.* 1.10.3) specifically asserts that theological reflection is not to start from any other (hypothetical or counterfactual) position. It is not to conceive of another God or Christ, other than the ones proclaimed by the apostles, in accordance with the Scriptures (*Haer.* 1.10.3). We are rather to seek out God's wisdom made manifest in the Christ preached by the apostles, "the power of God and the wisdom of God" (1 Cor. 1:24). Adam, as the apostle asserted, is always already a "type of the one to come" (Rom. 5:14), that is, a sketch or an imprint of the reality that is manifest in Christ. So, as Irenaeus puts it, Christ is in fact the beginning who appears at the end (*Haer.* 1.10.3).

For Irenaeus, the starting point for all theological reflection is the given fact of the work of Christ, his life-giving and saving death. In a very interesting way, this is confirmed by James Barr's study *The Garden of Eden and the Hope of Immortality*: Barr points out that it is only from the perspective of the crucified and exalted Christ that we can speak of a "fall" in Genesis and of the human race being held thereafter under sin and death.[13] Accordingly, in the passage we just looked at, Irenaeus speaks of God "arranging in advance the finding of salvation, which was accomplished by the Word through the sign of Jonah." This was already a given, though it was unknown to humans prior to the incarnation; they then receive an "unhoped-for salvation," not hoped for but divinely foreseen.

In one other part of his work, Irenaeus emphasizes his starting point in an even more startling fashion. Commenting on Paul's description of Adam as a "type of the one . . . to come" (*typos tou mellontos*, Rom. 5:14), Irenaeus says: "Since he who saves already existed, it was necessary that the one who would be saved should come into existence, that the One who saves should not exist in vain" (*Haer.* 3.22.3).

Creation and salvation, for Irenaeus, are not Plan A and Plan B. Rather, they cohere together as the one economy of God, which culminates in the work of Christ. God's saving plan can be understood and explained only from this starting point, which is at the same time the completion of the creative act begun in Genesis 1:26–27: "Let us make humankind in our image, according to our likeness." In the Gospel of John (19:30), when Christ says from the cross, "It is finished"—and then God rests from his works on the day that Byzantine hymnography says "is the blessed Sabbath"[14]—we should recall

---

13. James Barr, *The Garden of Eden and the Hope of Immortality* (Minneapolis: Fortress, 1993), esp. 89.

14. See the Doxastikon for Vespers on Holy Saturday; Greek and English text, in Michael Monos, ed., *The Services of Holy and Great Week* (Columbia, MO: Newrome, 2012).

what Pilate has just unwittingly stated, making clear what it is that is now finished: "Behold the human being" (John 19:5, my trans.).

This does not, however, mitigate human responsibility for the action of apostasy or the reality of the work of the devil in instigating it, for he is, as Irenaeus puts it, "the author of transgression." The devil's temptation, according to Irenaeus, is to offer what he could not give: Adam and Eve were beguiled through "the pretext of immortality" (*Haer.* 3.23.5; 4, preface 4). Trying to secure their life, they lost it; if they had lost it in the manner shown by Christ, they would have gained true immortality (cf. Matt. 16:25 and parallels).

So, for Irenaeus, death is the result of human apostasy, turning away from the one and only Source of life. It is instigated by the devil and thus is the expression of his dominion over the human race. But it is also embraced within the divine economy, the way in which everything fits together in God's hand. When viewing this from the perspective of the salvation granted by Christ through "the sign of Jonah," we can see that, as it was God himself who appointed the whale to swallow Jonah, so also the engulfing of the human race by the great whale was "borne" by God in his arrangement, his economy, which culminates in the finding of salvation.

But there is yet more! For Irenaeus, the newly created humans were inexperienced, and so they immediately gave way to temptation.[15] And, so Irenaeus continues:

> Such then was the patience of God, that human beings, after passing through all things and acquiring knowledge of death, then attaining to the resurrection from the dead, and learning by experience from whence they have been delivered, may thus always give thanks to the Lord, having received from him the gift of incorruptibility, and may love him the more, for "he to whom more is forgiven, loves more" [cf. Luke 7:42–43]. And may they know themselves how mortal and weak they are, but also understand that God is so immortal and powerful as to bestow immortality on the mortal and eternity on the temporal. And may they also know the other powers of God made manifest in themselves, and, being taught by them, may they think of God in accordance with the greatness of God. For the glory of the human being is God, while the vessel of the workings of God, and of all his wisdom and power, is the human being. (*Haer.* 3.20.2)

God thus is patient, while humans learn by experience their own weakness and death in their ungrateful apostasy. Knowing that having passed through

---

15. Cf. esp. *Haer.* 4.40.3, where Irenaeus mitigates the disobedience of humans by attributing it to a lack of care and inexperience, in contrast to the conscious sowing of tares by the devil; cf. *Haer.* 3.23.3.

this experience, and having an unhoped-for salvation bestowed upon them, they will remain ever more thankful to God, they are willing to accept from him the eternal existence that he alone can give. In this way humans become fully acquainted with the power of God. By being reduced to nothing, to dust in the earth, humans simultaneously come to know their total dependency upon God, allowing God to work in and through them, to deploy his power in them as the recipient of all his work. And both dimensions of this economy—the engulfing of the human and the salvation wrought by the Word—are simultaneously represented by Jonah, a sign of both the transgressing human race and its Savior.

By viewing death from the starting point of the work of Christ, the divinely foreseen sign of Jonah, Irenaeus can discern in the tragedy and absurdity of death an educational role within the divine economy: it enables humans to experience to the uttermost their weakness and mortality in their apostasy from God, the only Source of life, so that they might thereafter hold ever more firmly to God.

A little later in *Against Heresies* 3, Irenaeus draws out a further positive role for death, this time following Theophilus of Antioch.[16] If death has come into the world as a result of sin (cf. Rom. 5:12), death can also be seen as a restriction of sin. Death cuts sin short, lest sin be immortal and as such unable to be healed. Viewed in this way, death can be seen, not so much simply as an arbitrary penalty imposed for disobedience, nor as a consequence of human transgression, turning away from the Source of life and so becoming mortal, but as a limitation on sin itself. As such, subjection to death can be seen as an act of mercy. It puts an end to sin through the resolution of the human into the earth. It is in this way that Irenaeus describes the action of God in response to the apostasy:

> Wherefore also he drove him [Adam] out of paradise and removed him far from the tree of life, but not because he envied him the tree of life, as some venture to assert. Rather, having mercy on him, that he should not continue a transgressor forever, nor that the sin which surrounded him should be immortal, and evil interminable and irremediable. But God set a bound to his transgression, by interposing death and causing sin to cease, putting an end to it by the dissolution of the flesh into the earth. So the human being, ceasing at length to live to sin, and dying to it, might begin to live to God.[17]

---

16. Theophilus of Antioch, *Ad Autolycum* 2.25–26, trans. and ed. Robert Grant, Oxford Early Christian Texts (Oxford: Clarendon, 1970).

17. Irenaeus, *Haer.* 3.23.6; Gen. 3:22–24; Rom. 6:2, 10. This positive evaluation of death, as putting an end to sin through the resolution of humanity into the earth, recurs in later patristic writings, e.g., Gregory of Nyssa, *Oratio catechetica* 8. On this dimension of death, see Panayiotis

From this perspective, the subjection of humans to death was an act of mercy. Had humans been created in such a way as to be able to remain immortal after apostatizing from God (if, for instance, they possessed a life of their own, other than the one received from God), then sin and evil would also have remained immortal and thus irremediable, and so God's economy would have been frustrated, conquered by the serpent (cf. *Haer.* 3.23.1).

Death as Eucharistic in Our Becoming Human

There are two further aspects to the mystery of death, as expounded by Irenaeus, when seen in the light of the mystery of Christ: seeing it in eucharistic terms and seeing it as the culmination of our becoming truly human. The life in death, begun by dying to sin in baptism as a "likeness" of Christ's death (Rom. 6:5; cf. Eph. 4:13), finds fruition in the eucharistic self-offering of the Christian in their own bodily death in witness to Christ. This finds striking expression in Ignatius of Antioch, when he beseeches the Christians at Rome not to interfere with his impending martyrdom: "Suffer me to be eaten by the beasts, through whom I can attain to God. I am God's wheat, and I am ground by the teeth of wild beasts that I may be found pure bread of Christ."[18] He continues:

> It is better for me to die in Christ Jesus than to be king over the ends of the earth. I seek him who died for our sake. I desire him who rose for us. The pains of birth are upon me. Suffer me, my brethren; hinder me not from living, do not wish me to die. Do not give to the world one who desires to belong to God, nor deceive him with material things. Suffer me to receive the pure light; when I shall have arrived there, I shall become a human being. Suffer me to follow the example of the passion of my God.[19]

For Ignatius, undergoing death in witness to Christ, the "perfect human being" or the "new human being," is a birth into a new life, to emerge as did Christ himself, a fully human being.[20]

Irenaeus quotes the passage of Ignatius about becoming the wheat of God and takes the imagery further:

Nellas, *Deification in Christ* (Crestwood, NY: St. Vladimir's Seminary Press, 1987), 64–66. The positive *pedagogical* value of death within the whole economy seems to be particular to Irenaeus.

18. Ignatius, *To the Romans* 4, trans. and ed. Lake, *Apostolic Fathers*, vol. 1.

19. Ignatius, *To the Romans* 6.

20. Ignatius, *To the Smyrnaeans* 4.2; Ignatius, *To the Ephesians* 20.1.

The wood of the vine, planted in the earth, bore fruit in its own time, and the grain of wheat, falling into the earth and being decomposed, was raised up manifold by the Spirit of God who sustains all, then, by wisdom, they come to the use of human beings, and receiving the Word of God, become eucharist, which is the Body and Blood of Christ. Likewise also, our bodies, nourished by it, having been placed in the earth and decomposing in it, shall rise in their time, when the Word of God bestows on them the resurrection to the glory of God the Father, who secures immortality for the mortal and bountifully bestows incorruptibility on the corruptible [cf. 1 Cor. 15:53], because the power of God is made perfect in weakness [cf. 2 Cor. 12:9]. [This will take place] in order that we may never become puffed up, as if we had life from ourselves, nor exalted against God, entertaining ungrateful thoughts, but learning by experience that it is from his excellence, and not from our own nature, that we have eternal continuance, that we should neither undervalue the true glory of God nor be ignorant of our own nature, but should know what God can do and what benefits the human, and that we should never mistake the true understanding of things as they are, that is, of God and the human being. (*Haer.* 5.2.3)

There is clearly a close relationship between the processes that lead to the Eucharist and to the resurrection: It is by receiving the Eucharist, as we have made the fruits into the bread and the wine, and as the wheat and the vine receive the fecundity of the Spirit, that we are prepared for the resurrection effected by the Word. Then, just as the bread and wine receive the Word and so become the body and blood of Christ, the Eucharist, so also our bodies will receive immortality and incorruptibility from the Father. As such, death, within the overall economy of God seen in the light of Christ's passion, takes on a eucharistic dimension, alongside its educative and limiting function: God's saving plan as a whole can be described as the Eucharist of God.

Irenaeus, like Ignatius, also connects the eucharistic self-offering of the martyrs with their becoming human, for, as he puts it in the words with which we began, "the work of God is the fashioning of the human being" (*Haer.* 5.15.2). When Irenaeus says that "the glory of God is the living human being" (4.20.7), this is not simply an endorsement of what we might now think it is to be "fully alive" in this world. Rather, for Irenaeus, the "living human being" is the martyr, going to death in confession of Christ:

In this way, therefore, the martyrs bear witness and despise death, not through the weakness of the flesh, but by the readiness of the Spirit. For when the weakness of the flesh is absorbed, it manifests the Spirit as powerful; and again, when the Spirit absorbs the weakness, it inherits the flesh for itself, and from both of these is made a living human being: living, indeed, because of the participation of the Spirit; and human, because of the substance of the flesh. (*Haer.* 5.9.2)

The strength of God is made perfect in weakness, and so, paradoxically, it is in their death, their ultimate vulnerability, that the martyrs bear greatest witness to the strength of God. It is not that they reckon death to be a thing of no importance, Irenaeus emphasizes, but rather that in their confession they are vivified by the Spirit, living the life of the Spirit, who absorbs the weakness of their flesh into his own strength. When the Spirit so possesses the flesh, the flesh itself adopts the quality of the Spirit and is made like the Word of God (*Haer.* 5.9.3). The paradigm of the living human being is Jesus Christ himself, and those who follow in his footsteps, the martyrs, have flesh vivified by the Spirit.

Conclusion

In this way, then, without denying the catastrophic reality of death—that the creature brought into being by God to share in his own life and glory turned his back on his Creator and so ends up rotting in the grave—it is possible, nevertheless, to see the same reality embraced within the overarching economy of God. He makes death a means of bringing his creation, made from mud, to the full maturity of a human, made in the image and likeness of God, knowing both good and evil but rejecting the evil by turning in repentance to God. This, at the same time, demonstrates the wisdom and the power of God, a power that is made perfect in weakness.

This is possible, however, only if we start with Christ's own passion and the theological vision it opens up. Retrospectively, this vision infuses the whole of our human, and humanly created, condition, with the power of God, the power that he manifests on the cross. The goal of the economy, for Irenaeus, is that we are brought to a true understanding "of things as they are, that is, of God and the human being," so that we too might allow ourselves to be fashioned into the fullness of being human. The truth about God revealed in, through, and as Christ, the crucified and exalted Lord, coincides with the truth about humans. This transition, from seeing death as catastrophic to seeing it as embraced within the divine economy, is a transition that has been essential to Christian theology from the beginning. It is a transition from a merely human perspective to a properly theological perspective, thus indicating the transformative power of theological words and the importance of the task of theology. Joseph bore witness to this transition when his brothers fearfully approached him in Egypt, and he reassured them that while they thought they had sold him into slavery (which they had), in fact it was God at work, sending Joseph into Egypt "to preserve life" (Gen. 45:5). Peter makes this transition evident in his preaching: "This man [Jesus], handed over to you according to the definite plan and foreknowledge of God, you crucified and killed by the hands of those outside the law" (Acts 2:23). And the liturgy of John Chrysostom emphasizes this transition rhetorically when the priest says, "In the night in which he was given up," and then, as if correcting himself, adds, "no, rather, gave himself up." It is perhaps most poetically expressed in the hymn of John of Damascus now used in the funeral service:

> I weep and I wail when I think upon death, and behold our beauty, fashioned in the image of God, lying in the tomb, disfigured, dishonored, bereft of form. O marvel! What is this mystery which befalls us? Why have we been given over unto corruption, and why have we been wedded to death? Of a truth, as it is written, by the command of God, who gives the departed rest.[21]

It is a catastrophe: we should weep and wail. But it is also a marvel, a miracle, a mystery, a sacrament. We have been wedded to death by the command of God, no less. In all these ways, then, the earth that we are is being fashioned, "suffering," to use Barnabas's expression, into the image and likeness of God, into what is truly human, into the children of God, for whose birth the world is currently "in travail." But for our suffering, and ultimately our death, to be effective in this way, we too need to learn to raise the horizon and scope of our vision, to see things theologically, which, as Irenaeus reminds us, is to see things as they really are.

---

21. Idiomelon hymn, by John of Damascus, in the funeral service; Sticheron from the Aposticha, Friday Vespers, Octoechos, tone 8. See *Paraclitique ou Grand Octoèque*, trans. P. Denis Guillaume, 2 vols. (Rome: Diaconie Apostolique, 1979), 2:544.

5

THE ENEMIES OF GOD

Demons and the Persecuting Emperors in Lactantius

DENNIS P. QUINN

The impact of the Great Persecutions (303–11) was profound and long lasting for the early Christian community: it is palpable in the Christian literature of those who lived through it. The Christian intellectual Lactantius (ca. 240–ca. 325) survived the persecutions under the emperor Diocletian, and they greatly influenced his worldview. The lasting impact of the persecutions on Lactantius is especially visible in the first two books of his *Divine Institutes* (ca. 308–9) and in another entire work, *Deaths of the Persecutors* (ca. 314–15).[1] The remarkable pleasure Lactantius seems to take in describing the details of their deaths in that later work may strike the modern reader as a bit vicious. However, when seen within the context of acts of brutality meted out by the Roman Empire against Christians, Lactantius's rhetorical vitriol may seem modest by comparison. The persecutions helped provoke Lactantius's apocalyptic view of the world. For Lactantius, the persecutions

1. The best recent study on the historical context of Lactantius's thought is Elizabeth De-Palma Digeser, *The Making of a Christian Empire: Lactantius and Rome* (Ithaca, NY: Cornell University Press, 2000).

he witnessed were the final attacks by the devil and his demons against the righteous Christians, and Constantine in triumph was the savior of the empire, with God on his side.[2] As this essay intends to show, in many respects Lactantius's earthly vision of the persecuting emperors and the coming of Constantine parallels his cosmic view of the fall of the angels and Christ's redeeming power to bring God's peace to the world. The first indication of this can be seen in the *Divine Institutes*, and his ideas are more fully developed in *Deaths of the Persecutors*.

Lactantius's *Divine Institutes*

In book 2 of the *Divine Institutes*, Lactantius describes the origin of evil and the fall of the angels.[3] He declares, "Since God was very alert in his preparations and very skillful in execution, before God began this task of the world, he created good and evil."[4] This, on the surface, may seem to imply that, for Lactantius, God is the author of evil, a position so fervently disputed by Augustine a century later.[5] However, as Lactantius explains, God remains off the hook for originating evil. "Since nothing existed at the time apart from himself," he writes, "because the source of perfect good was in himself, as it always is, in order that good should spring from him like a stream and flow forth on and on, he produced a spirit like himself."[6] Although Lactantius does not identify this spirit in this passage, later he does indicate that this is the Word, the Logos, the Christ—a position that, if posited only a few decades later, would certainly raise suspicions of Arian heresy as a Christ who is *made* and not begotten. Then Lactantius goes on in his discourse to the origin of evil. He writes,

> [By] means of the one he made first, he made another, liable to corruption. In this one, the divine inheritance was not to abide. This spirit was poisoned by its own envy; it changed from good to evil, and of its own choice, a free choice granted by God, it claimed for itself a contradictory name. The source of all evil

2. The standard though dated work on Lactantius's demonology is Emil Schneweis, *Angels and Demons according to Lactantius* (Washington, DC: Catholic University of America Press, 1944). This book, so often cited by scholars addressing Lactantius's view of demons, pays little attention to the historical context behind his theological system.

3. Translation is taken from Lactantius, *Divine Institutes*, trans. Anthony Bowen and Peter Garnsey (Liverpool: Liverpool University Press, 2003).

4. Lactantius, *Divine Institutes* 2.8.3.

5. For the difference between Lactantius and Augustine on this topic, see Peter Garnsey, "Lactantius and Augustine," in *Representations of Empire: Rome and the Mediterranean World*, ed. Alan K. Bowman et al. (Oxford: Oxford University Press, 2002).

6. Lactantius, *Divine Institutes* 2.8.3.

can consequently be seen as jealousy. The spirit was jealous of the one who came before it, which consistently earned the favor and affection of God its father.[7]

Making a spirit "liable to corruption," possessing "free choice granted it by God," thereby ensured the existence of evil in the world, which, Lactantius explains, is necessary for there to be any hope for humanity's salvation.[8] Lactantius continues, "So that the pattern of God's purpose may be known, good cannot be known without evil, nor can evil without good, and wisdom is the knowledge of good and evil."[9] He emphasizes that this evil spirit, "which made itself evil instead of good," is what "the Greeks call the slanderer; we call it the prosecutor, because it brings before God the prosecution of crimes which it inspires itself."[10] Those who successfully resist the wiles of the devil and his minions and follow Christ shall win salvation. Evil exists so that it "may fight with good, so that vice may be set against virtue," all done in order that God has someone to punish and someone to honor.[11]

It is this battle of good versus evil that is at the heart of the Lactantian theology of Christ's coming to the earth. It is the demons' rise to power that prompted God to send his only Son. Lactantius writes: "When God saw that evil and the worship of false gods had grown so strong all over the world that his name by now had been almost removed from people's memories, . . . he sent them his own Son, the prince of angels, to turn them from wicked and empty patterns of worship to knowing and worshiping the true God."[12]

But Christ was only the first step in the process of expelling demons from the world. He left Christians with the power to finish the job. Lactantius argues that after Christ, the demons began to manipulate pagans to eradicate his followers. "[The people] do not do the persecution themselves: they have no reason to get angry with the innocent; it is those unclean, desperate spirits who know the truth and loathe it, insinuating themselves into their minds and egging them on to mad acts in their ignorance."[13]

The Roman Empire is a key player in this cosmic battle. The demons once controlled the empire by possessing emperors and leading some to take on demonic attributes themselves. As the power of Rome increased, the devil and his demons also gained power by attaching themselves to the names, rites, and statues of the Roman gods. For Lactantius, as for so many in the patristic

7. Ibid., 2.8.4–5.
8. Ibid., 2.8.5.
9. Ibid.
10. Ibid.
11. Ibid., 2.17.1.
12. Ibid., 4.14.17.
13. Ibid., 5.21.3.

tradition, Roman paganism was what enabled the demons to gain power in the empire. This began at the very beginning of Roman religion. Following common philosophical critiques of traditional myths and cults, Lactantius uses euhemerism to explain the origin of the gods and their cults as arising from tales of early human history.[14] He believes that masquerading as these gods, evil demons use their worshipers to bring about their plan to entice worshipers away from the one true God. So, entrenched in the very fabric of Roman civic religion before the coming of Constantine, demons held sway over the world.

Book 2 of the *Divine Institutes* describes how the angels sent to watch over humanity became smitten by human women, seduced them, and impregnated them, creating the "earthly demons" who would wreak havoc on the world.[15]

> As long as there is peace among the people of God, these spirits keep shunning the just for fear of them, and whenever they try to occupy a body and torment its soul, they are exorcised by the just and are put to flight in the name of the true God. When they hear that name, they tremble and cry out, and say they are being branded and beaten. When asked who they are and when they came and how they got into a man, they confess it all. So racked and tormented, they are forced away from the virtue of the divine name.[16]

This is why the demons are so angry with Christians, according to Lactantius. And since they cannot hurt the Christians themselves, they stir up pagan hatred against them in an attempt to break their resolve and challenge their faith. But, Lactantius continues, "If [demons] cannot achieve that, [they attempt] to remove [Christians] altogether from the earth, so that no one shall exist with the power to repress their evil."[17] As indicated above, the battle on earth between demons and Christians is a part of God's unfolding plan that will end in the destruction of the devil and the demons.

Lactantius's *Deaths of the Persecutors*

The demons were not about to roll over and give up easily; they needed coconspirators to help them, so they enlisted Roman emperors to enact the

14. Harold W. Attridge, "The Philosophical Critique of Religion under the Early Empire," *Aufstieg und Niedergang der Römischen Welt* 16.1 (1978): 45–78.

15. Lactantius, *Divine Institutes* 2.14.3–4. Lactantius borrows this demonology from the watchers tale in *1 Enoch* 6–11. For the evolution of this tale, see Paul D. Hanson, "Rebellion in Heaven, Azazel, and the Euhemeristic Heroes in 1 Enoch 6–11," *Journal of Biblical Literature* 96, no. 2 (1977): 195–233.

16. Lactantius, *Divine Institutes* 5.21.6.

17. Ibid.

persecutions. Likewise, God needed a compatriot in his plans for good; this task would be carried on the shoulders of Constantine. In *Deaths of the Persecutors*, as Hal Drake has pointed out, Lactantius draws a direct cause-and-effect relation between the persecuting emperors and their deaths, with Diocletian acting as the archvillain. The Lord meted out just punishment for those who tried to eradicate his people.[18] Indeed, Lactantius takes this even a step further by associating these emperors with the fallen angels. They too acted as the enemies of God; and as the demons are punished, the persecuting emperors too suffered for their transgressions.

Peter Brown defines demonology as "a map on which [Christians] plotted the disruptions and tensions all around them."[19] Indeed, Lactantius's theology posited Christ, working *for* the salvation of humanity, pitted against the demons that worked to keep people *from* salvation. Lactantius's demonology seeks to map this chaotic world through assigning blame for the persecutions to the cosmic powers of evil. The persecutors, he writes, "suffocate themselves in serving such woeful demons which God has condemned to eternal punishment."[20] Thus he places Christian misfortunes within a context that is ultimately under God's control through the act of exorcism. Christians, he reminds his readers, are well known for their abilities to cast out demons. "[By] using God's name against them you can drive them out and put them to flight."[21] The ability to cast out demons was something everyone in the Roman world could appreciate. Furthermore, as David Frankfurter recently wrote, "Demonologies seek to control—through order, through writing, through the ritual power of declaration—a chaotic world of misfortune, temptation, religious conflict, and spiritual ambiguity."[22] Indeed, Lactantius's demonology is about gaining control over the meaning of persecution. The main problem with the Roman world, according to Lactantius, was that it had been usurped by evil demons, and the only way to set the world right was for the empire to embrace the faith of the Christians, the exorcists par excellence.

Associating persecuting emperors with the devil and demons is an important component of Lactantius's demonology. Specifically, he explains how demons

18. Harold A. Drake, *Constantine and the Bishops: The Politics of Intolerance* (Baltimore: Johns Hopkins University Press, 2000), 115.

19. Peter Brown, *The Making of Late Antiquity* (Cambridge, MA: Harvard University Press, 1978), 75.

20. Lactantius, *Divine Institutes* 5.19.1. Bowen and Garnsay, in *Lactantius: Divine Institutes*, 14–21, provide a good introduction to his sources and note the scarcity of scriptural references in his writings. Discussions of demonology are no exception to this scarcity.

21. Lactantius, *Divine Institutes*, 2.17.11.

22. David Frankfurter, *Evil Incarnate: Rumors of Divine Conspiracy and Satanic Abuse in History* (Princeton: Princeton University Press, 2006), 26.

gained so much control of the world. For him, demons needed emperors to
enact their will. Thus all the persecuting emperors are shown to be in league
with the demonic. In *Deaths of the Persecutors*, Nero, the first persecuting
emperor, is described as "the forerunner of the devil."[23] Thus his unnatural
death and the chaos that it brought to the empire further demonstrate that his
death was a part of God's vengeance against him to vindicate God's people.
But Nero is an easy target: there are even pagan historians who treat him with
little sympathy. Domitian, also considered one of the bad emperors by many
Roman sources, was "instigated by evil demons to pursue righteous people."[24]
His demise too is ascribed to divine judgment, which vanquished his atten-
dant demons as well. Decius, the first to enact an empire-wide persecution,
is described as the image of Lucifer. Lactantius insists, "It seems as if he had
been raised to sovereign eminence, at once to rage against God, and at once
to fall." Once he gains power, Decius falls because he conspires against God
himself. At the end of his life he is surrounded, killed, stripped, and devoured
by beasts, a fit end for one whom Lactantius calls "the enemy of God,"[25] a
title reminiscent of his famous moniker for the devil as the "anti-God."[26]

Diocletian is particularly singled out as having demonic attributes. Considering that Lactantius lived through the persecutions under this emperor, it
comes as no surprise. Associating him with Nero and Decius, Lactantius calls
Diocletian "an enemy of divine religion,"[27] like demons who are "the enemies
of truth and in collusion against God."[28] This association of Diocletian with
Nero as being like the demons who controlled him exposes the rhetorical
dimensions of Lactantius's demonology.

The influence of the persecution on the demonology of Lactantius is nowhere more clearly demonstrated than within the incident that led to the
persecutions. While Diocletian presided over a *haruspicium* (divination), as
Lactantius describes it in *Deaths of the Persecutors*, some of the Christian
ministers in attendance made the sign of the cross over their foreheads in an
act of contempt for the demons being called upon. This forced the demons to
flee from the ritual, thereby preventing any readable signs from entering the
animals' entrails. Having thought that they botched the sacrifice somehow,
the augurs repeated the ceremony again and again. The priests concluded
that gods were offended by certain profane men and required that everyone

23. Lactantius, *Deaths of the Persecutors* 2, in *ANF* 7:302.
24. Ibid., 3.
25. Ibid., 4.
26. Lactantius, *Divine Institutes* 2.9.13.
27. Lactantius, *Deaths of the Persecutors* 11, in *ANF* 7:305.
28. Lactantius, *Divine Institutes* 2.16.9.

there make a sacrifice.[29] When some did not, Diocletian began seeking out those who refused to sacrifice, which inevitably led them to Christians who refused to do so, and the persecutions were begun. Although one may rightly be suspicious of Lactantius's explanation for the Great Persecutions, this encounter is a microcosm of Lactantius's point about the demonic powers: they are no match for the Christians.

Constantine is thus the polar opposite of a persecuting emperor. In the beginning of *Deaths of the Persecutors*, Lactantius describes the ascension of Constantine as sole emperor: "Behold, all our adversaries have been destroyed, tranquility is restored in the world, and the Church, once pummeled by persecution, now rises again; and the temple of God, once overthrown by the wicked, is rebuilt in greater splendor by the mercy of the Lord."[30] As the savior from persecution, Constantine is portrayed as almost Christlike. He is described as the bringer of peace to the world.[31] As Diocletian has ushered in an age of demonic power, Constantine brings an age of final deliverance. To demonstrate this even more clearly, Lactantius concludes *Deaths of the Persecutors* with the rise of Constantine and the world's liberation "from the machinations and assaults of the devil."[32] Lactantius emphasizes Constantine's "power and sovereign goodness in rooting out and utterly destroying the enemies of [God's] name."[33] The cosmic battle with the demonic has ended with the victory of Constantine: "The heavens are now become calm."[34] The victory of Constantine has "brought to an end the united devices of the wicked, and wiped off the tears from the faces of those who mourned."[35] Thus with Constantine's rise, Christ's work is done. The power of the demons is now severely limited—and for Lactantius, so also is Roman paganism. Of course, Lactantius is too optimistic in his estimation of the fall of paganism. The actual Christianization of the empire will be a much longer process.

Conclusion

Lactantius's view of demons in the world is inseparable from his understanding of the persecutions. The uncertain, bifurcated world for Christians during the Roman Tetrarchy (under Diocletian) soon gives way to a new world of

29. Lactantius, *Deaths of the Persecutors* 10, in *ANF* 7:304.
30. Lactantius, *Deaths of the Persecutors* 1, in *ANF* 7:301.
31. Ibid.
32. Lactantius, *Deaths of the Persecutors* 52, in *ANF* 7:322.
33. Lactantius, *Deaths of the Persecutors* 1, in *ANF* 7:301.
34. Ibid.
35. Ibid.

Christian dominance but doctrinal uncertainty. Thus Lactantius's demonology, so focused on the gods of the Roman cult, soon fades into the background of the history of Christianity, though echoes of it come time and again when Christians see the power of the devil and his demons gaining control in the world.[36] For Lactantius, however, demons ultimately fail, and the church, under Constantine's watch, will rise again to be "built in greater splendor by the mercy of the Lord."[37] Lactantius's demonology thus has a very practical function: to explain the reason for the persecution of the people of God and to provide a solution: the Christianization of the empire.

36. Frankfurter, *Evil Incarnate*, 31–72.
37. Lactantius, *Deaths of the Persecutors* 1, in ANF 7:301.

6

CHRISTUS VICTOR IN THE WORK
OF EPHREM, NARSAI, AND JACOB OF SERUG

GARY A. ANDERSON

No one can write about the theme *Christus Victor* without mentioning the classic work by Gustav Aulén.[1] In his work, Aulén lays out the early view of the church fathers on the atonement, which consists of a dramatic victory of Christ over the powers of Satan and death. This midrash-like expansion of the New Testament narratives is nicely illustrated in the icons of the resurrection wherein Christ is shown beating down the doors of Hades and crushing Satan underfoot so that he can secure the release of Adam, Eve, and other righteous figures from the Old Testament.[2] For Aulén, it was important

1. Gustav Aulén, *Christus Victor: An Historical Study of the Three Main Types of the Idea of the Atonement* (New York: MacMillan, 1969). The work appeared first in a Swedish edition in 1930. The English version (London: SPCK, 1931) has undergone numerous reprintings, a strong witness to its influence and popularity, as is the fact that many major theological libraries hold multiple copies of the work.

2. For an excellent treatment of the development of these icons, see Anna D. Kartsonis, *Anastasis: The Making of an Image* (Princeton: Princeton University Press, 1986). For the relationship of the icon to the patristic thought, see Gary A. Anderson, "The Resurrection of Adam and Eve," in *In Dominico Eloquio—In Lordly Eloquence: Essays on Patristic Exegesis in Honor of Robert Louis Wilken*, ed. Paul M. Blowers et al. (Grand Rapids: Eerdmans, 2002), 3–34, esp. 6–9.

to contrast this portrait of Christ's martial victory over the powers of sin with the more penitential, juridical view that obtained in the work of Anselm of Canterbury. The latter perspective, Aulén argued, with its overriding interest in securing satisfaction for the personal debt that accrued to one's sins, puts undue emphasis on the role that humans play in saving themselves.[3] In this essay I take a new look at this problem. It is my firm conviction that the imagery of Christ's victory over the power of sin is intricately linked to the world of Second Temple Judaism, a matter almost completely overlooked in the discussion of this topic. To keep such a Semitic flavor in view, I will consider how three Syriac authors use the New Testament to flesh out this theme. The grounding of this metaphor in Scripture cannot be grasped without careful attention to its Jewish roots.

Metaphors for Sin

Let me begin by juxtaposing two very different texts about the forgiveness of sins. The first is a well-known passage from the book of Leviticus that describes the culmination of the events that mark the atonement liturgy in ancient Israel.

> When [Aaron] has finished purging the Shrine, the Tent of Meeting, and the altar, the live goat shall be brought forward. Aaron shall lay both his hands upon the head of the live goat and confess over it all the iniquities and transgressions of the Israelites, whatever their sins, putting them on the head of the goat; and it shall be sent off to the wilderness through a designated man. Thus the goat shall carry on it all their iniquities to an inaccessible region; and the goat shall be set free in the wilderness. (Lev. 16:20–22 NJPS)[4]

The key feature to attend to is the function of the goat. Aaron puts both of his hands on the head of the goat and then confesses the sins of the Israelites. By doing this, he transfers the accumulated *weight* of these sins onto the goat so that it can "*carry* . . . all their iniquities." Next, the goat is sent off into the wilderness with all these sins loaded upon its back. The wilderness was a particularly fitting destination because it was imagined as being beyond the realm of the living, sometimes even as a portal into the underworld. If the sins

3. Aulén has been severely criticized on this point. For a critique of the work from a Protestant historical theologian, see John McIntyre, *St. Anselm and His Critics* (London: Oliver & Boyd, 1954); and for the perspective of an Orthodox systematic theologian, see David Bentley Hart, "A Gift Exceeding Every Debt: An Eastern Orthodox Appreciation of Anselm's *Cur Deus Homo*," *Pro Ecclesia* 7 (1998): 333–48.

4. For citations from the Old Testament in this essay, I am altering the translation when necessary to draw attention to the biblical metaphors for sin (as indicated by "alt.").

were sent there, this ritual presumes, they would be safely out of sight. And in the narrative world of the Old Testament, out of sight means out of mind. In a very real sense, we could say that this rite ritualizes what is affirmed more poetically in the Psalms: "As east is far from west, so far has He removed our sins from us" (103:12 NJPS).

The second text I notice is from the Gospel of Matthew. It is a parable that builds on a petition from the Lord's Prayer: "Forgive us our debts as we also have forgiven our debtors" (Matt. 6:12).

> For this reason the kingdom of heaven may be compared to a king who wished to settle accounts with his slaves. When he began the reckoning, one who owed him ten thousand talents was brought to him; and, as he could not pay, his lord ordered him to be sold, together with his wife and children and all his possessions, and payment to be made. So the slave fell on his knees before him, saying, "Have patience with me, and I will pay you everything." And out of pity for him, the lord of that slave released him and forgave him the debt. But that same slave, as he went out, came upon one of his fellow slaves who owed him a hundred denarii; and seizing him by the throat, he said, "Pay what you owe." Then his fellow slave fell down and pleaded with him, "Have patience with me, and I will pay you." But he refused; then he went and threw him into prison until he would pay the debt. When his fellow slaves saw what had happened, they were greatly distressed, and they went and reported to their lord all that had taken place. Then his lord summoned him and said to him, "You wicked slave! I forgave you all that debt because you pleaded with me. Should you not have had mercy on your fellow slave, as I had mercy on you?" And in anger his lord handed him over to be tortured until he would pay his entire debt. (Matt. 18:23–34)

Central to this parable is the notion that the sinner is someone who has incurred a debt. In this particular worldview, the debt can be overcome in two basic ways: either the holder of the bond graciously remits what was owed, or the debtor pays the full penalty.

At first glance it is striking how different these two narratives about the forgiveness of sins are. The gulf between the two Testaments seems large indeed. But a little investigation of the terrain below the surface of these stories will reveal why they take the shape they do. In the Old Testament are several different metaphors for describing the state of a sinner, but pride of place goes to the image of sin as a weight that the culpable soul must bear on one's back.[5] Conventional English translations often fail to bring this out, but a literal rendering of Leviticus 5:1 is quite instructive:

---

5. See my article, Gary A. Anderson, "From Israel's Burden to Israel's Debt: Towards a Theology of Sin in Biblical and Early Second Temple Sources," in *Reworking the Bible: Apocryphal and*

If a person incurs guilt—

    When he has heard a public imprecation and—although able to testify as
one who has either seen or learned of the matter—he does not give information,
then he shall bear the weight of his wrongdoing [*nāśāʾ ʿăwônô*]. (NJPS alt.)

Forgiveness, on the other hand, requires the offended party to remove the
weight of the sin. This perspective is well in view when Joseph's brothers beg
him to forgive them for trying to murder him earlier in the narrative:

    When Joseph's brothers saw that their father was dead, they said, "What if
    Joseph still bears a grudge against us and pays us back for all the wrong that
    we did him!" So they sent this message to Joseph, "Before his death your father
    left this instruction: So shall you say to Joseph, '*Take away the weight of the
    offense* [*śāʾ nāʾ pešaʿ*] and guilt of your brothers.'" (Gen. 50:15–17a NJPS alt.)

A heinous sinner is one loaded down with a considerable degree of wrongdoing; hence Isaiah describes Israel in one text as so weighted down with sin
that they would require a team of oxen to assist them in transporting this
burden.[6] Truly Israel was a people "*heavily laden* with the weight of iniquity
[*kebed ʿāwôn*]" (Isa. 1:4, my trans.).

    During the onset of the Second Temple period, due to the introduction of
Aramaic into the world of ancient Judaism, the dominant metaphor becomes
that of debt. This transformation is already in evidence in late biblical material
and the Dead Sea Scrolls, but there is perhaps no better way to illustrate this
momentous change than in the targums, ancient translations of the original
Hebrew into the idiom of Aramaic. In *Targum Onqelos*, every place where
we find the Hebrew expression "to bear the burden of one's sin," the targumist translates, *lě-qabbalat ḥôbâ*, "to assume a debt." So in Leviticus 5:1 the
Hebrew expression *wǝ-nāśāʾ ʿăwônô*, "so that he shall bear the weight of
his sin," becomes *wîyqabbel ḥôbêh*, "so that he shall assume his debt." And
similarly where we find the expression "to take away the burden of one's sin,"
the targumist regularly translates, *lě-mišbaq ḥôbâ*, "to remit a debt." And
so in Genesis 50:17, the targum renders the Hebrew expression *śāʾ nāʾ pešaʿ
ʾaḥêkā*, "remove the weight of the sin of your brothers," as *šǝbôq lěḥôbê ăḥāk*,
"remit the debt of your brothers."[7]

Related Texts at Qumran, ed. Esther G. Chazon et al. (Leiden: Brill, 2005), 3–9, and the literature
cited therein.

    6. So Isa. 5:18 NJPS, "Ah, those who haul sin with cords of falsehood / and iniquity as with
cart ropes!"

    7. I have cited *Targum Onqelos*, but the same sort of translation can be found in the other
targums.

Paul Ricoeur has argued that there is no such thing as a "sin" per se, that every culture mediates the notion of wrongdoing in the highly picturesque imagery of metaphor.[8] And from these basic metaphors, each culture will, in turn, construct the stories it wishes to tell about how sin is alleviated. In the examples that I have chosen, we can see how insightful his remarks are. In the Old Testament, where the primary metaphor for sin is that of a weight, the classic text about forgiveness involves a pack animal that bears that weight away. In the period of the New Testament, when the metaphor of weight in contemporary Judaism has been replaced by that of debt, it should occasion no surprise that a Jewish teacher living in Palestine in the first century would tell stories about the forgiveness of sins that involved debtors and creditors.

The Bond of Indebtedness in Rabbinic Judaism

The notion that sin is a debt that must be repaid is standard in contemporary Jewish texts. This is amply in evidence in the Dead Sea Scrolls.[9] But rather than turning there, I will push ahead a few centuries to a couple of rabbinic texts. The first comes from a traditional prayer spoken during the days leading up to Yom Kippur: "Erase, in your great mercy, all the bonds of our indebtedness."[10] This prayer, which is often cited as background to the Lord's Prayer in the New Testament, presumes that each of our sinful deeds results in the creation of a bond (*šəṭār*) that must be paid off. To get an even more colorful picture of the same, let us consider a midrash found in the fourth-century text *Genesis Rabbah* 82.13:

> "Esau took his wives, his sons and daughters, and all the members of his household, his cattle and all his livestock, and all the property that he had acquired in the land of Canaan, and went to another land *because of his brother Jacob*" (Gen. 36:6). R. Eleazar explained [the departure of Esau from his brother Jacob this way]: it was on account of the bond of indebtedness [*šəṭār ḥôb*]. R. Joshua said it was due to shame.

The midrash is struck by the fact that Esau, of his own free will, departs from the promised land while Jacob remains in it. Since the land had been

---

8. Paul Ricoeur, *The Symbolism of Evil* (Boston: Beacon, 1967).

9. See Anderson, "From Israel's Burden," 13–18.

10. This prayer can be found in any *Siddur* (Jewish prayer book); it follows the Amidah on Yom Kippur and is called *Avinu Malkenu*, "Our Father and Our King"; New Testament commentaries on Col. 2:14 frequently refer to it, including Hermann L. Strack and Paul Billerbeck, *Kommentar zum Neuen Testament aus Talmud und Midrasch*, 6 vols. (Munich: Beck, 1922–61).

given to Abraham and his offspring, Esau would seem to have a legitimate right to settle there even if he were to remain in a subordinate position to his brother. The text from the book of Genesis indicates that his departure was due to his brother Jacob (36:6) but says no more. The midrash steps into this void and provides us with a specification of the reason: Esau was wary of a bond of indebtedness. Though *Genesis Rabbah* says no more about what exactly this is, we can find the matter clarified in another tradition found in *Numbers Rabbah* 19.15.

> And Moses sent messengers from Kadesh to the king of Edom. "Thus says your brother Israel. 'You know all the hardships that have befallen us; that our ancestors went down to Egypt, that we dwelt in Egypt a long time, and that the Egyptians dealt harshly with us and our ancestors'" [Num. 20:14–15]. . . . Scripture states: "You know all the hardships that have befallen us." The messengers said to the king of Edom: "You know that the Holy One [Blessed be He!] said: 'You shall truly know that your seed will be sojourners in a land that does not belong to them, and they will be enslaved and afflicted for four hundred years' [Gen. 15:13]. Yet it was we who suffered slavery while you were free." "Our ancestors went down" for the purpose of suffering that affliction. We can compare this situation to two brothers against whom a bond of indebtedness was issued on account of their grandfather. One of the two paid that bond. After some time he asked his brother to loan him a certain item. He said to him, "You know that I paid that bond which was the responsibility of the two of us. So don't turn down my request to borrow said item from you."[11]

This text presumes an earlier midrashic tradition that Abraham had sinned when he expressed some doubts about God's ability to fulfill his promises.[12] In order to pay off the cost of this bond, Israel would be required to descend into Egypt and suffer for some four hundred years (Gen. 15:13) before being released and allowed to enter the land that had been promised to Abraham's seed in the first place. Esau was aware of this bond, and as a result he did not wish to remain in the land of Canaan with his brother Jacob and be forced to share his allotted punishment. He moved on to the land of Edom to avoid having to descend into Egypt. Yet Esau's departure did not exempt him from his obligation to repay the bond, for both he and Jacob were direct descendants of Abraham. Thereby arises the logic of the parable that our midrash tells:

11. Mosheh Aryeh Mirkin, ed., *Midrash Rabbah: Be-Midbar Rabbah* (Tel Aviv: Yavneh, 1987), 2:231–32.

12. See *Song of Songs Rabbah* 1.23. When Abraham asks how he can be sure that he will inherit the land that God has promised (Gen. 15:8), this is understood to be the sin that creates the bond.

There were two brothers who had to pay off a bond that was held against their grandfather. One of the brothers stepped forward and paid it on his own. As a result of his generosity, he later asked his brother to reciprocate by lending him an item he needed. And exactly so was the logic of Moses's plea to the Edomites when Israel sought to take a shortcut through their territory on the way to the promised land. We, the sons of Jacob, Moses declares, paid off the bond our ancestor Abraham owed by suffering for some four hundred years in Egypt. The least you could do now is grant us safe passage through your land.

The Bond of Indebtedness in Colossians 2:14

Colorful portrayals such as this are even more frequent in early Christian material, especially in writings that come from the Syriac milieu, where the idioms for sin and forgiveness are exactly the same as those found in Jewish material. The classic text derives from Paul's Letter to the Colossians and describes the saving work of Christ as akin to the voiding of a bill of indebtedness:

> When you were dead in trespasses and the uncircumcision of your flesh, God made you alive together with him, when he forgave us all our trespasses, *erasing the bond of indebtedness* that stood against us with its legal demands. He set this aside, nailing it to the cross. He disarmed the rulers and authorities and made a public example of them, triumphing over them in it. (Col. 2:13–15, emphasis added)

The key clause here is the statement that through the work of Christ on the cross, God was able "to erase the bond of indebtedness that stood against us." The term in Greek is *cheirographon*, and in Syriac it was translated as *šṭār ḥawbayn*. Both terms refer to a handwritten bond of indebtedness.

Early Syriac writers, very much like the rabbis, were fond of filling out this text so as to describe just how Christ voided this bond. Indeed, this Christian "midrashic" development culminates in the motif that Gustav Aulén aptly titled "Christus Victor." Yet the Syriac data severely qualifies a theme that lies at the very heart of Aulén's project. Aulén claimed that the classic patristic approach, which emphasized Christ's victory over the powers of sin and death, was to be sharply distinguished from the more juridical (and hence "legalistic") approach that was represented in such Latin thinkers as Tertullian and Cyprian. What was particularly offensive to Aulén was the emphasis on debt and the rendering of "satisfaction" for that debt. Yet within the Semitic background to the New Testament, the concepts are linguistically and conceptually inseparable. In both Jewish and Christian Aramaic, the noun that means "debt" (*ḥôbâ*) comes from a verbal root (*ḥab*) whose basic meaning is "to suffer defeat" either in battle or in the lawcourt. Because someone who loses in battle is obligated to pay tribute and someone who loses in court is often obligated to pay a fine, the verbal root came to have a very prominent secondary meaning as "obligated to pay." So when Adam is defeated (*ḥab*) by Satan in the garden of Eden, it was altogether natural for a Syriac thinker to imagine that he now was obligated to pay (*ḥayyab*) for the debt of his sin. And similarly the term for punishment, *pûr anût*, comes from a verbal root (*pera*) that means "to pay." In short, the concepts of defeat in battle and satisfaction for a penalty that is owed are part of a single linguistic package. They cannot be separated.

In contrast to *ḥab* is the Aramaic root *zakâ*, meaning, "to be victorious" in battle or the lawcourt.[13] A favorite title of Christ among the Syriac fathers is that of *zakyâ*, "the victor." But whom does this victory benefit? Those who have been defeated (*ḥab*) by the powers of sin and stand in a state of obligation (*ḥayyab*) to make satisfaction for their obligations.

New Testament scholars have noticed the patristic development of Colossians 2:14 but have been quick to point out that it is not relevant to the original intent of the author of the epistle. It must be conceded that there is more than a grain of truth here. There is no evidence that the author of Colossians thought that the bond that Christ voids on the cross had been signed by Adam. But let us shift our focus from the epistle itself to its place within the emerging Pauline corpus. For early readers of the letter were certainly not going to isolate this text from the larger fabric of Pauline theology in which it was embedded. In this light it is useful to bear in mind an observation that Adolf Deissmann made long ago. He remarked that Paul was quite fond of depicting the human predicament as one in which humans were enslaved to sin.[14] Consider these examples from the Letter to the Romans,

We know that our old self was crucified with him so that the body of sin might be destroyed, and we might no longer be enslaved to sin. (6:6)

But thanks be to God that you, having once been slaves of sin, have become obedient from the heart to the form of teaching to which you were entrusted. (6:17)

13. In Jewish Aramaic a nominal form of this root assumes the additional meaning of a "merit" or "credit" that accrues to one's account. So the important rabbinic concept of *zəkût 'abôt*, "the merits of the Patriarchs," a term denoting a form of "currency" that accrues from virtuous actions such as Isaac's willingness to lay down his life for God (Gen. 22). These meritorious actions generate a form of currency (*zəkût*) that can counterbalance the "debts" of sinful Israelites. Frequently in midrashic texts, Israelites will pray that God will ignore their "debts" and reckon by the "merits" of their ancestors.
14. Adolf Deissmann, *Light from the Ancient East* (New York: George H. Doran, 1927).

For Paul, the heart of our redemption consists in being freed from such servitude. This act of redemption is true to the etymology of the term: Christ literally "buys us back" (1 Cor. 6:20; 7:23). Deissmann was especially impressed by the language of Galatians 5:1—"For freedom Christ has set us free; stand firm therefore, and do not submit again to a yoke of slavery" (RSV)—because it reflects almost exactly the ancient documents of manumission found among the Greek papyri.

If we take the Pauline evidence at face value, it would not be unreasonable to argue that human sins have created in their wake a bond of indebtedness that must be repaid. Should one not be able to raise sufficient currency to cover the cost of the bond, then one would become enslaved. Christ's salvific act is defined by his overturning of this bond. Indeed C. F. D. Moule, who accepts the traditional attribution of Colossians to Paul, puts the picture together almost precisely in this fashion: "A *cheirographon* is an 'IOU,' a statement of indebtedness, personally signed by the debtor."[15] But how is the bond actually signed? Here Moule appeals to data found elsewhere in the Pauline corpus, specifically the opening chapters of the Epistle to the Romans: "The bond in question here is signed by men's consciences: for a Jew, it is his acceptance of the revealed Law of God as an obligation to abide by; for the gentile, it is a corresponding recognition of obligation to what he knows of the will of God. . . . This *cheirographon* is 'against us' because we have manifestly failed to discharge its obligations—no one felt this more keenly than Paul the Pharisee (cf. Rom. 7:16, 22, 23)." To arrive at what the church fathers saw, the only element we need to add to this picture is the evidence of Romans 5:12–21 that slavery to sin begins with Adam. Once that piece of the puzzle is in place, the picture that Jacob of Serug draws does not seem nearly as strange as it otherwise might. In commenting on the words from the Lord's Prayer, "forgive us our debts," he writes,

> To the father you cry when you pray that he come and set free
>   His sons who are enslaved to the Enemy of old.
> You say to him that I have been captured and sold.
>   I am a slave and have been enslaved among foreigners.
> Sin purchased me and I fell from the state of Freedom.
>   They led me away from you and I became a slave for naught.
> The Evil lord who purchased me yoked me with a harsh yoke
>   And disfigured me in a cruel form of slavery.
> I have been sold, O my Lord, how can I return to Freedom?
>   By my own will I came among those of this Evil lord.

15. C. F. D. Moule, *The Epistles of Paul the Apostle to the Colossians and to Philemon* (Cambridge: Cambridge University Press, 1957), 97.

> The devious serpent took my pen and wrote;
>   He and Eve wrote a bond [*štarâ*] of servitude and enslaved me.
> I consented and I who was once free became a slave
>   The Enemy who purchased me, bound me for naught.[16]

In this brief résumé of the plight of humanity, Jacob of Serug sounds the important Pauline theme of our servitude to sin that is represented by the bond that Adam and Eve sign in Eden. The one element we cannot find so clearly in Paul is the fact that Satan holds this bond. But the introduction of the figure of Satan should not occasion any surprise. For it is the nature of such bonds that the one who is obligated to pay must hand over the bill to his creditor.[17] The bond represents the rights that the creditor holds over the debtor. So naturally one must ask who holds the bond that Adam and Eve have signed. For the fathers, the answer was clear: the only fitting representative would be Satan.

If the picture of humanity's plight emerges with a certain degree of uniformity from this composite picture drawn from Paul's writings, the manner in which Christ will save humanity from its indebtedness is not uniform at all. It has been observed that although the church spent a considerable degree of time and effort in clarifying the nature of Christ's personhood, it showed no similar interest in defining how the atonement actually worked. As a result a variety of different proposals circulated in late antiquity. In the space that remains I will outline three different ways of accounting for how the bond that Satan possessed was overturned.

Narsai (d. 503): Satan Overreaches the Terms Set for the Bond

Narsai begins his account of the passion with a brief flashback to the moment of Christ's temptation in the desert.[18] This may surprise some modern readers, but it certainly would not have troubled Narsai's audience. For in the patristic

16. Paul Bedjan, ed., *Homiliae selectae Mar-Jacobi Sarugensis*, 5 vols. (Paris: Harrassowitz, 1905–10), 1:225; rev. ed. as *Homilies of Mar Jacob of Sarug*, ed. Paul Bedjan, with additional material by Sebastian P. Brock, 6 vols. (Piscataway, NJ: Gorgias, 2006). All Syriac translations in this chapter are my own.

17. See Tobit 5:3. In this text the document is not a bond of debt per se but a financial obligation of deposit. Tobit left a considerable amount of money in trust with a person by the name of Gabael. Tobit gets a handwritten receipt, a *cheirographon*, that will identify him as the one with a rightful claim to the money in the future.

18. For the text of his *Homily for the Great Sunday of the Resurrection*, see Narsai, "Narsai's Metrical Homilies on the Nativity, Epiphany, Passion, Resurrection and Ascension," ed. Frederick G. McLeod, PO 40 (1979): 136–61.

tradition, the conflict with Satan was imagined to have two principal staging grounds: the first was the temptation in the desert, and the second was the passion.[19] Early Christian readers had two strong exegetical reasons for linking these two events. First, already in the Gospel of Luke, it is said that after the temptations had run their course, Satan left Jesus until the "appropriate moment."[20] Even modern New Testament scholars are in general agreement that this means until the moment of the passion. Second, the fathers of the church generally thought the temptation scene to be a resumption of the temptation of Adam in the garden.[21] This typological reading was aided by the fact that in Eden, Adam and Eve succumb to the offer of fruit, whereas in the desert Satan offers Christ bread. The desire for food is the common factor that Satan is able to use to his advantage.

Narsai opens his homily with some general remarks about the incarnation. Christ assumes a body so that he can go forth to restore those whom the Strong One has taken captive. Though Christ is visibly indistinguishable from the other captives, he differs from them in that he has been armed with the hidden power of the Spirit, through which he will overcome the temptations that beset the body.

> His race was captive to the Evil One and Death, the tyrants who
>   rebelled.
> He gave himself to the struggle on behalf of his people.
> He went forth to the desert to battle the Evil One, conquered him,
>   and prepared himself for a struggle against Death, the insatiable
>   one.[22]
> He grappled with the Strong One over the desire for bread,
>   bound him, and cast him down through his enduring those
>   blandishments.

19. See the important article of Veselin Kesich, "The Antiochenes and the Temptation Story," StPatr 7 (1966): 496–502; and two monographs: Klaus-Peter Köppen, *Die Auslegung der Versuchungsgeschichte unter besonderer Berücksichtigung der Alten Kirche: Ein Beitrag zur Geschichte der Schriftauslegung* (Tübingen: Mohr Siebeck, 1961); and Martin Steiner, *La tentation de Jésus dans l'interprétation patristique de Saint Justin à Origène* (Paris: Gabalda, 1962).

20. Cf. the last verse of the temptation story (Luke 4:13): "When the devil had finished every test, he departed from him until an opportune time." Most commentators believe that this moment takes place during the passion; in support of this they cite Luke 22:3, "Then Satan entered into Judas, called Iscariot, who was one of the twelve." Hans Conzelmann goes the farthest here when he asserts that the interval of time between the temptations and the passion was a "Satan-free period." See his *Theology of St. Luke* (Philadelphia: Fortress, 1961), 16, 27–29, 80–81.

21. This position is also followed by some modern commentators. See, e.g., Joel Marcus, *Mark 1–8*, Anchor Bible 27 (New York: Doubleday, 2000), 169–71.

22. There appears to be a typographical error in the Syriac text; I have emended it.

The Spiritual One was defeated (*ḥab*) by the Corporeal One through
   spiritual power.
The body which trampled down the passions overcame the prince
   of the air.
The body that was contemptible derided and mocked the Strong One
   and removed the weaponry lest he use it to wage war on mortals.
"Be gone, Evil One, to your counterpart," he said to him.
   "Be gone, prepare other weaponry for Death.
Be gone, prepare deadly nets with the help of mortals,
   for your power is too weak on its own for the struggle.
Be gone, gather the children you have begotten by your stratagems.
   Arm them with slander as you are accustomed.
Summon lying comrades to assist you,
   for you are a liar and through lies you are accustomed to conquer."[23]

At the center of Satan's strategy lies the human "desire for bread." Unlike
Adam, however, Christ resists "those blandishments" and as a result binds the
strong man and casts him down. The first round in this struggle has drawn to
a close, but the fight has not yet come to completion. Christ goes on to taunt
Satan and to urge him to prepare better weaponry for his next engagement
with his comrade in arms, Death. Merely repeating the temptation of Adam
and Eve will be insufficient to overcome him. Christ suggests that Death make
use of the deadly nets that only mortals can provide. Here we have in view the
false witnesses who will be called to testimony against Jesus when he appears
before the high priest (cf. Mark 14:53–65 and parallels).

At this point Narsai skips directly to the events of Holy Saturday, the
moment when Christ descends to the abode of the dead. Narsai must continue his story without scriptural aids, for the Gospels are completely silent
as to what happens to Christ once he breathes his last breath. Yet the fathers of the church found hints that a larger cosmic struggle was going on
against the backdrop of the more mundane, historical events that Scripture
narrates. For example, in the Gospel of John, when Jesus begins to speak
in detail of his death, he remarks, "Now is the judgment of this world;
now the ruler of this world will be driven out. And I, when I am lifted up
from the earth, will draw all people to myself" (12:31–32). For Narsai and
other patristic readers, this verse indicated that the events of the passion
would take place on both a historical and a suprahistorical plane. What
happened on earth somehow mirrored what was transpiring elsewhere. The
fact that the Jewish high priest used false witnesses in an effort to find a way

---

23. Narsai, *Homily for the Great Sunday of the Resurrection*, lines 23–40.

to condemn Christ to death suggested that Satan would pursue a similar course.

> He remembered the breaking of the law in paradise
> and took refuge in this sin as his evidence.
> With the desire for fruit as a guarantee, he made his accusation.
> For this guarantee secured his enslavement of humanity, whom he acquired through eating.
> The signature of Eve and Adam he showed him.
> "Look! Your forefathers signed and handed this over. Read it carefully.
> The bond [*šṭarâ*] that Adam wrote for me in Eden when he succumbed to sin [*ḥab*].
> Because he did not repay it, he pledged his sons as interest.
> From the beginning, I acquired authority over mortals.
> It was not in secret that they wrote this bond and became enslaved as debtors.
> I did not capture your race through force but through love.
> They willingly became slaves.
> It was not solely Adam and his generation that became corrupt,
> rather his entire nature by necessity is bound by mortality.
> If you are corporeal and share the passions of the body,
> then examine your nature; know that you are bound by the bond of my lordship.
> There is no corporeal being, a possessor of limbs, that is not mortal,
> and if he is mortal, he is a slave to me and Death.
> Show me that you are not mortal, and I shall depart from you,
> but if you are mortal, your nature refutes the contention of your words.
> Show me the edict that Death issued to you that you are not mortal
> even though I don't accept such things from corporeal beings.
> You are corporeal. What need is there of words in this lawsuit?
> The nature of your body is entirely mortal and perishable."[24]

At this point, Satan appears to have Christ exactly where he wants him. For according to the tableaux on view here, when Adam and Eve succumbed to sin (*ḥab*), they signed a bond of indebtedness (*šṭār ḥawbâ*). In and of themselves, they were not able to repay this bond, and as a result the offspring of Adam and Eve were taken as a pledge toward the interest. As a surety or guarantee, Satan could point to the human will, which had a propensity for

---

24. Ibid., lines 45–68.

disobedience, or as Narsai puts it, for "desiring fruit." In this fashion, the sin of Adam is both a punctiliar moment in time whose aftereffects of sin continue to unfold through the centuries, and an example that each generation will reproduce within itself.

To make matters worse, the bond cannot be overturned by the somewhat conventional strategy of contesting the terms under which it was signed, for Satan makes it perfectly clear that Adam and Eve were not forced to sign this bond. Nay, rather, they did so out of their own volition.[25] There is one point, however, where Satan overstates his case. He claims that Adam's entire nature is "*by necessity* bound to mortality." If this were the case, then the simple act of assuming human flesh, Satan reasons, would make anyone "bound by the bond of my lordship." Yet Satan has earlier confessed that the guarantee of his rights over humanity was marked by their uncontrollable "desire for fruit." In the person of Jesus, however, this desire has been quenched by the Holy Spirit, who indwelled him.[26] As a result, Adam's nature, entirely and without remainder, was not bound to mortality. If God put on this body and made it his own, everything would be different. This legal codicil to Satan's claim to power would prove his undoing.

Once Satan has thought through his legal argument, he begins to press his case. He demands that Christ "fulfill his mortal obligations," for he is, after all, simply a human being. "Pay back," Satan insists, "just as the others do who are legally obligated [*hayyab*]." Christ, however, does not contest the matter. He acts before Satan just as he acted before Caiaphas: he keeps his peace. "In silence, I conceal my majesty from him / until he completes his treachery of putting me to death." For the sake of the economy of salvation, it is necessary that Satan overreach his stated rights. Only then can his grip over humankind be undone. So Christ lets Satan pursue his misguided thinking to its logical conclusion. At this key turning point in the trial, Christ lays out his case:

> If mortals are obligated to repay because they have sinned,
>   then I, who am clean of all such stain, who could enter a suit with
>   me?

25. In legal contracts from the ancient world, it was important to establish that the contracting parties entered the agreement by their own free choice. For if this was not the case, the contract could be contested in court at a later date. On this point see Yochanan Muffs, *Studies in the Aramaic Legal Papyri from Elephantine* (reprint, Leiden: Brill, 2003), 128–41. In our text, Satan makes it clear to Christ that Adam and Eve had freely chosen to sign this bond, making it all the harder to dissolve it.

26. So Narsai in his homily on the passion, "Our mortal nature was too imperfect to serve as its own redeemer. / The Self-subsistent One put on our nature and thereby freed our race." See Narsai, "Narsai's Metrical Homilies," 128, lines 659–60.

If it be that Adam having fallen into debt was taken in pledge because
    he took his advice,
        then I, whom he did not overpower for even a second, how could he
        enter a suit with me?
Therefore it is clear that his rash assault on me is wrong.
    He wields his royal scepter over mortals unjustly.
Though it is quite clear that I am free from his servitude,
    I shall willingly accept death due to his treachery.
He threatens and frightens me with death like other mortals,
    but by death I shall overthrow him from his rule.
With the weaponry of mortal passions he fights against me.
    But by my own sufferings I shall teach him that his weaponry is
    weak.
Because he thinks that Adam and all his offspring have been given in
    pledge,
    I shall wipe away the bond of his lordship from mortals.
By death he sealed the bond of indebtedness of the human race,
    and through death on top of a cross I shall rip it in two.
In the eyes of both angels and humanity I will void it,
    that legal verdict which he boasts about as if he were a victor.
I will demonstrate for those in heaven and earth
    the redemption of the living and their renewal, which is fulfilled in
    me.
I summon heaven and earth as reliable witnesses,
    and in the name of the hidden one, I shall seal my promise.
Those that can speak and the mute are mediators between me and the
    Evil One
    that he provokes a suit and dares to put me to death who am with-
    out any debts.
If he be at fault and thirsts for my death,
    then judge justly and rebuke his fault and expose his treachery.
See how I assume his wrongful judgment
    and show that death freely chose to overpower me.
I am descending to the depths of Sheol as though into the ocean.
    Swiftly I shall proclaim my victorious name.

If Adam's bond is guaranteed by an ongoing desire for forbidden fruit, then
clearly Christ cannot fall within its bounds if he is "clean of all such stain."
Through Christ's death on the cross, the originating terms of this bond are
voided. Christ can declare that on the cross he has ripped this bond in two,
by which he means it is null and void due to its misuse. Moreover, it is certainly significant that Death has freely chosen to take Christ; like Adam and

Eve, he consented willingly; there was no divine compulsion that could have forced his hands. As a result, his rights are lost in an incontestable fashion. And the whole salvific event has been witnessed by both heaven and earth, so the promise of Christ rests on far surer ground than the bond that Satan held, which could not claim such reliable witnesses.[27] The authority of sin and death has been broken. Since they have lost the battle (*hab*), Christ the victor (*zakyâ*) is free to share the spoils of his victory with his companions in faith.[28]

Jacob of Serug (d. 521): Christ Repays the Bond

Like Narsai, Jacob also sees the salvific action of Christ as a two-stage event. The process begins with the temptation in the desert and concludes with the passion. What is striking here, and what we do not see in Narsai, is that Satan actually falls during the temptations in the desert. One might have thought that the demise of Satan would take place either before his temptation of Adam, in which case we would imagine Satan as having been in possession of some sort of primordial glory that he loses as a result of his rebellion; or during the passion narrative itself, in which case Satan would lose the power he had gained over humanity through the atoning death of Jesus Christ. The surprising move to localize this fall in the temptation scene is necessitated, Jacob believes, by what Jesus says to the disciples after they have returned from their first apostolic mission to teach and heal in Jesus's name:

> The seventy returned with joy, saying, "Lord, in your name even the demons submit to us!" He said to them, "I watched Satan fall from heaven like a flash of lightning. See, I have given you authority to tread on snakes and scorpions, and over all the power of the enemy; and nothing will hurt you. Nevertheless, do not rejoice at this, that the spirits submit to you, but rejoice that your names are written in heaven." (Luke 10:17–20)

As Jacob understands the matter, Jesus is able to authorize the disciples to perform various works of wonder because he has already defeated the power of Satan earlier in his earthly life. Though the Gospels give no explicit reference to this, Jacob concludes that the only possible place in Jesus's life where

---

27. This point is made later, in lines 291–92: "That wrongful bond he brought forth and demonstrated legally / that it was not sealed with a signature before proper witnesses."

28. See lines 295–96, "And since I have conquered [*zk*] and the hater of our race has been defeated [*hab*] / I will allow my companions to share in the greatness of my victory."

Satan could have fallen would have been during his failed attempts to tempt Jesus to obey him. For it was during those temptations that Satan tried to lure Christ into the same trap into which he had lulled Adam.

Because the fall of humanity was due to eating a piece of forbidden fruit, the penalty for that sin could be paid only by abstaining from such a choice in the future. Fasting was the fit remedy for the human predicament.

> Fasting is the first remedy that was set up to heal the first lesion of the flesh.[29] Through eating came the fall, and from fasting came the rising again. The first commandment was, "Do not eat." That one who did not obey and ate was swallowed up by Death. And because he was defeated, became a debtor, and stumbled so as to fall, it became necessary that his debt be repaid by fasting and his stumbling be corrected so that he could rise from his fall.[30]

But the repayment of the debt was not by any means brought to a close during the period of fasting in the desert. It was simply the first act in a two-act play. The full terms of Adam's debt could not be brought to completion until the passion. Christ is uniquely able to repay the debt because Jacob believes that he is the true *heir* of Adam. The classification of Christ as "heir" derives from the opening paragraph of the Epistle to the Hebrews as well as the parable of the wicked tenants in the vineyard.[31] What is required, Jacob seems to be arguing, is that no mere mortal can fulfill the terms of the debt that Adam has bequeathed to humanity. As the uniquely fashioned "Son of the Father," he bequeathed a legacy that only another uniquely fashioned being can assume. In other words, satisfaction cannot be generated by currency that is generated below; salvation must have its origin in heaven.

On this view the bond of indebtedness required that currency be raised in order to be paid off. Given that the word for physical punishment in Syriac (*pûr anût*) derives from a verbal root that means "repayment of a debt," it was

29. In Syriac thought the mark of the fall was the change from an angelic constitution to a mortal human body. Here the lesions on the flesh indicate that onset of the mortal state. See the classic essay of Sebastian Brock, "Clothing Metaphors as a Means of Theological Expression in Syriac Tradition," in *Typus, Symbol, Allegorie bei den östlichen Vätern und ihren Parallelen im Mittelalter*, ed. M. Schmidt and C. Geyer (Regensburg: Friedrich Pustet, 1982), 11–37; as well as Gary A. Anderson, "Garments of Skin in Apocryphal Narrative and Biblical Commentary," in *Studies in Ancient Midrash*, ed. James L. Kugel (Cambridge, MA: Harvard University Press, 2001), 101–43.

30. This selection is from the *Homily on Fasting*. The Syriac text was edited by Frédéric Rilliet, "Jacques de Saroug: Six homélies festales en prose," PO 43 (1986): 568, 570.

31. See Heb. 1:1–4, esp. v. 2: "In these last days he has spoken to us by a Son, whom he appointed heir of all things, through whom he also created the worlds." For the parable of the vineyard, see Matt. 21:33–46 and parallels.

altogether logical that the suffering of Christ would come to be understood as providing the currency needed to pay off the debt of Adam.

> Then the Messiah entered and took the debt and put the sins upon himself so as to tear up the bond by his own person. He said: "I am the heir. I shall repay the debt that drowned the mighty, entangled the swift, bound the strong, and destroyed all generations and raised the entrance ways [?] of the noble ones. Neither Enosh, Noah, Melchizedek, nor Abraham was able to stand before the debt. What was demanded of Eve? Let her bond be read aloud. The virgin fell into debt; the son of a virgin repays it. The snake bit the young maiden; another young maiden gives the medicine for her cure.
>
> "The inheritance of these ruins has come upon me. I shall rebuild the house of Adam; as the Heir, I shall repay. On account of this, my Father had sent me: I shall be the heir to Adam. For He saw that there was no other heir who could repay his debts. I shall rebuild his ruins. I will not let our image be ruined in Sheol. I will not forsake our likeness nor allow them to be trodden underfoot in the mire by the champions of perdition. I am the heir. All which Adam owes [ḥayyab], I myself will repay."
>
> The bond of Adam was read aloud, and it was found that he owed [ḥayyab] the penalty of death on the grounds that he had eaten from the tree of knowledge. A heavenly voice was heard on this account which said: "You are of the dust and to the earth you shall return" [Gen. 3:19]. What sin could Adam have committed that his transgression could be so great? He shunned his lord, obeyed his wife, reached for the fruit, put his foot in the snare, breached the fence of the law, broke the yoke of the commandment, dug a deep grave, and opened the gate to death so that it might enter and corrupt creation.[32]

Jacob's emphasis on the necessity for Christ to repay the debt puts his soteriological schema in a different category from that of Narsai. For the latter, the bond was voided by Satan's act of overreaching. Narsai takes very little interest in the actual suffering that Christ would have to undergo during the passion. When those moments do appear in his writings, the point Narsai makes is how unjustly Satan has acted in his legal suit. He has used his bond to condemn an innocent man. Jacob, on the other hand, is not interested in elaborating the theme of a legal suit. In his view the bond of indebtedness "was onerous and justice was fierce. That which was demanded [of the human race] was great." The love of God is exemplified in Christ's willingness to step forward and pay this price in full. Only in this fashion could the bond be discharged.

For Jacob, this point is made clear during the trial before Pilate when Barabbas and Christ are placed before the people.

---

32. From the *Homily on Good Friday*. For the Syriac, see Rilliet, "Jacques de Saroug," 612.

"Then the judge said: 'Whom do you desire that I should release to you, Bar Abba or Jesus who is called the Messiah?' All of them cried out and said, 'Bar Abba'" [Matt. 27:17, 21]. A prophecy was spoken by these foolish ones. The truth was sung by liars. They proclaimed what was to happen without knowing what they were saying. For Jesus was crucified in place of Bar Abba. It was for him that Jesus had come to free him from the bonds. For our Lord was bound solely that Adam be freed. For what could this mystery mean that on that feast day the bound one was set free? Certainly this one was a type of Adam who was freed from his bonds on the feast day of the cross.

The merciful Father made Adam a son by grace so that he could be heir to his possessions. For this reason Adam is the son of the Father [i.e., "Bar Abba"]. When Adam had sinned, he was bound in Sheol. Yet when the great feast day on which he was set free from his bonds [came], a brigand was bound by the Hebrews. Even he was called Bar Abba. When Pilate asked them, "Whom do you wish that I set free for you?" they cried out and said, "Bar Abba." These people showed mercy on this brigand, for prophecy cried out that Adam should be freed.

The one who sets free the prisoners entered the prison, and a clamor arose from the people, for that one who was bound for his debts was to be set free. For how could it happen that the name of the one bound at that time was called Bar Abba unless it be that providence—so rich in understanding—willed that through the mouths of all the people there be a clamor for Adam? And so he was set free. "'Whom do you wish that I set free for you?' They cried out and said, 'Bar Abba.'"

It was a wicked desire but a beautiful clamor. Jesus was bound, and Bar Abba was freed. The innocent one was declared guilty while the one who was guilty was declared innocent. [Or: the innocent one owed a punishment while the one who owed a punishment was declared innocent.] The strong man was bound, the sinner went free. Our Lord was scourged while Adam was spared the scourgings. The Sun took hold of the pillar, and the flame was scourged with lashes. The champion bore the weight of the world and removed the ills of sinners by his sufferings. The rich one paid the debts of the sinners and tore up the bond which all generations had not the resources to repay. The crucified one renewed creation by his sufferings and reestablished the world without corruption by his afflictions. For this reason the church cries out in a loud voice, "Let it not be that I should boast except in the cross of our Lord Jesus, the Messiah," to whom be glory in all times and forever and ever. Amen.[33]

In this remarkable text Jacob of Serug makes an ingenious and unprecedented move in the history of exegesis. He understands the name of Bar Abba to be the key to understanding the trial before Pilate. The Aramaic name Bar Abba literally means "son of the father." This unusual name, Jacob

33. Rilliet, "Jacques de Saroug," 626, 628.

reasons, must be a subtle cipher for Adam, for only he was fashioned directly by the hands of the Father. This means that when Bar Abba and Christ are presented before the crowd, what is really on offer is a choice between the first and second Adam. The providential plan of God the Father requires that the second Adam suffer for the sins of the first, and it just so happens that as the economy of salvation unfolds, this is precisely what happens. The crowd, in an ironic fashion, does the bidding of the Father by releasing the first Adam and putting the second to death. "It was a wicked desire," Jacob observes, "but a beautiful clamor."

The events of the passion can be read at two levels. On the plane of simple historical fact we see a brigand and an innocent man. The brigand has committed crimes requiring a considerable amount of bodily suffering to pay them off. But he is released by the crowd in favor of an innocent man who will suffer unjustly. At the cosmic level, this brigand is none other than Adam himself. The punishment he owes has become our own tragic patrimony. Yet due to the workings of divine grace, Adam will not suffer as is his due. The second Adam will stand in his place and undergo the scourging that was his and our due. Christ, "the rich one," steps forward and repays "the debts of the sinners and [tears] up the bond which all [previous] generations had not the resources to repay."

Ephrem the Syrian (d. 373): The Old Bond Is Voided and a New Bond Is Written

Ephrem is certainly the most complex and profound thinker in the Syriac tradition. His construal of the atonement, though it shows numerous family resemblances to what is found in Narsai and Jacob, differs sharply from them. There are two important elements in view: the bond of indebtedness that stands against humanity and the enormous interest generated by almsgiving and other works of charity. The latter element we will put off for another time.

Let us begin with a consideration of how the bond of indebtedness works in *Carmina Nisibena* 35–42, the story of Christ's descent into Hades to despoil the kingdom of Death. The narrative opens with Christ preparing to offer his life back to his divine Father on the cross. Satan and Death confer as to what stratagem they should follow. They are puzzled over what to do because they cannot tell whether Christ is a man or God. If he is a man, then he is clearly susceptible to death since he falls under the terms of the contract that Adam signed in Eden: "Through writing Adam became gravely liable to death and sin; / by transgressing the command, he sealed a pledge."[34] Satan, whose task it is to tempt humans, finds that his wiles have no power over Christ. Even at night, while he is asleep, Christ's dreams remain completely pure of any hint of concupiscence.[35] In his despair Satan seems on the verge of giving up. Just then his underlings gather and exhort him to maintain the fight. Satan then reasons that if his own powers are too weak for direct combat, perhaps he should shift the confrontation to Christ's disciples.

> "By the words of this Jesus
> I can learn to fight against him.
> For he said that '[if] Satan is divided
> against himself, he will not endure' [Matt. 12:26]. Though he wishes
>   to fight with us
> he gives us a weapon against him. Go divide his disciples,
> for if they are divided, it is possible for you to be victorious.
> By means of the Snake and Eve, these weak ones,
> by means of his very own, I overcame the First Adam."
> Death answered and said to the Evil One:
> "Why do you neglect your former ways?
> You used to catch the contemptible and trifling
> just like the capable. But Jesus, who is greater than all,
> with what will you catch him? The taste of his arrows,
> which he cast in you, while being tested by you, causes you fear.
> You and I along with your servants,
> our congregation is (too) small for war with the son of Mary.
> If this contention [among the disciples] allows
> us to do anything, then I advise this:
> go forth and dwell in that disciple,
> that the head will speak with the heads. Dismiss your camp,
> go forth and incite the Pharisees. But don't speak as in a disputation,
> as you are wont to: 'If you are God, throw yourself from here.'

---

34. *Carmina Nisibena* 48.9. For the original Syriac, see E. Beck, *Des Heiligen Ephraem des Syrers, Carmina Nisibena* CSCO 240 (Louvain: Peeters, 1963).

35. In Narsai's account it was also the case that Satan discovered that Christ was free of the normal "desire for fruit" that defined Adam and his progeny (as discussed above in this essay). See Satan's thoughts as expressed in *Carmina Nisibena* 35.10:

> Bodily desire is in every body,
> for even when they sleep it is awake in them.
> He whose thoughts are clear while awake,
> I can make them turbid in a dream. The dregs of his body stir in him,
> by the impulses hidden within him. Whether awake or asleep,
> I can disturb [him]. This One alone was so clear,
> not even in a deep dream could I disturb him;
> even in his sleep he was clear and holy.

> With affection kiss him and turn him over;
> the envy and sword of the Levites shall drag him away."[36]

The irony of Satan's logic should not be missed. Christ remarked during his ministry that if Satan's house is divided, it cannot stand (see Matt. 12:25–26). Now Satan uses Christ's words against him in order to concoct a strategy that he believes will allow him to emerge victorious in the struggle. Judas will be the means of bringing discord into Jesus's inner circle.[37]

Death, at this point, has taken no active role in the plot, for he bears no responsibility for murder. His task is that of taking the sick, the infirm, and the aged. What nature offers him, he collects.[38] At first Death reasons that there is cause for fear since no being can repay the debt of Adam. "Neither Cherubim nor Seraphim are able," Death relates, "to repay his debt;

> there is no mortal among them that can give
> their soul on behalf of him. Who can open the mouth of Sheol
> and go down and bring him up from there?
> He whom Sheol has smitten, she conceals forever.[39]

Yet the death of Christ is unlike all other deaths because Christ does not fall under the bond of indebtedness that Adam signed in Eden. Because he is human, Jesus is granted entry into the kingdom of Sheol. Only someone

36. *Carmina Nisibena* 35.20–22.

37. This idea of Ephrem is clearly reflected in Narsai's account: "Be gone, Evil One, to your counterpart," [Christ] said to him. "Be gone, prepare other weaponry for Death. / Be gone, prepare deadly nets with the help of mortals, / for your power is too weak on its own for the struggle. / Be gone, gather the children you have begotten by your stratagems. / Arm them with slander as you are accustomed."

38. See *Carmina Nisibena* 38.3–4:
> It is before God that I serve,
> for there is no partiality before him.
> Who else has endured as I have?
> For I am reviled though I do good. I am requited oppositely
> from the good deeds that I do. Though my acts are good
> my name is not good. My conscience is at rest in truth;
> in God I take consolation;
> though he is good, he is cheated every day but endures it.
> The old I remove from all sufferings,
> likewise the young from all their sins.
> Inner turmoil I quell in Sheol;
> for in our land there is no iniquity. Only Sheol and Heaven
> are removed from sin. But iniquity is rampant
> on the earth which lies in between. Therefore he who is discerning,
> let him ascend to heaven.
> And if that be [too] hard, let him descend to Sheol, which is easy.

39. Ibid., 36.2.

who is truly man would have a key to fit the door of entry.[40] But because he is also God, there is no way that Death can retain him once he has secured his entrance. To his credit, Death recognizes the lordship of Christ and submits to him when he enters the kingdom of Sheol. As a token of his submission, Death provides Christ with Adam and pledges to return all of the rest of humanity when Christ comes again in glory. Thus Death says:

> Jesus, King, receive my petition.
> And with the petition take your pledge.
> Lead forth Adam, the great pledge,
> in whom all the dead are concealed. [It is] just like when I received him,
> when all the living were hidden in him. I give you this ancient pledge,
> the body of Adam. Go up from here and rule over all.
> When I hear your trumpet
> I will bring out the dead with my own hands at your coming [again].[41]

In consideration of these new circumstances, "Death rewrote [the contract]; Sheol stood surety with him: All whom they had snatched and plundered would be returned at the resurrection."[42]

On this view it is not Satan who holds the bond, a fact that many over the centuries have worried about, but Death. And Death, by holding this bond, is simply carrying out the will of God established in the garden of Eden. Once Death learns of who Christ is, he grasps for the first time what his true role is in the economy of salvation: "If this is only a figure of what is to come, then I, who thought I was a king, did not know that it was a *temporary* deposit that I was keeping."[43] Here the bond of indebtedness assumes a very different sort of meaning. One recalls the role such a bond plays in the book of Tobit. In this story Tobit left a rather substantial sum of money with Gabael (Tob. 1:14). To secure that deposit and to guarantee that he or his agent could retrieve the funds at a future date, a *cheirographon*, or "bond of indebtedness," was

---

40. See ibid., 37.9:
> If a man reads the prophets, he hears about just wars.
> If a man reflects on the stories of Jesus,
> he learns of pity and mercy.
> And if a man believes that Jesus is an alien (to this created world),
> it is a blasphemy to me. For an alien key
> could never fit the door of Sheol.
> There is only the one key, that of the Creator,
> which opened this door and will open it again at his coming [again].

41. Ibid., 36.17.
42. Ibid., 48.9.
43. Ibid., 37.3, emphasis added.

signed and served as a guarantee. Later in the narrative, Raphael is able to present this bond before Gabael and receive the entire sum back (5:3; 9:5). And a similar custom seems to be at work in Ephrem's account of Christ's descent into Sheol. Death erred in thinking that this bond was an interest-bearing note that gave him permanent rights to collect payment. It turns out that this bond only guaranteed his rights over a temporary deposit. Death does not overreach the terms of his bond, as we saw in Jacob of Serug; rather, he learns that the terms of his "fiscal" sovereignty are time-bound. In recognition of his error, Death provides Christ with Adam as a token of what he will return to Christ when he comes again. This change in circumstances requires that a new contract be written. Through Christ the promise is made that all will be raised again at his second coming. In his *Hymns on the Nativity*, Ephrem frames this construal of the atonement as a surprising if not shocking reversal: "Thanks be to the Rich One, who paid the debt in place of us all, something He did not borrow, but He signed and became indebted to us again."[44] Thus Death, who has erred, owes the debt of human life to Christ and will pay it at the Lord's second coming, and in turn Christ, the gracious one, has taken it upon himself to repay this life to humankind through the final resurrection.

There is much, much more to say about Ephrem's construal of Christ's victory than space will allow. Let it suffice to say that the manner by which Christ becomes indebted to us is equal to or exceeds in significance the way in which our own debt was released. Ephrem differs from Narsai and Jacob in making his story a two-pronged affair. To this theme I hope to return in a future essay. But for the time being, one chapter in this story has come to closure. As can be vividly seen in the work of these three Syriac writers, the impact of Second Temple and rabbinic Judaism is patent. The conception of sin as a debt that must be repaid, an idea that takes root in Second Temple Judaism, is the foundation upon which the doctrine of atonement is built. This important detail was missed by Aulén and by the numerous commentators on his legacy. A common criticism of Aulén has been that the theme of Christus Victor, for all of its powerfully dramatic character, is too unbiblical to be taken seriously.[45] Yet this criticism fails to take seriously the influence of a text like Colossians 2:14 and the powerful influence of the late biblical metaphor of sin as a debt that must be repaid.

---

44. *Hymns on the Nativity* 3.10. For the original Syriac, see E. Beck, *Des Heiligen Ephraem des Syrers, Hymnen de Nativitate*, CSCO 186 (Louvain: Peeters, 1959).

45. For an example of this sort of criticism, see the fine book of Colin Gunton, *The Actuality of Atonement: A Study of Metaphor, Rationality, and the Christian Tradition* (Grand Rapids: Eerdmans, 1989).

7

GREEK PATRISTIC PERSPECTIVES ON THE ORIGINS OF SOCIAL INJUSTICE

NONNA VERNA HARRISON

Let me begin with a caveat. "Social injustice" is a modern concept that did not exist as such in late antiquity. For the purposes of this essay, I take it to mean arbitrary and unjust inequalities that place some persons or groups of people at a disadvantage in relation to others. However, the kinds of inequalities commonly regarded as socially unjust today were sometimes regarded as just in the ancient Mediterranean world. The philosophical schools differed from each other on what justice is. Stoics believed that all humans are by nature equal, since all are endowed with *logos*, that is, with rationality that participates in the rationality pervading and organizing the world, making of its parts a harmonious whole. Marcia Colish summarizes their position well:

> It is inconceivable for the Stoics that there could be any conflict between the good of the individual, the good of the group, and the good of the universe, for the same *logos* permeates and rules them all. From this premise the Stoics work out a number of distinctive ideas in the field of social and political theory. The *logos* of each [human being] is the *logos* of every [human being]. In their common possession of reason, a fragment of the divine *logos*, all [humans] are by

nature equal. On this basis, the Stoics argue that slavery and sexual inequality are contrary to the law of nature.[1]

Though the later Stoics taught that people have a duty to live rationally and ethically within the roles society has allotted to them, even they considered inequalities as essentially unjust. As we shall see, Gregory of Nyssa's view is similar, though the theological foundation is different. For him, all humans are by nature equal because all are made in the image of God.

Aristotle, on the other hand, teaches that people are by nature unequal; some are inherently better than others, and some are by nature slaves. For him, justice is proportional, that is, it distributes the good things in life to people unequally in proportion to their differing levels of value. If people are unequal, he says, unequal shares are owed to them.[2] The inequalities he envisages are the differences of social class or role that exist in his classical Greek cultural world. He considers men and women, parents and children, free citizens and slaves, as by nature unequal. Again, unlike the Stoics, he even argues that the virtues proper to people in these various groups differ, and the different categories of people are capable of differing degrees of virtue. For him, only the free adult male citizen is capable of virtue in its fullness.[3] Although in today's world many would regard economic equality, equality of social or political status, or equality of opportunity as an ideal of justice toward which communities ought to strive, an Aristotelian would regard such equalities as unjust. Although Stoic ideas were common in late antiquity, hierarchies structured the entire social world in both the private realm of the household and the public realm of city and empire. Hierarchy was taken for granted as natural and normative in daily life. Many people would in practice have agreed with Aristotle's understanding of equality and justice, whether or not they knew anything of his writings.

When we speak of Greek patristic ideas of social injustice, then, we impose a modern value judgment on an ancient culture that had social ideals different from our own. Yet the question is fruitful. Like the Stoics and Aristotle, early Christian theologians have differing ideas about whether people are, or should be, by nature equal, and what this implies for the ways individuals ought to treat their neighbors and how communities ought to be structured.

Early Christians lived in a late Roman cultural world in which the social and relational character of human existence was taken for granted. They

1. Marcia Colish, *The Stoic Tradition from Antiquity to the Early Middle Ages*, 2nd ed., 2 vols. (Leiden: Brill, 1990), 1:36–37.
2. Aristotle, *Nicomachean Ethics* 5.3.
3. Aristotle, *Politics* 1.12–13.

belonged to the structured communities of household, city, and empire, as well as the church. Within these structures persons fulfilled differing and mutually interdependent prescribed roles based on gender, family, class, and regional and economic ties. Their roles were ranked hierarchically and connected by mutual responsibilities, often conceived, as in Aristotle's ethics, in terms of authority and obedience. People saw these social structures as landmarks in an already existing landscape they inhabited and did not envisage the possibility that they could be shifted. So except when they were building radical alternative communities within the ascetical movement, Christian pastors encouraged the faithful to live within their prescribed roles and find in their daily tasks opportunities to practice virtue and treat others with love and respect. This is especially true of John Chrysostom, who emphasizes the value of the existing hierarchical order. His homilies are so practical and contextual that it is crucial to understand their aims and possible impacts within their original cultural context.

Yet Stoic ideas were also commonplace in the late antique world, particularly the understanding that humans are by nature equal in certain respects, alike in sharing such qualities as rationality, freedom of choice, the capacity for virtue, and moral responsibility. Christians agreed with the Stoics on these points; both wanted to affirm that people are fundamentally alike, equal, and dignified in their common humanity. For Christians, who believe that Christ came to extend the same offer of salvation to every person, all share the same basic bodily and emotional experiences, the same moral freedom and responsibility, the same capacities for virtue or vice and for loving relationship with God and neighbor. All are sinners like Adam and Eve, and all are capable of receiving the same salvation. Every human faces the same divine judgment and the same possibilities of eschatological condemnation or glory, since everyone is capable of entering through grace into knowledge of God, communion with the Holy Trinity, and participation in divine life.

Given their common cultural context and theological commitments, early Christian anthropologies must thus negotiate and attempt to include both human equality and inequality and show how they relate to each other. We will examine how Origen, the Cappadocians, and John Chrysostom address this issue in quite different ways. When gnostic teachers pose radical questions about how the Creator of a world where people are born into conditions of unjust inequality can be good, wise, and just, Origen responds with his theory of preexistent intelligences that were originally alike and equal to each other. Gregory of Nyssa discards his predecessor's idea of preexistence but agrees with him that people are originally and fundamentally alike and equal. John Chrysostom, whose formation among the Antiochene exegetes differs from that of the Alexandrians and Cappadocians, believes that human community is by nature ordered hierarchically through relationships of authority and obedience, even in the original paradise. This essay describes how within their shared late antique and Christian setting, Gregory of Nyssa and John Chrysostom arrive at radically different conclusions about how "natural" equality and inequality function in grounding social and political life. Though their common cultural and imperial context limited the extent to which they could follow diverging paths in social and political practice, their differing anthropologies have significant theological and ethical implications that remain relevant today.

Origen

The Alexandrian theologian asks himself a pointed question about social injustice in *First Principles* 2.9. He inquires about what accounts for the wide discrepancies in people's living conditions. This question is particularly acute when people are born into privileged or disadvantaged circumstances that they presumably could not have brought upon themselves. Writing with the prejudices of an educator of upper-class youth, one steeped in Greek cultural traditions, he first observes differences of culture and social class.

> Among human beings, there are no small differences, for some are barbarians, others Greeks, and of the barbarians some are wilder and fiercer, whereas others are more gentle. Some moreover employ laws of the highest excellence, others poorer and ruder ones, while others follow inhuman and savage customs rather than laws. Some people are from the very moment of their birth in a lowly position, brought up in subjection and slavery, placed under lords and princes and tyrants; whereas others are brought up with more freedom and under more rational influences.[4]

Like others in the ancient world, Origen tends to think of diversities as if they can be ranked on a linear scale as better or worse, higher or lower, more or less advantageous. He is particularly concerned about differing cultural environments that vary in the resources and opportunities they provide for the development of good character and conduct. His implicit question is whether people's moral condition, which determines their relationship with God and their hope for the next life, is molded by the culture into which they are born

---

4. Origen, *First Principles* (= *Princ.*) 2.9.3, SC 252:356; G. W. Butterworth, trans., *Origen: On First Principles* (New York: Harper & Row, 1973), 131, alt.

rather than their own free choices, a situation he would regard as profoundly unjust. A little later he returns to this issue and ranks several cultures according to their moral impact. As a believer in biblical religion, he ranks the Hebrews first, followed by the Greeks, and contrasts them with foreigners, whom his culture imagined as practicing the worst moral outrages: "One is born among the Hebrews, with whom he finds instruction in the divine law, another among the Greeks who are themselves people of wisdom and no small learning, another among the Ethiopians, whose custom it is to feed on human flesh, others among the Scythians, where parricide is practiced as if sanctioned by law, or among the Taurians, where strangers are offered in sacrifice."[5]

Interestingly, Origen also identifies disability as a problematic kind of diversity: "Some have healthy bodies, others from their earliest years are invalids; some are deprived of sight, others of hearing or speech; some are born in such a condition, others lose the use of one faculty or another soon after birth or else suffer a like misfortune when fully grown."[6] All these inequalities of culture, class, and ability are troubling to Origen because they appear profoundly unjust, and since many of them are present at the beginning of people's lives, it would be easy to conclude that God created the unfair inequities. Origen takes pains to reject such reasoning and appeals to the mystery of divine judgment. Yet he does not find apophatic reserve to be a sufficient answer. His theological approach, here and elsewhere, is characteristically to ask searching questions and suggest tentative answers, taking care not to claim that they are anything more than conjectures.

In *First Principles* 2.9, Origen is concerned to respond to gnostic teachers like Valentinus and his follower Basilides, whom he names explicitly.[7] It is they who have raised the question of unjust human inequalities. Their explanation is that souls have come into this world as a result of a subordinate deity's mistake and a precosmic fall. They further believe that some people are born spiritual by nature, others merely carnal, and others in an intermediate condition.[8] To respond, Origen has to vindicate the Creator's goodness, power, wisdom, and justice; and he needs to reaffirm the freedom, moral capacity, and responsibility of all human beings. He proposes an alternative theory of human preexistence, as follows. God created all intellects alike, free and equal, but through inattention to God they fell by their own choice to varying degrees and became souls. God then created diverse forms of embodiment for them, a

5. Origen, *Princ.* 2.9.5, SC 252:362; Butterworth, 135, alt.
6. Origen, *Princ.* 2.9.3, SC 252:356–58; Butterworth, 131, alt.
7. Origen, *Princ.* 2.9.5, SC 252:360–62. He also names Marcion, probably incorrectly.
8. For a brief description of Valentinus's context, life, and teachings, see Everett Ferguson, ed., *Encyclopedia of Early Christianity*, 2nd ed. (New York: Garland, 1997), 2:1155.

different situation for each according to their merit, both as punishment and as education, so that all could in the end return to contemplation of God.[9] The Creator also organized these embodied souls into a single harmonious cosmos and history. In most cases, then, inequalities at birth result from the fallen soul's own free choices in its preexistent state together with God's wise but inscrutable plan for redeeming and restoring that soul in the age to come.

For Origen, the end is like the beginning; the final stage of the eschaton will restore the original state of alikeness and unity.[10] From this perspective, all inequality and all diversity as such belong to a flawed and transitory phase of human identity, though they are valuable in serving God's pedagogical purposes. However, Origen's belief in preexistence is a double-edged sword from the viewpoint of social justice, in the same way that the theory of karma allows some people in India to make a case for the caste system. Karma means cause and effect, such that one's condition in the present necessarily results from one's own past action, perhaps in a previous life, and likewise one's every action in the present will affect one's future situation, though maybe not until a life to come. Notwithstanding his critics' accusations, Origen rejects belief in reincarnation;[11] yet his theory, like the theory of karma, affirms a continuity in personal existence from before birth through the present life into a life after death. Framing our present human experience within this larger context enables him to affirm that justice prevails in the world as a whole and in the history of each person's whole existence. Yet such a theory can easily be used to justify unjust inequality and discrimination within this life as deserved on account of greater sin in a previous existence. Like high-caste Hindus despising "untouchables," Valentinians could denigrate people outside their circle as by nature carnal, thus justifying disregard or mistreatment of them, or at least lack of concern for their salvation. A follower of Origen, too, could justify prejudice against foreign cultures, slaves, and the disabled on the grounds that they deserve their disadvantages because of sins they committed before their birth. At least in the text we have examined, Origen's theological speculations have not led him to critique his own cultural prejudices. The distinguished fourth-century Origenist exegete and theologian Didymus of Alexandria lost his eyesight as a boy.[12] There is no historical evidence by which we could answer this question, but I wonder what he thought of this part of Origen's theology.

9. Origen, *Princ.* 1.6.2, SC 252:196–200.
10. Origen, *Princ.* 3.6.3–4, SC 268:240–44.
11. John A. McGuckin, ed., *The Westminster Handbook to Origen* (Louisville: Westminster John Knox, 2004), 205–7.
12. See Richard A. Layton, *Didymus the Blind and His Circle in Late Antique Alexandria* (Urbana: University of Illinois Press, 2004).

Gregory of Nyssa

At the Oxford Patristics Conference in August 2003, Graham Gould presented a paper surveying "Moral and Ascetical Passages in Gregory of Nyssa's *Contra Eunomium*, Book I." In one of the texts from his first book *Against Eunomius*, as Gould explains, Gregory proposes a rational argument to refute the neo-Arian's claim that although the Son is not truly God in an orthodox sense but is created, he nevertheless has inherited the Father's authority over all creation. Gregory's argument that this claim is untenable is based on a political theory with two potentially radical presuppositions: (1) humans are ontologically equal and united to each other through kinship, and (2) inequalities of power must be grounded in corresponding ontological inequalities to have stability and lasting credibility. This important passage is worth quoting at length.

> Suppose their [the Eunomians'] assertion is granted, that while not truly Son he has become heir to the Lord of all, and having been created and made, he governs his kindred. How, then, is it that the rest of creation will accept and not rebel at being pushed into the subordinate place by its own kin? Being in no way inferior in nature, since it is itself created just as he is, creation would then be condemned to slavery and subjection to what is akin to it. Such a thing resembles tyranny, when power is not given to a superior being, but while remaining naturally of equal honor, the creation is divided into slave and master. So one part of it rules while the other is subordinate. Yet the one who has been allotted greater honor than those like him has won this higher rank by luck as in a raffle.[13]

This argument is not simply an ad hoc debater's point scored against Eunomius. It has significant parallels in Gregory's other writings, though with one crucial difference. Here he refers to all created beings, in contrast to God, as akin and equal to each other by nature, since his context is the standard pro-Nicene ontological division between Creator and creation. Yet the political illustration really fits more appropriately within a discussion of human social arrangements. This is a clue that Gregory may have in mind parallel ideas he expresses elsewhere in key anthropological texts.

In *Against Eunomius* 1, Gregory speaks of the created world as a unity; all creatures are alike and equal in their creaturehood and are united by ties of

---

13. Werner Jaeger, ed., *Gregorii Nysseni Opera* (Leiden: Brill, 1952–), 1:178. Henceforth cited as *GNO*. Translations not otherwise attributed are my own. For *Contra Eunomium* 1, I have consulted and reworked Stuart Hall's version in Lucas F. Mateo-Seco and Juan L. Bastero, eds., *El "Contra Eunomium I" en la producción literaria de Gregorio de Nisa: VI Coloquio Internacional sobre Gregorio de Nisa* (Pamplona: Ediciones Universidad de Navarra, 1988).

kinship. An unjust distinction between ruler and ruled arbitrarily divides this cosmic unity by violating the natural kinship and equality that hold it together. In *The Creation of Humanity* 16, Gregory speaks of humankind as a unity, a single nature created in God's image, in which all members are alike and equal.

> As a particular human being is enclosed by the size of his body, . . . so, it seems to me, the whole fullness of humanity was encompassed by the God of all through the power of foreknowledge, as if in one body. And the text teaches this which says, "And God created the human, . . . in the image of God he created him" [Gen. 1:27 RSV alt.]. For the image is not in [just] part of human nature, . . . but such power extends equally to all the human race. A sign of this is that . . . all have the power of rational thought and deliberation, and all the other things through which the divine nature is imaged in that which has been created according to it. The human being manifested at the first creation of the world and the one that will come into being at the [final] consummation of all are alike, equally bearing in themselves the divine image. Because of this, the whole [of humankind] was named [in Gen. 1:27] as one human being, since to the power of God nothing is either past or future; what will be is encompassed equally with what is now present by the energy that rules all. So the whole nature, extending from the first to the last, is, as it were, one image of the Existing One. The distinction between male and female was fashioned last [Gen. 1:27b], added to what was formed.[14]

This famous text shows how Gregory regards humankind throughout time, space, and the eschaton as a single whole whose unity is foundational and is constituted by the divine image, which all people possess equally and in the same way. For Gregory, the divine image defines what is authentic to human identity. He is saying that unity and equality are central to being human, and people are alike in possessing crucial characteristics such as reason that bind them together. The context of protology and eschatology is important. Like Origen's intelligences, Gregory's humans are by nature alike and equal at the beginning and at the end, though he rejects his Alexandrian predecessor's belief in preexistence.[15] Notice that just as unjust power relationships sunder the unity of creation in *Against Eunomius* 1, in *The Creation of Humanity* 16 the gender distinction sunders the unity of humankind. I have discussed Gregory's understanding of gender elsewhere[16] and will not pursue it further here. My point now is to observe a broader pattern. For Gregory, the inequalities

---

14. Gregory of Nyssa, *The Creation of Humanity* 16, PG 44:185B–D.
15. Gregory of Nyssa, *The Creation of Humanity* 29, PG 44:233C–236A.
16. Verna E. F. [Nonna Verna] Harrison, "Male and Female in Cappadocian Theology," *Journal of Theological Studies* 41 (1990): 441–71.

and divisions intrinsic to social injustice are not present in the original human nature that God has created, nor will they be present in the eschatological restoration of God's original creative plan. They have been added to the human condition subsequently and go against our original nature.[17]

In a famous discussion of slavery, the *Fourth Homily on Ecclesiastes* addresses the issue of social class in a similar way. Gregory again speaks of the image of God as central to the human identity that all people share. He cites Genesis 1 to demonstrate the absurdity of owning slaves as he scolds the owner directly.

> "I acquired slaves and slave girls" [Eccles. 2:7]. What are you saying? You condemn to slavery the human being, whose nature is free and self-ruling, and you legislate in opposition to God, overturning what is according to the law of nature. For upon the one who was created to be lord of the earth and appointed to rule the creation, upon this one you impose the yoke of slavery, as if he were resisting and fighting the divine precept. You have forgotten the limits of your authority, a rule limited to dominion over the nonrational animals. For Scripture says, "Let them rule birds and fish and quadrupeds and reptiles" [Gen. 1:26, my trans.]. How can you bypass the slavery within your power and rise up against the one who is free by nature, numbering one of the same nature as yourself among the four-legged and legless beasts?[18]

This text shows that Gregory sees his image theology as having ethical implications here and now. He is discussing not protology or eschatology but present unjust conditions. He asserts that all humans alike share the royal dignity, freedom, and equality that characterize the divine image. Following Genesis 1:27, he observes that it is natural for humans to have nonrational animals as slaves and pointedly contrasts this with the unnaturalness of humans enslaving other humans. As in *The Creation of Humanity* 16, the unity in question pertains to humankind rather than to creation as a whole. Yet here again he speaks of this unity as sundered in violation of nature. Again he addresses slave owners, accusing them as follows: "You have divided the nature itself, making some live as slaves and others as lords," though God created all humans according to the divine image and likeness.[19]

Gregory uses the theology of the image to make a related ethical point in his second homily on *Love of the Poor*, where he defends the human dignity

17. On the topic of Gregory of Nyssa and other church fathers on social injustice and the image of God, see also Nonna Verna Harrison, *God's Many-Splendored Image* (Grand Rapids: Baker Academic, 2010), 89–102.

18. *GNO* 5:335. On the responsibility of humans, made in God's image as stewards of God, to care for the animals and the earth's ecosystem, see my *God's Many-Splendored Image*, 123–46.

19. *GNO* 5:336.

of homeless social outcasts who are disabled and disfigured by leprosy, as he reminds his audience of their duty to take care of them. In the middle of a lengthy description of such a person's miserable bodily condition and way of life, we find the following observations: "He is a human being, created according to the image of God, appointed to rule the earth, having within his power the service of the nonrational animals. In this misfortune he has indeed been changed to such an extent that from his appearance it is doubtful whether his visible form with the identifying marks it bears is clearly that of a human being or of some other animal."[20]

Just as it is scandalous for the slave to have to play the role of a nonrational animal, it is an outrage that illness and mistreatment have blurred the distinction between a human and a beast. In both cases one bearing the divine image is denied the respect intended by God. Divisions of class and social status have sundered the unity and solidarity intrinsic to the humanity shared by owners and slaves, by those secure in their houses and those wandering homeless in the countryside.

The passage in *Against Eunomius* 1 cited above makes the same point about the beasts too, showing, as we suggested, that the concept at issue is really more anthropological than cosmic: "The human being was not equal in honor to the inferior nature when he was allotted rule over the nonrational animals. Rather, as superior in reason he is lord of the others, promoted because his nature was advantageously different."[21] The text also offers a striking political observation based on Gregory's anthropology: "The reason why human governments suffer frequent changes is that it is not acceptable to one of equal worth by nature to be excluded from an equal share with the superior, but there is an innate natural desire in every one to become equal to the ruling power, when it is akin to them."[22]

Gregory did not envisage revolutionary changes in the social structures taken for granted in his time any more than his contemporaries did. The recognition that social structures themselves undergo transformation throughout history is a modern discovery. Yet he no doubt observed that Roman emperors and other high government officials often kept their offices for only a short time, and power frequently passed to others in disorderly ways. Perhaps he seeks an explanation for such political instability. He finds its root in inequality itself, which is unstable because it conflicts with underlying human ontology. His writings about gender, poverty, and slavery show further that he sees the

---

20. Gregory of Nyssa, *De pauperibus amandis orationes duo*, ed. Arie van Heck (Leiden: Brill, 1964), 26.
21. *GNO* 1:178.
22. *GNO* 1:178–79.

essential equality of human beings as having clear ethical implications. For him, violation of humankind's natural unity and equality results in social injustice. Political instability follows because unjust social arrangements lack grounding in authentic human nature.

John Chrysostom

Like Aristotle, however, John Chrysostom regards hierarchy and relationships of authority and obedience as foundational in human identity. He believes that when people are related to each other as equals, this causes instability and disorder, whereas clearly defined hierarchical relationships, in which one leads and the other accepts subordinate status, bring peace and harmony. He finds the same pattern in every kind of human community, in church, household, city, and empire alike.[23] In *Homily 20 on Ephesians* he cites this theory as supporting women's subordination in marriage. "Where there is equal authority," he declares, "there is never peace. A household cannot be a democracy, ruled by everyone, but the authority must necessarily rest in one person."[24] He equates democracy with anarchy and chaos, and as Valerie Karras observes, "He applies monarchist political theory to the question of [women's] submission."[25]

Chrysostom explains his political theory further in *Homily 23 on Romans*, where he discusses Paul's exhortation in Romans 13 to submit to civil authorities. He explains that while God does not approve of all rulers, since some are tyrannical oppressors, he does mandate that some should rule over others, and he gives them the power by which they rule. The reason for this, Chrysostom believes, is that equality results in disorder.

> For that there should be rulers, and some rule and others be ruled—and that all things should not just be carried on in confusion with people swaying like waves in this direction and that—this, I say, is the work of God's wisdom. . . . For since equality of honor often leads to fighting, [God] has made many forms of rule and subjection, such as husband and wife, child and father, old and young, slave and free, ruler and ruled, teacher and student.[26]

23. David C. Ford, *Women and Men in the Early Church: The Full Views of St. John Chrysostom* (South Canaan, PA: St. Tikhon's Seminary Press, 1996).

24. PG 62:141; Catharine P. Roth and David Anderson, trans., *St. John Chrysostom on Marriage and Family Life* (Crestwood, NY: St. Vladimir's Seminary Press, 1986), 53.

25. Valerie Karras, "Male Domination of Women in the Writings of St. John Chrysostom," *Greek Orthodox Theological Review* 36 (1991): 131–39, esp. 135.

26. PG 60:615. The first half of this translation is by J. B. Morris and W. H. Simcox, *Saint Chrysostom: Homilies on the Acts of the Apostles and the Epistle to the Romans*, NPNF¹, ed. Philip Schaff (Grand Rapids: Eerdmans, 1956), 11:511, alt. The second half is my own.

Notice how this hierarchical principle extends to all forms of human community and relationship, in the private as well as the public sphere. Chrysostom then supports his argument with two analogies between human community and other natural life systems. He first asserts that within the human body not all parts are alike: some limbs or organs rule while others are ruled. Even here, he understands diversity as necessarily entailing inequality and the corresponding relationships of authority and obedience. His second analogy is with the nonrational animals. Here, in contrast to Gregory of Nyssa, he states that humans are like rather than unlike them. Just as bees, wild sheep, birds, and fish live in groups in which all are subordinate to one that is the leader, he says, humans should do the same.

Chrysostom then makes his underlying principle explicit: "For anarchy, wherever it may be, is altogether evil, and a cause of confusion."[27] *Anarchia* literally means the lack of rule, hence the absence of a ruler. Without one person vested with authority over the others, Chrysostom believes, there will inevitably be disorder and conflict. He drives this point home a little later in the same homily.

> [The ruler] is a benefactor to you in things of the greatest importance, since he provides peace and the civic institutions. For countless good things come to states through these rulers; and if you were to remove them, all things would go to ruin, and neither city nor country, nor private nor public buildings, nor anything else would stand, but all would be turned upside down, while the more powerful would devour the weaker.[28]

It appears Chrysostom cannot imagine any middle ground between monarchical authority and a complete absence of structure in community life, or foresee the possibility of other formal or informal arrangements for creating and sustaining structure. So he would not see inequalities of social or political power or status as unjust.[29] He does not envisage that people can sometimes get along as equals, as brothers and sisters, though he does sometimes describe and praise ideal friendships, such as that of David and Jonathan.

27. PG 60:615.

28. PG 60:617; Morris and Simcox, *Saint Chrysostom*, 513. Chrysostom's fear is echoed, probably unknowingly, by that of a later monarchist political theorist, Thomas Hobbes, who warns of "a warre . . . of every man, against every man" in the absence of absolutist authority, a condition in which human life would be "solitary, poore, nasty, brutish, and short" (Thomas Hobbes, *Leviathan*, ed. Richard Tuck, rev. student ed. [Cambridge: Cambridge University Press, 1996], 88–89).

29. Chrysostom probably views economic inequalities differently, given his zealous concern for the poor.

Of course, Chrysostom is careful to distinguish among diverse kinds of unequal relationships. Like everyone in his hierarchically structured culture, for instance, he is well aware of the difference between an honorable Roman matron's deference to her husband and the cowering obsequiousness of a slave living in fear of corporal punishment.[30] As I have shown elsewhere in discussing his understanding of marriage,[31] his ideal of human community is a complete unity of mind and purpose in household, city, church, or empire character-ized by such harmony, consensus, mutual respect, and love that hierarchical structures function as free collaboration among equals. Leaders still lead and followers still obey, yet they work together on every level, so that the leaders share their dignity and mode of existence fully with the followers. In paradise, for example, Eve shares so fully in Adam's cosmic sovereignty that through her union with him and sharing in his work, she also is fully sovereign. He remains the center and source of the authority, and she has no authority apart from him. Yet this inequality pales into insignificance because of their unity and love, and both partners benefit, together with the natural world they lovingly manage on behalf of God. This is ultimately how Chrysostom envisages hierarchical structures as enabling and supporting peace and harmony. Yet unequal human relationships remain foundational for him even when, through God's grace and human leaders' right use of authority, they undergird a kind of equality.

On the other hand, for him the presence of sin intensifies natural hierarchical relationships into radical inequality, as with masters and cringing slaves, wives who need to live like slaves, or authoritarian governments and their subjects. In *Sermon Four on Genesis*, Chrysostom observes that in a fallen world all these harsh social arrangements serve the divine will and benefit humanity because they restrain evil and preserve order.[32] The chaos and conflict he fears in the absence of a ruler are surely caused by pervasive human wrongdoing. In the absence of sin, Chrysostom believes, people will defer to God and each other, so hierarchical structures will function beneficially and harmoniously.

Different Starting Points

Though they agree in many areas, on the point we are examining the diver-gence between Gregory of Nyssa and John Chrysostom is striking. In terms

30. On this difference, see Kate Cooper, *The Virgin and the Bride: Idealized Womanhood in Late Antiquity* (Cambridge, MA: Harvard University Press, 1996).

31. "Women and the Image of God according to St. John Chrysostom," in *In Dominico Eloquio—In Lordly Eloquence: Essays on Patristic Exegesis in Honor of Robert Louis Wilken*, ed. Paul M. Blowers et al. (Grand Rapids: Eerdmans, 2002), 259–79.

32. Chrysostom, *Sermon Four on Genesis*, SC 433:220–38.

of what is most essential to being human, Gregory sees people as inherently equal, and for him hierarchical relationships must be understood in terms of an underlying equality. For John people are inherently hierarchical, and equality must be understood in terms of inequality. Because they differ about the kinds of relationships that are most profoundly natural to human community, these two theologians have opposite understandings of what causes the political instability that so easily disrupts social harmony. Gregory says instability results when one person tries to impose unwarranted authority over his equals and they naturally resist. John says it arises when subordinates disrupt hierarchical order by refusing to obey their natural superiors.

These divergences reveal the two authors' political and theological convictions. Yet they also reflect the fact that Gregory's and John's anthropological reflections start from different contexts. Gregory's model of human community, like that of his fellow Cappadocians, is the ascetical movement, in which Christian men and women established radical forms of alternative community that sought to follow the teachings of the gospel. Ascetics emphasize the divine image and likeness common to all people and work to develop the human capacities for virtue and sanctification that all share. In this setting, differences of gender, ethnicity, wealth, ability, and social class become unimportant compared with the vocation to grow into Christlikeness, which all are called to. Hence, Gregory regards unity, equality, and alikeness as central to human identity. The exegetical starting point Gregory shares with the other Cappadocians and the Alexandrians also supports this view. Their anthropological reflection begins with the humans created in accord with Genesis 1:26–27a, who are defined by God's image and likeness, which is equal, alike, and common to all.[33]

Chrysostom, like his fellow Antiochene exegetes, begins his anthropological reflection with the creation account in Genesis 2, where, in the Septuagint version, Adam is created first and then Eve is created from his side to be his helper.[34] This story is important in affirming the communal dimension of human identity, but when read in isolation it depicts a community that is asymmetrical and hierarchical from the outset. Adam remains the center while Eve is oriented

33. See, e.g., Basil's two homilies on the creation of humankind, SC 160; Gregory of Nazianzus, *Poem* 1.1.6 *On the Soul*, trans. and ed. Claudio Moreschini and D. A. Sykes, in *St. Gregory of Nazianzus*, Poemata Arcana (Oxford: Oxford University Press, 1997), 32–41; and Gregory of Nyssa, *The Creation of Humanity*, PG 44:125–256.

34. On the Antiochenes Diodore of Tarsus, Theodore of Mopsuestia, and Theodoret of Cyrrhus, see my "Women, Human Identity, and the Image of God: Antiochene Interpretations," *Journal of Early Christian Studies* 9, no. 2 (2001): 205–49. Chrysostom's reading of the two creation stories in his *Homilies on Genesis* follows the same pattern as his colleagues' interpretations.

toward helping him. This impression of primordial inequality is diminished when Genesis 2 is read in terms of the first creation account, in Genesis 1, but the Antiochenes read Genesis 1 as summarizing in advance the creative work described in Genesis 2. Correspondingly, Chrysostom's model for human community is not the ascetic community but the family, that is, in effect, an idealized version of the late antique household, where unequal people fulfill their hierarchically structured social roles in a spirit of love and service to others.

Eschatological Convergence

Despite their differences in theory, in practice Origen, Gregory of Nyssa, and John Chrysostom all lived and functioned in the same late antique Mediterranean world. They all took existing social structures as givens, including the civic and religious practice of philanthropy, which mandated that wealthy aristocrats provide for the poor.[35]

Further, they agree about the end more than they do about the beginning. Though they diverge in protology, they converge in eschatology, which may appear surprising given what we have seen thus far of their views on human identity. All three are agreed that the kinds of arbitrary inequalities people today regard as social injustice will be absent in the age to come. Origen envisages the final consummation as a restored community of intelligences who are alike and equal in their contemplation of God.[36] Gregory of Nyssa hopes for a time when all evil has been purified away, when humans are alike and united in eternal growth, sharing divine life more and more and forever becoming more Christlike.[37] John Chrysostom compares differences in social and economic status to masks that actors wear to identify their characters in a play. When this life is over, such inequalities drop away from human identity, just as when the play ends and the masks are removed, revealing the actors' true faces.[38] All three fathers agree that in the age to come people will differ in rank, if they do, because of their differing degrees of virtue and the rewards corresponding to them.[39]

35. Peter Brown, *Power and Persuasion in Late Antiquity: Towards a Christian Empire* (Madison: University of Wisconsin Press, 1992), 71–117; Susan R. Holman, *The Hungry Are Dying: Beggars and Bishops in Roman Cappadocia* (New York: Oxford University Press, 2001).

36. Origen, *Princ.* 3.6.4, SC 268:244.

37. Gregory of Nyssa, *On Those Who Have Fallen Asleep*, GNO 9:66.

38. John Chrysostom, *Second Sermon on the Rich Man and Lazarus*, PG 48:986; cf. Gregory of Nyssa, *On Those Who Have Fallen Asleep*, GNO 9:64–65.

39. For a thoughtful discussion of virtues and rewards, see Gregory of Nazianzus, *Oration* 14.1–5, PG 35:860–64.

John Chrysostom, who lived with monks in the caves near Antioch as a young man, admired the ascetics who lived, to the extent possible, in anticipation of the eschaton. Though the household is the model for human community in his protology, in his eschatology the monastery becomes the model, as it is throughout Cappadocian anthropology. Gregory of Nyssa and John Chrysostom even agree that the gender distinction is absent in the soul and will be absent in the resurrection body.[40]

All are agreed, further, that Christians are called to model their lives to some extent in anticipation of the eschaton. Their hopes, not only their origins, shape their present moral obligations. In his homily *Holy Pascha*, Gregory of Nyssa speaks of how the feast's joy is a participation in the joy of the future resurrection, which is made present liturgically. He then says that the way to celebrate the feast is to free prisoners, forgive debtors, and liberate slaves, and that those slaves who are not freed must be given honor instead of disgrace. He adds that the resurrection brings provision to the poor and healing to the disabled.[41] At this point in the homily it is unclear whether he refers to the grace of the present feast, to the future resurrection, or to both. Baptism, which in the early church was frequently done at Pascha (Easter), is another occasion to anticipate that for which Christians hope. In one of his *Baptismal Catecheses*, John Chrysostom exhorts everyone to come to baptism, since Christ offers the same grace to all in the sacrament and thereby bestows on all the same new human identity.

> *Come to me*, he says, *all you that are weary and are carrying heavy burdens* [Matt. 11:28]. What a gracious invitation, what ineffable goodness! *Come to me all*, not only rulers but also those ruled, not only rich but also poor, not only free but also slaves, not only men but also women, not only young but also old, not only those with healthy bodies but also the maimed and those with mutilated limbs, all of you, he says, come! For such are the Master's gifts. He knows no distinction of slave and free, nor of rich and poor, but all such inequality is cast aside. *Come*, he says, *all you who are weary and are carrying heavy burdens!*[42]

Ultimately, Christ is the one who makes people what they are meant to be and orders their community life with compassion, justice, and boundless generosity. The honor he bestows on every human person is what judges all forms of social injustice in our sinful world and mandates that communities in all cultures move toward the justice of God's eternal kingdom.

40. John Chrysostom, *Homily 6 on Colossians* 4, PG 62:342. Chrysostom's Antiochene colleagues agree with him on this. See my "Women, Human Identity, and the Image of God."

41. Gregory of Nyssa, *Holy Pascha*, GNO 9.1:250–51.

42. John Chrysostom, *First Instruction* 27, SC 50:122; Paul W. Harkins, trans., *St. John Chrysostom: Baptismal Instructions*, ACW 31 (New York: Paulist Press, 1963), 33, alt.

8

SYMPATHETIC PHILOSOPHY

The Christian Response to Suffering according to John Chrysostom's Commentary on Job

DOUGLAS FINN

When contemplating the suffering of Job, John Chrysostom asks, "Do you not see, beloved, that those who are cut cry aloud? And do we therefore rebuke them? Not at all. Rather, we pardon them."[1] Many in the culture of Chrysostom's day, in reflecting upon how one should react to suffering, would have had recourse to a Stoic understanding of the inevitability

I hereby thank my teachers Blake Leyerle and Fr. Brian Daley, SJ, and my friend and colleague Fr. Andrew Hofer, OP, for their gracious help in critiquing earlier drafts of this essay.

1. John Chrysostom, *Commentary on Job* (= *Comm. Job*) 51.1–3; 3.1.15–18 (SC 346:198). Translations from the Greek of Chrysostom's *Commentary on Job* are my own and derive from *Kommentar zu Hiob*, trans. and ed. Ursula Hagedorn and Dieter Hagedorn, PTS 35 (Berlin: de Gruyter, 1990). There is a second critical edition of the text: John Chrysostom, *Commentaire sur Job*, trans. and ed. Henri Sorlin, with the assistance of Louis Neyrand, SJ, SC 346 and 348 (Paris: Cerf, 1988). The first part of each parenthetical reference to a quote from Chrysostom's commentary consists of page and line numbers and corresponds to the critical edition of 1990. The second reference is to chapter, section, and line number, respectively, of 1988. The volume and page numbers from Sorlin's edition in Sources chrétiennes (SC) then follow in parentheses.

of misfortune and tragedy. They would have extolled the one who maintains equanimity amid the vicissitudes of life. Chrysostom himself follows this line of thinking to an extent,[2] but when he interprets Job's plight, he finds such unflinchingness and self-restraint ultimately inadequate and, frankly, inhumane. In contrast, he sets forth a philosophy, a life, lived according to the teachings of the gospel. With regard to suffering, this philosophy exhibits a truly humane character, compassionately taking into account human weakness and consequently requiring those who would philosophize to comfort those who suffer.

In this essay I explore how John Chrysostom interprets the figure of Job in his commentary. In particular, my investigation focuses on the correct reaction to suffering and how this is determinative for true philosophy. For Chrysostom, philosophy must exhibit sensitivity to human nature. Job's human nature, in fact, is central to his example of philosophy. The philosopher is marked by the traits of sympathy and philanthropy. Because Job exemplifies these qualities, he anticipates the highest ethical teachings of the law and the gospel and thus represents a unique example for the members of Chrysostom's congregation to emulate.

The analysis begins by introducing Chrysostom's little-known commentary on Job. We then explore the first reason for Job's excellence in Chrysostom's eyes: his humanity. A comparison with some other contemporary reactions to suffering helps throw the uniqueness of Chrysostom's interpretation into relief. Following this comparison, the essay examines the substantive character of Job's excellence as a moral exemplar. Finally, I try to place Chrysostom's *Commentary on Job* into its broader theological and exegetical context. Chrysostom situates the book of Job in an Old Testament hermeneutical project intended to show the historical trajectory of God's love for humankind, his philanthropy, and his caring accommodation for human weakness as evidenced in Scripture and ultimately in the incarnation. As a figure whose simultaneously philosophical and humane reaction to suffering anticipates the teachings of the gospel, Job figures significantly into Chrysostom's Old Testament exegetical strategy. Perhaps more importantly, Job finds a place in the larger project of which scriptural exegesis is the essential part: the pastoral formation of the Christian community.

2. Francis Leduc, "Penthos et larmes dans l'oeuvre de Saint Jean Chrysostome," *Proche-Orient chrétien* 41, no. 1 (1991): 222–23; for other parallels between the Stoics and Chrysostom with regard to suffering, see also K. Elser, "Der heilige Chrysostomus und die Philosophie," *Theologische Quartalschrift* 76 (1894): 568–69; and Anne-Marie Malingrey, *"Philosophia": Étude d'un groupe de mots dans la littérature grecque, des Présocratiques au IVᵉ siecle après J.-C.*, Études et Commentaires 40 (Paris: Librairie C. Klincksieck, 1961), 273.

Background to Chrysostom's *Commentary on Job*

Chrysostom's *Commentary on Job* has come down to us in an unfinished form and a somewhat rough style, probably as notes meant for a series of future sermons.[3] The text evidently was either composed by Chrysostom himself in draft form or drawn together by his assistants from shorthand notes he left behind.[4] For many years its authenticity was questioned, but the work of Léon Dieu[5] and its editor Henri Sorlin has well established Chrysostom's authorship, based on external attestation as well as internal features (thematic and exegetical parallels as well as stylistic idiosyncrasies).[6]

The commentary is significant because it represents one of the few extant works of Antiochene exegesis on the sapiential books of the Hebrew Bible and has been relatively neglected by the scholarly community.[7] Furthermore, it is of great interest to any student of Chrysostom's thought. Numerous themes and figures to which Chrysostom devotes much attention in his other, more well-known works feature prominently in the commentary: for example, Job's wife, the devil, human nature, suffering, detachment from worldly goods, sympathy, wealth and poverty, the education and upbringing of children, sin, free will, the nature of friendship, the angels, the divine nature, and divine providence.[8]

And, of course, there is the figure of Job. As Sorlin observes, we can find in Chrysostom's corpus "vraiment . . . un thème de Job,"[9] truly, Job is a theme. Of all the figures of the Hebrew Bible, Job earns the most mention in Chrysostom's works.[10] Yet within Chrysostom's vast homiletic oeuvre, there is, according to Sorlin, only one other homily that explicitly takes Job as its topic of interest: *An Exposition concerning the Struggles and Contests of the Blessed and Just Job.*[11] Consequently, the *Commentary on Job* emerges as an important single work on this figure of pivotal interest to Chrysostom.

3. Sorlin, *Commentaire*, 35n1.

4. Hagedorn and Hagedorn, *Kommentar zu Hiob*, 38.

5. Léon Dieu, "Le commentaire de Saint Jean Chrysostome sur Job," *Revue d'histoire ecclésiastique* 13 (1912): 650–68.

6. See Sorlin, *Commentaire*, 35–69.

7. Robert C. Hill, *Reading the Old Testament in Antioch*, Bible in Ancient Christianity 5 (Leiden: Brill, 2005), 106, declares, "[Chrysostom's commentary on Proverbs] and the other sapiential commentaries deserve editing and further study."

8. Sorlin uses some of these thematic similarities to buttress his argument in favor of the commentary's authenticity. He provides notes on several of them; see *Commentaire*, 53–65, 53n2, 88n2, 98n1, 106n1, 156n1, and so forth.

9. Ibid., 58.

10. Ibid., 58–59; cf. n. 1 above.

11. In PG 63:477–86; see Sorlin, *Commentaire*, 70–71.

Job's Humanity

The importance of Job to Chrysostom is evident at the very outset of his commentary. Chrysostom's Greek text of Job reads: "There was a certain man in the land of Ausis, whose name was Job" (Job 1:1a). Chrysostom comments: "See the first praise: he was a human. For this is certainly not meager praise, to be a human."[12] Such a striking opening underscores the importance of Job for understanding Chrysostom's theological anthropology. It is Job's humanity that makes his victory over Satan so glorious, and it is this humanity that makes Job an example for others to follow. Job suffers greatly, but he is able to temper the emotions he feels with philosophical restraint. He exhibits detachment from worldly goods yet shows at the same time a genuine concern for others. Because these virtues reveal his true humanity, Job can serve as a model for Chrysostom's congregation.

One reason why Job's human nature features so prominently in Chrysostom's commentary is his typically Antiochene optimism concerning human nature and its potential for good.[13] Commenting on the biblical text, which states that Job is "blameless, just, true, God-fearing, keeping himself from every evil deed" (Job 1:1b LXX), Chrysostom points out Job's virtue and his own conviction of human nature's inherent goodness. "Where are those," Chrysostom asks, "who say that nature inclines more toward evil?"[14] The source of Job's virtue is his fear of God. Like Job, true humans fear God and strive after true things rather than the fleeting elements of this world. Chrysostom argues, "The one who does not fear God is not a human, but rather a false human being."[15] True humanity is shown not only in words but also in deeds.[16] The connection between one's way of life and the knowledge of God is decisive for an appreciation of Job's example of philosophy: "Then [Scripture] says that the cause of all [Job's] good traits was that he feared God. Because of those good traits Job came to know God. For a good life leads to the recognition of God, just as a careless life leads to the opposite. The knowledge of God is discovered through one's way of life and becomes the guardian of that way of life."[17] For Chrysostom, virtue, rather than mere

12. *Comm. Job* 3.11–12; 1.1.2–3 (SC 346:84).
13. Hill, *Reading*, 177–82, examines the "careful—if sometimes uneasy—balance of the respective roles played by divine grace and human effort in the moral life" struck by the Antiochene pastors in their Old Testament commentary. For them the fall did not damage human nature or its exercise of free will.
14. *Comm. Job* 3.26–27; 1.1.17–18 (SC 346:84).
15. *Comm. Job* 4.15–17; 1.1.35–37 (SC 346:86).
16. *Comm. Job* 4.11–12; 1.1.31 (SC 346:86).
17. *Comm. Job* 4.19–22; 1.1.39–43 (SC 346:86).

speculation, leads the way to knowledge of God and to true humanity. Job exemplifies this path of steadfast and pious virtue. *Hich Irenaeus* . Job's human perfection is manifested in his suffering and finitude. The theme of human weakness dominates much of the book of Job and, accordingly, a great deal of Chrysostom's commentary. It furnishes Chrysostom with the means whereby he can make sense of Job's seemingly contradictory reactions to his plight: on the one hand, constant trust in God's providence and detachment from all worldly things; on the other, the forlorn cries of a soul struggling to understand why he suffers. The focus on human weakness and the appropriate response to it enables Chrysostom to interpret Job as a true philosopher: one who is indeed human, yet who realizes and fulfills that human nature by fearing God and imitating divine compassion (*philanthrōpia*) through his acts of charity toward others.

Job epitomizes philosophy in his practice of virtue. Before exploring Chrysostom's development of this theme, we should first determine how Chrysostom generally employs the term *philosophia* in his works and what its range of meaning includes.

Philosophia in Chrysostom

The term *philosophia* and its related forms exhibit a wide range of meanings in Chrysostom's works.[18] On the one hand, the concept of philosophy is often used by Chrysostom and other Christian authors to refer to pagan Greek philosophy. This sense is particularly clear in his early work *Adversus oppugnatores vitae monasticae* (*Against the Opponents of the Monastic Life*), where he praises some pagan philosophers for their practice of reason and virtue. On this rare occasion in which Chrysostom speaks of the pagan philosophers in favorable terms,[19] it becomes apparent that philosophy is never

18. See the treatments of Chrysostom's use of the term *philosophia* in Ivo auf der Maur, OSB, *Mönchtum und Glaubensverkündigung in den Schriften des Hl. Johannes Chrysostomus*, Paradosis: Beiträge zur Geschichte der altchristlichen Literatur und Theologie 14 (Freiburg, Switzerland: Universitätsverlag Freiburg Schweiz, 1959), 87–92; and Malingrey, "*Philosophia*," 263–88 (chap. 8). See also G. J. M. Bartelink, "'Philosophie' et 'Philosophe' dans quelques oeuvres de Jean Chrysostome," *Revue d'ascétique et de mystique* 36 (October–December 1960): 487–92. For a wider survey of early Christian use of the term *philosophia*, see Malingrey's aforementioned work and Gustave Bardy, "'Philosophie' et 'Philosophe' dans le vocabulaire chrétien des premiers siècles," *Revue d'ascétique et de mystique* 25 (April–December 1949): 97–108. For further literature regarding philosophy and the early Christian fathers, see Jean-Louis Quantin, "A propos de la traduction de *philosophia* dan l'*Adversus oppugnatores vitae monasticae* de Saint Jean Chrysostome," *Revue des sciences religieuses* 61, no. 4 (October 1987): 187n1.

19. Malingrey, "*Philosophia*," 267. For a thorough treatment of both the implicit and explicit significations of the word *philosophia* in Chrysostom's *Against the Opponents of the*

something abstracted from one's way of life. Thus the ascetic or monastic life can also be described as philosophical.[20] This narrower use of the term may have been, in part, the result of the younger Chrysostom's desire to withdraw from the world and live as an ascetic. His later engagement as a pastor in Antioch and Constantinople broadened his understanding of Christian philosophy to include those living in the world as well.[21] This later inclusiveness is evident, as auf der Maur observes, in the diverse group of biblical figures whom Chrysostom sets forth as examples of the philosophical life, a group that includes both Old and New Testament figures, men and women, Samaritans, and even the good thief who was crucified alongside Jesus.[22] Thus, while philosophy is usually a way of life informed by Christian principles, Chrysostom can use the term to describe Jews and pagans. Its use corresponds, roughly, with a life lived in accordance with solid values and right purpose.

Philosophy, then, entails the cultivation of self-restraint and strength of soul. The philosopher is one who abstains from seeking transitory worldly goods and pleasures. But such abstention, however indispensable, only constitutes what Chrysostom calls external philosophy, a way of life equally accessible to pagans and Jews as well as Christians. Philosophy also has an internal dimension. One must rein in errant or disordered passions and desires, thus seeking to maintain equilibrium of soul amid the vicissitudes of life. For the Christian, such philosophical self-control is guided, if not made possible, by the correct knowledge of God and his ultimate rewards and punishments. This is the second part of Christian philosophy for Chrysostom. Truly to philosophize means to meditate upon God, Christ, death, the resurrection, and the afterlife, and to bring them to bear on one's life. These two moments in Chrysostom's understanding of philosophy play a decisive role, as we will see, in his positive interpretation of Job.

But there is more to say about Chrysostom's nuanced use of philosophy. In several places he argues that philosophy (i.e., self-restraint and detachment) must be practiced in moderation.[23] Both too little and too much are deleterious. This

---

Monastic Life, especially with regard to pagan Greek thought, see Quantin, "Traduction," 187–97.

20. Chrysostom, Adversus oppugnatores vitae monasticae 2.2 (PG 47:333); 2.8 (PG 47:344); 3.20 (PG 47:384).

21. Malingrey, "Philosophia," 284–86, nonetheless notes that, even in Against the Opponents of the Monastic Life, the philosophy of Christ is available to all, ascetic or not: Adversus oppugnatores vitae monasticae 3.15 (PG 47:372).

22. Auf der Maur, Mönchtum, 89–90; as exemplars of philosophical living, Chrysostom cites Adam, Job, Abraham, Sarah, Anna, the Samaritan woman, Moses, Samuel, Saul, David, the three youths in the fire, the mother of the Maccabees, the Magi, Lazarus, the Canaanite woman, the woman with the flow of blood, and others.

23. Chrysostom, Homiliae in epistulam ad Romanos 14.9 (PG 60:535); 22.4 (PG 60:613); Homiliae in Acta apostolorum 43.3 (PG 60:306); Homiliae in epistulam ad Titum 6.2 (PG 62.697).

Deleterious = Damaging

critique of philosophy practiced immoderately (*pera tou metrou*) relates directly to Chrysostom's efforts to advance a philosophy compatible with gospel teachings and the pastoral needs of his congregation. Elsewhere, Chrysostom employs the verb *philosophein* to signify a sort of useless chattering,[24] which in many instances can cause pain precisely by its display of indifference and accusatory speculation.[25] These seem to be the meanings Chrysostom has in mind when he has Job accuse his friends of philosophizing in the face of another's sufferings.

Chrysostom's praise of philosophical restraint is thus tempered by sensitivity to human vulnerability. This desirable sensitivity is manifested in "love of humanity" (*philanthrōpia*), "sympathy" (*sympatheia*), "pity" (*eleos*), and "sharing in suffering," or "showing compassion" (*synalgein*). Job's excellence, for Chrysostom, manifests itself in the proper combination of philosophy and sympathy for human nature. Job deserves praise for enduring a horrific situation in which "no one is sympathetic [*sympathēs*], no one takes pity [*eleēmōn*], no one shares in [his] suffering [*synalgōn*]."[26] A brief comparison with other contemporary responses to suffering reveals the unusual properties of Chrysostom's exegesis. We turn first to Gregory of Nyssa's *Life of Saint Macrina*.

Gregory of Nyssa's *Life of Saint Macrina*

The issues of Christian philosophy and the role of grief loom large in Gregory of Nyssa's *Vita sanctae Macrinae* (*Life of Saint Macrina*). Nyssen labels the way of life led by his sister Macrina and those women who join her in communal ascetic practice as "philosophical" and "unworldly."[27] In their practice of virtue, they strove to replicate the angels by freeing themselves from worldly concerns. J. Warren Smith notes that Nyssen uses the term "philosophy" in the same sense as Plato does in his *Phaedo*.[28] In that work

24. Chrysostom, *De virginitate* 35.1.17, in *La virginité*, ed. Herbert Musurillo, SJ, trans. Bernard Grillet, SC 125 (Paris: Cerf, 1966), 208; *Homiliae in Joannem 5:19* 2 (PG 56:250); cf. auf der Maur, *Mönchtum*, 91.

25. Cf. Chrysostom, *De sacerdotio* 4.9, in *Sur le sacerdoce*, trans. and ed. Anne-Marie Malingrey, SC 272 (Paris: Cerf, 1980), 280: "*en tais allotriais philosophein symphorais* [to . . . speculate upon another's misfortunes]," in John Chrysostom, *Six Books on the Priesthood*, trans. Graham Neville (Crestwood, NY: St. Vladimir's Seminary Press, 2002), 126.

26. *Comm. Job* 45.11–12; 2.11.15–16 (SC 346:184).

27. Gregory of Nyssa, *Vita sanctae Macrinae* 11.6, in *Vie de sainte Macrine*, trans. and ed. Pierre Maraval, SC 178 (Paris: Cerf, 1971), 174. English quotations of this work, unless otherwise noted, are taken from *St. Gregory of Nyssa: Ascetical Works*, trans. Virginia Woods Callahan, FC 58 (Washington, DC: Catholic University of America Press, 1967), here 170.

28. J. Warren Smith, "A Just and Reasonable Grief: The Death and Function of a Holy Woman in Gregory of Nyssa's *Life of Macrina*," *Journal of Early Christian Studies* 12, no. 1 (Spring 2004): 66.

philosophical practice is characterized as a preparation for death, when the soul is freed from the body. The philosopher strives for a foretaste of this freedom by turning the mind from the needs of the body in the practice of *sōphrosynē*.[29] In Nyssen's case, however, the philosophical practice of virtue is less about readying oneself for liberation from the body than about anticipation of eschatological glory and incorruption.[30]

In the pursuit of virtue, reason (*logismos*) must be master over the drives (*pathē*) issuing from the lower nonrational parts of the soul or from wrong judgment. Whenever passion overwhelms reason, it disrupts the proper functioning of both soul and body.[31] Such disorder obtains, for instance, when Gregory's mother, Emmelia, grieves after learning of her son Naucratius's death in a hunting accident. With Emmelia's "reason giving way to passion," "nature won out even over her."[32] She lost her breath and fainted. Smith argues that Nyssen here "means that it was [Emmelia's] natural revulsion of death, which deprives us of loved ones and of life itself, that felled her."[33]

Macrina, by contrast, maintains her composure during the time of mourning. Through rational dialogue, patient endurance, and the introduction of an ascetic regimen, she helped stabilize and coach her mother on the path to virtue. Macrina too was faced with the death of a loved one, but she transcended the weakness of her nature and helped rid her mother of the disruptive passion of grief.[34] In a passage of interest to us, in view of Chrysostom's *Commentary on Job*, Gregory reports that Macrina kept her mother from yielding to grief's natural impulse: she did not "cry out against the evil or tear her clothes or lament over her suffering or stir up a threnody of mournful melodies."[35] The main problem with grieving over the dead, in Nyssen's view, is that it betrays a loss of hope in the immortality and resurrection of the soul and the body.[36]

Yet when Nyssen describes Macrina's resistance of grief, it is not, as Smith observes, in terms of "the stoic sage whose disinterest in the world

29. Plato, *Phaedo* 63E–64A.
30. Smith, "Reasonable Grief," 68.
31. Ibid., 69.
32. *Vita sanctae Macrinae* 9.17–20 (SC 178:170; Callahan, *St. Gregory*, 169).
33. Smith, "Reasonable Grief," 70.
34. *Vita sanctae Macrinae* 10.17–24 (SC 178:174; Callahan, *St. Gregory*, 170).
35. *Vita sanctae Macrinae* 10.8–10 (SC 178:172; Callahan, *St. Gregory*, 170). Interestingly, the one mention of Job in *The Life of Saint Macrina* passes over the fact that he tears his garment and curses the day of his birth. Perhaps Nyssen does not allow Scripture to inform his understanding of philosophy as much as Chrysostom does. Nyssen's *Life of Moses* similarly seems to omit the less positive parts of Moses's biography in favor of a narrative of uninterrupted progress in virtue.
36. Smith, "Reasonable Grief," 74.

Parhos = pity

has exempted her from experiencing any emotional turmoil."[37] Christian philosophy, as exemplified by Macrina, does not entail utter insensitivity. At the news of her brother Basil's death, Macrina's soul was affected emotionally.[38] But this, along with the deaths of her other brother and mother, purified her soul and made manifest the greatness of her reasoning faculty (*dianoia*),[39] the part of the soul that constitutes the image of God and is thus completely rational and not subject to *pathos*. Macrina's victory consisted in keeping in check each *pathos* she experienced.[40] Her reasoning was impassible.[41] Macrina is here compared to Job, who despite the illness covering his body, "by means of his power of reasoned reflection did not allow his perception to incline towards his pain, but kept the faculty which felt the pain in the body, and would neither blunt the edge of his concentration upon his own proper activity nor interrupt the conversation when it embarked on higher matters."[42] Both Macrina and Job still felt *pathē*, but they turned their reasoning consciousness away from the pain and sickness of their shriveling bodies and toward the things of heaven.[43]

By drawing this parallel, Nyssen reads Job in light of a philosophy that, through its ascetic practice of virtue and the contemplation of heavenly things, seeks to move beyond human nature (*anthrōpinēs physeōs*) and the *pathē*.[44] He describes Macrina in her last moments of life as having "transcended the common nature"[45] to such a degree that it "was as if an angel had by some providence taken on human form, an angel who had no relation with or similarity to the life of the flesh and for whom it was not at all unreasonable to remain detached since the flesh was not part of her experience."[46] Nyssen can ultimately speak this way of Macrina because his purpose is to portray her as a holy woman whose life of philosophy, indeed whose very presence, conveys a sense of hope in the resurrection and humankind's future angelic existence. Macrina has overcome the weakness of human nature and become akin to humankind in its resurrected state. She

suffering -▷ we become heavenly.

37. Ibid., 72.

38. Thus *epathe tēn psychēn*, in *Vita sanctae Macrinae* 14.11–12 (SC 178:188; Callahan, *St. Gregory*, 173).

39. *Vita sanctae Macrinae* 14.20–23 (SC 178:190; Callahan, *St. Gregory*, 173).

40. Smith, "Reasonable Grief," 72.

41. Thus *en apatheia tēn dianoian*, in *Vita sanctae Macrinae* 22.29–30 (SC 178:214).

42. *Vita sanctae Macrinae* 18.3–7 (SC 178:198–200); English translation from *The Life of Saint Macrina*, trans. Kevin Corrigan, Peregrina Translations Series 10; Matrologia Graeca (Toronto: Peregrina, 1987), 42, alt.

43. See Corrigan, *Life*, 70–71nn36 and 46.

44. *Vita sanctae Macrinae* 17.27–30 (SC 178:198; Callahan, *St. Gregory*, 175).

45. *Vita sanctae Macrinae* 22.21 (SC 178:214; Callahan, *St. Gregory*, 179).

46. *Vita sanctae Macrinae* 22.26–31 (SC 178:214; Callahan, *St. Gregory*, 179).

not only exemplifies but actually mediates a foretaste of humanity's future impassibility.[47]

Philosophy for Gregory of Nyssa, as manifest in his *Life of Saint Macrina*, makes no room for grief, a disordered passion. Hence we see an explicit condemnation of such visible displays of grief as the rending of one's garment. Consolation should raise one *above* common human nature, which fears death and loss and thus impedes hope in the resurrection. Nonetheless, Nyssen's depiction of philosophy does not preclude emotional sensibility, as long as it is governed by reason.

In contrast to Nyssen's depiction of Macrina, whose very presence seems almost sacramental in the salutary effect she wields upon those around her, Chrysostom focuses on scriptural figures as moral exemplars worthy of imitation. This is perhaps why, although Chrysostom, like Nyssen, considers it necessary that reason (*dianoia, logismos*) govern the emotions, he considers it so important to highlight Job's humanity—as evidenced by his emotional displays of grief—and hence his imitability. Job is a philosopher in part because he so obviously shares in our common human nature.

Gregory of Nazianzus's *Epistle 165* to Stagirius

Chrysostom's view of philosophical moderation, that neither irrational emotion nor rational, philosophical restraint should exceed their limits, is not without precedent.[48] Another of the Cappadocian Fathers, Gregory of Nazianzus, expresses this position aptly in a letter to the Sophist Stagirius:

> I learn that you are acting unphilosophically [*aphilosophōs*] with regard to misfortune, and I do not extol this. For it is necessary to write the truth, especially to a man who is a friend and makes a pretense of the good and beautiful. . . . I praise neither extreme lack of feeling [*to lian apathēs*] nor excessive affectivity [*to agan peripathēs*], since the former is inhumane [*apanthrōpon*], and the latter unphilosophical [*aphilosophon*]. The one treading the middle way ought rather to appear more philosophical [*philosophōteron*] than those who are utterly ungovernable [*tōn agan aschetōn*] and more humane [*anthrōpikōteron*] than those who philosophize without measure [*tōn philosophountōn ametrōs*].
>
> Had I written to some other person, I might perhaps have had need of a lengthier discussion. It would have been necessary to offer sympathy [*sympathein*] in some things, exhortation in others, perhaps even reproach. For showing

47. Smith, "Reasonable Grief," 71–72.
48. For the issue of keeping grief within bounds, see Leduc, "Penthos et larmes," 243–44.

compassion [*synalgein*] is suitable for consolation, and a state of sickness requires treatment by someone healthy.[49]

In the remainder of the letter, Gregory argues that proper philosophy in the face of suffering strives to raise itself above attachment to the fleeting pleasures of this world and to recognize that God allows sufferings as a means to a salutary end. As we will see, Chrysostom expresses much the same view in his *Commentary on Job*. With these two examples of contemporary Christian responses to suffering in mind, let us turn to Chrysostom's explication of Job as a philosophical exemplar.

Job's Excellence as a Model for Others

A Balance between Philosophy and Emotion

With mighty rhetorical force, Chrysostom recounts the disasters that befall Job in quick succession. Finally, after receiving news of the deaths of his children, Job stands up and tears his cloak (Job 1:20a). Whereas Gregory of Nyssa, through Macrina, would forbid such a display of grief, Chrysostom offers a compassionate explanation: "Do not consider this matter to be a defeat, beloved. This shows most of all the victory. For if he had done nothing, he would have seemed to be without sympathy, but now he is at once a philosopher, a father, and a God-fearing man."[50] Job's submission to God's will immediately afterward, when he falls to the ground and claims that, as he came naked into the world, so will he exit it (Job 1:20b–21), confirms for Chrysostom the appropriateness of Job's twofold reaction of grief and philosophical restraint: "Do you see how the magnitude of the misfortune does not overwhelm the God-fearing man? . . . He showed emotion [*pathos*]; he showed piety. And it was impossible that he, being human, not be pained at what had happened, just as it was impossible that he, being Job, be embittered. And in the former case he showed his nature, in the latter his devotion."[51]

Chrysostom dwells on Job's immense pain at his loss. He does not exhort his listeners to suppress feelings of sorrow and mourning during times of tragedy but insists that these feelings be expressed with the proper attitude of piety. Chrysostom observes that people often allow the blow of tragedy and the ensuing despondency (*athymias*) to seize their tongues, with the

---

49. Gregory of Nazianzus, *Epistula 165*, in Gregory of Nazianzus, *Briefe*, ed. Paul Gallay, GCS 53 (Berlin: Akademie Verlag, 1969), 119–20, with my trans.
50. *Comm. Job* 25.18–20; 1.21.2–5 (SC 346:136).
51. *Comm. Job* 26.24–25; 26.27–27.2; 1.23.6–7, 10–14 (SC 346:138–40).

result that they blaspheme in spite of reason's (*dianoias*) protests.[52] With Job such is not the case. Chrysostom concludes that, when a person harbors bad thoughts about God, the cause is not the circumstances, be they fortune or misfortune, wealth or poverty, but rather a bad state of mind and purpose (*dianoias ponēras*).[53]

Chrysostom thus stresses the need to probe not just the words that one utters but also the state of mind from which they emerge. And this he does when Job, having been reduced to a horrifying state of illness, curses the day of his birth (Job 3:1–3). He calls attention to Job's human nature: "Do you not see, beloved, that those who are cut cry aloud? Do we then rebuke them? Not at all. Rather, we pardon them. If he had not cried out these things, he would have seemed not to share in our common [human] nature."[54] This, it is worth noting, stands in contrast to Gregory of Nyssa's impression of Macrina before her death, when she no longer seemed to him to share in the common nature. Nyssen would have considered an outburst on Macrina's part as a failure of the tests she faced, whereas Chrysostom views Job's forlorn cries as part of the educational process leading to victory. Just as a doctor inflicts pain during an operation in order to help the patient heal,[55] so God, in testing Job, allows for extremely painful measures. It is natural that Job should cry out. Indeed, it is imperative that Job should cry out, for if he did not, he would not appear human. If that were the case, his victory over Satan in this trial would not be so glorious,[56] nor would he be an example that Chrysostom's listeners could follow.

Chrysostom then examines the source of Job's curse (Job 3:1–3). These words derive, he says, from despondency, not from some evil or blasphemy.[57] He reaches this conclusion by observing first and foremost that God has pronounced Job just.[58] Job curses not God or God's act of creation but only the day of his birth,[59] a day that cannot be destroyed because it lies in the past and is consequently nonexistent.[60] These are not accusatory words but words of

---

52. *Comm. Job* 31.20–23; 1.26.13–16 (SC 346:150).

53. *Comm. Job* 32.28–33.21; 1.26.51–53 (SC 346:152).

54. *Comm. Job* 51.1–4; 3.1.15–18 (SC 346:198).

55. Hagedorn and Hagedorn, *Kommentar zu Hiob*, 51n79.

56. Chrysostom brings the import of Job's victory into even greater relief by an explicit contrast with the devil's fall: "This immediately upset the devil, that Job is called God's servant. God thereby reproaches the devil and strives to turn him around: 'You were also previously a servant, and you are without a body, but he has a body and is on earth, while you were in heaven'" (*Comm. Job* 16.25–29; 1.11.26–30 [SC 346:116]).

57. *Comm. Job* 51.17–19; 3.1.35–36 (SC 346:200).

58. *Comm. Job* 51.8–15; 3.1.24–33 (SC 346:200).

59. *Comm. Job* 53.22–25; 3.4.23–26 (SC 346:204–6).

60. *Comm. Job* 51.19–21; 3.1.36–38 (SC 346:200).

one who is suffering and searching for the reason for his pain.[61] Additionally, Chrysostom does not fault one who, amid such pain, longs for death as a final respite.[62] To be sure, Job's piety is even more evident in that he does not defy God's commandment and kill himself.[63] Indeed, the words that betray Job's yearning for death reveal Job's *philosophia*, since he recognizes the limits of human nature. When Job muses how in death he would lie next to the wealthy and powerful kings and lords of the earth (3:13–15), Chrysostom praises him: "See that even in misfortune [Job speaks] philosophical words. In no way did wealth assist them. In nothing did power benefit them. Death prevails over all."[64] And when Job cries out that what he had feared has now befallen him (3:25), Chrysostom exclaims: "And it is certainly amazing that with a pure and untouchable life he expected the opposite [i.e., misfortune], and not only expected, but feared it, keeping in mind what had happened in the past as with Abraham. But should we who every day pass our lives in evil not expect the opposite [i.e., misfortune]? See how even before his trial Job philosophized!"[65] Even in good times, according to Chrysostom, Job avoided an inflated and naive confidence, since he understood that human life and worldly things are transitory. Job kept in mind God's power and justice.

Through his emphasis on Job's nature, then, Chrysostom can hold together Job's emotion and his reasoning. The obvious displays of grief on Job's part, such as tearing his cloak, imbue his example of philosophy with credibility. They show that God did not create him insensitive (*anaisthēton*) to pain. God permits Job to be overcome by emotions (*ta pathē*) in order that we might see how well he restrains himself while suffering.[66] The depth of his agony is incontestable. Job's sensitivity to pain, his human vulnerability, only underscores the greatness of his nature. It is all the more amazing that Job has learned about God and brought that knowledge to bear on his life through only the illumination of his natural reason (*tēs physeōs tous logismous lampontas*).[67] Job's human nature, as it manifests itself in his grief and suffering, is thus essential for his claim to philosophy. His vigilant mind-set, piety, and humility helped rein in potentially errant thoughts and words, so that an otherwise understandable sense of despondency did not issue in blasphemy. Precisely in this crucial juncture of sympathy, wisdom, and virtue lies Job's philosophy.

61. *Comm. Job* 53.15–16; 3.4.15–16 (SC 346:204).
62. *Comm. Job* 52.25–30; 3.3.18–23 (SC 346:202).
63. *Comm. Job* 53.12–14; 3.4.13–15 (SC 346:204).
64. *Comm. Job* 54.19–21; 3.4.48–51 (SC 346:206–8).
65. *Comm. Job* 58.6–10; 3.7.15–20 (SC 346:214).
66. *Comm. Job* 26.4–8; 1.21.14–18 (SC 346:138).
67. *Comm. Job* 3.2–3; prologue 4.8 (SC 346:82).

Doxology = A liturgical hymn to praise God.

The Elements of Bad Philosophizing

Chrysostom's characterization of Job as a philosopher occurs in the context of criticizing other types of philosophizing. He takes issue with a Stoic attitude[68] that would open the door to those who accuse God of capricious injustice. Job first attributes all things to God, who can accordingly give and take as he sees fit. Only afterward does he say, "Blessed be the name of the LORD" (Job 1:21). If Job had begun his speech with the doxology, Chrysostom contends, then it would have seemed as if Job were "simply philosophizing,"[69] that is, as if Job would endure whatever God does, be it just or not. As it is, however, Job does not "simply" philosophize; rather, he presents right and just arguments for God's actions and providence in the world, thereby silencing those who would accuse God of injustice. One must recognize all that one has been given as a gift from God, even if possession of that gift is brief.[70] Hence we see that for Chrysostom, philosophy entails more than just enduring what one cannot control. It also includes exhibiting trust and faith in God's wisdom and justice, and in his love of humankind manifest in the tests by which he strengthens people in virtue.[71]

As we have seen, however, trust in God does not preclude lamentation.[72] Had Job not cried out and torn his garment when he learned of the collapse of his wealth and the deaths of his children, he would have seemed to be without feeling. Chrysostom goes to great lengths to describe the depth of Job's suffering, but he concedes that, to measure accurately the magnitude of another's suffering, one must experience such a trial oneself.[73] Job's friends come to visit under the pretext of wanting to comfort him, but their accusatory speeches only exacerbate Job's pain and intensify his feelings of isolation. Like a well-trained doctor who cuts open wounds, one needs the proper expertise in order to behave in a manner fitting to the misfortune. Many, like Job's companions, only make matters worse out of either malice or ignorance.[74]

68. Here I follow the Hagedorns' interpretive translation of "simply philosophizing" as "being of stoic impassibility" (*Kommentar zu Hiob*, 30).

69. *Comm. Job* 30.22; 1.25.44 (SC 346:148).

70. *Comm. Job* 30.13–28; 1.25.34–50 (SC 346:146–48).

71. See *Comm. Job* 15.6–7; 1.9.67–69 (SC 346:112), where God, out of his love for humankind, his philanthropy, brings good out of the trials caused by demons; similarly *Comm. Job* 21.1–15; 1.16.22–39 (SC 346:126), where the same love (*agapēs*) that led God to call Job just and blameless also leads him to permit the devil to harm him, in order that the fact of Job's suffering might testify to his virtue.

72. "The LORD gave, and the LORD has taken away" (Job 1:21).

73. *Comm. Job* 39.26–28; 2.7.22–24 (SC 346:170).

74. *Comm. Job* 58.17–59.1; 4.1.3–18 (SC 346:218).

When Job responds to his friends in 16:3–5, Chrysostom interprets him as saying: "I wished . . . that your situation was like mine and that you were in my place. And I would be able to shake my head and do these things which you do to me. Then you would learn not to philosophize before the misfortunes of another."[75] What exactly is the problem with the friends' philosophizing? As the Septuagintal text reads, "You tread upon me without pity" (Job 6:21a), Chrysostom adds: "Without sympathy [asympathōs], . . . reprovingly, accusingly."[76] The friends miss the point that suffering need not be the consequence of sin but can be a test intended to strengthen faith; their speeches are deleterious because they develop into an indifferent philosophy, speculation at the expense of others' misfortune, ultimately devoid of sympathy.[77]

Chrysostom further views sensitivity to suffering as part of a philosophy practiced in proper measure. Job was moderate, insofar as he ripped his garment only at the news of his children's deaths. "But if one of the philosophers," Chrysostom continues, "in making demands beyond measure, would say that he ought not do these things, let him learn that even Paul cried [Acts 21:13], and that Jesus himself shed tears [John 11:35]. Let him know what it means to mourn for children [paidōn sympatheia]."[78] Chrysostom clearly considers a philosophy that seeks to suppress natural human reactions to tragedy, thus being devoid of sympathy, as excessive and incompatible with the Christian gospel.

The gospel teaches the proper balance of philosophical restraint and sympathy for human nature. Job's example is one that anticipates these precepts and thus renders him an excellent model of virtue for Chrysostom's Christian audience. Job proleptically fulfills the gospel in that he demonstrates restraint and the fear of God, but Christ and Paul also give evangelical warrant to

75. *Comm. Job* 121.15–17; 16.2.6–10 (SC 348:22).

76. *Comm. Job* 81.4; 6.12.2 (SC 346:270).

77. Job's friends are mistaken when they assert that he suffers on account of his sin. Elsewhere, however, Chrysostom is clear that one ought to have compassion especially for those who suffer just punishment from God. This, he argues, is a true testament of one's humanity and philosophy, that one can sympathize even with those who arouse the greatest revulsion in the upright heart: "We see men-slayers, wicked men, suffering punishment, and we are distressed, and grieve for them [daknometha kai algoumen]. Let us not be philosophical beyond measure [Mē hyper to metron philosophoi ōmen]: let us show ourselves full of pity [eleēmones], that we may be pitied; there is nothing equal to this beautiful trait: nothing so marks to us the stamp of human nature [ton anthrōpinon . . . charaktēra] as the showing of pity [to eleein], as the being kind to our fellow humans [to philanthrōpon einai]" (Homiliae in Acta apostolorum 43.3 [PG 60:306; NPNF¹ 11:266]). When set against this view of philanthropic, sympathetic philosophy, Job's friends appear in an even more inhumane light, because they did not even know for sure that Job was guilty.

78. *Comm. Job* 27.7–10; 1.23.19–22 (SC 346:140).

Job's sensitivity to pain and suffering. After Job declares that, just as he came naked from his mother's womb, so he will also perish (Job 1:21), Chrysostom comments: "See how he distances himself, see how he removes himself from the mourning. . . . See the apostolic words once again fulfilled through his deeds: 'For we brought nothing into the world, so that we can take something out [of it]' [1 Tim. 6:7]. See such words as are spoken are of use not only to him but also to us."[79] For Chrysostom, therefore, Job is first and foremost an example of philosophy, and as such a true human being, on account of his pious response to suffering.

Job's Virtue toward Others: His Philanthropy

This fear of God brings with it knowledge of the Creator. In fact, Chrysostom states that observation of God's creation leads not only to mere knowledge of God but also to true philosophy.[80] Yet philosophy is lived knowledge of God. For this reason, Chrysostom argues that not only from the order of creation but also from God's very nature and deeds one must conclude that God hates evil and loves humankind (philanthrōpos). Acting out of a natural aversion to evil rather than a fear of punishment, people ought therefore to imitate God's philanthropy.[81] Moreover, the fear of God requires humility and detachment from worldly things. To Job's question "How can a mortal be just before God?" (Job 9:2b), Chrysostom replies, paraphrasing Job's words: "'I know that on account of sins I suffer these things,'—do you see the philosophy, how he is not haughty?—'and I know that there is a great distance between me and God.'"[82]

While Job's detachment from worldly things helps him endure his trial, it does not prevent him from being engaged in the world. To the contrary, Chrysostom observes, it keeps him from clinging to his many possessions and enables him to share them generously with the orphan, the widow, and the sick.[83] Job imitates God's philanthropy in his humane treatment of others. With regard to the treatment of his servants, Job shows himself philanthropic (philanthrōpos) and not violent.[84] In these acts of charity, Job's humility is once again manifest, as he does not seek praise or fame and even readily confesses his sins to all people. In Chrysostom's words: "That is the greatest

79. *Comm. Job* 28.2–7; 1.23.40–45 (SC 346:142).
80. *Comm. Job* 163.8–9; 31.11.6–8 (SC 348:140).
81. *Comm. Job* 174.11–16; 34.4.6–11 (SC 348:170).
82. *Comm. Job* 92.10–12; 9.1.10–2.2 (SC 346:308).
83. *Comm. Job* 162.14–32; 31.10.1–18 (SC 348:138).
84. *Comm. Job* 164.12–13; 31.14.3–5 (SC 348:142).

philosophy, the standard of virtue, to hide one's good deeds, but to parade in the open one's sins. People today do the opposite."[85]

The care that Job shows for others extends not merely to their bodies but also to their souls. Chrysostom argues that Job is disappointed in his wife because she has encouraged him to curse God and die, a grievous impiety that runs contrary to the way he has educated her. Job is sensitive to how much she, as a wife and mother, also suffers, and in scolding her he strives to educate her, to change the bad attitude that produced her blasphemy.[86] Similarly, according to Chrysostom, Job feels pain not only because he lost his children but also because he lost "students of his piety."[87] In the same vein, when Job's friends come to visit him, Job's pain is greater because he realizes that word of his condition has spread far and wide. He is distressed, Chrysostom contends, not because of his longing for fame and glory, but rather because he fears that those whom he earlier helped, whom he has comforted, might become unsettled and scandalized when they hear of his plight and that he himself has no one to comfort him.[88] In his tireless care for others, Job stands in stark contrast to his friends, who can only babble useless pseudo-wisdom to their suffering companion.

Thus we see that, for Chrysostom, Job exemplifies the appropriate mixture of philosophy, philanthropy, and sympathy. He is an anticipation of the gospel, of "the grace and the philanthropy of our Lord Jesus Christ,"[89] so Christians are to imitate his example. Job can serve as a model because he is really human. He too suffers pain; he too has *sympatheia*. As a true human, he recognizes in humility the finitude and transitoriness of his condition vis-à-vis his incomprehensible creator. This realism in the face of human weakness and death is not the occasion for resignation and defeat but the opportunity to achieve true humanity through the fear of God and practice of virtue. Chrysostom points precisely to Job's virtue of soul: "Let no one say: Such and such a one was [only] human. See, Job was also a human. Do you see the piety of nature? He was human, and he could maintain virtue faithfully. In the dwelling of clay he manifested such piety."[90]

If Job could demonstrate such virtue and piety, so too could the members of Chrysostom's congregation who shared in the same humanity. Chrysostom thus employed the figure of Job as part of his pastoral program of ethical

---

85. *Comm. Job* 164.30–165.2; 31.15.18–20 (SC 348:144).
86. *Comm. Job* 47.17–20; 2.14.2–6 (SC 346:190).
87. *Comm. Job* 27.16; 1.23.29 (SC 346:140).
88. *Comm. Job* 49.2–20; 2.17.17–37 (SC 346:192–94).
89. *Comm. Job* 200.10–11; 42.9.18–19 (SC 348:240).
90. *Comm. Job* 17.10–13; 1.11.44–48 (SC 346:118).

instruction. This pastoral focus is evident in his massive homiletic output, and it consistently governed his method of scriptural commentary,[91] the primary locus of which was the homily. One of Chrysostom's primary goals in commenting on Scripture was the improvement of his congregants' behavior. Chrysostom makes this explicit in his second homily on the obscurity of the Old Testament: "The reason we comment on Scripture is not only for you to get to know Scripture but for you also to correct your behavior: if this does not occur, we are wasting our time in reading it out, we are wasting our time in explaining it."[92] Toward that end, Chrysostom underscores Job's excellence as a model of the proper Christian reaction to suffering. This raises the question, though, why an Old Testament figure is accorded such prominence. The answer lies, I think, in Chrysostom's understanding of the relationship between the two Testaments of Scripture and in his consequent exegetical strategy for the Old Testament. In the final section of the essay, then, let us examine briefly how Chrysostom situates Job into his broader project of Old Testament commentary.

Job's Excellence as an Example of Chrysostom's Use of the Old Testament

We have begun to see how, in Chrysostom's view, Job's life of virtue anticipates the ethical teachings of the gospel. In what space remains, I suggest how this reading of Job fits into Chrysostom's understanding of the Old Testament as a whole.[93] It becomes clear that the practice of philosophy that we have elucidated is linked to an entire theology of Scripture, a theology that especially guides Chrysostom's project of Old Testament commentary.

Accommodation (Synkatabasis) as the Key to Chrysostom's Scriptural Hermeneutic

Robert C. Hill has argued that Chrysostom conceived of the Old Testament as a gesture of God's love and care for humankind within the broader

---

91. Hill, *Reading*, 107, 183–92, 195–97; cf. Robert C. Hill, "St. John Chrysostom: Preacher on the Old Testament," *Greek Orthodox Theological Review* 46, nos. 3–4 (2001): 267–86.

92. Chrysostom, *Homilies on the Obscurity of the Old Testament* (= *Obscurit.*) 2.7.51–53, in *Omelie sull'oscurità delle profezie*, trans. and ed. Sergio Zincone, Verba Seniorum 12 (Rome: Edizioni Studium, 1998), 148; this work is cited below as *Omelie*; the English translation is taken from John Chrysostom, *Homilies on the Obscurity of the Old Testament*, in *Old Testament Homilies*, vol. 3, trans. Robert C. Hill (Brookline, MA: Holy Cross Orthodox Press, 2003), 43.

93. Here, unfortunately, I can only gesture at the broader theological and exegetical context of his *Commentary on Job*, leaving aside a more detailed analysis until a later date.

incarnational trajectory of salvation history. For Chrysostom, Hill argues, "The Scriptures, like the Incarnation, come to us as a gesture of divine considerateness,—*synkatabasis*—a loving gesture, with nothing patronizing about it, nothing to suggest 'condescension.'"[94] In reaching out to humankind in its limitedness, God reveals his love for humankind, his *philanthrōpia*. The purpose of accommodation (*synkatabasis*) is to guide embodied humans gradually, by means of the very materiality of scriptural language, from the material things of this world to the spiritual things of heaven. Ultimately, God's accommodation of humankind in Scripture finds its "prime analogue . . . [in] that (other) Incarnation of the Word in the person of Jesus."[95]

The Obscurity of the Old Testament as Synkatabasis and the Impetus to Philosophia

In his first homily on the obscurity of the Old Testament, Chrysostom links the reading of Scripture to one's life practice. Those who encounter difficulty in reading and applying the sacred texts are akin to those who permit "the soul to be submerged by the passions and suffer shipwreck, whereas experienced people practiced in nobly bearing such things, like a steersman at the tiller, put their mind above the passions and do not stop adopting every means until they guide the vessel towards the tranquil harbor of sound values [*philosophias*]."[96] In these first paragraphs of his homily on the Old Testament, Chrysostom has drawn the essential connection between reading Scripture and training in philosophy.

Chrysostom provides explicit reasons for the enigmatic nature of the Old Testament. Some have to do with the nature of the text itself, others with limitations on the part of its hearers or readers.[97] We will look primarily at the reasons that address the question of divine *synkatabasis* and the cultivation of philosophy. Chrysostom first raises the issue of obscurity by pointing to the relative clarity of doctrine in the New Testament:

94. Hill, *Reading*, 36–37; our treatment here of *synkatabasis* is unfortunately but necessarily brief. For thorough treatments of this concept in Chrysostom, see David M. Rylaarsdam, *John Chrysostom on Divine Pedagogy: The Coherence of His Theology and Preaching* (Oxford: Oxford University Press, 2014); and Margaret M. Mitchell, *The Heavenly Trumpet: John Chrysostom and the Art of Pauline Interpretation*, Hermeneutische Untersuchungen zur Theologie 40 (Tübingen: Mohr Siebeck, 2000).

95. Hill, *Reading*, 39.

96. *Obscurit.* 1.1.24–31 (*Omelie*, 64; Hill, *Homilies*, 8–9).

97. Robert C. Hill, "Chrysostom on the Obscurity of the Old Testament," *Orientalia christiana periodica* 67, no. 2 (2001): 371–83, divides them into objective and circumstantial reasons.

The Old Testament, in fact, resembles riddles, there is much difficulty in it, and its books are hard to grasp, whereas the New is clearer and easier. Why is it, someone will ask, that they have this character, apart from the fact that the New talks about more important things, about the kingdom of heaven, resurrection of bodies and ineffable things that also surpass human understanding?[98]

In the second homily, however, Chrysostom advocates a theory of continuity and development between the two Testaments. Commenting on 2 Corinthians 3–4, where Paul interprets the veil covering the glory of Moses's face with reference to the law, Chrysostom argues that the lofty teachings of the New Testament were present already in the Old but were covered over by its obscurity, as if by a veil:

> Likewise the Law, too, since at that stage [the Jews were] incapable of learning the perfect doctrines characterized by sound values [*philosophias*], both those about Christ and the New Testament (all these being stored in the Old Scripture, as in a treasure), had a veil, out of considerateness [*synkatabainōn*] to them and to preserve all these riches for us, so that when Christ came and we turned to him the veil would be taken off.[99]

Here Chrysostom speaks explicitly of God's *synkatabasis*, his considerateness toward and accommodation of the Jews, who were not yet ready to receive the truths of the New Testament. This gesture of divine accommodation forms part of a larger trajectory of God's love for humankind in its weakness:

> Since, you see, some were bound to ask, Why did Christ not come with divinity revealed instead of being clad in flesh, the explanation was given to all these in advance through the face of the servant [Moses]: if Jews could not bear to look upon the servant's glory that came to him later, how would they have managed to look upon the divinity clearly revealed afterwards?[100]

The incarnation is the culmination of God's grand gesture of accommodating love for humankind.

Chrysostom thus maintains the continuity of the law and the gospel of Christ against those who would try to set them in opposition.[101] The law retains significance for the Christian community. He underscores that knowledge of the truths contained in Scripture must translate into the right practice of

---

98. *Obscurit.* 1.3.6–11 (*Omelie*, 74–76; Hill, *Homilies*, 13).
99. *Obscurit.* 2.1.49–60 (*Omelie*, 110–12; Hill, *Homilies*, 27).
100. *Obscurit.* 1.6.62–67 (*Omelie*, 98–100; Hill, *Homilies*, 23).
101. *Obscurit.* 1.7.57–59 (*Omelie*, 104; Hill, *Homilies*, 25).

philosophy in one's life. The Old Testament and its law play an indispensable role in this philosophical training: "The one [the law] shows the way to
this great value system [*tē megalē tautē philosophia*], the other [the gospel of
Christ] takes them from that point to the very summit."[102] The very "kinship
of the Law with grace"[103] enables Chrysostom to appropriate countless Old
Testament figures as examples of a philosophical way of life in anticipation
of Christ.[104]

Situating the Book of Job in the History of God's Synkatabasis

God's adaptable care and foresight for humans are clear both in the person of Job himself and in the story of his virtue. At the beginning of his
Commentary on Job, Chrysostom investigates Job's historical context. He
argues that even though Job was a descendent of Esau, his ancestry in no way
hindered his practice of virtue. But because he was not of the line of Jacob,
he inhabited a foreign land. Thus we learn that God has "sent teachers to all
people."[105] Indeed, God extended the duration of Job's plight and made him
a spectacle (*theatron*) for all to see, so that all people might recognize the
material evidence of God's love.[106]

To the question of why God would expose a just man to the whims of
Satan, Chrysostom answers: "'So that the devil might be silenced,' God says,
'so that the just one might appear more brightly, so that I might leave behind
for those who come later the medicine of patience for affliction.'"[107] The example of Job's trial can aid all those who suffer, especially those over whom
God has lovingly set the devil as a harsh and terrifying pedagogue, so that
they might remain vigilant. Throughout the suffering that Satan inflicts, God
strengthens those who love him.[108]

God's providential care is further evident in the transmission of the story of
Job. Chrysostom situates the story in Israel's history: "When the Jews were in
Egypt, and this land [Palestine] was without guides, they had the example of

102. *Obscurit.* 1.7.59–61 (*Omelie*, 104; Hill, *Homilies*, 25).

103. *Obscurit.* 1.7.53 (*Omelie*, 104; Hill, *Homilies*, 25).

104. Robert C. Hill, "Chrysostom as Old Testament Commentator," *Estudios bíblicos* 46,
no. 1 (1988): 74, notes that Chrysostom often interprets Old Testament figures as moral exemplars worthy of imitation rather than as pivotal figures in salvation history. But is it not perhaps
precisely their practice of philosophy, their incarnation and anticipation of the teachings of
the gospel, that invests them, in Chrysostom's view, with such significance in the trajectory of
God's incarnate love?

105. *Comm. Job* 2.3–4; prologue 2.5–6 (SC 346:80).

106. *Comm. Job* 2.11–27; prologue 3.1–20 (SC 346:80–82).

107. *Comm. Job* 21.3–5; 1.16.25–27 (SC 346:126).

108. *Comm. Job* 14.28–15.7; 1.9.58–69 (SC 346:112).

Job."[109] This is significant for Chrysostom because it puts Job prior to Moses and the law. Although Job was a foreigner and predated Moses, he knew about God. In fact, even Job's friends had some idea of God. But who taught them? In accordance with his positive anthropology, Chrysostom hints at a natural knowledge of God available to all. He instructs his listeners, "Observe how from the beginning the knowledge of God was clear everywhere."[110] And then he points to the book of Job's role in helping spread this knowledge: "For it seems to me that [Job] lived before the Law—it is immediately clear—such that one might reasonably say that this book was the first to teach and announce the knowledge of God, but clearly, to be sure, through a life of patience."[111] The knowledge of God, for Chrysostom, cannot be abstracted from one's daily way of life. This insight is at the heart of true philosophy.

Chrysostom has thereby given us a sense of where, historically, he locates the figure of Job and the text narrating his struggles. While in his homilies on the obscurity of the Old Testament he describes how the law was God's loving means of teaching the Jews about himself in a way commensurate to their ability to learn, he now identifies an even earlier stage of divine pedagogy. Through the story of Job, God has provided a means of coming to know him that is available to all people: the practice of the virtue of patient endurance. Despite its early place in Chrysostom's biblical chronology, Job's example is in no way obsolete. Rather, Job's historical priority to the law and Christ invests his example of philosophic virtue with a unique significance in the scriptural witness to God's accommodating love for humankind.

Conclusion: Job as a Figure of Evangelical Philosophy

In the figure of Job, therefore, Chrysostom finds a human being through whom God lovingly offers philosophy even before giving the law. Job has learned about God and brought that knowledge to bear on his life through the illumination of his natural reason.[112] He had no teacher. His life of virtue and patience is a model for people of all stripes. Chrysostom exhorts his listeners: "See . . . the one who pursued virtue prior to the Law as if it were the time after the Law."[113] He cites 1 Timothy 1:9, "For the just one the Law is not established," thereby signaling that Job's virtue already exceeds the law.

109. *Comm. Job* 2.28–30; prologue 4.2–3 (SC 346:82).
110. *Comm. Job* 2.5–6; prologue 2.6–7 (SC 346:80).
111. *Comm. Job* 2.7–10; prologue 2.9–12 (SC 346:80).
112. *Comm. Job* 3.2–3; prologue 4.8 (SC 346:82).
113. *Comm. Job* 2.30–3.2; prologue 4.3–6 (SC 346:82).

Chrysostom can thereupon ask, "Whence does he exemplify the practice of the Gospel, whence such great patience?"[114] For Chrysostom, Job's example of patience and virtue, of humane and sympathetic philosophy amid such horrific suffering, anticipates the highest ethical teaching of both the law and the gospel. Job, the man whom no one taught, is swept up into the whole continuous movement of divine pedagogy, of *synkatabasis*, God's loving accommodation of weak humans so that they might know him. Job anticipates Christ's example and teachings. "Do you see," Chrysostom asks, "that Christ came as a teacher of nothing new or foreign?"[115]

The figure of Job thus appears at the heart of Chrysostom's Old Testament exegetical strategy and, by extension, his overall pastoral program. This is indeed the significance of Job for Chrysostom: as a figure who practiced Christ's teachings even before the law and the gospel, he represents an example open to both Jew and Christian, even, one might say, to all those outside (or prior to) the law and the gospel. Through the figure of Job, John Chrysostom shows God to be a truly *humane* God and the Christian gospel to be the truly *humane* philosophy.

The virtue evident in this philosophy, in keeping with its human character, calls not only for resilience in the face of adversity but for true *sympatheia*, true shared feeling with one's fellow humans. Personal suffering demands piety and humility, a detachment from worldly things, and a faith in the God who not only punishes the wrongdoer but also tests his faithful. Those who suffer are not to be reproached when they cry out, when they shed tears, or when they mourn, but rather, they are to be comforted. Job's friends make the mistake of thinking they understand God's ways. But Chrysostom makes clear that they would in fact, like Job, exhibit more philosophy and more wisdom if they humbly admitted that they cannot grasp the mystery of God's providence in the world and instead practiced virtue and cared for others. Indeed, just as God shows his love for humankind by his providential creation and governance of the universe, so, according to Chrysostom, the one practicing true human philosophy should care for others. Chrysostom can therefore contend that for his listeners and readers it is "the greatest philosophy" to have examples of God's punishments and tests always present in their minds.[116] These are instances of his love for humankind. Chrysostom upholds Job as one of the best examples of a human being, yet more than a human, a philosopher, and still more: a philosopher with sympathy for his fellow humans.

---

114. *Comm. Job* 2.4–5; prologue 4.10–11 (SC 346:82).
115. *Comm. Job* 3.7–8; prologue 4.13–14 (SC 346:82).
116. *Comm. Job* 130.24; 19.12.7 (SC 348:48).

9

John Chrysostom
on the Man Born Blind (John 9)

Nonna Verna Harrison

As they walk together, not far from the Jerusalem temple, Jesus and his disciples see a man blind from his birth, a beggar. So the disciples ask Jesus, "Rabbi, who sinned, this man or his parents, that he was born blind?" (John 9:2). In other words, when was the sin committed that was punished with this disability? Underlying their question is a cultural attitude that a disability is a curse and that a person who has one should be ashamed and deserves to be discriminated against. This was certainly the attitude in the Greco-Roman world, where the disabled were forbidden from being priests because people believed the gods would be insulted by the service of a person so imperfect.[1] Judaism sometimes had similar attitudes.[2] The Pharisees in John 9 certainly do, as we shall see. But Jesus has a more positive perspective, and the man born blind in this chapter ably demonstrates that such a person can possess faith and virtues. John Chrysostom, who writes eloquently about the ethics

---

1. Robert Garland, *The Eye of the Beholder: Deformity and Disability in the Graeco-Roman World* (Ithaca, NY: Cornell University Press, 1995).
2. Judith Z. Abrams, *Judaism and Disability: Portrayals in Ancient Texts from the Tanach through the Bavli* (Washington, DC: Gallaudet University Press, 1988), 16–70.

of Scripture, draws out the implications of this chapter in his *Commentary on Saint John the Apostle and Evangelist*, homilies 56–59.[3] This essay examines the views of disability expressed in John 9, guided by Chrysostom's comments.

The disciples' question "Who sinned?" raises difficult theological issues as well as expressing problematic cultural attitudes. Chrysostom's comment is blunt: "The question was a mistake. For how could he have sinned before he was born? Or how, if his parents sinned, could he have been punished?"[4] In other words, the disciples' proposed alternatives are wrong, so Jesus rejects both of them. He replies, "Neither this man nor his parents sinned" (John 9:3a). Chrysostom draws the conclusion that, for the most part, disability is not caused by sin. He admits that sin can at times cause it because of what Jesus said to the paralytic in John 5:14: "See, you have been made well! Do not sin any more, so that nothing worse happens to you." But a disability from birth cannot be caused by the disabled person's sin. As Chrysostom explains, this is because punishment belongs to the one who sinned, not to someone else, even one as close as a parent.[5] Nor was the blind man's soul alive and thus capable of sin in a preexistence of any kind before his birth. It is true that a few of the rabbis whose conversations are preserved in the Talmud believed in some kind of preexistence or reincarnation, though they probably lived in the fourth century or later.[6] If such ideas already existed within Judaism in Jesus's earthly lifetime, they could lie behind the disciples' question. Yet *their* Rabbi rejects such opinions out of hand.

The Healing

Jesus states the following reason for the man's blindness: "He was born blind so that God's works might be revealed in him" (John 9:3b). However, this verse is not saying that every disabled person glorifies God by living with impairments. The Lord knows that he is about to accomplish a great work of God: "He spat on the ground and made mud from the saliva and spread the mud on the man's eyes, saying to him, 'Go, wash in the pool of Siloam.' . . . Then he went and washed and came back able to see" (9:6–7). The man humbly accepts Jesus's instructions. It may not be easy for him to find his way as he

3. In PG 59:305–28; trans. Sr. Thomas Aquinas Goggin, *St. John Chrysostom: Commentary on Saint John the Apostle and Evangelist, Homilies 48–88*, FC 41 (Washington, DC: Catholic University of America Press, 1959), 85–124; this work is cited below as Goggin.

4. PG 59:305.

5. PG 59:306–7.

6. Jack Bemporad, "Soul: Jewish Concept," in *Encyclopedia of Religion*, edited by Lindsay Jones, 2nd ed. (Farmington Hills, MI: Macmillan Reference, 2005), 12:8556–61.

walks from the centrally located temple precincts to Siloam, at the edge of the city. He may first have to find somebody to guide him there, but he simply agrees and does it. He does not need a guide on the way back.

Later in the chapter, the healed man remarks, "Never since the world began has it been heard that anyone opened the eyes of a person born blind" (John 9:32). When Jesus uses mud and saliva in this healing, perhaps he follows current medical practice. But the Fourth Evangelist often wove profound symbolic meanings into his stories, and as Chrysostom explains, here Christ is doing on a small scale what God did according to Genesis 2:7, when he created humans from the earth:

> Since they had heard that God made man by taking dust from the ground, it was for this reason that he also made clay in this way. In truth, if he said: "I am the One who took dust from the ground and fashioned mankind," it would seem offensive to his hearers, while if this was demonstrated by a concrete example, it would no longer give offense in the future. . . . Indeed, it was no small glory for Him to be regarded as Creator of the world. For by this miracle the rest of His claims were also substantiated, and from the part the whole was likewise established. . . . Man is more honorable than all the rest of creation, and the eye is more honorable than the other parts of our body. Because of this He created [the blind man's] vision, not out of nothing, but in the way he did.[7]

Healing a person blind from birth was indeed an act of creation, not simply a repair. Contemporary medical science knows more clearly how difficult it would be than was known in the first century. When a boy is born, he can only see far enough to behold his mother's face when held in her arms. It will take several years of practice for him to learn to use his eyes, to make the connections among nerves and his brain that will enable him to see well. Medical technology is working on building an artificial eye that would enable a blind person to see at least light and darkness. This might work for one who lost vision in adulthood, but not for one who was born blind, who never developed the infrastructure of nerves for seeing in the first place. Indeed, Chrysostom in his own way hints at these facts:

> Furthermore, not only did [Christ] fashion eyes, not only did He open them, but He also endowed them with power to see. And this is a proof that He also breathed life into them. Indeed, if this vital principle should not operate, even if the eye were sound, it could never see anything. And so He both bestowed the

7. PG 59:307–8; Goggin, 89–90, alt.

power to see by giving the eyes life, and also gave the organ of sight completely equipped with arteries, and nerves, and veins, and blood, and all the other things of which our body is composed.[8]

This passage contains another echo of Adam's creation in Genesis 2:7: "Then the LORD God formed man from the dust of the ground, and breathed into his nostrils the breath of life, and the man became a living being."

Arguments

The man who has been healed of lifelong blindness "came back" to the temple area "able to see" (John 9:7). Yet he is not met with congratulations but challenged by his Jewish neighbors and then by Pharisees. These arguments occupy most of the chapter, through verse 34. The way he responds to these challenges is impressive. First, his neighbors and people who have seen him begging ask each other whether he is in fact the one who was born blind. He uses his eyes and finds his way around so effortlessly that they wonder if he is the same man. "He kept saying, 'I am the man'" (9:9). Chrysostom comments, "He was not ashamed of his former affliction, nor did he fear the anger of the crowd, nor did he hesitate to appear in public in order to proclaim his Benefactor."[9] If he were ashamed of his disability, as one could easily be in that culture, he would have kept silence and tried to "pass" as somebody else. But he is of an honest character, full of courage and faith in Christ, and wants to give Christ public credit for the gift he has given. Chrysostom returns to these points about the man's character throughout his homilies on John 9. The man gives forthright, truthful answers to those who question him, and as a result they continue to engage him in argument.

When his neighbors and acquaintances ask how he has been healed, he explains, "The man called Jesus made mud, spread it on my eyes, and said to me, 'Go to Siloam and wash.' Then I went and washed and received my sight" (John 9:11). Then they ask him where Jesus is, and he replies, "I do not know" (9:12). To begin with, he does not know much about Jesus except that he has given the amazing gift of sight. However, as the arguments continue, he is pressed by his interlocutors to arrive at a more and more exalted view of who Jesus is.

Then the acquaintances bring Pharisees to talk to him, perhaps hoping they can clarify matters. Since the healing has occurred on a Sabbath, they

8. PG 59:308; Goggin, 91–92.
9. PG 59:312; Goggin, 99.

dispute among themselves: "Some of the Pharisees said, 'This man is not from God, for he does not observe the sabbath.' But others said, 'How can a man who is a sinner perform such signs?' And they were divided" (John 9:16). At this point, some of them had a favorable view of Christ. As Chrysostom says, "They were being educated by the miracles."[10] Then, as a group, the Pharisees try to get the man who was healed to settle their argument; they ask him who he thinks Jesus is. He replies, "He is a prophet" (9:17). The Pharisees do not like this answer, so they continue to investigate and argue. Meanwhile, perhaps at their request, some Jews ask the man's parents three questions: whether he is their son, whether he was born blind, and how he has come to see. They answer that he is indeed their son and was born blind, but to avoid getting in trouble, they do not answer the third question. "Ask him," they said; "he is of age. He will speak for himself" (9:21).

Since his parents have not satisfied them, the Pharisees question the man born blind a second time, stating aggressively, "We know that this man [Jesus] is a sinner" (John 9:24) because, in their opinion, he does not keep the Sabbath. As Chrysostom explains,[11] the man born blind replies as an eyewitness, reporting only what he knows from his own experience. He knows from the miracle Jesus has worked that he is not a sinner, but the man has no prior experience of Jesus's conduct. So he says in a conciliatory way, "I do not know whether he is a sinner. One thing I do know, that though I was blind, now I see" (9:25). He bases his claim about Jesus entirely upon what has indisputably happened to him. The Pharisees have no reasoned answer to this assertion, so they again speak aggressively, "What did he do to you? How did he open your eyes?" (9:26). Chrysostom, himself a master rhetorician, observes that the man born blind is winning the argument and notes that he now presses his case further: "Because he had defeated them and laid them low, he finally ceased speaking mildly."[12] He refused to answer their question about the healing, having answered it before: "I have told you already, and you would not listen. Why do you want to hear it again? Do you also want to become his disciples?" (9:27). This is splendid Johannine irony. The man is probably thinking of what he himself wants to do. Not surprisingly, the Pharisees react with an angry accusation: "You are his disciple, but we are disciples of Moses. We know that God has spoken to Moses, but as for this man, we do not know where he comes from" (9:28–29). By this time the man

10. PG 59:313; Goggin, 101.
11. PG 59:318; Goggin, 110–11.
12. PG 59:318; Goggin, 111.

must be taking their insult as a compliment, and he is further emboldened. He answers with a theological argument about Jesus based on the healing: "Here is an astonishing thing! You do not know where he comes from, and yet he opened my eyes. We know that God does not listen to sinners, but he does listen to one who worships him and obeys his will. Never since the world began has it been heard that anyone opened the eyes of a person born blind. If this man were not from God, he could do nothing" (9:30–33). Notice how he turns the Pharisees' own argument against them, namely, that God does not listen to sinners but listens to his obedient worshipers.

The Pharisees no longer engage with what he has said but instead respond with an ad hominem attack: "You were born entirely in sins, and are you trying to teach us?" (John 9:34). They use his disability to attack him, even though it is no longer there. Since he was born blind, they say he was actually born a sinner, and his parents no doubt are sinners too. Their pride is offended that someone from such a background would dare to try to teach them. Contrast this attitude with how Jesus responds to his disability at the beginning of the chapter: "Neither this man nor his parents sinned."

From Blind Beggar to Apostle

The Pharisees "drove him out" (John 9:34). He is probably expelled from the temple, and maybe also the synagogue, from which his parents feared being expelled if they confessed Jesus too boldly (9:22). The man born blind can no longer be a beggar, he has no livelihood, and now he has been rejected by leaders of the Jewish community. As a matter of religious obligation, Jewish people gave alms to disabled beggars, especially in or around the temple. Now able bodied, the man has lost his place in society, lowly as it was.

Then Jesus takes the initiative and finds him again. John Chrysostom eloquently explains what happens:

> Those who endure some terrible suffering and are insulted for the sake of truth and the confession of Christ are the ones particularly held in honor by him. . . . If we are insulted for God's sake, we shall be honored both in this world and in the next. Furthermore, since they had thrown him out of the temple, Jesus found him. The Evangelist pointed out that He came there for the purpose of meeting him. And what a reward He conferred on him: the best of blessings. And I say this because He made Himself known to him who before did not know Him and included him in the company of His own disciples.[13]

13. PG 59:321–22; Goggin, 120–21, alt.

Jesus immediately gives him a new community and a new place in it. He calls this man as he, in John 1, has called Andrew and Peter, Philip and Nathanael. It is clear from his dispute with the Pharisees that the man with the opened eyes has the truthfulness, courage, intelligence, and articulate speech of an apostle. He now has the opportunity to travel with Jesus and learn from him directly. He is not one of the Twelve, whose names we know, but is it not likely that he becomes one of that larger group of apostles whom Luke names as the "seventy-two" (Luke 10:1–17 marg.)?

At his second meeting with Jesus, he sees him for the first time, but, given the good hearing and good memory a person born blind develops, he probably recognizes his voice. He listens openly and respectfully, though he does not yet really know who the Lord is. Jesus asks him, "Do you believe in the Son of God?" (John 9:35 marg.).[14] Eager to learn, he answers, "And who is he, Lord? Tell me, so that I may believe in him" (9:36 marg.). Then the Lord reveals himself to him: "You have seen him, and the one speaking with you is he" (9:37). Christ invites the man to believe in him but does not order him to believe. As Chrysostom says, he asks whether he believes "not out of ignorance, but that the athlete who bore many sufferings would be granted a crown."[15] He invites him to reveal his own faith, the faith that has sprung from the healing of his eyes, has grown through facing the challenges of the Pharisees, and is now coming to fullness. "He said, 'Lord, I believe,' and he worshiped him" (9:35–38). Chrysostom observes, "By this action the man showed his belief in Christ's divinity, for he added the prostration in order that no one might think that what he said was merely words."[16] Chrysostom understood the Greek of John 9:38 as saying that the man expresses his worship in a physical action, such as kneeling and bowing his forehead to the ground. So to him the blind man's confession is equivalent to the confession of Thomas when he saw Christ after the resurrection: "My Lord and my God!" (John 20:28).

14. This is what Chrysostom's text says, PG 59:322, an important point reflected in his interpretation of the text. Many biblical versions, including the RSV and NRSV (cf. marg.), say "Son of Man," an exalted title as Dan. 7:13–14 and Jesus use it, yet this title is ambiguous when compared to "Son of God." The standard scholarly version of the original, *The Greek New Testament*, ed. Kurt Aland et al., 2nd ed. (New York: United Bible Society, 1968), 363–64, says *Sy pisteueis eis ton huion tou anthrōpou?* Yet the footnote cites many more manuscripts that say *huion tou theou* than the reading chosen, including one by Chrysostom, probably cited above. According to *The New Testament in the Original Greek: Byzantine Textform 2005*, ed. Maurice A. Robinson and William C. Pierpont (Southborough, MA: Chilton, 2005), 219, the contemporary Greek version likely closest to what Chrysostom knew reads *Sy pisteueis eis ton huion tou theou?*

15. PG 59:322; replacing Goggin's weak paraphrase, on 121.

16. PG 59:311; Goggin, 122.

Jesus then speaks of how this man has obtained sight, while the Pharisees have become blind (John 9:39–41). Here, according to Chrysostom, he speaks of "two kinds of sight and blindness: one physical, the other spiritual."[17] Christ healed the man blind from birth first of physical blindness, then also of spiritual blindness. As his perceptions unfold, he continues to be receptive and cooperative. His example shows that physical blindness, and by implication other kinds of disability, is not tied to sin, nor is it shameful. As Chrysostom says earlier, "Evil does not consist in the misfortunes of this life, as also good does not consist in the blessings of this life, but sin is the only evil, and disability is in reality not an evil."[18] When the Pharisees ask Jesus in John 9:40, "Surely we are not blind, are we?" Chrysostom observes that they are concerned only with the things of the senses and are "ashamed of physical blindness."[19] In these homilies, John Chrysostom shows the same appreciative and compassionate attitude toward the disabled that he shows toward the poor throughout his writings. And indeed, the disabled often are poor.

The Blind Rabbi

In John 9, the Pharisees are portrayed as gravely deficient, not only in their attitude toward Christ, but also in their attitude toward people with disabilities, especially blindness. John's negative portrayal may in general be unfair to them, given that they and Jesus held enough theological views in common to find many grounds for arguing with each other, like rabbis disputing over the meanings of Scripture. So the Pharisee Saul of Tarsus could become Paul the apostle.

Yet most of the spiritual descendants of the Pharisees became the rabbis who preserved and reconstituted Judaism after the fall of the temple in AD 70. The rich diversity of their voices interpreting and disputing over Scripture and the Jewish way of life is preserved in the talmudic literature (ca. AD 200–500). Unlike the temple priesthood governed by rules in Leviticus, rabbis were mostly laypeople, as the Pharisees were, and could have disabilities themselves. They expressed differing views on issues of disability. In contrast with John's portrayal of uniformly negative Pharisaic attitudes toward blindness, I will share one story from the Babylonian Talmud about three rabbis who respond to it much more positively. One of them is the chief rabbi of the time, named in the talmudic text simply as "Rabbi":

17. PG 59:323; Goggin, 122.
18. PG 59:307; Goggin, 88, alt.
19. PG 59:323; Goggin, 123.

Rabbi and Rabbi Ḥiyya were on the road. When they reached a certain town they said, "Is there a sage here? Let us go and greet him!" The people said to them: "There is a sage here and he is blind." Rabbi Ḥiyya said to Rabbi: "You sit. I will go and greet him so that you don't degrade your exalted status." But he prevailed over him and they went together. When they were taking their leave [of the blind sage], he said to them: "You have received the one who is seen, but who does not see. May you merit to be received by the One who sees, but who is not seen." Rabbi said to Rabbi Ḥiyya: "If I had followed your advice, you would have kept me from this blessing!"[20] (Ḥagigah 5b)

As a courtesy, the chief rabbi and his companion like to visit the rabbis in towns they pass through on their journey. This gives local rabbis a chance for conversation and consultation with senior colleagues. So people tell them that the rabbi in their village is blind. Rabbi Ḥiyya regards blindness as shameful and worries that the man's shame would spread to his illustrious companion if he visited, so to spare him, Rabbi Ḥiyya offers to make the visit alone. But Rabbi disagrees, they dispute about it, and the senior colleague wins the argument. It would be interesting to know what they said to each other, but the Talmud does not record their conversation.

So the two go together to see the blind rabbi. At the end of their visit the gracious host gives a blessing to his guests. They all belong to a culture in which blessings are considered to be concretely effective. He says, "You have received the one who is seen, but who does not see." They have received him as a colleague and entered into dialogue with him, for which he is thankful. Then he turns this saying around: "May you merit to be received by the One who sees, but who is not seen," that is, the invisible God. The blind rabbi's subtle point is that all the rabbis, in fact all people, are like himself in relation to God. All are seen by God, all can enter into dialogue with him through prayer, but nobody can see him. The blind rabbi is, in effect, an example to everybody. Moreover, he has edified the chief rabbi, who remarks that the visit has brought the blessing to both himself and Rabbi Ḥiyya. Rabbi Ḥiyya's shame about blindness has been corrected by the other two rabbis. At their parting, all three are honored through the blessing. The blind rabbi, like the blind apostle in John 9, is honored for speaking wisdom.

20. Quoted in Julia Watts Baker, "Reading Talmudic Bodies: Disability, Narrative, and the Gaze in Rabbinic Judaism," in *Disability in Judaism, Christianity, and Islam: Sacred Texts, Historical Traditions, and Social Analysis*, ed. Darla Schumm and Michael Stoltzfus (New York: Palgrave Macmillan, 2011), 5–27, esp. 18–19. This article provides a good overview of approaches to disability in talmudic literature.

Conclusion

John the Evangelist and John Chrysostom exemplify a Christian belief that there is nothing shameful about physical disability. Above all, God is never offended when people with disabilities seek to serve him. Like the anonymous village rabbi in Ḥagigah 5b, John's man born blind could serve in a ministry of teaching and exhortation. Another example is the monk and biblical teacher in fourth-century Alexandria who went down in history as Didymus the Blind.[21]

Although the ancient Greeks and Romans thought the gods would be offended if a disabled person served as a priest, and Judaism, too, excluded them from the priesthood because they were "blemished," the Christian church explicitly rejected this opinion. In the Apostolic Canons, a collection of regulations used in the early church and ratified by the Council of Nicaea and subsequent ecumenical councils, it is stated, "If anyone has lost an eye or has a lame leg but in other respects is worthy of the episcopate, he may be ordained, since a defect of the body does not defile a person, but pollution of the soul does." Bishops were the highest rank of Christian priesthood. However, people with more severe disabilities were excluded because they would have practical difficulties in doing a bishop's work: "Yet if a person is deaf or blind, he may not be made a bishop, not as if he were defiled by this, but so that the affairs of the Church may not be hindered."[22] As an apostle, the man born blind who received his sight would have been called to travel to places new to him, which could have been very difficult without eyesight. His vocation must have become much easier for him to fulfill with the sight Christ granted him. Yet we must recognize, as John's Jesus recognized—as Chrysostom, the chief rabbi in Ḥagigah 5b, and the authors and editors of the Apostolic Canons would have agreed—that his earlier blindness was never itself a diminution of his humanity.

21. See Richard A. Layton, *Didymus the Blind and His Circle in Late Antique Alexandria* (Urbana: University of Illinois Press, 2004).

22. Apostolic Canons 77 and 78, quoted in John H. Erickson, *The Challenge of Our Past: Studies in Orthodox Canon Law and Church History* (Crestwood, NY: St. Vladimir's Seminary Press, 1991), 64n35, with English updated in translation.

10

THE DEATHS OF MACRINA AND MONICA IN GREGORY OF NYSSA'S *LIFE OF MACRINA* AND AUGUSTINE'S *CONFESSIONS*

The Female Philosopher and the Problem of Christian Grief

REGINA L. WALTON

Macrina and Monica: the names of these contemporaries, virgin and widow, are inextricably linked with their famous kinsmen. The narratives of the lives and especially the deaths of these holy women are bound up with the theological questions of brother and son. Macrina, older sister of Gregory of Nyssa and Basil of Caesarea, died in 380 at the age of fifty-six, on her family's estate in Cappadocia, which she had converted into a monastery. Monica, mother of Augustine of Hippo, died in 387 at the age of fifty-four while traveling with her family in Ostia, one year after her son's conversion. Both Gregory of Nyssa and Augustine were professional rhetoricians before they were bishops. As we approach their texts, therefore, we must remember that, as Elizabeth Clark writes, "far from uncovering 'the women themselves,' we encounter literary set pieces by male authors"[1] and "that we deal, always, with representation."[2] Though they were historical figures known intimately by those relatives who wrote about them, Macrina and Monica are also characters playing many different roles in Nyssen's and Augustine's texts.

This essay explores the way in which Gregory's and Augustine's representations of sister and mother are bound up with philosophical questions of the role of the emotions in the Christian life. The two theologians also use the death scene of each woman to work out what I call the problem of Christian grief: Is it permissible to grieve for someone who dies in the hope of the resurrection? And if so, is it possible to grieve without giving over to an immoderate wave of passion? Is there such thing as "reasonable grief"?

Macrina and Monica as Historical and Philosophical Figures

Gregory and Augustine have a double relationship with Macrina and Monica: they are connected both physically through bloodlines and spiritually through membership in the body of Christ. These familial relationships were spiritually formative for them. Gregory repeatedly calls Macrina his teacher, and though Augustine in the *Confessions* credits his friends Simplician and Theodore with the intellectual stimulus for his conversion,[3] he recognizes the many occasions his mother acted as, to use George Herbert's phrase, an "engine against the Almighty," praying and lamenting ceaselessly on his behalf. Indeed, Augustine writes, "she suffered greater pains in my spiritual pregnancy than when she bore me in the flesh."[4]

Both women appear in biographical narratives and philosophical dialogues, Macrina discoursing for nearly seventy pages in *The Soul and the Resurrection*, and Monica appearing in *Vita beata* and *De ordine*. In the dialogues especially, the women often function as "types," Macrina as a classical philosopher and Monica as representative of the Spirit-inspired wisdom of the humble Christian believer.

As J. Warren Smith writes, "Through her ascetic piety and chastity, Macrina embodies the angelic life which is humanity's eschatological destiny."[5]

1. Elizabeth A. Clark, "Holy Women, Holy Words: Early Christian Women, Social History, and the 'Linguistic Turn,'" *Journal of Early Christian Studies* 6, no. 3 (1998): 416.

2. Elizabeth A. Clark, "The Lady Vanishes: Dilemmas of a Feminist Historian after the 'Linguistic Turn,'" *Church History* 67, no. 1 (March 1998): 30.

3. Garry Wills, *Saint Augustine: A Life* (New York: Penguin, 1999), 58.

4. Augustine, *Confessions* (5.8.15), trans. Henry Chadwick, Oxford World Classics (Oxford: Oxford University Press, 1992), 83; this translation is cited as Chadwick.

5. J. Warren Smith, "A Just and Reasonable Grief: The Death and Function of a Holy Woman in Gregory of Nyssa's *Life of Macrina*," *Journal of Early Christian Studies* 12, no. 1 (1994): 58.

Macrina's persona in the dialogue is modeled after Socrates in the *Phaedo* and Diotima, Socrates's female teacher in the *Symposium*.[6] However, due to her sex, Gregory adds some qualifiers to her philosophical resume. Despite the numerous complex arguments Macrina makes in *The Soul and the Resurrection*, Nyssen writes in the *Vita* that she was taught at home not from the poets, which were considered a bad influence on a young girl, but from the Bible, learning all the Psalms by heart.[7] Her wisdom comes not from formal education but from God. She has dedicated her life to the pursuit of philosophy, and she lives out this commitment not by traveling to study with rhetoricians and philosophers but through prayer, Scripture reading, and ascetic acts in her rural retreat.[8]

Augustine values Monica's contributions to the dialogues in which she is named, though he first has to convince her to join them. In chapter 11 of *De ordine*, Monica checks in on the progress of the dialogue but protests when Augustine wants her entrance and her question recorded by their stenographer. Monica says, "What are you doing? In those books which you read, have I ever heard that women were introduced into this kind of disputation?" Augustine acknowledges how she could have gathered this impression but tells her that he does not care and that "in olden times, women, too, have worked on the problems of philosophy. And your philosophy is very pleasing to me."[9] It is likely that Monica was illiterate; she has heard Augustine and his friends reading aloud, as was their custom.[10]

In response to one of Monica's points in *Vita beata*, Augustine writes, "At these words, she so exclaimed that we, entirely oblivious of her sex, believed that some great man was with us. Meanwhile I understood, as well as possible, from what source those words came and how divine was the source."[11] Later in the dialogue, Augustine refers to Monica directly: "'Do you all see,' I asked, 'that a great difference exists between many and varied doctrines

6. Ibid., 62; and Clark, "The Lady Vanishes," 24.

7. Gregory of Nyssa, *The Life of Saint Macrina*, trans. Kevin Corrigan (Toronto: Peregrina, 1987), 28; this work is cited below as *Life*.

8. Ibid., 31.

9. Augustine, "Divine Providence and the Problem of Evil," in *The Writings of St. Augustine*, trans. Robert P. Russell, vol. 1, FC 2 (New York: CIMA, 1948), 269–71. For a list of philosophically involved women in the Hellenistic world, see Arnaldo Momigliano, "The Life of St. Macrina by Gregory of Nyssa," in *On Pagans, Jews, and Christians* (Middletown, CT: Wesleyan University Press, 1987), 207.

10. Augustine comments: "Whose books I see are known to you, whenever we read them"; in "Divine Providence and the Problem of Evil," 269.

11. "The Happy Life," in Augustine, *Selected Writings*, trans. Mary T. Clark, CWS (New York: Paulist Press, 1984), 174–75.

and a soul wholly devoted to God? For whence come those words which we admire unless from Him?'"[12]

Macrina, having dedicated herself to philosophy and asceticism, is portrayed as disputing with a high level of theological knowledge, while Monica makes more humble contributions from a more traditional standpoint. Both women are portrayed as mouthpieces for the divine, possessing a direct connection with God that the more highly trained men lack.

Clark has commented on the phenomenon of women presented as teachers of wisdom in early Christian *Vitae* and other texts, connecting it back to the *Life of Anthony*, whose wisdom was also God-given instead of being acquired in philosophical schools. "The ascetic as philosopher is a literary topos," she writes. The woman philosopher "provides a tool with which men can 'think' the values of their culture. . . . [Diotima in the *Symposium*] stands for something else—namely, as a trope for Socrates himself, the quintessential philosopher. She is not a true female 'Other' to the male philosopher, but 'a masked version of the same.'"[13] Macrina, in *The Soul and the Resurrection*, "ponders the acceptability of a modified Origenism that skirts 'dangerous' theological points," provides a "shaming" device for ascetically lax Christian men, and is a living example of Gregory's teaching of someone who, through virginity and asceticism, has taken steps to restore the pure "image of God," which includes moving beyond gender divisions.[14] Though Clark does not discuss Monica directly, Augustine's portrayal of his mother's participation in the dialogue fits with Clark's assessment of women as teachers of wisdom. In the two dialogues, Monica is not *a* woman, but Woman, an uneducated but devout "soul wholly dedicated to God." However, while Monica may stand in for more than herself the historical person, she represents not the ascetic as philosopher but the ordinary pious Christian as philosopher. This is a significant adjustment of the literary topos away from the spiritual elite toward common urban Christian experience.

Macrina and Monica on the Passions

The description of both women as teachers of wisdom with a direct connection to the divine is quite possibly their only similarity. They are each other's emotional inverse, two mothers of the church on opposite ends of the spectrum of the passions. Macrina, virgin and abbess, is so otherworldly as to seem cold

12. Ibid., 187.
13. Clark, "The Lady Vanishes," 22, 25–26.
14. Ibid., 27, 29–30.

and heartless in the face of others' grief. Monica, on the other hand, takes "attachment parenting" to a whole new level, as her love for her son and the emotions it evokes in her become an obstacle to her own spiritual growth.

Macrina in her *Vita* is the model virgin ascetic. When Gregory, after an absence of nine years, returns to the family home to visit her, he finds her "in the grip of a grievous sickness, but she was resting not on a bed or a couch, but on the ground, on a plank covered with sack-cloth, with another plank supporting her head and designed to serve instead of a pillow."[15]

Macrina and the virgins in her care are already participating in the life to come, "removed from all life's vanity and fashioned in harmonious imitation of the life of the angels."[16] She is so spiritually advanced that at the beginning of the *Vita*, Gregory wonders if he can still call her a woman, "for I do not know if it is appropriate to apply a name drawn from nature to one who has risen above nature."[17] Gregory—unlike Augustine, who calls his mother's faith "virile"[18]—is not saying that Macrina has been promoted to masculinity for her ascetic accomplishments; instead, she has actually transcended embodied gender itself.

Macrina also rises above nature at the death of her younger brother Naucratius, killed in a hunting accident, whose corpse was brought back to the family estate, overwhelming their mother, Emmelia, with grief: "By means of her own reasoned reflections she lifted her mother up together with her and placed her beyond suffering, guiding her to patience and courage by her own example."[19] Macrina is so "apathetic" that in *The Soul and the Resurrection* she initially describes emotions as warts on the soul.[20] Gregory objects with lauded biblical examples of eagerness, anger, fear, and sorrow, and Macrina tempers her position, saying that emotions are instead on the boundary of the soul. Not one for tea and sympathy, Macrina rebukes Gregory when he begins to tell her of his episcopal troubles with the emperor Valens. "Will you not put an end," she asks, "to your failure to recognize the good things that come from God?"[21]

Where Macrina is dispassionate to the point of callousness, Monica spends much of the *Confessions* weeping over Augustine. While both Gregory and Augustine point out that weeping over sins is the only consistently acceptable form of tears, Augustine makes clear that his mother was overly attached to

---

15. *Life*, 41.
16. Ibid., 36.
17. Ibid., 26.
18. Augustine, *Confessions* (= *Conf.*) 9.4.8, trans. Chadwick, 160.
19. *Life*, 35.
20. Gregory of Nyssa, *On the Soul and the Resurrection*, in *Saint Gregory of Nyssa: Ascetical Works*, trans. Virginia Woods Callahan, FC 58 (Washington, DC: Catholic University of America Press, 1967), 219; this work is cited below as Callahan.
21. *Life*, 45.

him: "As mothers do, she loved to have me with her, but much more than most mothers; and she did not understand that you were to use my absence as a means to bring her joy. She did not know that. So she wept and lamented, and these agonies proved that there survived in her the remnants of Eve, seeking with groaning for the child she had brought forth in sorrow."[22]

Monica's affection goes beyond what Augustine considers "normal" attachment. Where Macrina has transcended her gendered nature and has returned to a "prelapsarian image of God," Monica is overly identified with Eve after the fall. Monica's devotion to Augustine and his spiritual welfare is symbolized by her copious tears; a priest, irritated that she will not stop begging him to visit Augustine, famously tells her, "It cannot be that the son of these tears should perish."[23] Through synecdoche, Monica's tears represent her as a whole. Macrina, however, sternly reprimands Gregory for weeping on seeing her on her deathbed so soon after their brother Basil's death.[24]

There are heroic aspects to the characterizations of both Macrina and Monica: Macrina, in her asceticism, is several times described as a victorious athlete, while Monica's persistent love for and lamentation over her wayward son, which becomes a kind of paradoxical ascetic practice, is eventually heard by God beyond her expectations. However, traces of excess exist on both sides. While both Gregory's *Vita* and his dialogue *The Soul and the Resurrection* are full of praise for his sister, her somewhat extreme view of the relation of emotions to the soul needs to be modified.[25] Monica's lamentations and prayers for Augustine are eventually answered, but her attachment to Augustine as her son, and not just as a lost soul, is disproportionate. From the perspective of their episcopal interlocutors, there is a sense in which Macrina's otherworldliness and Monica's this-worldliness must each be tempered.

Death and Grief as Theological and Moral Problems

In the deaths of Macrina and Monica, the personal intersects with the theological. The amount of space given to Macrina's death in the *Vita* and the

22. Augustine, *Conf.* 5.9.15, trans. Chadwick, 82.
23. Augustine, *Conf.* 3.12.21, trans. Chadwick, 51.
24. Callahan, 198.
25. For a full discussion of the evolution of Macrina and Gregory's views on the emotions, see J. Warren Smith, *Passion and Paradise: Human and Divine Emotion in the Thought of Gregory of Nyssa* (New York: Crossroad, 2004); and Rowan Williams, "Macrina's Deathbed Revisited: Gregory of Nyssa on Mind and Passion," in *Christian Faith and Greek Philosophy in Late Antiquity*, ed. Lionel R. Wickham and Caroline P. Bammel, Supplements to Vigiliae Christianae 19 (Leiden: Brill, 1993), 227–46.

placement of Monica's death at Ostia at the very end of the biographical portion of the *Confessions* together demonstrate the importance these events held for Gregory and Augustine. The bishops are not only "working through their grief," as we might say using the language of psychology, but working through grief itself: Can it have a valid place in the emotional life of the Christian? Or does Christ's death and resurrection necessarily evict grief from the heart of the believer? Is grief as an emotional experience now out of bounds for Christians? And is there a way that grief, like lust, can somehow be redirected toward the divine?

Macrina, chastising her brother at the beginning of *The Soul and the Resurrection*, says, "It is not right to grieve for those who are asleep, since we are told that sorrow belongs only to those who have no hope."[26] Augustine comments more fully along these lines in the *Confessions*: "We did not think it right to celebrate the funeral with tearful dirges and lamentations, since in most cases it is customary to use such mourning to imply sorrow for the miserable state of those who die. . . . But my mother's dying meant neither that her state was miserable nor that she was suffering extinction. . . . Why then did I suffer such sharp pains of inward grief?"[27]

How is one to grieve properly for a Christian person? Is there anything to grieve, since the Christian who has died is now dwelling in the bosom of Abraham? And what is to be done with the intense feelings of sorrow that arise despite this knowledge? Robert C. Gregg defines this problem as "the morality of grieving," a question of ethics.[28]

Gregory and Augustine explore this ethical dilemma in the *Vita* and the *Confessions* by setting up various scenarios of grieving in the narratives, some of "bad," out-of-control, or unbalanced grief, and some of "good" or right, orderly, and moderate grief. Gregory and Augustine also describe their own experience of grieving and the tension that remains even after they have concluded that their actions were appropriate.

The Death of Macrina in Vita Macrinae

In *Vita Macrinae* (*The Life of Macrina*), it is the deaths of Macrina and Gregory's brother Naucratius, a young man who had chosen the life of a hermit, which provide the catalyst for appropriate and inappropriate grief.

26. Callahan, 198. Gregory is citing 1 Thess. 4:13.
27. Augustine, *Conf.* 9.12.29, trans. Chadwick, 174.
28. Robert C. Gregg, *Consolation Philosophy: Greek and Christian* Paideia *in Basil and the Two Gregories*, Patristic Monograph Series 3 (Cambridge, MA: Philadelphia Patristic Foundation, 1975), 83.

When the messenger arrives at the family estate and delivers the bad news of Naucratius's death to Emmelia, Macrina's mother, she becomes overwhelmed. Gregory writes, "Perfect though she was in every virtue, nature prevailed all the same even over her. She became breathless and speechless and fainted away on the spot, reason giving way to grievous shock, and she lay under the assault of the dreadful news like an athlete of noble stock felled by an unexpected blow."[29]

Gregory is setting up a foil for Macrina. Although Emmelia is not a "weak, undisciplined woman of low birth," her reason is supplanted by the unexpected ordeal.[30] Emmelia's life was ordered according to virtue and reason, but this surprise test of her mettle has felled her. By contrast, Macrina is able to pull her mother "from the depths of her grief," teach her to be brave and not "give vent to her suffering in any base or womanish way" (i.e., by customs of public lamentation and wailing associated with lower-class women).[31] Gregory observes that Macrina's nature also experienced suffering over the death of her beloved brother, but she was victorious over it, "like an undefeated athlete, who does not cringe at any point before the onslaught of misfortune."[32] Indeed, Smith describes Macrina's primary pastoral role in the *Vita* as grief counselor, first to her mother and then also to Gregory.[33]

Throughout the *Vita*, Gregory wrestles with his own grief during the approaching death of his sister and then, after she dies, struggles to behave in the impassive, reasoned way in which she has urged him. He is not alone in this struggle: Macrina's community of virgins is present as well. Macrina's rebukes help keep the grief of the group around her in check while she is alive, but after she dies, Gregory and the community falter under the weight of their sorrow. Unlike Macrina, who views grief as irrational, Gregory reflects that the grief of the virgins makes sense: "The maidens' grief seemed to me to have a just and reasonable cause. For they were not bewailing the loss of some ordinary acquaintance or physical attachment, . . . but it was as if they had been cut off from their hope in God and from the salvation of their souls."[34] The virgins have lost their bridge between the present life and the life to come, and so they cry out, "The lamp of our eyes has been extinguished; the light to guide our souls has been carried off."[35] But looking at Macrina's face reminds Gregory of her instruction, and he shouts over the wailing of the maidens that

29. *Life*, 34.
30. Smith, "Reasonable Grief," 70.
31. *Life*, 34.
32. *Life*, 39.
33. Smith, "Reasonable Grief," 60.
34. *Life*, 51.
35. Ibid.

they should conduct themselves in the orderly and graceful fashion she taught them. Instead of lamentation, they should sing psalms together, channeling their wild grief into liturgical order. Macrina has instructed that the only appropriate time for weeping is during prayer. During the funeral, the virgins manage to contain themselves for a time, but as Macrina's body is about to be put in the tomb of her parents, wailing breaks out, and Gregory and the bishops must once again try to funnel the public display of grief into psalm-singing. Although Gregory, in contrast to his sister, concludes that there are times when grief can be "just and reasonable," public lamentation is liable to carry the rational soul away on a river of immoderate sorrow and so must be directed into contained, orderly forms such as psalm-singing.

The Death of Monica in the Confessions

In the *Confessions*, Augustine presents his own youthful love of tragic theater, his grief over the death of his friend, and Monica's grief at his covert departure for Rome as three kinds of inappropriate, or disordered, grief. As a student at Carthage, Augustine is "captivated by theatrical shows." Reflecting back, Augustine is critical of the desire to witness tragic events one would never wish to go through, and to feel pleasure at this sort of removed pain.[36] It is this pleasurable wallowing in pain that is the reason he condemns his grief at the death of a close friend during his Manichaean days: "Only tears were sweet to me, and in my 'soul's delights' weeping had replaced my friend."[37]

Against the Stoics, Augustine argues that the emotions are fundamental parts of the human person and that ignoring them makes us not more divine but less human. Augustine uses three aspects of his own emotions to evaluate them: the source or object of the emotions, the experience of the emotions themselves, and the result or goal of the emotions.[38] By these criteria, his love of the theater, his grief over his friend, and Monica's grief at Augustine's voyage are not worthy forms of sorrow. The source of his experience of pleasure from tragic theater is immoderate love of what is not real. The experience is taking pleasure in another's (though fictional) misfortune, and the result does not make Augustine a more compassionate person. His grief in the loss of his friend is caused by attachment to an impermanent relationship: the experience is again a kind of pleasure in pain, and the result is debilitating.

---

36. Augustine, *Conf.* 3.2.2, trans. Chadwick, 35.
37. Augustine, *Conf.* 4.4.9, trans. Chadwick, 58. The term "soul's delights" is a reference to Psalm 93:19 Vulgate (94:19).
38. Kim Paffenroth, "The Young Augustine: Lover of Sorrow," *Downside Review* 118, no. 412 (July 2000): 221–22.

Likewise, Monica's grief stems from an immoderate attachment to her son, which manifests itself as her inability to let him go, resulting in much pain and consternation at their separation, even though this separation is ultimately for Augustine's good.

Monica's deathbed is the scene of appropriate, ordered grief, though not without the presence of the kind of tension that Gregory experienced with the wailing maidens. At the conclusion of Augustine and Monica's mystical conversation at Ostia, Monica tells him that he is a Christian, her hope in this world has been fulfilled, and so she no longer sees a reason to live.[39] Soon afterward she, like Macrina, contracts a fever. In her illness she tells her sons to bury her at Ostia and not in the tomb of her husband at their home in North Africa; Augustine interprets this as a sign that his mother's nature has finally transcended the earthly attachments, including the attachment to her son, to which she had previously clung, and she is focused only on heavenly things.[40]

At her last breath with her two sons and grandson at her side, the boy Adeodatus cries out. All present silence him. Like the wailing virgins in the *Vita Macrinae*, Augustine recognizes that his son's cry is "the voice of my heart," expressing what he struggles to suppress. As in Macrina's community, after the crying has been checked, someone begins to chant a psalm and all join in.[41]

Although Augustine feels as if "my life were torn to pieces, since my life and hers had become a single thing," he manages for a time to fool those around him into thinking that he is not grieved. The recognition that emotions have such power over him, "though they are a necessary part of the order we have to endure," is an additional grief to him.[42] After trying to "sweat out" his grief through a bath to no avail, he finds some relief through sleeping. On waking and remembering a poem by Ambrose, he feels free to weep before God. He writes, "I was glad to weep before you about her and for her, about myself and for myself. Now I let flow the tears which I had held back so long so that they ran as freely as they wished. My heart rested upon them, and it reclined upon them because it was your ears that were there, not those of some human critic who would put a proud interpretation on my weeping."[43] Like Gregory, Augustine has come to an understanding of certain kinds of grief as "just and reasonable," though his acceptance of his own tears, about his situation and not only for his sins, is distinct from Gregory's. Still, Augustine weeps only once, for "a fraction of an hour," and in the next paragraph says that

39. Paraphrased from Augustine, *Conf.* 9.10.26, trans. Chadwick, 172.
40. Augustine, *Conf.* 9.11.28, trans. Chadwick, 173.
41. Augustine, *Conf.* 9.12.29–31, trans. Chadwick, 147–75.
42. Augustine, *Conf.* 9.12.31, trans. Chadwick, 175.
43. Augustine, *Conf.* 9.12.33, trans. Chadwick, 176.

his heart is now healed of that wound. Even a rightly ordered sorrow must be tempered by moderation and control of the emotions. However, this brief time of weeping and crying out to God from the depths of his grief brings about a renewed awareness of his own weakness and dependence on God. As Augustine declares in this section, this is a fitting way to honor one who shed so many tears for his sake.

Conclusion

Macrina and Monica, with their contrasting modes of life and divergent approaches to emotion and worldly attachment, represent exaggerated versions of two paths to holiness for early Christian women. Gregory and Augustine engage them both as personalities and as literary types in their own theological wrestling with attachment, asceticism, and the place of grief in Christian experience. The bishops' relationship to grief, like their relationships to their kinswomen and foremothers in faith, remains complex. They grant grief an uneasy place in the believer's heart, recognizing that in this life it is not always possible to subordinate the passions to reason, but are still deeply suspicious of the sway this powerful emotion can have over the Christian. The expression of grief, especially in public, undermines faith in the life to come by privileging the bonds of earthly relationships. Yet the departed sister and mother played formative roles in the second births of Gregory and Augustine, and so demonstrations of grief at their passing also honor the incarnate presence of Christ to which their lives bore witness.

11

Evil, Suffering, and Embodiment in Augustine

David G. Hunter

Few topics, if any, were of greater significance to the theology of Saint Augustine than the theme of this book. If we can believe Augustine's own account in the *Confessions*, inquiry into the origins and nature of evil animated his intellectual development from his earliest years. Search for the cause of evil had led him to the Manichaean sect in his early twenties, and disenchantment with the Manichaean account of God and evil led him eventually to abandon its tenets nearly a decade later. Reading the "books of the Platonists" at Milan in his early thirties, Augustine tells us, provided him with a convincing metaphysical account of God and evil, one that finally detached him from Manichaean materialism and paved the way for his ultimate conversion to catholic Christianity. In the final decade of his life (that is, from roughly 420 to 430), Augustine's engagement with followers of Pelagius and the so-called Semi-Pelagians led him (perhaps reluctantly) to dwell on the darkness of evil in the human heart and the mysterious workings of divine grace and predestination. From his earliest to his latest writings, some features of the problem of evil seem always to have exercised his mind.[1]

Since the topic of Augustine and evil opens up such wide horizons, it is necessary to limit my discussion here to manageable proportions. I focus on a period of life and a selection of writings somewhere between Augustine's first philosophical dialogues and his final polemical treatises. Specifically, I examine his discussion of evil in works composed roughly between 410 and 420. My choice of this decade of Augustine's life is not arbitrary. Augustinian scholars usually look to the year 396 as the crucial watershed in Augustine's theological development, and there is good reason to do so. As Augustine himself observed in his *Retractations*, when he wrote his two books *To Simplicianus* (the successor of Ambrose, bishop of Milan) in response to questions on the apostle Paul, he had finally grasped the overwhelming power of grace in freeing humans from their sinfulness.[2] The best-known fruit of this conversion of 396 was the *Confessions*, which presented Augustine's reading of his own early life in terms of the inexorable attraction of divine grace.[3]

Why, then, should I start my account a decade after the *Confessions* and nearly fifteen years after his books *To Simplicianus*? The reason is that there appears to be a cluster of writings from around 410 onward in which Augustine began to reflect in a new way on the nature of human embodiment, and these reflections, I argue, had a profound impact on his treatment of the problem of evil, particularly in its manifestation as human, moral evil. These reflections are found initially in his *Literal Commentary on Genesis* (esp. book 9, composed around the year 410), but the repercussions of this development can be most clearly seen in the middle books of his *City of God* (books 11–14), composed between 417 and 420.[4] My aim in this essay is to suggest that Augustine's new reflections on human embodiment—which show a more positive view of the body and its relationship with the soul—gave a new and, this time, more permanent shape to his grappling with the problem of evil.

1. Cf. John M. Rist, *Augustine: Ancient Thought Baptized* (Cambridge: Cambridge University Press, 1994), 261, who observes that the question of the origin of evil "was the most important and most enduring challenge to Augustine throughout his life."

2. Augustine, *Retractationum libri II* 2.1.1 (CCSL 57:89–90): "In cuius quaestionis solutione laboratum est quidem pro libero arbitrio uoluntatis humanae, sed uicit dei gratia." *To Simplicianus* = *De diuersis quaestionibus ad Simplicianum*.

3. Cf. Robert A. Markus, *Conversion and Disenchantment in Augustine's Spiritual Career*, Saint Augustine Lecture 1984 (Villanova, PA: Villanova University Press, 1989), 22, who states: "His rereading of Saint Paul in the mid-390s is one of the great divides of Augustine's intellectual development. It marks the end of his belief in human self-determination and the beginnings of the theology of grace he would deploy against Pelagius."

4. I follow the dates given by Goulven Madec, *Introduction aux "Révisions" et à la lecture des oeuvres de saint Augustin* (Paris: Institut d'Études Augustiniennes, 1996), 162–64.

God and Evil

Before proceeding to that critical decade in Augustine's thought, I observe that several features of his teaching on God and evil never changed. There are certain options that Augustine always considered unacceptable, and on these matters his thought remained consistent from his earliest to his latest writings. These ideas will be very familiar to most of you, since they are found in the *Confessions* and were commonplaces in the Christian literature inspired by Platonic philosophy.[5] Yet they are worth recalling here because they provide the stable framework within which the developments I later sketch took shape.

The first of these points is that God can never do evil in any way. By definition, God is supreme Goodness. As Augustine put it in his early treatise *Free Will*, "To hold God supreme is most truly the beginning of piety; and no one holds Him supreme who does not believe him to be omnipotent and absolutely changeless, Creator of all good things, which He Himself transcends in excellence, and the most just Ruler, as well, of all that He has created."[6] After struggling in his earlier years with the Manichaean notion of the good God as vulnerable to invasion by the forces of evil, Augustine was determined never again to allow that the transcendent God might be affected in any way by the presence or persistence of evil.[7] While modern theologians might be inclined to deal with the problem of evil by positing either mutability or passibility within God, this was an option that Augustine would not entertain, and this was largely a legacy of his anti-Manichaean (i.e., Platonist) philosophical mind-set.

Another position that Augustine held as axiomatic, at least from the time of his conversion to the teachings of the Platonists, was that all created beings, by virtue of their creation by a good God, must be good. Even though corruption might harm or diminish the good in created things, in their essential being they remain good. As Augustine put it in the *Confessions*, even the possibility of corruption showed that created things were good, for if they had no good to corrupt, they could not be corrupted: "Therefore as long as

need good to have bad.

5. Parallels to all of the points in the next three paragraphs can be found in the writings of Gregory of Nyssa. See, e.g., his *Oratio catechetica* 5–6.

6. Augustine, *De libero arbitrio* 2.12, trans. Anna S. Benjamin and L. H. Hackstaff, *Saint Augustine: On Free Choice of the Will*, Library of Liberal Arts (New York: Macmillan, 1964), 6; cf. Augustine, *De natura boni* 1: "The Supreme Good beyond all others is God. It is thereby unchangeable good, truly eternal, truly immortal"; trans. John H. S. Burleigh, *Augustine: Earlier Writings*, LCC (Philadelphia: Westminster, 1953), 326.

7. In *Confessions* (= *Conf.*) 7.1.1, Augustine says that even prior to reading the *libri Platonici* he was convinced that God must be "incorruptible and inviolable and unchangeable."

they exist, they are good."[8] The corollary of Augustine's recognition of the essential goodness of all created things (that is, of all that exists) was the insight—again derived from Neoplatonic sources—that evil could not have existence as a "substance." Again, Augustine put it succinctly in the *Confessions*: "Accordingly, whatever things exist are good, and the evil into whose origins I was inquiring is not a substance, for if it were a substance it would be good. Either it would be an incorruptible substance, a great good indeed, or a corruptible substance, which could be corrupted only if it were good."[9] All being, Augustine insisted, is good by virtue of its being.

This second principle of Augustine's led inexorably to a third: if God and all existing things are good, then evil itself must be a "nothing," a lack or a privation of the being or goodness of a thing. In the case of rational creatures (humans or angels), this loss of goodness can be attributed only to a movement of the will, to a "perversity" in the literal sense of a "thorough turning away" from the source of being and goodness that is the supreme substance or God.[10] The possibility of a turn to the worse arose because all things were created out of nothing and were, by that fact, mutable. But the actual defection from good was the fault of the will. From his earliest to his latest writings, Augustine always insisted that the cause of evil could be neither God nor the created world itself but only the perverse will of a rational creature that chooses to reject or turn away from the divine source of its own being.[11]

If these three points formed the stable framework of Augustine's metaphysics of evil, the stability of his views ended there. For in the first two decades of his literary career—between the dialogues at Cassiciacum (386) and the *Literal Commentary on Genesis* (begun 405)—Augustine's thinking on the nature of this perverse will underwent significant development. In a brilliant (and, I think, still underappreciated) essay, Robert A. Markus has traced the evolution of Augustine's reflections on the primal sin—pride—that began

---

8. Augustine, *Conf.* 7.12.18, trans. Henry Chadwick, *Saint Augustine: Confessions* (New York: Oxford University Press, 1991), 124; this translation is cited as Chadwick.

9. Augustine, *Conf.* 7.12.18, trans. Chadwick, 124–25. For a later statement of this view, see *De Genesi ad litteram* 8.14.31.

10. Cf. Augustine, *Conf.* 7.16.22.

11. As J. Patout Burns has observed, this point, which Augustine first developed at length in *De libero arbitrio*, was already a step away from the positions of Ambrose and other Platonists: Augustine "separated himself from the tradition, however, by insisting that the temptation was not related to the bodily condition of humanity. . . . Augustine refused to admit a conflict between mind and bodily appetite in the original world order. He insisted that this division arises from and punishes a sin of the spirit." See his essay "Augustine on the Origin and Progress of Evil," in *The Ethics of St. Augustine*, ed. William S. Babcock, JRE Studies in Religious Ethics 3 (Atlanta: Scholars Press, 1991), 67–85, esp. 77.

with the devil and eventually fractured both the human heart and human community. Building on the work of Oliver O'Donovan, Markus has argued that Augustine's understanding of pride changed in important ways between his writing of the early philosophical dialogues and the composition of the *Literal Commentary on Genesis*.[12] Although pride was always the primal sin for Augustine, in the early works he tended to view pride as a violation of the divine order of the cosmos, a deliberate turning away from higher to lower goods. This perspective is still evident in the *Confessions* where Augustine describes evil thus: "I inquired what wickedness is; and I did not find a substance but a perversity of will twisted away from the highest substance, you, O God, towards inferior things, rejecting its own inner life and swelling with external matter."[13] *Pg 150.*

By the time of the *Literal Commentary*, according to Markus, Augustine's understanding of pride had shifted from this hierarchical concern to a more social one. Pride had become a perverse self-love that seeks its private good over the common good. As Markus has put it:

> Augustine's thought in his fifties [when he composed the *Literal Commentary on Genesis*] began to be dominated by the notion that the roots of sin lie in the self's retreat into a privacy which is deprivation: the self is deprived of community. All community—with God, with one's fellows, and even with one's own self—is fatally ruptured by sin. The radical flaw in human nature is now transcribed in terms of a retreat into a closed-off self.[14]

The social character of Augustine's new understanding of pride is especially evident in the following passage from the *Literal Commentary on Genesis*, to which Markus has pointed. Here Augustine described this new sense of pride (and its opposite) as two types of love, which in turn have formed "two cities":

> There are, then, two loves, of which one is holy, the other unclean; one turned towards the neighbor, the other centered on self; one looking to the common good, keeping in view the society of saints in heaven, the other bringing the common good under its own power, arrogantly looking to domination; one subject to God, the other rivaling Him; one tranquil, the other tempestuous; one peaceful, the other seditious; . . . one wishing for its neighbor what it wishes for itself, the other seeking to subject its neighbor to itself; one looking

12. Markus, *Conversion and Disenchantment*, 24–42, acknowledging his debt to Oliver O'Donovan, *The Problem of Self-Love in Augustine* (New Haven: Yale University Press, 1980).

13. Augustine, *Conf.* 7.16.22, trans. Chadwick, 126.

14. Markus, *Conversion and Disenchantment*, 31–32.

for its neighbor's advantage in ruling its neighbor, the other looking for its own advantage.[15]

These two loves, Augustine suggested, created two cities: one, the city of the just; the other, the city of the wicked. In his *Literal Commentary*, Augustine even promises to write someday about these two cities, "if the Lord is willing," a promise he was able to keep during the next decade as he composed *The City of God*.

What, you may ask, does all this have to do with "evil, suffering, and embodiment," the topic of my discussion? Quite a lot, I would say. In his account of the shift in Augustine's understanding of pride, Markus has offered some tantalizing hints—though only hints—of another development in Augustine's thought, one that pertains directly to the question of evil and embodiment:

> The aim of the whole discussion of sin and pride in Book XIV of the *City of God* is to shift the stress from sin as the result of the soul's entanglement in the flesh to sin as the result of the will's own decision. Augustine registers this shift by the strenuous effort he makes to establish that the biblical category of the "flesh" is not sensual indulgence, not a case, in other words, of the superior allowing itself to be seduced by the inferior, but a fault within the mind itself. Sin is a matter of pride rather than sensuality.[16]

These comments of Robert Markus point toward another development in Augustine's thought: Augustine's new understanding of pride as the perverse choice of a private good over a public one was accompanied (perhaps even preceded) by an increased emphasis on the soul—not the body—as primarily responsible for sin. Augustine's exoneration of the body from responsibility for sin, while not entirely new in 410, was part of a far-reaching revolution in his thought that first reached its full expression in the later books of the *Literal Commentary on Genesis*. This new emphasis on the original harmony of body and soul, then, became the context within which Augustine treated the problem of evil and human suffering. In Augustine's new vision—the vision of the decade from 410 to 420—all human evil and suffering came to be seen as a fracturing of the original unity and harmony of creation, a

15. *De Genesi ad litteram* 11.15.20, trans. John Hammond Taylor, SJ, *St. Augustine: The Literal Meaning of Genesis*, ACW 42 (New York: Newman, 1982), 147; this translation is cited as Taylor.

16. Markus, *Conversion and Disenchantment*, 32. See also his essay "*De civitate Dei*: Pride and the Common Good," in *Proceedings of the PMR [Patristic, Medieval, and Renaissance] Conference 12/13* (Villanova, PA: Augustinian Historical Institute, Villanova University, 1987–88), 9: "Sin is pride rather than sensuality; and sensuality [is] the consequence and the penalty of pride."

gaping fissure between body and soul, caused by the pride of the soul. I first say a word about this new positive sense of embodiment and then turn to the question of the impact of sin upon it.

Creation and Embodiment

Numerous scholars have noticed that Augustine's *Literal Commentary on Genesis* marked a significant turning point in his understanding of the body and its place in God's original creation. Those who have studied the development of his views on sex and marriage, such as Peter Brown and Elizabeth Clark, have observed that it is only in book 9 of the *Literal Commentary* that Augustine finally accepted the notion that God originally intended Adam and Eve to "increase and multiply" in a physical way even before their sin. This was a significant step away from some of the Greek fathers and away from some of Augustine's own Latin contemporaries, who tended to consider procreation to be a consequence of the fall, merely an act of compensation to humanity for the mortality brought about by sin. As Peter Brown has observed, after the *Literal Commentary* "Augustine invariably wrote of Adam and Eve as physical human beings, endowed with the same bodies and sexual characteristics as ourselves. God had created them for the joys of society. . . . Compared with the notions of many of his most vocal contemporaries, it was a singularly sociable and full-blooded vision."[17]

Other scholars, more concerned with philosophical questions, have pointed to the years around 410 as the period when Augustine began to emphasize that a natural relationship existed between the soul and the body, an intimate union analogous to marriage. John Rist, for example, has observed that in *Letter 140*, composed in 412, "Augustine spoke of the 'sweet marriage bond [*dulce consortium*] of body and soul,'" citing Ephesians 5:29 ("No one hates his own flesh" [NABRE]).[18] In contrast to the Platonism of Porphyry—who demanded that everyone must "flee the body" (*omne corpus fugiendum est*)—and even repudiating his own earlier infatuation with Neoplatonism,[19] the later Augustine

17. Peter Brown, *The Body and Society: Men, Women, and Sexual Renunciation in Early Christianity* (New York: Columbia University Press, 1988), 400–401. Essential on this question are the essays of Elizabeth A. Clark, "'Adam's Only Companion': Augustine and the Early Christian Debate on Marriage," *Recherches Augustiniennes* 21 (1986): 139–62; "Heresy, Asceticism, Adam, and Eve: Interpretations of Genesis 1–3 in the Later Latin Fathers," in her *Ascetic Piety and Women's Faith: Essays on Late Ancient Christianity* (Lewiston, NY: Edwin Mellen, 1986), 353–85.

18. Rist, *Augustine*, 111.

19. See *De civitate Dei* 10.29, where Augustine attacks Porphyry on this point; and Rist, *Augustine*, 97.

insisted that a human is a true union of the two "substances" of body and soul, a union best characterized by the word "person" (*persona*). Indeed, as Rist has argued, by the year 411, "Augustine became almost as hostile to 'spiritual' reductionism as he had been since his conversion to 'material' reductionism."[20]

Even the scholars who accept the theories of Robert O'Connell—that for much of his life Augustine held that human embodiment resulted from a "fall" of the soul into the body—acknowledge that a radically different teaching is present in the *Literal Commentary on Genesis*.[21] Again, Rist has summarized this point nicely: "According to the *Literal Commentary*, Adam had an 'animal' body before the fall, that is, he was a mixture of soul and body and so did not fall *into* body. His fall was *with* his body [emphasis added], and so in a different way was ours. . . . The *Confessions* may be the latest major work of Augustine in which he thought that we are souls *fallen into* [Rist's emphasis] rather than with a body."[22] The consensus of contemporary scholarship is that the key insight in this new phase of Augustine's development is that body and soul belong together and that this was God's intention from the beginning of creation.

In the remainder of this essay I take this scholarly consensus as a point of departure to explore the implications of Augustine's new understanding of embodiment for his teaching on evil and its influence. I suggest that there are three areas of human experience in which Augustine tended to emphasize the impact of sin: sex, politics, and death. By examining these three examples of how evil has affected human life, particularly in its embodied character, I believe we can arrive at a richer and more nuanced account of his teaching than most previous commentators have recognized.

Sex and Sin

It would be a great understatement to claim that Augustine's views on sex have attracted negative attention from some modern scholars. In books such as Ute Ranke-Heinemann's *Eunuchs for the Kingdom*, Augustine's teaching

20. Rist, *Augustine*, 101; on 100, Rist points to *Letter 137*, composed in 411, as the point at which Augustine first uses the term "person" for the body-soul relationship.

21. In his recent study of the O'Connell thesis, *Saint Augustine and the Fall of the Soul: Beyond O'Connell and His Critics* (Washington, DC: Catholic University of America Press, 2006), 211, Ronnie J. Rombs has remarked: "The later books of the *De Genesi ad litteram* and *The City of God* reveal a mature Christian metaphysics within which there is no place for a Plotinian ontological fall. Individuation and plurality, Augustine insists, are the result of the creative will of God."

22. Rist, *Augustine*, 112.

on sexual desire and sin has been subjected to nearly systematic misrepresentation. We are told by Ranke-Heinemann, for example, that the man "who fused Christianity together with hatred of sex and pleasure into a systematic unity was the greatest of the Church Fathers, St. Augustine. . . . Augustine was the father of a fifteen-hundred-year-long anxiety about sex and an enduring hostility to it. He dramatizes the fear of sexual pleasure, equating pleasure with perdition in such a way that anyone who tries to follow his train of thought will have the sense of being trapped in a nightmare."[23] It is difficult to square these harsh judgments with anything that Augustine actually says, especially if one takes seriously the developments that began with the *Literal Commentary on Genesis*. Augustine hated neither sex nor pleasure, and more than most of his contemporaries, he taught that both sex and pleasure were good creations of a good God.[24]

What Ranke-Heinemann and other critics of Augustine have in mind is the fact that Augustine did come to believe that the sin of Adam and Eve had damaged human nature and that one symptom of this damage was a disorder in the way that sexual desire, or libido, now operates in humans. This is a topic to which I turn in a moment. But it is critical first to look closely at Augustine's teaching on the creation of sex and the body in order to properly understand the impact of sin upon them.

I begin with a passage from *The City of God*, in which Augustine describes the original reason why God created all humans from one. Noticing the difference between the way God created other animals (several members of the species all at once) and the way God created humans (all from one), Augustine argues that the reason for the latter is to produce a solid social bond—first between the original couple, and then among their descendants:

> God therefore created only one single man: not, certainly, that he might be alone and bereft of human society, but that, by this means, the unity of society and the bond of concord might be commended to him more forcefully, mankind being bound together not only by similarity of nature, but [also] by the affection of kinship. Indeed, God did not even create the woman who was to be united with the man in the same way as He created the man. Rather, it pleased Him to create her out of the man, so that the human race might derive entirely from the one man.[25]

23. Ute Ranke-Heinemann, *Eunuchs for the Kingdom of Heaven: Women, Sexuality and the Catholic Church* (New York: Doubleday, 1990), 75, 78.

24. See, e.g., *De bono coniugali* 16.18, where Augustine explicitly acknowledges that the pleasure accompanying eating and sex is, in itself, not morally problematic.

25. *De civitate Dei* 12.12, trans. R. W. Dyson, *Augustine: The City of God against the Pagans*, Cambridge Texts in the History of Political Thought (Cambridge: Cambridge University

Here Augustine stresses that the purpose of the creation of all humans from one was precisely to establish a social bond characterized by "unity" and "concord," first between Adam and Eve, and then among all the members of the human race. Even though God foreknew that humans would sin and that human society would become more fractured by wars than any animal kingdom ever could be, Augustine insisted that "God had caused the human race to be derived from one man, in order to show how highly he prizes unity in a multitude."[26] No matter how discordant human society may become, Augustine argued, the example of Adam should stand as a reminder of that original unity, "either to prevent discord from coming into existence, or to heal it where it already exists."[27] Again, as he puts it in book 12 of *The City of God*: "God chose to create one individual for the propagation of many, so that men should thus be admonished to preserve unity among their whole multitude. Moreover, the fact that the woman was made for him from his side signifies clearly enough how dear the union between a man and his wife should be."[28] For the later Augustine, it is clear that the purpose of the creation of man and woman as physical and physically sexed beings was precisely to establish community—both personal and social—in which harmony and unity might flourish. This was the purpose of God's original blessing and command to "increase and multiply" (Gen. 1:28 Vulgate), Augustine said, and most importantly, this blessing has not been abrogated, despite the pernicious effects of sin. As Augustine states in the *Literal Commentary on Genesis*, "It is by virtue of this blessing that the earth is now filled with human beings who subdue it."[29] So much for Ute Ranke-Heinemann and Augustine's "enduring hostility" to sex!

But, of course, something did go wrong, according to Genesis, and we cannot escape Augustine's novel reading of the fall and its impact on the bodies and sexuality of the first humans. What went wrong, according to Augustine, was precisely a fracture of the original unity and harmony between body and soul that characterized the first humans. Pride was at the root of the first sin, and for Augustine, this pride led to disobedience. Adam and Eve were commanded not to eat of the "tree of the knowledge of good and evil." There was nothing noxious about the fruit of this tree itself, Augustine insists. What was evil was the disobedience of those who violated the command. Since the first parents were placed in a state of dependence on God, it was only fitting that

---

Press, 1998), 533; this translation is cited as Dyson. Already in *De bono coniugali*, Augustine had articulated this theme.

26. Augustine, *De civitate Dei* (= *Civ.*) 12.23, trans. Dyson, 534.
27. Augustine, *Civ.* 12.28, trans. Dyson, 539.
28. Augustine, *Civ.* 12.28, trans. Dyson, 539; cf. the similar view in *Civ.* 14.1.
29. Augustine, *De Genesi ad litteram* (= *Gen. litt.*) 9.3.5, trans. Taylor, 73.

they should have been given some commandment so that they could exercise the virtue of obedience and thereby please the Lord. "I can truthfully say," Augustine states, "that this is the only virtue of every rational creature who lives his life under God's rule, and that the fundamental and gravest vice is the overweening pride by which one wishes to have independence to his own ruin, and the name of this vice is disobedience. There would not, therefore, be any way for a man to realize and feel that he is subject to the Lord unless he is given some command."[30]

What follows, of course, is disobedience, and this disobedience proceeds from the arrogance of a creature that tries to be like God. Augustine's own account of this fall is worth repeating because it stresses the element of the first sin (the willful disobedience) that was so repugnant to him:

> It is impossible for the will of a man not to come tumbling down on him with a thunderous and devastating crash if he so exalts it as to prefer it to that of the One who is his superior. This is what man has experienced in his contempt of God's command, and by this experience he has learned the difference between good and evil, that is, the good of obedience and the evil of disobedience, namely, of pride and contumacy, of the perverse imitation of God, and of pernicious liberty. The tree which was the occasion of this experience for man received its name from what happened there. . . . For we would not feel evil except by experience, since there would be no evil unless we had committed it.[31]

For Augustine, the primal sin was the free choice of Adam and Eve to reject their creaturely dependence on God and to opt for their own private good. By attempting to take their salvation into their own hands, so to speak, they had rejected the grace of God and turned in upon themselves. The effect of their disobedience was to lose the grace that God had given to preserve their bodies from death and to live in peace with themselves and all the rest of creation. And here we have come to the problem of embodiment.

Vulnerability to death, for Augustine, was not the only effect of the sin of Adam and Eve. At the moment of their sin, the first parents experienced another wound as well: a disordered motion or movement that he calls the "concupiscence of the flesh." It was the presence of this new impulse in their bodies that caused Adam and Eve to feel shame at their nakedness. As Augustine put it, "As soon, then, as they had violated the precept, they were completely naked, interiorly deserted by the grace which they had offended by pride and arrogant love of their own independence. Casting their eyes on their

---

30. Augustine, *Gen. litt.* 8.6.12, trans. Taylor, 42.
31. Augustine, *Gen. litt.* 8.14.31, trans. Taylor, 53–54.

bodies, they felt a movement of concupiscence which they had not known."[32] Not only did the bodies of Adam and Eve become liable to disease and death, like other animals, but they also became "subject to the same drive by which there is in animals a desire to copulate and thus provide for offspring to take the place of those that die."[33] Although the sin of Adam and Eve in no way involved sexual relations, the effects of this sin were felt directly in the "animal instinct" (*bestiale motum*) now present in their bodies.

We are here at the crux of the problem of sin and embodiment that has troubled so many modern readers of Augustine. Is sexual desire, as it is now experienced in the human body, something evil, a symptom or product of the original sin of Adam and Eve? This was precisely the issue at the center of Augustine's last great controversy with the Pelagian bishop Julian of Eclanum, during the final decade of his life (420–30). I do not wish to engage in a detailed analysis of that conflict, nor do I wish to defend Augustine's account of the corruption of human nature. But I do point out that Augustine's teaching is not as outrageous as it first appears, especially when it is viewed in the light of his fuller understanding of creation and embodiment. First, we must acknowledge that Augustine always maintained that the original purpose of sex, the procreation of children, remained something good. As I noted earlier, he explicitly stated that the original blessing to "increase and multiply" remained in force even after original sin. Second, it is important to notice that Augustine never said that the "animal instinct" (the *bestiale motum*) was something evil in itself. Humans have animal bodies, and now that these bodies have become mortal, it is good and "natural" for people to experience the instinct for procreation. What Augustine could not accept, what he saw as "evil" and an effect of original sin, was the way in which these instincts assert themselves and are experienced apart from any assent by the mind or will. In other words, it was the fractured state of the human person—the tension, if you will, between the body and the soul—that was the real "evil" brought about by sin. In the case of sex (Augustine liked to use the example of male erections), the natural instincts even controlled the bodily parts apart from the consent of the mind or will (as in the case of impotence). This, to Augustine, was a sure sign that some unfortunate chasm had opened up between the body and the soul, one that was not part of God's original intention for the human race. This split within the person—the soul's loss of control over the body in this crucial area of human experience—was, for Augustine, a just punishment (though a self-inflicted punishment) for the

---

32. Augustine, *Gen. litt.* 11.31.41, trans. Taylor, 164.
33. Augustine, *Gen. litt.* 11.32.42, trans. Taylor, 165.

pride and disobedience of Adam and Eve. By opting for autonomy, the first humans had lost control even over themselves.[34]

But there is yet a third consideration that should somewhat temper our judgments on Augustine's teaching, one that will lead into my next topic, the impact of sin on human social relations. When Augustine spoke of the "lust" or "concupiscence of the flesh," he sometimes meant specifically this experience of disruptive sexual desire. Quite often, however, the "lust of the flesh against the spirit" referred to any one of a number of other disordered impulses of the human heart. In book 14 of *The City of God*, Augustine devoted a lengthy discussion to the issue of what it means to "live according to the flesh" and to "live according to the Spirit." Starting with Paul's list of vices in Galatians 5:19–21, he observed that the apostle included many vices pertaining strictly to the mind and not involving fleshly pleasures at all, such as idolatry, hatred, wrath, and sedition.[35] The devil himself, Augustine declared, is the prime example of living "according to the flesh," yet he is not a physical being at all and is supremely proud and envious.[36] The "works of the flesh," Augustine concluded, cannot refer primarily to bodily experiences but must refer to the corruption caused by the prior sin of the soul. To live "according to the flesh," therefore, is to live "according to oneself" (*secundum se*), that is, according to humanity rather than according to God. It is, essentially, the vice of pride.[37]

We have returned here to the point raised earlier by Markus: if pride lies at the root of a vicious self-love—one that ignores the common good and looks to domination—then, for Augustine, the fractured unity of body and soul experienced in sexual desire was merely a microcosm (though also the starting point) of the broader social fractures wrought by sin. It was practically inevitable, therefore, that Augustine's new insights into sin and embodiment in his *Literal Commentary on Genesis* would eventually lead him to reflect on the social and political dimensions of sin. In other words, *The City of God* was, quite literally, the logical outcome of the *Literal Commentary on Genesis*. So let us briefly follow Augustine's logic as he moved from sexual to social sin.

Sin and Society

In the remainder of this essay, I can offer nothing like a full account of an Augustinian political theology or full exposition of *The City of God*. I can,

---

34. Cf. Augustine, *Civ.* 14.15.
35. Ibid., 14.2.
36. Ibid., 14.3.
37. Ibid., 14.3–4; cf. Markus, *Conversion and Disenchantment*, 32.

however, point to certain ways in which the issue of embodiment is woven into Augustine's account of the progress of social sin in *The City of God*. We must begin with the recognition that the very separation of the sexual and the social may be an anachronism. In the opening paragraphs of *The City of God*, Augustine describes the earthly city (the community of those seduced by pride) in terms that recall the self-inflicted punishment of sexual concupiscence: "That city, . . . when it seeks dominion, is itself dominated by the lust for dominion [*libido dominandi*] even though all nations serve it."[38] Later, in book 14, he repeats similar sentiments: "In the earthly city princes are as much dominated by the lust for domination as the nations which they subdue are by them."[39] Margaret Miles once observed that the tendency to separate the "lust of the flesh" in a sexual sense (*libido carnalis*) from the "lust for domination" (*libido dominandi*) is a recent, modern invention. As Miles argues, Augustine "did not assume or envision any division between them."[40] That is to say, the *libido dominandi* of the earthly city is merely the social extension of the more personal lust of sexual desire. The fracture between the body and soul, therefore, is writ large in the fracture of the body politic.

Augustine envisioned clear parallels between the two forms of lust. After Eden, both social life and sexual life have become problematic. Though both are grounded in the original, creative will of God, both have become corrupted by evil. While both continue to function as goods within God's providence, both the sexual and the social lives of humans have become weakened by self-love and pride. Social unity and harmony, as we saw earlier, were the original purpose of human procreation, and that purpose has not changed, despite the damage done by sin. But social life, like sexual life, is shot through with the effects of self-willed agents, just as the body has been riddled with competing lusts and desires.[41] And yet, as Augustine indicated, both social life and sexual life have become essential instruments in the process of salvation, for God willed that the Savior should be born from the people of Israel, who

38. Augustine, *Civ.* 1, preface.

39. Ibid., 14.28.

40. Margaret R. Miles, *Augustine on the Body*, AAR Dissertation Series 31 (Missoula, MT: Scholars Press, 1979), 68. Miles acknowledges and cites the foundational work of Gerald Bonner, "Libido and Concupiscentia in Augustine," StPatr 6 (1972): 303–14.

41. The connection between the manifestations of evil in the sexual and social spheres is evident, one might argue, even today. For example, the English expression "sexual conquests" implicitly acknowledges a violent or at least manipulative element in sexual promiscuity. Even more tragically, the use of rape as a weapon of war to humiliate conquered populations attests to the overlap between sexual and political expressions of evil.

had been propagated by sexual intercourse.[42] As Augustine put it in book 19 of *The City of God*, "How could the City of God have first arisen and progressed along its way, and how could it achieve its proper end, if the life of the saints were not social?"[43]

A concrete example will help to illustrate the point. According to Augustine, the original reason for sexual copulation was to produce human beings with ties of kinship (of blood), so that the bonds of society would be stronger than if people had been created independently of one another. But Augustine was not encouraged by the history of the first siblings. The first founder of the earthly city was a fratricide. Overcome by envy, Cain slew his brother Abel, who was a citizen of the eternal city. To Augustine, it was no surprise that this crime became what he calls an "archetype" that was mirrored at the founding of Rome in the slaying of Remus by his twin brother, Romulus.[44] Both cases of fratricide show the power of envy and self-will (the "lust of the flesh") to sever the bond of kinship created by sexual union. As Augustine noted at a later point in *The City of God*, citing the words of Cicero, "There is no treachery more insidious than that concealed under a pretense of duty or by the name of kinship."[45]

Augustine could have left the matter there, but the lesson he ultimately drew from the stories of the two fratricides is that social strife will exist even among those who are good and between members of the heavenly city. In this life, even within a good person, "the flesh lusts against the Spirit, and the Spirit lusts against the flesh." As a result, social conflicts will remain, even among those who are destined to be saints. "While they are still making their way towards perfection," Augustine writes, "and have not yet attained it, there can be strife among them inasmuch as any good man may strive against another because of that part of him with which he also strives against himself."[46] The internal division caused by sin, "the concupiscence of the flesh," simultaneously cuts more deeply and extends more broadly than the fissure between the body and the soul evident in disordered sexual desire. For Augustine, the struggle to turn from the "lust of the flesh" to the "lust of the Spirit," to move from self-satisfaction to joy in another, to embrace the common good rather than the lust for domination—that is a lifelong task, one that can be accomplished

---

42. See Augustine, *Contra Secundinum Manichaeum* 22 (CSEL 25.2:940): "Since it was necessary that Christ come in the flesh, both the marriage of Sarah and the virginity of Mary served to propagate that flesh."

43. Augustine, *Civ.* 19.5, trans. Dyson, 925.

44. Augustine, *Civ.* 15.5.

45. Augustine, *Civ.* 15.5, quoting Cicero, *In Verrem* 2.1.13.

46. Augustine, *Civ.* 15.5, trans. Dyson, 640–41.

only with the aid of divine grace. In this life, social harmony and peace, like the integration of sexual desires, remain something incomplete, the object of eschatological hope, not present possession.

Sin and Death

This brings me to the final example of Augustine's teaching on the impact of sin on the body: death. Fortunately, given the limits of my essay, this topic can be treated more briefly because Augustine's thought in this area is clearer than on the earlier topics. Moreover, the question of Augustine's view of death has been the object of some notable studies.[47] Here, too, we are dealing with a matter in which there has been some development in Augustine's thought. In his early writings, when he was still very much under the influence of Platonic philosophy, Augustine echoed the philosophical tradition in regarding death as a good. In an early work, *The Greatness of the Soul*, Augustine could speak of death as "the sheer flight and escape from this body, . . . now yearned for as the greatest boon."[48] By identifying the death of the body as a good, Augustine gave his assent to two classic Platonic teachings: that the soul is the true identity of the person and that the body is the source of the evils experienced by the soul. The teaching had been given Christian approbation by Ambrose, who wrote an entire book, *The Good of Death* (*De bono mortis*), in which he essentially echoed the Platonic teaching.

By the time he composed book 13 of *The City of God*, which has been called "a short treatise on the subject of death,"[49] Augustine had moved far beyond this position. As we have seen, at least from the time of the *Literal Commentary on Genesis*, Augustine had come to accept the union of the body and soul as constituting one "person." Moreover, he now held that the evils suffered by the soul were not the result of its imprisonment in the body, as the Platonic tradition (in both its Christian and non-Christian varieties) held. For Augustine, the evils of the soul derive from its own willful self-assertion in abandoning its union with God. After the fall, the coexistence of body and

---

47. Éric Rebillard, *In hora mortis: Évolution de la pastorale chrétienne de la mort au IVe et Ve siècles dans l'Occident latin* (Rome: École française de Rome, Palais Farnèse, 1994); John Cavadini, "Ambrose and Augustine *De bono mortis*," in *The Limits of Ancient Christianity: Essays on Late Antique Thought and Culture in Honor of R. A. Markus*, ed. William E. Klingshirn and Mark Vessey (Ann Arbor: University of Michigan Press, 1999), 232–49.

48. Augustine, *De quantitate animae* 76, cited in Miles, *Augustine on the Body*, 106; cf. Robert J. O'Connell, *St. Augustine's Early Theory of Man, A.D. 386–391* (Cambridge, MA: Belknap Press of Harvard University Press, 1968), 204, who notes that "the *Dialogues of Cassiciacum* regularly refer to death as the moment when the soul is liberated from the toils of the body."

49. Cavadini, "Ambrose and Augustine," 232.

soul was characterized by sufferings of many kinds, which Augustine took to be a just punishment for sin. But it was sin, and not the union of body and soul in itself, that caused these sufferings. These reflections led Augustine to a new and decidedly un-Platonic approach to death.[50] Now he came to see the separation of the body and soul as a genuine evil, suffered by humanity as a result of original sin.

In *The City of God*, Augustine directly addresses the character of death in the light of his new emphasis on the original and natural harmony of body and soul:

> As regards the death of the body, then—that is, the separation of the soul from the body—it is a good to no one while those who are said to be dying are suffering it. For a sensation of anguish, contrary to nature, is produced by the force that tears apart the two things which had been conjoined and interwoven during life; and this sensation persists until there is a complete cessation of all that feeling which was present by reason of the union of soul and flesh.[51]

Even when circumstances intervene to shorten the period of suffering involved in death—for example, a swift blow to the body or some other quick snatching away of the soul—Augustine insists that death must be seen as an evil and indeed as a punishment for the primal sin. In Augustine's mature reflections on death, I argue, we have another example of the way in which his new thought on embodiment led to a reconsideration of the impact of evil. Like the existence of sexual concupiscence, death fractures the original fellowship of body and soul. The separation of body and soul, like the treachery of siblings or the disorder of sexual desire, is something "contrary to nature," a perversion of the original creation. It is an evil, though one that will be redressed ultimately at the resurrection of the dead.

Conclusion

At the beginning of this study, I observed that one of the constant elements in Augustine's teaching on evil is his insistence that God cannot be the cause of evil. Only the willful perversity of a rational creature, a turning of the will away from God, can bring about the defects in human nature that we all experience as real. The problem, one might say, is anthropological, not theological. The consequence of the original disobedience, Augustine believed,

---

50. According to Cavadini, Augustine's approach to death in *Civ.* 13 was a deliberate repudiation of Ambrose, *De bono mortis*.

51. Augustine, *Civ.* 13.6, trans. Dyson, 547.

was the disobedience of one's own body, manifest in sickness, aging, and, finally death: "For what is man's misery if not simply his own disobedience to himself, . . . that is, his very mind, and even his lower part, his flesh, does not obey his will. Even against his will his mind is often troubled; and his flesh endures pain, grows old, and dies, and suffers all manner of things which we should not suffer against our will if our nature were in every way and in all its parts obedient to our will."[52] For Augustine, the alienation of sin is evidenced, par excellence, in the alienation of the soul from the flesh. Hope and healing, therefore, could come only from another incarnation.

It is paradoxical that Augustine the former Manichaean and Augustine the convert to Neoplatonism should eventually develop a theology of evil and suffering that virtually requires salvation by means of the embodiment of God, the incarnation. For Augustine, Jesus is the model of divine humility, taking on our feeble humanity and healing its pride. For Augustine, Jesus is the one example of a fully integrated union of body and soul, a "person" in the full sense of the word. In *The City of God*, Augustine can even present the emotions that Jesus experienced—grief, anger, joy—as proof that emotions can be natural and good.[53] We should remember this side of Augustine when we hear him dismissed (as he so often is) as a Platonist or a crypto-Manichaean.

Finally, by way of evaluating the relevance of Augustine's theology, I shall first state the obvious. Many features of his teaching are no longer tenable: our contemporary understanding of evolution and the origin of species requires a radical rethinking of the mythic characters of Adam and Eve and their contribution to human evil and suffering. But, again paradoxically, the success of contemporary science and the failure of Augustine's science may lead to a better understanding of the biblical story and a chastened reappropriation of Augustine's theology. For the myth of Adam and Eve was never really "about" the natural origins of the human race. It was, as Augustine saw, a story about who humans are *now* in their alienation from God, community, and themselves. We still have much to learn about Genesis and ourselves from Augustine of Hippo.

---

52. Augustine, *Civ.* 14.15, trans. Dyson, 612–13.

53. Augustine, *Civ.* 14.9. In this chapter Augustine also argues that the Stoic idea of living "without passion" (*apatheia*) is a corruption of true humanity.

12

THEODORE OF MOPSUESTIA
AND THE PEDAGOGY OF DESTRUCTION

ERIC PHILLIPS

It is a commonplace in patristic theology, and even in the Bible, that God uses suffering to get people's attention and spur them on to repentance and holiness. Also fairly common is the related but more unsettling idea that God sometimes will *destroy* a group of sinners outright, while sparing others so that they might learn from the catastrophe. In the course of his commentaries on the Psalms and the Minor Prophets, Theodore of Mopsuestia develops this second theme from an ad hoc observation into a characteristic feature of divine Providence and its plan for human salvation. In this essay, I explain his ideas in their Old Testament context and then show how they resurface in his eschatology.

Pedagogical Suffering in the Old Testament

In the Old Testament, the first kind of pedagogical suffering is the kind to which Israel is frequently subjected. At its most extreme, it involved the sack of Jerusalem and seventy years of captivity in Babylon. Even in the middle of that disaster, however, God was preserving them, moderating punishment.

"The inrushing Babylonians," Theodore says, would have killed everyone "had not the help of the Lord been extended, who had decreed that we learn from that chastening, not that we die entirely."[1] For the sake of the patriarchs, for the sake of David, and for the sake of Christ, God had promised not to destroy Israel. He would always leave a sizeable remnant alive so that they could learn from his punishments. But God had made no such promises regarding the gentiles.

Theodore identifies two main reasons why God would smite the gentiles in the Old Testament: first, it was often necessary in order to protect Israel from them; second, as long as God was defending Israel anyway, it was a great opportunity to teach the gentiles a salutary lesson. The first reason actually works to the gentiles' good also, since Christ is going to come from Israel, and Christ will save all nations. Yet Theodore does not dwell on this explanation in his commentaries. It is a hallmark of his exegetical practice to avoid christological readings of the Old Testament as much as he can. He does not always deny their validity, but he thinks it is the job of the interpreter to explain what the prophets *meant* to say to their own people in their own historical context, not simply to read the Christian revelation back into every passage. Theodore wants to show that Israel's favored status was beneficial to the gentiles even centuries before Christ was born. He wants to make the case that God was not acting *only* in wrath, *only* with the Israelites' interests at heart, or even *only* with Christ in mind when he drowned Pharaoh's army and slew the Assyrians besieging Jerusalem.

Theodore makes this case by expanding on a theme that runs throughout the Old Testament: "Then you/they shall know that I am the LORD" (cf. Exod. 6:7; 7:5; etc.). When this is said of the Israelites, it is a case of divine Providence reinforcing the message of the law. But sometimes it is said of pagan nations, who do not know Moses. In these cases, Theodore explains,

1. Comment on Ps. 122:3a LXX (123:3a English), Theodore of Mopsuestia, *Theodori Mopsuesteni Expositionis in Psalmos*, ed. Lucas de Coninck and Maria Josepha d'Hont, CCSL 88A (Turnhout: Brepols, 1977), 368. This comment is preserved in the *Epitome* of Julian of Eclanum's Latin translation of Theodore's commentary, which survives in three partial forms. We have the original Greek for Pss. 32–80 (33–81), along with some fragments from the first part of Ps. 31 (32). For Pss. 1–40 (1–41) we have Julian of Eclanum's Latin translation, which grows fragmentary toward the end, and then we have an *Epitome* of this Latin translation— possibly also by Julian—that begins in the middle of Ps. 16 (17) and runs through the end of the Psalter. The surviving Greek and Latin for Pss. 1–80 (1–81), excluding the *Epitome*, can be found in *Le commentaire sur les Psaumes (I–LXXX)*, ed. Robert Devreesse (Vatican City: Biblioteca Apostolica Vaticana, 1939); and in *Theodore of Mopsuestia: Commentary on Psalms 1–81*, trans. Robert C. Hill (Atlanta: Society of Biblical Literature, 2006), which reproduces Devreesse's edition. The surviving Latin, including the *Epitome*, can be found in CCSL 88A (cited above in this note).

the divine punishments actually *take the place of* the law. When the psalmist prays in Psalm 9, "Lord, establish a lawmaker over [the nations]," he comments:

> When . . . they suspect that they have no Lord, and that no censure of law restrains them, on account of this they do not fear to sin either, nor do they consider that they will be judged for actions done evilly. Thus when they have noticed vengeance for iniquity committed against us [i.e., against Israel], they will know and acknowledge that there is a Judge and Lord in common for them and us, that is He whom we confess and know, who has remained severe for our vindication. So, when punishment has been applied, they may be forced to acknowledge the deserts of the work they carried out against us. This will itself take the place of the Law among them. That is, the punishments that have been applied will teach them so that they may know that they are slaves and subject to the Lord, who is accustomed to judge against sinners most severely.[2]

Since the nations look to idols and demons instead of God, they do not believe in the One who both sees all their wicked deeds and cares about enforcing justice on them. They have enough understanding of morality to know what is right and what is wrong, if they bother to think about it, but no firm reason—either love for God or fear of God—to choose the right. So they do not conceive of righteousness as a matter of *law* at all, or associate it with a divine Lawgiver and Judge, until God punishes them for violating it.

Of course, God would have had abundant opportunity to punish the gentiles even if he had not committed himself to Israel's defense. Israel was not the only small nation attacked by a cruel empire, nor was God indifferent to the plight of the others. "The LORD judges the peoples," says the psalmist in Psalm 7, and Theodore explains, "That is, by the examination of his judgment he weighs how just the causes of wars are that diverse nations have in common between themselves."[3]

Israel as Interpretive Key to Suffering

Yet punishment is not sufficient by itself to teach. People had already managed to ignore the Creator despite the ever-present wonder of his creations, and to ignore rational morality when it conflicted with their desires. What was to stop them from drawing the wrong conclusions when God punished them, too? Judgment works as pedagogy only if there is a lesson for it to reinforce.

---

2. Comment on Ps. 9:21 LXX (9:20 English), in Theodore, *Expositionis in Psalmos*, 47–48. Biblical citations are henceforth to the LXX with English in parentheses if different from LXX.

3. Comment on Ps. 7:9 (7:8), in ibid., 35.

This is where Theodore saw Israel as being most useful to the gentiles of Old Testament times. A catastrophe might not be enough, by itself, to teach them to recognize their Creator, but if it befell them while they were trying to destroy the only nation on earth that claimed to worship one God alone, the Creator of heaven and earth, that was different. Israel was the key by which the gentiles could interpret and learn from their sufferings.

Theodore's commentary on the book of Jonah offers a good example of his insistence on this point. In the Hebrew version, the sum total of Jonah's message to the Ninevites is "Forty days more, and Nineveh shall be overthrown!" (Jon. 3:4b). In the Septuagint the prophecy is just as pithy and even more urgent: "*Three* days more, and Nineveh will be destroyed" (emphasis added). If the interpreter keeps strictly to the text, it seems that the Assyrian inhabitants of the city are moved to repentance solely out of fear of punishment, with no further information—and that they are so moved *immediately*, so that the whole huge city can meet a three-day deadline. Theodore recognizes that a special act of divine Providence is required to make this feasible: "He caused them all to become immediately attentive to the voice of the prophet, even though no one knew who he was, nor had they seen him accompanied with marvels so as to be struck with admiration of him."[4] But even with God himself causing the Ninevites to take Jonah seriously, Theodore cannot believe that a bare, unexplained *threat* could have made them turn to God:

> The verse "The men of Nineveh believed in God" also brings out that he did not carelessly say only, "Three days more and Nineveh will be destroyed." They could never have believed in God on the basis of this remark alone, from a completely unknown foreigner threatening them with destruction and adding nothing further, not even letting the listeners know by whom he was sent. Rather, it is obvious he also mentioned God, the Lord of all, and said he had been sent by him; and he delivered the message of destruction, calling them to repentance.[5]

The Israelites had a necessary role to play when God chose to teach the gentiles through punitive means. Without the interpretive context that only they could provide, the lessons would be missed.

Thus it was that the best opportunities the gentiles had to learn true religion in Old Testament times were those occasions on which they menaced Israel,

---

4. From the introduction to the comments on Jonah, in Theodore of Mopsuestia's *Commentary on the Twelve Prophets*, trans. Robert C. Hill, FC 108 (Washington, DC: Catholic University of America Press, 2004), 190–91.

5. Comment on Jon. 3:5, in ibid., 202.

and God destroyed them for it. Theodore identifies four such events as the ones that had the greatest influence on the gentile world: (1) the deliverance of Israel from Egypt, by means of plagues and the drowning of the Egyptian army; (2) the deliverance of Judah from the Assyrians in the days of Hezekiah; (3) the return of the people from Babylon and their defeat of Gog's Scythian hordes soon afterward (more on this in a moment); and (4) the success of the Maccabean revolt.

The formula is clearest in the case of the Assyrians, because of the speech given by Sennacherib's representative, the Rabshakeh, which makes explicit the theological implications of the standoff.[6] It lists nations the Assyrians have already smashed, observes that their gods were no help to them, and concludes that neither will the God of Israel be any help to Judah. To Theodore's mind, this is a direct propositional denial of God's existence. In fact, he says that Psalm 14:1 (LXX), "The fool has said in his heart, there is no God," is a prophecy of the Rabshakeh's speech, and he goes on to explain how the fool's destruction disproves his words:

> Have they not been taught by the teacher of things "that God is in the just generation," that is, in the race of the people of Israel? . . . How might the Assyrians "know that God is in the just generation"? Without doubt, that plague by which they were struck proved most clearly by its magnitude that God is in the middle of the just, since the wrath by which they were extinguished surpassed by its novelty and wonder all the things which had been done previously by the power of God. For in one point of time, 185[,000] were destroyed, as an angel was smiting. Well then did he say, "Do they not know?" since the Assyrian had said, "Who rescues your land from my hand?" and since he had said, "Will the God of Jerusalem liberate from my hand?" and many things similar to these, through which he denied that God is.[7]

The scale and miraculous nature of the slaughter prove that there is a God who is displeased with the Assyrians. The fact that this destruction comes upon them when they are besieging Jerusalem, not one of the countless other cities they had attacked, proves that this God is *Israel's* God, and that the temple in Jerusalem is *God's* temple. The gentiles must conclude that those who want to know God, or at least learn to avoid his wrath, will need to learn their theology from Israel.

According to Theodore, each of the four major deliverances made a lasting and cumulative impression on the gentile world. In his commentary on

6. See 2 Kings 18:17–35; 2 Chron. 32:1–22; and Isa. 36:4–20.
7. Comment on Ps. 13:5 (14:5), in *Expositionis in Psalmos*, 68.

Psalm 134, he says that the power God exerted to bring Israel out of Egypt "shined in almost the whole world, the suppliants being guarded and the impious being punished."[8] When Psalm 76:11 says that the nations will bring tribute to God, Theodore explains it as a direct result of the miracle that saved Hezekiah from the Assyrians, "not only because they were astounded at what had happened, but also because they were giving thanks. For when he had publicly dealt with all the Assyrians himself, and nearly destroyed them, their death was the common freedom of all [nations]."[9] Then when the Jews had returned from the Babylonian captivity, Theodore claims that their miraculous defeat of Gog and his Scythians had an even more powerful effect on the rest of the gentiles:

> A general astonishment at the novelty of what happens will seize all people everywhere. For those settled in different places and behaving as different nations will use one language, as it were, and with one accord confess the God of the Israelites to be God. And all established under one yoke, as it were, they will believe service under him to be a blessed thing on the basis of what you [Israel] are due to be granted by me [God].[10]

But the reader might wonder: When did that happen? When did the many pagan nations of the Old Testament ever unite in confessing the God of Israel to be the true God? And who is this Gog? When did Israel ever repel a Scythian invasion? These are excellent questions, and they lead us to a fascinating answer.

Theodore's Historical Revisionism

In most of his surviving commentaries, Theodore explains Old Testament prophecies by assigning them to some established event in the pre-Christian history of Israel. So one psalm might foretell the Assyrian attack on Jerusalem in the days of Hezekiah, while an oracle might foretell the return from Babylon. As he gets to the last few Minor Prophets, however, two things happen. First, he overruns the date of the Babylonian captivity. Halfway through the Twelve, he starts dealing with prophecies that were made *after* Judah was carried off, and he does not see how everything they predict can be applied to the Maccabean revolt. Second, in some of them he encounters passages

---

8. Comment on Ps. 134:8 (135:8), in *Expositionis in Psalmos*, 378, from the *Epitome*.
9. Comment on Ps. 75:12b–13 (76:11b–12), in *Le commentaire sur les Psaumes (I–LXXX)*, 508–9.
10. Comment on Zeph. 3:8–9, in *Commentary on the Twelve Prophets*, 302–3.

that predict a degree of peace and prosperity for Israel and of worldwide concern for the true worship of God, prophecies that he cannot assign to any recorded historical events. He tries, but the best he can come up with is a passage from the *Antiquities* of Josephus[11] that tells how many pagans in the Persian Empire circumcised themselves out of fear after Esther foiled Haman's plot against the Jews.

There are two main ways that Christians have interpreted these prophecies. The traditional method, practiced by most of Theodore's contemporaries, has been to understand them spiritually and apply them to the coming of Christ and the growth of the church. The method practiced by modern interpreters of the dispensationalist school is to understand them as references to events that are *still* future, even for us—things that will happen just before the end of the world. Theodore chooses neither of these options and selects a third method. In the absence of history to link to the prophecies, he uses the prophecies to *construct* a plausible history. According to Ezekiel 38, Israel was supposed to be attacked at some time by a prince named Gog, of the land Magog (v. 2), who would come from the north with a great army of horsemen (v. 15). This attack was not recorded in any source, sacred or secular, but Theodore thought some of the Minor Prophets were predicting it too, and he was absolutely dedicated to a hermeneutic that demanded Old Testament fulfillments for Old Testament prophecies. So he simply asserted that it had happened. Soon after the return of the Jewish exiles from Babylon, he claimed, a huge army, more terrible than anything Israel had faced before, swept down upon the sorely weakened nation and was destroyed by the power of God.

And Theodore invents not just battles. He does the same thing with verses such as Micah 4:1–3, which prophesy that "many nations" will go "in the last days" (KJV) to Mount Zion to worship the Lord and learn his law. The result is that he posits the existence of a Pax Judaica from the time the Jews rebuilt the temple until roughly the time of Christ, an Old Testament golden age in which Israel faithfully followed the law, and the gentile nations sent gifts and pilgrims to Jerusalem instead of invading armies. This period of peace was interrupted only by the Seleucids and some recidivistic neighbors at the time of the Maccabean revolt, and Theodore treats that exception in a way that firmly establishes the rule.[12] The gentile nations attacking Israel are no longer ignorant of God's law, he says—not at that late date. Rather, they are rebelling against it in much the same way the Israelites often had.

---

11. Josephus, *Antiquitates judaicae* 11.6.13, referred to in Theodore's comments on Ps. 101:23 (102:22), in *Expositionis in Psalmos*, 330, from the *Epitome*.
12. Pompey's "interruption" in 63 BC goes unmentioned.

"Awful punishment will befall the Philistines for *abandoning* the worship of God."[13] In his commentary on Psalm 47, which he identifies as a hymn of praise predicting the Maccabees' victory, Theodore actually suggests that the very nations Israel had just beaten would be rejoicing afterward in their own defeat. "All nations, clap your hands," the psalm says, and Theodore explains: "He says 'all nations' not in a generic way [*haplōs*], but because they had defeated both neighboring [armies] and the armies of Antiochus, and since many were utterly vanquished, the power of God also became clear to many."[14]

The pedagogy of destruction was a big success, in other words. All the nations that knew of Israel's deliverances (and had not been destroyed) transformed over time from ignorant pagans into tentative monotheists with a great interest in the temple and its divinely appointed rites—or so Theodore says. As Robert C. Hill observes, "In Theodore's view, *to historikon* requires insistence on historicity, not evidence of it."[15]

Theodore's Eschatology

Of course, even given Theodore's historical revisionism, there is one significant drawback to this kind of pedagogy: it works only on the survivors. The ones who are actually destroyed have no opportunity to learn from their own destruction. In the broader context of his theological system, however, Theodore has an answer for this too. Although he recognizes that millions have died in their sins, he believes in universal human salvation, and he turns again to the pedagogy of destruction to explain how this might be possible.

In 2 Thessalonians 1:9, the apostle Paul says that those who have not obeyed the gospel "will suffer the punishment of eternal destruction." In his commentary on that book, Theodore takes the word "eternal" to signify not duration but character. It means that the torments of hell do not develop by stages, gradually meting out punishment. Instead, they "complete the ruin instantaneously, because they are not of time, but of eternity."[16] Hell involves

13. Comment on Zech. 9:2–7, in *Commentary on the Twelve Prophets*, 364–65, emphasis added.

14. Comment on Ps. 46:2–3 (47:1–2), in *Le commentaire sur les Psaumes*, 307.

15. *Commentary on the Twelve Prophets*, 392n111.

16. *Theodori episcopi Mopsuesteni in epistolas B. Pauli commentarii*, ed. H. B. Swete (Cambridge: Cambridge University Press, 1880–82), 2:45–46. Rowan Greer's translation in Theodore of Mopsuestia, *The Commentaries on the Minor Epistles of Paul* (Atlanta: Society of Biblical Literature, 2010), published since this essay was prepared, does not support my reading here: "The destructions are exterminations that accomplish ruin in time, yet are not temporal, but for eternity" (501). In order to arrive at this rendering, however, Greer translates *ex tempore* (instantaneously) as if it were *in tempore* (in time) and *quod* (because) as if it were *tamen* (yet);

instant, radical destruction. But there is a big difference between the sinner who is destroyed in this life and the sinner who is destroyed in hell. The former dies because he is mortal; the latter has already died and been resurrected. He is immortal now. So this is destruction without death. The damned can no longer evade their lessons by expiring in the midst of them. Instead, they will learn from their own extremities the same lessons that in this life only the survivors could have learned. Here is Theodore's explanation of the process:

> In the future age, those who have chosen good things here will receive the enjoyment of good things, with praise. But as for the evil ones, who for all the time of their life were perpetrating evils, when they shall have tasted the force and fear of the punishments, and [when by] choosing good things they shall have learned that they remained in evils as long as they sinned, not in goods, and [when] through these things they have attained to the knowledge of the best teaching, the fear of God, [and] have been taught to apprehend him with a good will, then they shall at last merit the enjoyment of divine generosity.[17]

In Theodore's rather Pavlovian conception of hell, the human sufferers begin to notice that they gain respite from their torments when they desire good things, and return to torments when they desire evil things. Eventually this treatment will condition them to want good things, at which point God will give them what they now want and confirm their wills in that good state for the rest of eternity.

So we end this essay in a surprising place. Having seen good evidence of the lengths to which Theodore is willing to go in his quest to interpret Scripture in the most un-Origenist way possible, we now find that despite their diametrically opposed hermeneutics, they agreed on universal salvation. Or they almost agreed. Giuseppe Assemani, the editor of the text from which this quotation comes, alleges that Theodore is teaching the error of Origen,[18]

---

cf. the Latin: *interitus sunt exterminii perditionem perficientes ex tempore, quod non ad tempus, aeterno sunt.* Yet I find Swete's explanation convincing: "Theodore, following in the steps of Diodore, held the future punishment of the wicked to be remissible upon their repentance. . . . But he may nevertheless have regarded it as objectively eternal, inasmuch as it belongs to a life not measured by periods of time, and as much as this is implied in his comment on the present verse" (2:46n20).

17. The argument continues: "Indeed, it never would have said 'until you render the last farthing' [Matt. 5:26] unless it could be done, and completing the punishments for sins, we should be freed from them. Nor would it have said, 'He will be beaten with many [stripes]' and 'He will be beaten with few [stripes]' [Luke 12:47–48], unless they were going to have an end at last, once they had completed a punishment commensurate with [their] sins." Giuseppe Simone Assemani, trans. and ed., *Bibliotheca orientalis Clementino-Vaticana* (Rome: Typis Sacrae Congregationis de Propaganda Fide, 1719–28), 3:323, right column.

18. Ibid., 3:323, left column.

but there is an important difference between what Theodore is saying and what Origen said, in that Origen extended his speculation even to the salvation of the devil. Theodore does not do this, and indeed cannot, because he understands the destruction wrought by death to be a necessary part of the process of salvation: "God well knew that mortality is an advantage for men. For if they remain without death, they will fall everlastingly."[19] Since the devil is immortal, he cannot be remade and must "fall everlastingly." The sense in which any of the angels can be "saved" is limited, extending only to the good angels who, thanks to the work of Christ, are rescued from futility and able to serve humanity joyously again, since in so doing they are really serving Christ and thereby serving God.[20] When it comes to the human race, however, Origen and Theodore agree on the end result, if not the mechanism by which it is achieved.

19. Comment on Gen. 2:17, by Theodore of Mopsuestia, *Fragmenta in Genesin*, PG 66:640C–D. The translation comes from Richard A. Norris, *Manhood and Christ* (Oxford: Clarendon, 1963), 183.
20. See Frederick G. McLeod, *The Roles of Christ's Humanity in Salvation: Insights from Theodore of Mopsuestia* (Washington, DC: Catholic University of America Press, 2005), 124–43.

13

THE WORD AND HIS FLESH

Human Weakness and the Identity of Jesus
in Greek Patristic Christology

BRIAN E. DALEY, SJ

"But you—who do you say that I am?" (Mark 8:29, my trans.). Jesus's blunt question to the disciples, it is often said, remains one of the driving questions of Christian faith: the question, for all those who desire to follow him, of how we understand his identity. For the church of the first several centuries, this question was, to a large degree, raised and focused by the scandal of his human weakness: his suffering and death, of course, but also his human growth and his human needs, as witnessed by the New Testament, as well as the limits his finite human nature imposed on his actions and knowledge. If he is truly the Messiah of Israel and the eschatological giver of God's Holy Spirit, as early Christians were generally ready to confess, what sense can one make of his human ordinariness and obscurity, his human vulnerability and mortality? And if those limiting qualities are taken to be essential to the narrative of how he has actually become humanity's Savior and Lord—if his death, as Jesus himself suggests on the road to Emmaus (Luke 24:26), is in fact the divinely ordained prelude to his resurrection and entry into messianic glory—how must one conceive of *him* as the subject of that narrative?

The classical understanding of Christian orthodoxy—formed in the early church over seven or eight centuries of preaching and controversy and expressed in a growing stream of biblical commentary, theological argument, creedal confessions, and conciliar formulas—was and continues to be that Jesus is himself the Son of God: the eternal Word "by whom all things were made" (cf. John 1:3), who in time has become a human among humans, in order to transform and liberate the humanity he has made his own, even to offer humanity a share in the life of God. Classical Christian orthodoxy confesses that the Jesus who revealed God's will and God's love in works and words of power is "one and the same" as the Jesus who slept in the boat, who wept for Lazarus, and who suffered on the cross: God the Son, humanly "personalizing" the transcendent fullness of the divine Mystery in the body and mind, the relationships and limitations, of his own fully human life. The Second Council of Constantinople (553) expresses this central, irreducible paradox of Christian orthodoxy in the clear, if confrontational, terms of a canonical ultimatum:

> If anyone says that the Word of God who performed miracles was someone other than the Christ who suffered, or says that God the Word was *with* the Christ "born of a woman" (Gal. 4:4) or was *in* him as one in another, but does not confess that our Lord Jesus Christ, the Word of God made flesh and made human, is *one and the same*, and that both the miracles and the sufferings which he voluntarily endured in the flesh belong to the same one, let that person be anathema.[1]

What I suggest in this essay is that this classical understanding of the single, paradoxical identity of Jesus developed precisely as part of an ongoing struggle on the part of the early church to grasp and express the saving meaning of his real human limitations and human sufferings, assuming that they are proper to a subject who is not simply and exclusively a human being. Taking these limitations seriously—limitations that include his human passivities, his ability to experience grief and to suffer and die—was always a challenge for early believers, because such passivities seemed to conflict both with his role as God's herald and Savior and with the paradigmatic character of his human behavior. Yet the alternative was to disregard the contents of the gospel narrative and to depreciate his humanity in a serious way.

1. Second Council of Constantinople, canon 3, trans. Josef Neuner and Jacques Dupuis, *The Christian Faith in the Doctrinal Documents of the Catholic Church* (New York: Alba House, 1982), 159, alt., emphasis added.

Through the process of protracted, often sharply polemical reflection on the implications of this paradox, early Christian theologians developed a grammar for language about Jesus that staked out the conditions for *identifying* him in the fullness of apostolic faith—for saying, as far as human and Christian speech can say, just who and what Jesus is, how the reality of God is involved through him in the history of the world, and what God has done for us in him. Only in knowing his identity, patristic Christology suggests—only in being able to name Jesus for who and what he is—do we begin to understand our own human identity and our ultimate vocation.

Clearly it is impossible here to offer a full summary of the growing sense of both the complexity and the simplicity of the identity of Jesus in the writings of those fathers considered to represent the mainstream of early Christian orthodoxy. Here I offer four "snapshots," four brief and impressionistic characterizations, of the ways four Greek theologians from the second to the seventh century—Irenaeus, Athanasius, Cyril of Alexandria, and Maximus the Confessor—invite us to conceive of the identity of Jesus. My hope is that this will both provide us with a sense of developing consistency within the early classical tradition of Christology, building on the New Testament witness yet moving well beyond it philosophically and theologically, and that it will provoke us to deeper reflection for ourselves.

Irenaeus of Lyons

Writing from the frontier region of Gaul around the year 185, Irenaeus tried, in his massive work *Against Heresies* (*Adversus haereses*), to confront the recurrent "gnostic" tendency in religious thought, which had already made its presence felt in the small circle of Christian believers, and which continues in various ways to have its appeal: the tendency to deconstruct the continuity and credibility of the public world and of the institutions and religious traditions in which we live; to look on matter and the body, as well the responsibilities we bear toward the material and bodily world, as part of an illusory realm, the creation of a lesser god, the fruit of a superhuman conspiracy, or a cosmic mistake; and to see human freedom, the redemption of the human spirit from illusion and enslavement to history, as possible only through a radically revisionist narrative of our origins, which calls us to disregard the accepted realities of daily life and find our meaning within ourselves, in the secret "enlightenment" communicated to an elect few. For Christian gnostics of the second century, such as the Valentinians, the source of this redeeming knowledge was thought to be the Savior Jesus:

not the earthy Jewish prophet of the four Gospels, but the representative of an archetypal *plērōma* of heavenly actors, whose doings long antedate the history of the material world, and who engage in this present history only to rescue from it those few who can see the illusion of matter, flesh, and human institutions for what it is.[2]

Irenaeus's concern, through all the twists and turns of his proclaimed "unmasking and refutation" of gnostic teaching, is to argue for the unity and religious relevance of what ordinary Christians regard as the real world—the unity of God as Creator and Savior and the unity of the biblical narrative, the created universe, the human person, and the worldwide church and its message—and to insist that it is in *this* world, in *this* history, in *this* body, for all their limitations, that the gospel of redemption through Christ is already on the way to fulfillment. Only in such a unified framework of time and space is there an intelligible form to the story of human alienation and hope, a convincing proclamation of good news. And in this unified narrative, the identity of Jesus as both divine Word and fleshly human being is clearly the paradoxical heart of the story of salvation, the link between source and goal, promise and fulfillment.

So in book 3 of *Against Heresies*, Irenaeus criticizes the gnostics for being unaware "that [God's] only-begotten Word—who is always present with the human race, united to and mingled with the work of his hands,[3] according to the Father's pleasure, and who became flesh—is himself Jesus Christ our Lord, who did also suffer for us and rose again on our behalf."[4]

By experiencing in himself every stage and aspect of human growth, while communicating to his own body and to the human family in solidarity with him God's own incorruptible life, Irenaeus's Word-made-flesh becomes the unique Mediator, the only one capable of restoring friendship and *communio* between humanity and its Creator.

In explaining Jesus's work of mediation in book 4 of *Against Heresies*, Irenaeus lays special emphasis on the revelation of God's glory—of God's life-restoring presence to the human mind and senses—which only Jesus, as Word and Son in human form, can achieve. For Irenaeus, it is the revelation of God in the historical, fleshly Jesus that is the heart of redemption.

2. See, e.g., *The Treatise on Resurrection* (*To Rheginus*) (Nag Hammadi I,3) 46.22–34; 47.31–48.20; *The Apocryphon of John* (Nag Hammadi II,1) 23.21–36; *The Dialogue of the Savior* (Nag Hammadi III,5) 140.10–142.16; *The Concept of Our Great Power* (Nag Hammadi VI,4) 46.7–47.9.

3. The Greek word here is *plasma*, meaning that which is shaped by God's hands, thus expressing "creation" in its most palpable sense.

4. Irenaeus, *Against Heresies* (= *Haer.*) 3.16.6, trans. Alexander Roberts and James Donaldson, in *ANF* 1:442, alt.

For the manifestation of the Son is the knowledge of the Father; for all things are manifested through the Word. . . . For the Lord taught us that no one is capable of knowing God, unless he be taught of God—that is, that God cannot be known without God—but that this is the express will of the Father, that God should be known. . . . For by means of the creation itself, the Word reveals God the Creator; and by means of the world, [reveals] the Lord as maker of the world; and by means of the formation [of the human creature, reveals] the craftsman who formed him; and by the Son [reveals] that Father who begot the Son. . . . And through the Word himself who had been made visible and palpable, the Father was shown forth; and although all did not equally believe in him, still all did see the Father in the Son: for the Father is the invisible of the Son, but the Son is the visible of the Father. And for that reason everyone called him "the Christ" while he was present [on earth], and named him "God."[5]

By revealing his splendor in the incarnate Word, God communicates life to mortal creatures, draws them into the vital *communio* of his own radiance.

In identifying the saving work of Christ with his presence on earth as incarnate Word, God made real flesh, Irenaeus even looks beyond Christ's revelatory role to connect his person with the continuing sacramental life of the church. So in book 5 of *Against Heresies*, he emphasizes the importance of the Eucharist, taken in this life to be our bodily nourishment, as a pledge of the fullness of the redemption that will be achieved for us in the resurrection of our own material, mortal bodies. It is only because the Word of God has actually become flesh and blood himself, he insists, that the Eucharist, the food that conveys his flesh and blood to us in liturgical signs, can be for us a promise of everlasting life.

If [our flesh] does not attain to salvation, then neither did the Lord redeem us with his blood, nor is the cup of the Eucharist the communion of his blood, nor the bread which we break the communion of his body. For blood can only come from veins and flesh, and whatever else makes up the substance of a human person. When the Word of God actually was made this, he redeemed us by his own blood. . . . When, therefore, the mingled cup and the manufactured bread receive the Word of God, the Eucharist becomes the body of Christ, and from these things the substance of our flesh grows and is supported. How, then, can they affirm that the flesh is incapable of receiving the gift of God, which is life eternal?[6]

Here as before, Irenaeus emphasizes the complex identity of Jesus, God's eternal Word who has made our limited, visible, material nature his own, as

5. Irenaeus, *Haer.* 4.6.3–6, in *ANF* 1:468–69, alt.
6. Irenaeus, *Haer.* 5.2.2–3, in *ANF* 1:528, alt., following a Greek fragment.

itself the key to the church's present faith in him as Savior, and to the church's hope that our flesh will share in the salvation he offers. For gnostic Christians, the passible and limited body and the whole visible bodily order of fragile human relationships and limiting human institutions constitute the world from which Christ came to save us by secret knowledge. Irenaeus, by contrast, and with him the growing consensus of Christian tradition, proclaims the body, the church, and the world as forming together the locus of salvation, precisely because in the person of Jesus the life-giving Word has made all of these things his own.

Athanasius of Alexandria

It is no exaggeration to say that Athanasius's whole long career as bishop and theologian was occupied with the church's fourth-century struggle to identify who and what Jesus is. Born in the closing years of the third century, Athanasius was elected bishop of Alexandria in 328, three years after the presbyter Arius had been excommunicated by the Council of Nicaea, essentially for his insistence that the Son of God is himself the first and noblest of creatures. But the issues raised by Arius and his followers were not resolved by Nicaea's creed and canons. From the early 340s until his death in 373, Athanasius continued to fight for a strong conception of Jesus's identity as fully divine, giving an increasingly explicit emphasis on the importance of the Nicene Creed's formulation that the Son is "of the same substance as the Father."

Undoubtedly, both Arian and Nicene approaches to Jesus's identity were the agenda of theological families, rather than organically developed theological systems; undoubtedly too, as Nicaea's "substance" language was accepted, understood, and eventually extended to include the Holy Spirit's relationship to the Father, this understanding grew slowly throughout the fourth century and found varied expressions among different authors.[7] Still, the thinking that Athanasius opposed throughout his career had a relatively consistent pattern: the well-established tradition of Platonic and earlier Christian thought that saw God's activity in the world as communicated in steps, and that conceived of the Son and the Holy Spirit, God's mediating agents in creation, as themselves produced, even "created" by a wholly transcendent Father, as God's first steps in self-communication. As such, Son and Spirit were understood

---

7. There is abundant literature in English on the fourth-century controversies surrounding Arius and Nicaea. See, e.g., John Behr, *The Nicene Faith* (Crestwood, NY: St. Vladimir's Seminary Press, 2004); and Lewis Ayres, *The Faith of Nicaea* (Oxford: Oxford University Press, 2004).

to participate in the Father's being and operations to such a preeminent extent that they might legitimately be called "divine," even "like the Father in all things"; but they were seen as less than the Father in their being, simply because the Father alone is the primordial source of all that is.

Part of the Arian argument, it seems, came from scriptural references to the limitations of knowledge professed by Jesus, the Word made flesh, in passages such as Matthew 24:36, as well as from the New Testament witness to Jesus's ability to grow and change (e.g., Luke 2:52)—both seen as features not of divine substance but of the world of "becoming."[8] Similarly, the suffering of Christ was seen as a crucial part of the vulnerability and limitation that prove the creaturely status of the Son.[9]

Against this Arian view, Athanasius argued with increasing energy throughout his life for a view of the Word—and in his later works, also of the Spirit—as fully equal with the Father in being and life, fully one reality with the Father, precisely because both Word and Spirit accomplish within creation what only God, and not a creature, can do. For Athanasius, God's transcendent Logos, or active Reason, eternally generated by the Father within the divine Mystery itself, is commissioned to be the Father's active and ordering presence in the world. God, as God, is totally "other" than creation; nothing that belongs to the created realm (which for Athanasius means what is brought into being from nothing) can be called "divine" in the strict sense. So God the Word and God the Spirit, whom baptismal faith instinctively recognizes as divine because they impart to creatures a share in divine life, must be seen as *other* than creation, but not *distant* from it: not part of creation, yet so actively involved in it, so present to it for its good, that they can direct, order, and heal it from within. This presence to creation of the Word, who is not a creature, is realized most fully, Athanasius argues, in his incarnation.[10]

In Athanasius's decades-long campaign to refute the Arian position in all its many shades and to promote a strong sense of the Son's full status as

8. This complex of ideas held by Arius and his associates is most clearly attested in the encyclical letter of Alexander of Alexandria and his clergy, contained in Socrates's *Ecclesiastical History* 1.6.4–6 (see Hans-Georg Opitz, ed., *Athanasius Werke* [AW] III/1:8.2–10 [= Urk. 4b.8–10]; trans. J. Stevenson, *A New Eusebius* [London: SPCK, 1987], 343). (Urk. identifies the document number in Opitz's *Early Arian Documents* [German: *Urkunden*]: http://www.fourthcentury.com/urkunde-chart-opitz/.) The most penetrating analysis of Arius's theological position and its philosophical and cultural roots remains Rowan Williams, *Arius: Heresy and Tradition*, rev. ed. (Grand Rapids: Eerdmans, 2002).

9. Opitz, AW III/1:25.15–22 [= Urk. 14.37].

10. For helpful synthetic presentations of Athanasius's theology, see Alvyn Petterson, *Athanasius* (London: Geoffrey Chapman, 1995); Khaled Anatolios, *Athanasius: The Coherence of His Thought* (London: Routledge, 1998).

God, even after he has made a human form or "body" his own,[11] the scandal of Jesus's limitations and sufferings, as well as their crucial importance to his identity as Savior, plays a critical, if complex, role. This is made clear in what are considered his earliest works: the pair of apologetic treatises written probably in the early 330s, known as *Against the Pagans* (*Contra gentes*) and *The Incarnation* (*De incarnatione*).[12] Like a fourth-century anticipation of Anselm's *Cur Deus Homo?*, these essays offer an elaborate argument for the plausibility of the Christian conception of an incarnate, saving, crucified Logos by telling the story of how humanity, originally created to participate in the ordered rationality of the divine Logos, and so to share in the divine quality of incorruptibility by knowing God, lost that gift by fatal choices. Humanity therefore needed to be redeemed, reshaped in God's image, endowed again with unending life, by the Word's coming to share in our world, our wounded physicality, and even our death.

In the early chapters of *The Incarnation*, Athanasius poignantly describes the effects of human sin on the descendants of Adam and Eve, depicting sin as a growing epidemic that has robbed humanity of its rationality and vitality and reduced it to being dominated by greed and violence, like other animal species. Then Athanasius points out the only remedy left to the Logos, as just and compassionate Creator: to take on human corruptibility and mortality himself, and to overcome death in his own person, through his identity as incarnate Word. "To this end," he writes, the Word "took to himself a body capable of death, that it, by partaking of the Word who is above all, might be worthy to die in the place of all, and might, because of the Word which had come to dwell in it, remain incorruptible, and that from then on corruption might be kept from all by the grace of the resurrection."[13]

In this treatise, Athanasius identifies the saving effect of the Word's incarnation in two principal ways: as his restoration of vital energy within the vulnerable human community "in putting away death from us and renewing

---

11. Athanasius has been criticized by some twentieth-century scholars for thinking of the incarnate Word simply as "the Word and his body," without taking seriously his human soul or interior life. See R. P. C. Hanson, *The Search for the Christian Doctrine of God* (Edinburgh: T&T Clark, 1988), 448, who goes so far as to call this a "space-suit Christology," in which Jesus is seen as simply "putting on" human flesh as an instrument for action in an alien environment. For a critical response to this view, see Alvyn Petterson, *Athanasius and the Human Body* (Bristol: Bristol Press, 1990); Khaled Anatolios, "'The Body as Instrument': A Reevaluation of Athanasius' Logos-Sarx Christology," *Coptic Church Review* 18 (1997): 78–84.

12. For a discussion of the dating of these treatises, and an argument for what is now the most widely accepted date—around 330—see Anatolios, *Athanasius*, 26–27.

13. Athanasius, *The Incarnation* (= *Inc.*) 9, trans. Archibald Robertson, in *Christology of the Later Fathers*, ed. E. R Hardy (Philadelphia: Westminster, 1954), 40–41, alt.; this translation is hereafter cited as Robertson.

us again";[14] but equally as the revelation to fallen human minds of the Word's power and presence, restoring to them the similarity to himself that makes them rational and holy, by manifesting again in the human world the Word's own holiness and rationality.[15] Like Irenaeus,[16] Athanasius is convinced that the Word's self-revelation in human terms itself opens up the new possibility of human participation in God's immortality.[17] Even Jesus's death on the cross—for ancient minds, the principal obstacle to belief in his divine identity—Athanasius describes as a moment of revelation: only a real death, a death inflicted by the violence of others, a death in public view, could qualify as the prelude to definitive resurrection and victory. "He accepted on the cross, and endured, a death inflicted by others, and above all by his enemies, which they thought dreadful and ignominious and not to be faced; so that when this also was destroyed, both he himself might be believed to be the life, and the power of death might be brought utterly to nought."[18] Jesus's passion reveals most forcefully, for Athanasius, the cost to God of his decision to restore humanity by taking our weakness to himself, but also its effect on faith.

Athanasius returns to the troubling issue of the weakness and mortality of the incarnate Word in his *Third Oration against the Arians*, written probably in Rome toward the end of his second exile, in 345–46. In this somewhat rambling treatise, he deals in detail with the scriptural arguments of Nicaea's opponents against the notion that the Word, generated by the Father and capable of incarnation, even of suffering, could be "of the same substance" as the Father. Athanasius's refutation of Arian exegesis follows a single form: the one Mystery proclaimed in the Gospels is that indeed "the Word has become flesh," the divine Son has taken on a body such as ours, to communicate through that human body a new revelation of God and new vitality; therefore the passages in Scripture that ascribe to the Son weakness or ignorance, or even a creaturely dependence on God, are to be taken as referring to his acquired humanity, his "flesh," and not to his core identity as God the Word. If Arians point to his human weaknesses as "ground for low thoughts concerning the Son of God," they must also "from his divine works recognize the Word who is in the Father, and hence renounce their self-willed irreligion"![19] The gospel narrative presents us with a Jesus whose identity is

14. Athanasius, *Inc.* 16, trans. Robertson, 45.

15. Ibid. See also Athanasius's description of the original grace, the "second gift" bestowed on the human race at its beginning but soon lost by the misuse of the human will: ibid., 3.

16. For this connection, see Khaled Anatolios, "The Influence of Irenaeus on Athanasius," StPatr 36 (2001): 463–76.

17. See, e.g., Athanasius, *Inc.* 54, trans. Robertson, 65.

18. Athanasius, *Inc.* 24, trans. Robertson, 49, alt.

19. Athanasius, *Orations against the Arians* 3:55, trans. John Henry Newman, NPNF[2] 4:423.

complex, paradoxical; yet for Athanasius that identity is itself both the key to right interpretation of Scripture and its central message of salvation.

Athanasius goes on to apply this principle to Jesus's physical and mental suffering, in Gethsemane and on the cross:

> Wherefore of necessity when he was in a passible body, weeping and toiling, these things which are proper to the flesh are ascribed to him, together with the body. . . . And as to his saying, "If it be possible, let the cup pass" [Matt. 26:39], observe how, though he thus spoke, he rebuked Peter, saying, "You are not thinking the things that are of God, but those that are human" [Matt. 16:23]. For he willed what he deprecated—and that was why he had come; but *his* was the willing (for this was why he came!), but the terror belonged to the flesh. Therefore as a human being he utters this speech also; and yet again, both were said by the same one, to show that he was God, willing this himself, but that having become human, he had a flesh that was in terror. For the sake of this flesh he combined his own will with human weakness, that by destroying this he might, in turn, make humans undaunted in face of death.[20]

Athanasius is not yet ready—as Augustine and later Maximus the Confessor would be—to acknowledge explicitly in the incarnate Word two naturally distinct wills, two fully operative (if utterly incommensurate) levels of psychological and cognitive activity. For him, the decisive, conscious agent in the life and works of Christ, even in his moments of most abject suffering, is the Word who is divine. Fear, pain, ignorance, mortality are all proper to "flesh"—*our* flesh, humanity in its fallen state, deprived of the clarity of vision and incorruptibility of life that God had intended for us when he originally shaped us in the image of the Son. Yet Athanasius repeatedly argues that the Word, by making these weaknesses of "the flesh" his own, has begun to transform and heal them. So he sees in Gethsemane and Calvary the testing place of the saving identity of Jesus: there Jesus experiences as his own a true human terror, a sense of abandonment in the face of death, yet he remains willing to carry out the eternal plan of sacrificial love, which is both his own and his Father's.[21]

Cyril of Alexandria

Athanasius's learned and strong-minded successor in the first half of the fifth century, Cyril of Alexandria, exerted perhaps the most formative influence

20. Athanasius, *Orations against the Arians* 3:56–57, trans. Newman, *NPNF*[2] 4:424, alt.
21. This is emphasized not only in the present passage but throughout *The Incarnation*: see esp. 27–32, 46–55.

on what have become the classic Christian language-rules for speaking of the complex identity of Jesus the Savior. Taking "body" and "flesh" in the fullest sense of their biblical usage, to signify not only biological materiality but also mind, feelings, and will, Cyril speaks of the human Jesus not as an "assumed man," as some of his Antiochene contemporaries would do, but as "one Christ along with his flesh, the same at once God and a human being."[22] Cyril's emphasis on the radical unity of Christ as subject of all that is predicated of him, and on the divine Word as the basis and central focus of that unity, is rich with implications for his portrait of Jesus. In his celebrated *Third Letter to Nestorius* (of Constantinople), written in the autumn of 430—a manifesto on the orthodox understanding of the Savior as the basis for continuing communion in faith and sacrament between the two prelates and their churches—Cyril insists that this sense of Jesus's unity as subject is the warrant for our worship of him, "without separating and parting the human and God as though they were mutually connected [only] by unity of rank and sovereignty."[23] An awareness of this unity enables the participant in a eucharistic liturgy to recognize in the sacramental gifts "not mere flesh (God forbid!) or the flesh of a man hallowed by connection with the Word, but the truly life-giving flesh belonging properly to God the Word himself."[24] It presents Christ's priestly sacrifice on the cross, identified as such typologically in the Letter to the Hebrews, as the Son's offering of his own body to the Father, "for us and not for himself."[25] And it provides the real justification for Cyril's insistence, throughout his quarrel with Nestorius, on the importance to orthodoxy of Mary's traditional title, "God-Bearer" (*Theotokos*), since the church believes that the eternal Word of God "united what is human to himself in his own concrete individuality [*kath' hypostasin*] and underwent fleshly birth from her womb."[26]

The dispute between Cyril and the representatives of the Antiochene exegetical and theological tradition—Nestorius, Theodoret of Cyrus, and their teachers Diodore of Tarsus and Theodore of Mopsuestia—was not primarily a dispute about the fullness of Christ's humanity, as has sometimes been suggested in the past: a dispute in which the Antiochenes were primarily concerned with emphasizing that humanity, while the Alexandrians only offered it lip

22. Cyril, *Third Letter to Nestorius* 12, anathema 2, trans. and ed. Lionel R. Wickham, *Cyril of Alexandria: Select Letters* (Oxford: Clarendon Press, 1983), 28–29.
23. Cyril, *Third Letter to Nestorius* 4, trans. Wickham, 19.
24. Cyril, *Third Letter to Nestorius* 7, trans. Wickham, 23, alt.
25. Cyril, *Third Letter to Nestorius* 9, trans. Wickham, 25.
26. Cyril, *Third Letter to Nestorius* 11, trans. Wickham, 29, alt.

service.[27] Rather, the main differences seem to lie in different senses of the relevance of history and time to salvation, and of the ontological and existential boundaries between God and the world. For Antiochenes such as Theodore or Theodoret, the saving and transforming encounter of humanity with God, with all the freedom from corruptibility, passion, and sin that it promises, is a gift reserved in its fullness for the eschatological future, a new "state" (*katastasis*) that at present is realized only by the risen Christ, yet pointed to by Scripture and the symbols of the church's worship. The world in which we presently live is separated by an unbridgeable gulf from God and his eternity, in the Antiochene view, and the main task of theology is to keep its language about God pure from anything that might confuse these realms, or imply some limitation or circumscription of God's being.[28] For Cyril and his followers, on the other hand, the news of the incarnation of the Word is precisely that the God who is ontologically "other" than creation has now become personally present within it, has made a human creature his own embodiment, united it to his own concrete existence or *hypostasis*, identified himself with the full individual nature of a man, so that the creative and healing energies proper to God are now accessible in time, in the person of Christ and in the church that is his body. Although in his polemical treatises against Cyril, Theodoret as a result lays strong emphasis on the importance of keeping the Word free from any suggestion of sharing in human suffering, Cyril insists with equal force that the Christian message of salvation rests on the paradoxical but literal ascription of human suffering—acquired through incarnation—to God the Word. So he writes, again in his *Third Letter to Nestorius* of 430: "We confess that the very Son begotten of God the Father, the Only-begotten God, impassible though he is in his own nature, has, as the Bible says, suffered in flesh for our sake [1 Pet. 4:1], and that he was in the crucified body making the sufferings of his flesh his own, in an impassible way."[29]

27. See the critique of this widespread conception by John McGuckin, *St. Cyril of Alexandria: The Christological Controversy; Its History, Theology, and Texts* (Crestwood, NY: St. Vladimir's Seminary Press, 2005), 205.

28. For a discussion of the eschatological orientation of Antiochene thought, see esp. Günter Koch, *Die Heilsverwirklichung bei Theodor von Mopsuestia*, Münchener theologische Studien 31 (Munich: Max Hueber, 1965); Günter Koch, *Strukturen und Geschichte des Heils in der Theologie des Theodoret von Kyros*, Frankfurter theologische Studien 17 (Frankfurt am Main: Knecht, 1974); Joanne McWilliam Dewart, *The Theology of Grace of Theodore of Mopsuestia* (Washington, DC: Catholic University of America Press, 1971).

29. Cyril, *Third Letter to Nestorius* 6, trans. Wickham, 21, alt. For recent discussion of Cyril's position on the "impassible suffering" of God the Word in the controversy with Nestorius and Theodoret, see John J. O'Keefe, "Impassible Suffering? Divine Passion and Fifth-Century Christology," *Theological Studies* 58 (1997): 39–60; Joseph Hallman, "The Seed of Fire: Divine Suffering in the Christology of Cyril of Alexandria and Nestorius of Constantinople," *Journal*

Cyril's reason for insisting on this living paradox of a divine Word who suffers, not as God, but still truly suffers in his own flesh, as Warren Smith has pointed out,[30] is not simply to head off the Antiochene criticism that his portrait of Christ compromises the divine attribute of impassibility. Rather, it is central to his soteriology that the Word made flesh should indeed suffer what we humans suffer, but that he suffer it in a way free from the elements of compulsion, self-preoccupation, and fear that normally accompany our own experience of pain and weakness.[31] Christ is fully human, yet human in a freer and more virtuous way than we can be—in a way that offers us both a model and an unattainable norm—because he is himself God the Son. As Cyril remarks in his *Scholia on the Incarnation*, "He has reserved to his [human] nature that it should be superior to all."[32]

In an interesting fragment of book 7 of his *Commentary on John* (written before the controversy with Nestorius began), Cyril makes this same point with reference to human grief, with which Jesus is said to have struggled at the death of his friend Lazarus (John 11:33–34). The Fourth Gospel tells us that Jesus "was indignant and was troubled" (my trans.) as he stood before Lazarus's tomb. Cyril writes:

> Since Christ was not only God by nature, but also a human being, he suffers in a human way along with everyone else. But when grief begins to be stirred up in him, and the holy flesh is inclined to shed tears, he does not allow it to suffer this in an unrestrained way, as usually happens with us. "He was indignant[33] in the Spirit" [John 11:33]: that is, in the power of the Holy Spirit he rebukes his own flesh, so to speak. . . . For this is the reason the Word of God, powerful in every way, came to be in flesh—or rather, came to *be* flesh: that by the activities

---

of Early Christian Studies 5 (1997): 369–91; J. Warren Smith, "Suffering Impassibly: Christ's Passion in Cyril of Alexandria's Soteriology," chapter 14 of the present volume.

30. Smith, "Suffering Impassibly."

31. See Cyril, *Second Oration to the Royal Ladies* (PG 76:1393B).

32. Cyril, *Scholia on the Incarnation of the Only Begotten* 37; text edited by Philip E. Pusey, *Cyrilli archiepiscopi Alexandrini Opera* (reprint, Brussels: Culture & Civilisation, 1965), 6:574–75; trans. Philip E. Pusey, *St. Cyril, Archbishop of Alexandria: Five Tomes against Nestorius* [etc.] (Oxford: Parker, 1881), 232–33.

33. The Greek word in John 11:33, *embrimaomai*, is usually translated as indicating deep emotion: "deeply moved" (RSV), "greatly disturbed" (NRSV), "greatly distressed" (NJB). The original meaning of the verb is "to snort," and it is used for horses; yet in its (fairly infrequent) application to humans, it appears to mean "to express anger," "to rebuke indignantly," as in Dan. 11:30 LXX; Mark 1:43; Matt. 9:30. Whatever case can be made for the various modern English softenings of John 11:33, Cyril clearly understands the verb to mean that Jesus "rebuked" his own flesh, in the power of the Holy Spirit, for its tendency to be undone by grief. It is in response to this inner, divine rebuke that his human nature is then said to be visibly "troubled" but ultimately healed of this weakness.

of his own Spirit he might strengthen the weaknesses of the flesh, and set this nature free from an earthbound way of thinking, and might reshape it to be concerned only with what pleases God. For surely it is an illness of human nature to be tyrannized by grief; but this, too, has been abolished first in Christ, along with our other illnesses, that [its abolition] might come over from him to us.[34]

In the complex subjective identity of the Word made flesh, the inner dialogue between these two complete and wholly different realms of being leads to a new subordination of what is human to God, and to new human freedom from the tyranny of our passions—a freedom now accessible to us all through Jesus's own person.

Maximus the Confessor

The immediate solution to the bitter fifth-century dispute between Cyril of Alexandria and the Antiochene theologians over how to conceive and express the identity of Jesus—although by no means a final, comprehensive solution—was the formulation of Christian faith in his person hammered out by the Council of Chalcedon in 451, and appended to the normative creeds of Nicaea and Constantinople I as a kind of hermeneutical key. Rejecting any formulation that might suggest a permanent separation or an indiscriminate confusion of the human and the divine in Jesus, insisting on the full reality of both levels of his existence as a single person, the language agreed on at Chalcedon confesses him to be

> one and the same Son, our Lord Jesus Christ: the same one perfect in divinity and perfect in humanity, truly God and truly human, . . . recognized in two natures without confusion, without change, without division, without separation, with the difference between the natures in no way removed through the union; rather, the distinctive property of both natures is preserved and comes together in a single *persona* and a single concrete individual [*hypostasis*].[35]

The language of the Chalcedonian formula was carefully woven together from a variety of earlier conciliar and theological texts, representing both sides

34. Fragment on John 11:33–34, ed. Philip E. Pusey, *Sancti Patris nostri Cyrilli archiepiscopi Alexandrini in D. Joannis Evangelium* (Oxford: Clarendon, 1872), 2:279–80. For a discussion of Cyril's understanding of the person and saving work of Christ in this commentary, see Lars Koen, *The Saving Passion: Incarnational and Soteriological Thought in Cyril of Alexandria's Commentary on the Gospel according to St. John*, Studia doctrinae Christianae Upsaliensia 31 (Uppsala: Acta Universitatis Upsaliensis, 1991).

35. Norman P. Tanner, ed., *Decrees of the Ecumenical Councils*, vol. 1, *Nicaea I to Lateran V* (London: Sheed & Ward, 1990), 86.

of the debate as well as earlier stages of agreement between them.[36] Yet the formula offered a divided Eastern Christendom little respite from the bitter disputes of the 430s and 440s. For theologians sympathetic to the Antiochene tradition, for ecclesiastical politicians looking for consensus, and for most Western theologians, it seemed a welcome and evenhanded compromise; but for the great majority of monks, clergy, and faithful outside of the main cities of the Eastern Empire, as well as for a number of Eastern Christian intellectuals of the late fifth century, it was an equivocation, a failure to acknowledge the centrally divine identity of the Savior as the core of even his human experiences and acts. For those who rejected the Chalcedonian formula, in the fifth century and afterward, only the terminology of Cyril's later letters, centered on the formula "one nature of the Word, made flesh," captured the vital, mutually expressive unity of the human and the divine elements that determined the identity of Jesus.[37]

In the second quarter of the seventh century, the Emperor Heraclius's efforts to reunify the Eastern Empire led to new efforts on the part of his court bishops to find a way of construing the official Chalcedonian Christology that might be acceptable to dissident Christians. Patriarch Sergius of Constantinople (in office 610–38), borrowing a phrase from Pseudo-Dionysius's *Letter 4*, cautiously advanced the theory that all the human activities of Christ, mental and bodily, were manifestations of "a single theandric operation [*mia theandrikē energeia*]," flowing forth from God's power and using his human nature as a created instrument. Sergius seems quickly to have refined this position in a somewhat more psychological direction, arguing in letters from the late 620s onward that the human experiences and actions of Jesus all express the single *will* and operation of the Second Person of the Trinity, even though they do so through the instrumentality of the complete human nature that God the Son has made his own. It was in response to this attempt to reread Chalcedon yet again that Maximus the Confessor was to make his name and then bear final witness with his life.

Maximus was a well-educated native of Constantinople, born about 580, who had spent some years as a bureaucrat at the imperial court. He became a monk about 613 and eventually moved west with other Byzantines to escape the

36. For an analysis of the text, see Aloys Grillmeier, *Christ in Christian Tradition*, 2nd ed., vol. 1 (London: Mowbray, 1975), 543–54, and the literature cited there.

37. For details of the reactions to Chalcedon, see esp. Aloys Grillmeier, *Christ in Christian Tradition*, vol. 2.1 (Atlanta: John Knox, 1985) and vol. 2.2 (Louisville: Westminster John Knox, 1994); Patrick Gray, *The Defense of Chalcedon in the East (451–553)* (Leiden: Brill, 1979); William H. C. Frend, *The Rise of the Monophysite Movement* (Cambridge: Cambridge University Press, 1972).

Persian invasion of western Asia Minor, settling in Carthage around 628–29, where he kept up a lively theological correspondence throughout the Greek-speaking world. For Maximus, Sergius's new interpretation of the Chalcedonian formula amounted to a tacit denial of its central affirmation about the identity of Jesus: the completeness of his two utterly incommensurate, fully functioning realities—that of God and that of a human—yoked together in the unique historical particularity of a single individual. Every nature, Maximus argued, to be completely itself, must be completely operational—a nature, after all, in classical Aristotelian terminology, is a substance (a definable kind of being, a "what") considered as a principle of operation. And since willing and desiring are integral to all intellectual natures, forming part of what we mean by consciousness, to deny that Jesus possesses a full human will (*thelēma physikon*), which by natural impulse seeks its own human welfare, is to deny the fullness of his human nature, affirmed by the tradition of faith and canonized at Chalcedon. So Maximus writes to Marinus, a Cypriot deacon, in 642:

> Every being that is rational by nature is clearly also by nature able to will. And if [Jesus] had, as a human being, a natural will, surely he willed those things, in accordance with his substance, that he himself, as God the Creator, had placed within that nature for its own continued existence. He did not come to do violence to the nature that he, as God and Word, had made. He came, rather, to divinize completely that nature, which he willed to have as his own.[38]

For Maximus, as for Athanasius three centuries earlier, the test case of Jesus's identity in the Gospels, in terms of consciousness and will, is the scene of his agony in Gethsemane. But while Athanasius construed that story in terms of a tension between the Word and his "flesh," Maximus sees at play simply an instance of what is implied more broadly by the Christology of Chalcedon: Jesus's two natures, with all their faculties and operations, remain intact and distinct, but his single hypostasis—his unique individual *way* (*tropos*) of being God and being human—gives a different modality to both his eternal existence as Son of God and his historical existence as son of Mary. Jesus is, as Maximus remarks in several places, "divine in a human way and human in a divine way."[39] For the human will and the other human faculties of Jesus, this divine modality, communicated by the divine hypostasis whose nature it is, brings that human nature to its own creaturely perfection. So he writes of the Gethsemane scene, in *Opusculum* 7, that in Jesus's prayer for

---

38. Maximus, *Opusculum* 7 (PG 91:77B–C).

39. See, e.g., *Letter 15* (PG 91:573B); *Letter 19* (PG 91:593A2–B1); *Opusculum 4* (PG 91:61B–C); *Opusculum 7* (PG 91:84B–D); *Disputation with Pyrrhus* (PG 91:297D–298A).

deliverance there was a clear expression of his humanity's natural dynamism toward self-preservation:

> On the other hand, that it [Jesus's human will] was completely deified and in agreement with the divine will, that it was always moved and formed by it and remained in accord with it, is clear from the fact that he always carried out perfectly the decision of his Father's will, and that alone. So, as a human being, he said, "Not my will, but your will be done" [Luke 22:42]. In this he offered himself to us as a model and norm for putting away our own wills to fulfill God's will perfectly, even if we should see death threatening us as a result. . . . He had, then, a human will. . . . Constantly and completely divinized by its assent to, and its union with, the Father's will, it was, to put it precisely, divine by union, not divine by nature; so it truly became, and so it should be called. But it never departed from its natural constitution by being divinized.[40]

In a number of his writings, Maximus stresses that it is precisely the unique structure of Jesus's person that contains and reveals the promised eschatological structure of human salvation.[41] In the identity of Jesus, Maximus discovers the full reality of grace, laid open to us in the divine modality of Jesus's humanity, and sees there at the same time the full realization of human nature as it was created to be. "Divinization," a hallowed term in the Greek patristic tradition for the goal of God's gracious work in redeemed humanity, is thus for him both a gift beyond the resources of human nature and the full realization of what God intends human nature to become. It has first been achieved, Maximus argues, in the person of Christ.

Concluding Reflections

In the four Greek fathers whose treatment of Christ we have briefly surveyed here, it is his human weakness—his ability to suffer and die and the limitation of his energy, strength, and intellect—which raise the greatest challenge to the church's proclamation of his lordship and stimulate the most profound theological reflection on what it might mean to say, with the centurion at Calvary, "This person truly was Son of God" (Mark 15:39, my trans.). Irenaeus's opposition to gnostic portraits of Christ clearly rests on an affirmation of the central importance of Jesus's inner-worldly materiality—a

40. *Opusculum* 7 (PG 91:80D, 81D).
41. See *To Thalassius*, Question 60 (CCSG 22:73.10–19). Maximus's collection of responses to Thalassius, mainly dealing with questions of scriptural interpretation, dates from his early years in Carthage, 630–633.

realm that for gnostic thought was irreducibly alien to God—for the full message of salvation. Athanasius, two centuries later, sees in the suffering of Jesus the full proof that God's Word has taken on the complex, damaged human reality that Athanasius calls "flesh" and has begun to transform it by making it the vehicle of revelation and renewed life. Cyril of Alexandria, along with his fifth-century contemporaries, develops a more nuanced technical vocabulary for speaking of the identity of Jesus—of what is single and what is twofold in his identity, and how they are related—and argues that in the very act of making our human weakness his own, the Son of God has begun to transform us, to give us virtue and life in place of sin and death, simply by being both God and fully human at once. Maximus the Confessor, in the seventh century, continues to reflect on the structure of Christ's person, using the vocabulary of Cyril and the Council of Chalcedon; for Maximus, Christ's will is especially the place in which human freedom begins to share in the transcendent freedom of God, and to choose, by the grace that Christ communicates, the destiny for which God created humanity in the beginning.

All of these portraits of the person of Christ are way stations in a continuing process of Christian reflection on who Jesus really is and what he means for us: reflections on the identity and work of Jesus that are rooted in the narrative of the Gospels and the apostolic witness, and that constantly return to the New Testament for judgment and verification. These patristic readings of the Gospels are framed, certainly, by certain particular New Testament affirmations about Jesus that set the hermeneutical conditions for reading the longer narratives of his life and work: by the schema of the self-emptying and glorification of one who in the beginning is "equal with God," formulated in Philippians 2:5–11; by the portrait of Jesus, Son of God and high priest, who "learned obedience through what he suffered," presented in Hebrews 4:14–5:10; and perhaps above all by the affirmation, in the opening verses of the Fourth Gospel, that the Word who "was in the beginning with God . . . became flesh and lived among us" (John 1:2, 12). Yet patristic reflection on the person of Christ clearly expresses a tradition of faith and understanding that moves into realms of discourse and conceptuality that the New Testament writers could never have imagined or understood, a tradition that continues to evolve wherever Christians receive and think about the gospel. As Athanasius argues in defense of the creedal language of Nicaea, the fact that both the supporters and the opponents of Arius could use similar scriptural texts and phrases to undergird their opposed positions made it necessary for the council to employ "strange" terms—terms taken from philosophy and science rather than Scripture—as interpretive norms for ensuring that the

Scriptures themselves would be understood in the way the Christian tradition had always taken them, and as the New Testament's apostolic authors had intended them.[42]

If we ourselves are to make sense of the classical Christian understanding of Jesus's identity that emerges in these and other early Christian writers, we must keep several cautions in mind. The two distinct "substances" or "natures" that early theology sees in the person of Christ are, of course, two wholly incommensurable realities—not two parallel species of being competing for central stage. The one does not rule out the other. And the one "person" the church recognizes as "owning" these two substances or natures is not classically understood in the way modern Westerners conceive of a person, defined by being a unique and self-contained pole of consciousness and free decisions, capable of forming relationships with other, equally distinct persons. In the classical understanding of both the triune God and of Jesus Christ, "persons" or hypostases are irreducible individual subjects of predication and attribution; yet the heart of both these Mysteries, for Christian faith, is that the three related "persons" in God share a single consciousness and will, a single substance, and that the one "person" of the incarnate Word possesses both an infinite divine mind and will, and a complete human mind and will like our own. For the post-Chalcedonian understanding of the person of Christ, the Mystery of the gospel is that God the Son—"one of the Holy Trinity"—is "selved" in the full human knowledge and freedom of the Son of Mary and expresses in Jesus's human life and actions what it is to be Son of the Father and giver of the Spirit. The one who is "God from God, light from light," in Nicene language, has lived out in a human life, in a human body and mind, with all their inherent vulnerability and promise, what eternal Sonship means, so that we too, who call Jesus "Lord," might also dare to call God "Father" and to live in his Spirit as God's sons and daughters.

In a famous passage in its Pastoral Constitution on the Church in the Modern World (*Gaudium et Spes*), the Second Vatican Council makes this same link between the identity of Jesus and the identity to which all of us are called, in grace: "In reality it is only in the Mystery of the Word made flesh that the mystery of humanity truly becomes clear. For Adam, the first human, was a type of him who was to come, Christ the Lord. Christ, the new Adam, in

---

42. See Athanasius, *Defense of the Nicene Definition* 18–24, esp. 21: "Let anyone who is ready to learn recognize that, even if these expressions are not found this way in the Scriptures, still—as we have said before—they contain the sense derived from Scripture, and by giving it expression they signify it to those whose hearing is completely attuned to piety." Cf. Origen, *First Principles* 1, preface 2.

the very revelation of the Mystery of the Father and of his love, fully reveals humanity to itself, and brings to light its very high calling."[43]

In the Greek Fathers we have surveyed here, that same Christian intuition is expressed with increasing clarity and wonder. In the person of Jesus—a human who, at the moment of his most abject human weakness and suffering, is recognized as "truly Son of God"—the ancient faith of Christians finds both the pledge of God's indomitable love and the form of our human vocation. The identity of Jesus, however we parse it, is meant to be the pattern and promise of our own identity.

43. *Gaudium et Spes* 22, trans. Paul Lennon, in *Vatican Council II*, ed. Austin Flannery (Northport, NY: Costello, 1996), 185.

14

Suffering Impassibly

Christ's Passion in Cyril of Alexandria's Soteriology

J. Warren Smith

etween the outbreak of the *Theotokos* controversy in 428 and the Council of Ephesus of 431, Cyril of Alexandria addressed a short treatise titled *On the Right Faith* to the emperor Theodosius II's wife, Eudocia, and his sister, Pulcheria. This was the third such treatise Cyril wrote in the hope of gaining imperial support in his dispute with Nestorius. A little more than halfway into the work, Cyril asserts that Nestorius's two-subjects Christology confers upon the human subject of the incarnation "equality of worth and power . . . with God the Word." To suggest that the divine subject and the human subject share an equality of power and worth, Cyril claims, strips the Word of the power proper to his divine nature, conferring on the Word the weakness of human nature. The absurd implication of this suggestion, Cyril explains, is an affirmation of the paradoxical nature of the incarnation.

> It would consequently be fitting also for the Word to fear death, to look upon danger with suspicion, to weep in temptations, and in addition to learn obedience by what he suffered when tempted. Nevertheless, I think it completely

foolish either to think or say this, since the Word of God is all-powerful, stronger than death, beyond suffering, and completely without a share in fear suitable to man. But though he exists this way by nature, still he suffered for us. Therefore, neither is Christ a mere man nor is the Word without flesh. Rather, united with a humanity like ours, he suffered human things impassibly [*pathoi apathōs*] in his own flesh. Thus these events became an example [*hypotypoein*] for us in a human fashion, as I said to begin with, so that we might follow in his steps [*tois ichnesin autou epakolouthēsomen*].[1]

According to John J. O'Keefe,[2] Cyril finds himself on the horns of a dilemma. On the one hand, he wants to give priority to the biblical narrative— which declares that the divine Christ suffered and died—over the Antiochenes' philosophical concern with God's impassibility. Yet on the other hand, Cyril does affirm the paradoxical character of the incarnation. What is particularly frustrating about this passage is that Cyril does not follow up this provocative suggestion by explaining what it might mean that Christ "suffered impassibly." Were this an isolated instance of the expression, one could dismiss it as a onetime, unsuccessful flirtation with the rhetoric of paradox. However, in later works, such as *Scholia on the Incarnation of the Only Begotten*,[3] and *The Unity of Christ*,[4] Cyril continues to employ the expression. Therefore we must take the phrase "suffering impassibly" to be a serious component of Cyril's thought and so must explore the logic behind this nuance of his Christology. Nestorius dismissed the term as Cyril's weak attempt to conceal his true theological move, namely, abandoning the doctrine of divine impassibility.[5] Recent interpreters have treated the enigmatic expression simply as expressing Cyril's desire not to be labeled a theopaschite. Therefore Cyril adopts the paradoxical language of "suffering impassibly," which attempts to assert two necessary claims about the incarnation, that the Christ in the fullness of the hypostatic union genuinely suffered, and yet that the divine did not suffer.[6]

---

1. Cyril of Alexandria, *Ad reginas de recta fide oratio altera* 163, trans. Rowan Greer (unpublished), 33; PG 76:1393B. This translation is cited as Greer.

2. John J. O'Keefe, "Impassible Suffering? Divine Passion and Fifth-Century Christology," *Theological Studies* 58 (1997): 9–60.

3. Cyril, *Scholia on the Incarnation of the Only Begotten* 35, PG 75:1409D.

4. Cyril, *Quod unus sit Christus*, SC 97:776–77.

5. See Paul Gavrilyuk, "*Theopathei*: Nestorius' Main Charge against Cyril of Alexandria," *Scottish Journal of Theology* 56, no. 2 (2003): 190–207. Gavrilyuk notes that while Nestorius acknowledged Cyril's explicit affirmation of the impassibility of God's nature, he objected that a nature cannot be both capable of suffering and also impassible. Cf. Nestorius, *Liber Heraclidis* 1.3. Thence arises the key christological issue for Nestorius: since the divine nature is impassible, one cannot make God the subject of Christ's suffering in the flesh.

6. O'Keefe, "Impassible Suffering?," 51. The Arian argument was that if the Word were the subject of every human operation, then the Word whose predicates are *kata physin* would be

Similarly, John McGuckin says that for Cyril "impassible suffering" was his attempt "deliberately to [maintain] both sides of the paradox with equal force and absolute seriousness of intent, refusing to minimize either reality."[7] As Rowan Greer has put it, Cyril's religious concern—affirming the reality of Christ's passion—takes priority over any interest in being philosophically or theologically coherent.[8] Certainly these conclusions are correct.

Yet my concern is that saying Cyril simply resorts to paradox, leaving us with this mysterious expression, does not explain why the expression is a true paradox—a *seeming* contradiction—and not simply an outright contradiction in terms that are wholly incoherent and theologically unhelpful. The thesis I argue here is that the phrase *pathoi apathōs* should be interpreted in its strict grammatical sense, that is, *apathōs* is functioning adverbially to qualify the character of *pathoi*. But "impassible suffering" is a theologically helpful category only if we can grasp how *apathōs* qualifies or limits the character of the Word's passion. It is my position that Cyril's idea of "impassible suffering" is a conscious step toward equating impassibility with immutability: Christ experiences suffering without being changed by the experience. Moreover I hope to show that "impassible suffering" is important in Cyril's thought for two reasons: (1) it preserves the inviolability of the divine in the hypostatic union, and (2) it illustrates the character of Christ's sanctification of human nature. "Impassible suffering" is not a property singular to the divine nature, but through the indwelling of the divine Word in the incarnation it becomes an attainable ideal that Christ's followers are to imitate. To do this I need to look at three things: (1) Cyril's Christology, which provides the framework for our investigation; (2) Cyril's understanding of suffering and the sense in which Christ even during the passion escapes the effects of suffering; and (3) the soteriological significance for us of Christ's impassible suffering.

---

limited and affected by Christ's suffering at the level of his nature. Cyril, following Athanasius, expresses the double judgment of Scripture in terms of a double predication. The first predication refers to the natural predicates of the Word; the second predication is an economic predication, i.e., it names the predicates that the Word truly possesses as a result of the incarnation; yet the former are not compromised by the latter. See Francis A. Sullivan, *The Christology of Theodore of Mopsuestia* (Rome: Universitatis Gregoriana, 1956), 162.

7. John McGuckin, *Cyril of Alexandria: The Christological Controversy; Its History, Theology, and Texts* (Leiden: Brill, 1994), 185.

8. Joseph M. Hallman similarly comments that Cyril's lack of interest in philosophy can be observed in his early willingness to ascribe emotions to the immutable and impassible God. Being faithful to the biblical narrative has priority over being philosophically rigorous. See "The Seeds of Fire: Divine Suffering in the Christology of Cyril of Alexandria and Nestorius of Constantinople," *Journal of Early Christian Studies* 5, no. 3 (1997): 371.

Cyril's Christology: Incarnation as Hypostatic Union

The heart of Cyril's Christology is his insistence that Jesus is no mere man through whom the Word of God speaks. He is the incarnate Deity—the divine and human natures inextricably bound together in the unity of a single person or hypostasis possessed of a single personality. Cyril conceives of the hypostatic union of the divine and human, not as the conjoining of two separate substances, but as substantial unity in which there is one substance, the Word, who governs the humanity he has assumed. Cyril's tendency to speak of "one substance" is merely his insistence that there is one subject of the incarnation, the Word. The source of much confusion for Cyril's interpreters arises from his use of "nature" to denote the single subject of the incarnation and alternatively the two elements in Christ Jesus.[9] Ultimately Cyril moves toward Chalcedon's final proposal when he chooses to speak of the two natures *from which* the union is made instead of the two natures *in which* the union consists.[10]

Cyril's doctrine of the hypostatic union was driven by two soteriological concerns. First, the Word must be divine in order to free us from death; and second, the Word must genuinely experience suffering and death in order to conquer death itself and provide an example for his disciples who would imitate the Lord's passion in their own martyrdom. These two soteriological concerns are necessarily linked. For the hypostatic union that divinizes human nature, thereby freeing it from corruption and death, also sanctifies the soul in a way that enables it to master the baser passions of fear proper to our human nature and thus stand fast in the face of temptation and persecution.

Cyril understands Christ's conquest of death through the divinization of human nature as the result of the *communicatio idiomatum*, the communication of attributes from his divine nature to his human nature and vice versa. The incarnation of the Word frees humanity from death by communicating the incorruptibility of the divine nature to corruptible and passible human flesh. Even as water though cold by nature "all but forgets its own nature" when placed in a kettle set upon an open flame, becoming warm through the transfer of the fire's energy, so too our bodies, which are naturally corruptible, abandon their weakness when mingling with the divine nature of the Word, which is life.[11] Christ overcomes corruption by revealing the archetypal image

9. Richard A. Norris, "Toward a Contemporary Interpretation of the Chalcedonian Definition," in *Lux in Lumine*, ed. Richard A. Norris (New York: Seabury, 1966), 71–72.

10. See Rowan Greer, *The Captain of Our Salvation: A Study in the Patristic Exegesis of Hebrews* (Tübingen: Mohr, 1973), 320.

11. *Commentary on John* 4.2, in Philip E. Pusey, *Sancti Patris nostri Cyrilli archiepiscopi Alexandrini in D. Ioannis Evangelium* (Oxford: Clarendon, 1872), 1:362A–B; cited below as Pusey.

of human nature, thereby restoring what was lost in Adam, namely, the Holy Spirit,[12] who seals the image of the incorruptible God upon our human nature.[13] As the flower that sprang from the stem of Jesse (Isa. 11:1–3), Christ is the one in whom human nature "blossomed again, . . . acquiring incorruption, and life, and a new evangelical mode of existence."[14] But in order for the Word to communicate its incorruptible nature to our flesh, it is not enough, Cyril says, for the Word to exist in a "casual conjunction"[15] to humanity, as Nestorius claimed; rather, the Word must be fully united to our human nature. This, Cyril explains, is why John wrote in the prologue to his Gospel, "And the Word *became* flesh." It would not have been enough simply to say that the Word "came into flesh"; rather, John says that the Word "became flesh" "in order to exclude any idea of a relative indwelling, as in the case of the prophets and the other saints. He really did become flesh, that is to say, a human being."[16] Cyril proceeds to qualify the Word's "becoming flesh" by insisting that John should not be misinterpreted to suggest that a change occurred in the Word. That is, the Word did not give up his divine nature. For this reason John adds "and dwelt among us." Therefore the divine and human, though fully united, remain distinct,[17] without confusion or mixing.[18] Yet though distinct, they are inseparable, except at a conceptual level.[19] Thus in Christ the two united natures exist side by side, forming the composite character and personality of Jesus.

12. Cyril, *Commentary on Isaiah*, PG 70:313C.

13. Cyril, *Commentary on John* 1.9, Pusey, 1:91A–B.

14. Cyril, *Commentary on Isaiah*, in *Cyril of Alexandria*, trans. Norman Russell (London: Routledge, 2000), 82–83; PG 70:313A; cited below as Russell.

15. Cyril quotes Nestorius: "There is no division in the conjunction, or in the dignity, or in the sonship. There is no division in his being Christ, but there is division between the divinity and the humanity." See Cyril, *Against Nestorius* 2.6, trans. Russell, 148; ACO 1.1:6.42. Although Nestorius claimed that there was one indivisible Christ, this "indivisible conjunction," Cyril contends, is only "a casual joining of one thing to another" either by spiritual concord or physical proximity.

16. Cyril, *Commentary on John* 1.9, trans. Russell, 106; Pusey, 1:95E.

17. "We do not . . . say that the Word who is from the Father was transformed into the nature of flesh, or that the flesh changed into the Word. For each remains what it is by nature, and Christ is one from both." Cyril, *Commentary on John* 1.9, trans. Russell, 117; Pusey, 1:363B.

18. "Our discussion of the union does not ignore the difference [between the humanity and divinity] but nevertheless puts the division aside, not because we are confusing the natures or mixing them together, but because the Word of God, having partaken of flesh and blood, is still thought of as a single son and is called such." See Cyril, *Against Nestorius* 2.6, trans. Russell, 148; ACO 1.1:6.42–43.

19. "For after the Incarnation they [i.e., the human and the divine] are not divisible, except insofar as one knows that the Word that came from the Father and the temple that came from the virgin are not identical in nature. For the body is not consubstantial with the Word of God." See Cyril, *Commentary on John* 4.2, trans. Russell, 115; Pusey, 1:361B.

The hypostatic union has consequences for both the divine Word and the humanity of Christ. The primary effect of the incarnation upon the Word is that the Word experiences the weakness of human nature. One of Cyril's favorite texts to support this point is the Christ hymn in Philippians 2. For Cyril, the Word does not *empty himself* of his transcendent power or glory. Rather, Cyril interprets *kenōsis* to refer to that which the Word takes on himself, his humanity. In his *Commentary on Isaiah*, Cyril remarks that "having brought himself down to the level of self-emptying, [the Word] should not repudiate the low estate arising from that self-emptying, but should accept what is full by nature on account of the humanity, not for his own sake, but for ours who *lack everything*."[20] When the Word became flesh, taking a body for his very own, he experienced, along with the infirmities of embodiment, the full range of human emotions, which accompany our mortal nature, including fear and timidity.[21] Cyril, in opposition to Apollinaris, maintains that Jesus possessed a human soul.[22] Since the soul, as Apollinaris maintained, is the source of the *physis* of a thing, Cyril having accepted the presence of a human soul in Jesus has trouble retaining Apollinaris's one-nature formula to express the unity of Christ.[23]

Indeed for Cyril, Christ's suffering is no mere by-product of the Word's union with human flesh; rather, it is the necessary means to accomplish the goal of the incarnation.[24] Since Christ is the Son who became for us high priest by offering himself on the cross as the perfect sacrifice fully sufficient for the expiation of all sin, he had to suffer and die. It was necessary for the divine Word to "suffer for us in his own flesh"[25] in order that, as Hebrews 2:14–15 says, "through death he might destroy the one who has the power of death."

20. Cyril, *Commentary on Isaiah* 2.4, trans. Russell, 83; PG 70:313C, emphasis added.
21. Cyril, *Commentary on John* 8, Pusey, 2:703E–4A.
22. Cyril, *Ad reginas de recta fide oratio altera* 9, PG 76:1345D.
23. See Aloys Grillmeier, *Christ in Christian Tradition*, vol. 1, *From the Apostolic Age to Chalcedon (451)*, trans. John Bowden, 2nd ed. (Atlanta: John Knox, 1975), 474–76.
24. Robert L. Wilken, *Judaism and the Early Christian Mind: A Study of Cyril of Alexandria's Exegesis and Theology* (New Haven: Yale University Press, 1971), 182, contends that within the Christ-Adam typology Christ truly suffers, but his suffering is unique; Christ's passion is effectively but not qualitatively different from our suffering. In other words, as I will argue later, Christ's impassible suffering becomes an example for his disciples of how they can face the suffering of martyrdom; yet, as Wilken rightly points out, Christ's passion is unique because his suffering is ultimately salvific in its effect.
25. For our confidence in Christ as high priest is because the sacrificial offering was the one who alone is without blemish. Cyril rhetorically asks Nestorius, who denied that the divine Word suffered, "By whom, then, are we justified? Is it not in him who suffered death according to the flesh for our sake? Is it not in our Lord Jesus Christ? . . . But if we believe that he who 'suffered in the flesh' is God, and that it is he who became our High Priest, we have not erred in any way." See Cyril, *Against Nestorius* 3.2, trans. Russell, 165; ACO 1.1:6.61.

The hypostatic union affects not only the divinity of Christ but also his humanity. For in him our humanity partakes of both the life-giving and the sanctifying power proper to the divine nature. The corollary of the Word's humiliation in the *kenōsis* of the incarnation is the exaltation of human nature. Commenting on 2 Corinthians 8:9, "He was rich, yet for your sakes he became poor," Cyril explains that Christ's condescension effected a "great exchange" between God and humanity. For while the Word "submitted to the limits of humanity, . . . thereafter man's nature might come to possess the lofty honors of the divine majesty in Christ and put off the shame of poverty."[26] In *Against Nestorius*, Cyril poetically describes the effect of the inseparable hypostatic union: the brilliance of the divine nature adheres to the human nature in the person of Christ Jesus as the shimmering brilliance inheres in the pearl or as the sweet fragrance exists as a quality inseparable from the lily.[27]

It is precisely the *simultaneity* of the Word's *kenōsis* that endures human suffering and the Word's empowerment of his assumed humanity that Cyril seeks to express in the phrase *pathoi apathōs*. Cyril's Christology forces him to acknowledge that in the fully integrative unity of the divine and human in Christ, the divine Word genuinely experiences the limitations of our humanity, including suffering, and at the same time preserves the perfection of his divine nature, including its impassibility. He does this in order to heal fallen human nature. Therefore the adverb *apathōs* is intended to qualify the character of Christ's suffering, to convey the idea that Christ's suffering did not compromise the very power of the divine Word. For this power was necessarily at work in Christ's passion to redeem humanity. To understand what characteristics of suffering the word *apathōs* is intended to exclude from Christ's passion, it is necessary for us now to examine Cyril's understanding of suffering and its effects on those who suffer.

The Nature of Suffering and Christ's Impassibility

Suffering, for Cyril, is problematic, especially if attributed to the Deity, because suffering entails *change*. Perhaps Cyril's clearest declaration of what "suffering" means is found in his explanation of why the incarnate Word cannot be said to suffer, properly speaking. Commenting on John 1:14, Cyril explains the evangelist's addition of the phrase "and dwelt among us":

> Having stated that the Word of God became flesh, he is anxious in case anyone out of profound ignorance should assume that the Word has abandoned his

26. Cyril, *Ad reginas de recta fide oratio altera* 6, trans. Greer, 4; PG 76:1344A.
27. Cyril, *Against Nestorius* 2, Proem, ACO 1.1:6.33–34.

own proper nature and has in reality been transformed into flesh and has suffered, which is impossible, for with regard to its mode of being the divine is far
removed from any kind of change or alteration into something else.[28]

Here Cyril explicitly denies that it is possible for God to suffer since the divine
nature is immutable. While the creature who comes into being is inherently
subject to change, God belongs to the realm of the eternal and so is, as Cyril
puts it, "far removed from any kind of change or alteration," which are the
effects of suffering. Moreover, suffering produces change that is degenerative.
If the Word actually became flesh, it would be a change from the perfection
of the uncreated nature to the imperfection of the created nature.

That suffering is degenerative change was the commonplace opinion in
late antiquity. Even in cases where experiences of physical pain or discom-
fort produced salutary change, these episodes were viewed as remarkable
precisely because the effect of the suffering was the opposite of what was
expected. They are the exceptions that prove the rule. One example is
found in the second-century orator Aelius Aristides's *Orationes sacrae*.
Aristides's ascending career as an orator was derailed when at the age of
twenty-six he fell incurably ill. Becoming a devotee of Asclepius, the god of
medicine and healing, he followed a harsh regimen of treatments inspired
by the deity in order to purge his body of its sickness. On one occasion, as
he traveled in Smyrna in the middle of winter, Asclepius appeared to him
in a vision and commanded him to bathe in the icy waters of a river whose
banks were lined with frost-covered pebbles. A crowd, including doctors,
gathered on the banks to watch the spectacle. After swimming for some
time and splashing himself with water, Aristides came out of the river; yet
to the surprise of everyone, including Aristides himself, he showed no ill
effects of the swim.

> When I came out, [he said,] all my skin had a rosy hue and there was a lightness
> throughout my body. . . . My mental state was also nearly the same. For there
> was neither, as it were, conspicuous pleasure, nor would you say it was like
> human joy. But there was a certain inexplicable contentment which regarded
> everything as less than the present moment. . . . Thus I was wholly with the god.[29]

28. Cyril adds, "The theologian [i.e., John] therefore very aptly added at once: 'and dwelt
in us,' so that realizing that he was referring to two things, the subject of the dwelling and that
in which the dwelling was taking place, you should not think that the Word was transformed
into the flesh, but rather that he dwelt in flesh." Cyril, *Commentary on John* 1.9, trans. Russell,
106; Pusey, 1:96B–C.
29. Aristides, *Orationes sacrae* 48.21–23, quoted in Judith Perkins, "The 'Self' as Sufferer,"
Harvard Theological Review 85, no. 3 (1992): 253.

The atypical nature of this case highlights two key characteristics of suffering. First, unlike the normal effects of exposure to such freezing temperatures, which would include turning blue or white with frostbite and a loss of mobility due to a lack of blood circulating to the limbs, Aristides's body preserves its rosy coloration. His body, far from being sluggish, is light, and he moves with ease. Second, and for our purposes more important, Aristides's mental faculties, rather than being clouded or unable to focus, remain unchanged. This episode stands out as exceptional precisely because he does not experience the freezing cold as the cause of suffering that would normally impair both his physical strength and agility and his mental stability. Although Aristides was exposed to threatening environmental forces that are often the source of suffering, he does not describe himself as having suffered precisely because he experienced neither the adverse physical effects nor the deleterious mental changes that are the common result of such exposure.

In contrast to Aristides, Cyril's Christ does suffer; yet Cyril insists that he does not experience the deleterious effects normally associated with suffering. In other words, Cyril's Christ does suffer, but he does not change. For change cannot be admitted in the divine nature. Commenting on Isaiah's vision of God in the temple, Cyril explains the symbolism of God's being "seated on a throne, high and lifted up" (Isa. 6:1 KJV). The throne is described as "set on high" to represent "the glory of God's rule, . . . transcending every intelligible nature." That God is seated on the throne, as opposed to standing on his feet and moving, indicates God's "steadfastness . . . and the enduring nature and immutability of God's blessing." Here the term "immutability" refers not just to "God's blessing," meaning the divine disposition toward humanity, but also to the divine nature itself. For immediately Cyril, after quoting Baruch 3:3, "For you are enthroned forever, and we are perishing forever," contrasts our created nature, which is subject to limitation and to decay, with One who is seated upon the throne, "Wisdom, who is craftsman and creator of all things. That is to say, her immutability is unshakable."[30] Thus Wisdom's immutability stands in contrast to our decay and corruption.

Even during the incarnation, Cyril insists, the divine nature retained its immutability. Of particular concern to Cyril in the dispute over Mary's status as "Mother of God" was his insistence that the incarnation entailed the birth of God, yet that such a birth did not compromise God's impassability. According to Nestorius, if one were to speak of Mary as *Theotokos*, it would imply that the eternal God was born, came to life, and therefore experienced change.[31]

---

30. Cyril, *Commentary on Isaiah* 1.4, trans. Russell, 74–75; PG 70:173B.
31. O'Keefe, "Impassible Suffering?," 52.

Cyril replies, "Since he was born in human nature, he endured what belongs to it without thereby suffering in any respect the slightest harm. . . . Just as, since he is lord by nature, he remained what he was even when he was born in the form of a servant."[32] This denial of Nestorius's charge is interesting because Cyril is using the term "suffer" in the sense of experiencing harm, as deleterious change. His point is that although Christ was indeed born, he did not suffer from his birth. This is a very curious comment given that earlier in *On the Right Faith* he uses the term "suffering" to refer to the process of birth. He writes, "For he who in his own nature was in no way poor was poor as a man, and he who is truly rich suffered this quite suitably—that is, the Word from God the Father when he was born like us."[33] This is curious because it means that in the latter passage he says that Christ suffered inasmuch as he was "born like us," but in the former passage he says that Christ though born as we are did not suffer any harm. Either this is a blatant contradiction or Cyril is simply using the term "suffer" in two different ways. The latter fits with Cyril's sense of *kenōsis*, namely, enduring the limitations of our nature and all the accompanying hardships. The former refers to the consequences of that experience of human hardships. In other words, Christ truly underwent human birth and all that goes with it; but contrary to Nestorius's claim, the richness and power and glory of his divinity were not lessened in the experience.

Moreover, the claim that in the incarnation Christ had to endure all the vicissitudes of embodiment but was not "the slightest harmed" is a very curious thing to declare about someone who underwent the tortures of crucifixion and died. Cyril's point is that although the hypostatic union enabled the Word to experience human suffering, this suffering did not harm the Word in the sense of compromising the unchangeable character of the divine. Cyril employs a number of metaphors to illustrate how the Word in union with the flesh may be said truly to suffer yet remain unchanged in his divine nature.[34] One image is that of the immortal human soul united to a mortal body. In death the person who is composed of soul and body suffers and dies. Consequently, the soul is said to experience suffering in the flesh. But even though the soul truly suffers death in the flesh, it does not change in its essential nature. The soul remains immortal. So too the Word suffers in his flesh but is unchanged in his divine nature by the

32. Cyril, *Ad reginas de recta fide oratio altera* 38, trans. Greer, 30; PG 76:1388B.
33. Cyril, *Ad reginas de recta fide oratio altera* 6, trans. Greer, 4; PG 76:1344B.
34. For a helpful list and analysis of the various metaphors, see Steven A. McKinion, *Words, Imagery, and the Mystery of Christ: A Reconstruction of Cyril of Alexandria's Christology* (Leiden: Brill, 2000), 214–24.

suffering.[35] This affirmation of Christ's immutability is the most basic meaning of *pathoi apathōs.*

Apathōs carries not only the qualification that Christ did not undergo any change of character or power as a result of his experience of suffering but also the sense that Christ's suffering is not forced upon him by external forces to which he needed to yield.[36] In other words, that which is possible not only changes but also is subject to change imposed on it externally. If Christ were passible in this sense, as we are, it would mean that in the incarnation he had emptied himself of the absolute power of his divine nature and thus was not fully God. Cyril wants to qualify the character of Christ's suffering so as not to jeopardize the autonomy of the Godhead. He comments that the incarnation is a kind of "middle position" in which the Word neither soars to the heavenly heights, detaching himself from our limitations, nor submits to the complete domination of human weaknesses. He writes, "Not that this self-emptying is sufficient to overwhelm by force, so to speak, him who with the Father is king of the universe, for the only begotten is never forced against his will. Rather, it was of his own accord, out of his love for us, that he accepted the self-emptying and persevered with it."[37] Here Cyril follows the Johannine theme that Christ did not have his life taken from him but laid it down voluntarily. Thus Christ's experience of suffering from birth to the tomb is not imposed on him but is something he allows to happen. For Cyril, the voluntary nature of Christ's suffering transformed the cross from a moment of supreme tragedy to one of glory. He interprets the comment in John 7:39 that "Jesus was not yet glorified" to refer to his crucifixion. Similarly, when Jesus prays to the Father, "Glorify your Son" (John 17:1), he is, according to Cyril, in effect asking, "Allow me to suffer in a voluntary fashion."[38] Because Christ "accepted suffering voluntarily for our sake when it was in his power to avoid it, this acceptance of suffering for the good of others is a sign of extraordinary compassion and the highest glory."[39] Christ suffers impassibly in that his suffering is the consequence neither of any weakness nor of any external necessity, but it occurs solely within the parameters of the strength of his divine power and out of the compassion of his divine mercy.

Most important for Cyril, Christ's immutability was manifest in his preservation of his unimpeachable devotion to the Father's will. He endured physical abuse as well as degrading insults from the very ones he came to liberate. Yet

35. Cyril, *Scholia on the Incarnation of the Only Begotten* 33, PG 75:1405A–B.
36. I am grateful to Dr. Phillip Cary for this helpful insight.
37. Cyril, *Commentary on John* 11.9, trans. Russell, 125; Pusey, 2:970A.
38. Cyril, *Commentary on John* 8, Pusey, 2:706A.
39. Cyril, *Commentary on John* 8, trans. Russell, 121; Pusey, 2:705D–E.

in spite of such demeaning treatment, Christ's benevolence toward humanity remained unchanged. In his Isaiah commentary, Cyril explains that the prophet's words, "Before the child knows good and evil, he will reject evil and choose the good" (cf. Isa. 7:15–16), bear witness to the goodness proper to Christ's divine nature, which directs his actions even before, in his humanity, he understands the difference between good and evil. Jesus's intuitive grasp of the good can be attributed only to his divinity; for the divine nature "is ever inaccessible to wickedness. And it repudiates the ways of viciousness, for it is not put to the test from that quarter, nor does it experience any annoyance, for it rejects wickedness by virtue of its nature."[40] This is a crucial passage. Here Cyril asserts not only that Christ was good by nature but also that this goodness was an immutable goodness. Thus he could not even be tempted to viciousness. When Cyril says that Christ's natural goodness does not allow him to "experience any annoyance," he is suggesting that amid all the insults and abuse that he received from the high priest and the Roman procurator, still Christ was not tempted to return evil for evil. Rather, Christ was "irrevocably fixed on the good."[41]

Perhaps the most vivid illustration of Christ's suffering the passions of human nature and yet remaining fixed with respect to the good is found in Cyril's account of Jesus's experience in the garden of Gethsemane. Here Cyril sees Christ's two natures existing side by side, in tension and in conflict about the ordeal that awaits. In his prayer, Jesus speaks out of the impulses of both natures. Yet every time his humanity recoils from its duty, it is checked by his immutable divinity, which will not deviate from the determined course. Commenting on Jesus's request to have this cup taken from him, Cyril observes that the Word, who is immortal, incorruptible, and life itself, cannot "cower before death." Yet by virtue of the hypostatic union he experiences all things proper to the flesh, including its revulsion at the threat of death. Thus, in his humanity, Jesus cowers before death. It is perfectly natural for Jesus as a human being to experience fear of death even as he would hunger or feel weariness or any other physiological disturbance. Yet Cyril goes on to say that, though Jesus experienced the full range of emotions that all mortals feel, he was not disturbed by them to the degree that we are. The implied difference is that in the case of most people, once the emotion is aroused, it seizes control over the soul. In the case of Christ, however, he masters the emotion and "immediately reverts to the

40. Cyril, *Commentary on Isaiah* 1.4, trans. Russell, 79; PG 70:205B.
41. Cyril, *Commentary on Isaiah* 1.4, trans. Russell, 80; PG 70:205C.

courageous attitude that is appropriate to him."[42] Commenting on Jesus's words, "The spirit indeed is willing, but the flesh is weak" (Mark 14:38), Cyril says the weakness of the flesh aroused a fear in him that "fell very short of the dignity appropriate to God," but then adds, "That is why he added a most spirited defense to what he had just said, declaring that the flesh is weak because of what is proper to it, and belongs to it by nature, whereas the spirit, by contrast, is willing because it knows that it can suffer nothing that can harm it."[43] In addition to declaring that the strength of the divine will reins in Christ's human instincts for self-preservation, Cyril implies that Jesus controlled the impulses of his baser appetites by the power of *thymos*, that is, the spirited faculty of the soul. But he goes on to explain how the divine will places a check on the impulses of his human nature; it was through the recognition that though he will suffer, he will suffer nothing that can harm him. Christ is able to prevail over his passion because of the strength of his spirit, which recognizes its ultimate invulnerability to death. Not only is Christ's courage rallied with the thought that death will not ultimately hurt him, but more importantly, he is committed to fulfilling the redemptive purpose of his incarnation.

Cyril is quick to explain that Jesus's apprehension in the face of his imminent passion is wholly natural for human nature and so is not a sin.[44] Nor does the presence of timidity imply for Cyril that Jesus possesses two wills that are in conflict. Jesus's prayer in the garden, "Take away this cup from me; . . . nevertheless not my will but yours be done" (cf. Mark 14:36), is problematic; it could be read to imply that, while the Father's will was that Jesus should die, Jesus's own will was inclined to evade death. Thus he asks the Father to deliver him from the cross. Cyril insists, however, that in the hypostatic union Christ is one person; and though in his humanity Christ is inclined to avoid death, his final human choice is perfectly in accord with the divine will. Cyril writes, "Christ, however, despising death and the shame that comes from suffering, focused only on the achievements resulting from suffering, . . . the death of all departing from our midst."[45] In fact, Jesus's wish to be freed from his passion conflicted with his will, which was set upon the liberation of humanity from death. The conflict was merely about the means necessary to achieve this end. He was willing to bear the dishonor, insults, and tortures "at the hands of the Jews." Yet "if it had been possible for him to achieve what he earnestly desired for us without suffering, he would not

42. Cyril, *Commentary on John* 8, trans. Russell, 120; Pusey, 2:704B.
43. Cyril, *Commentary on John* 4.1, trans. Russell, 113; Pusey, 1:332B–C.
44. Cyril, *Commentary on John* 8, Pusey, 2:703E.
45. Cyril, *Commentary on John* 8, trans. Russell, 120–21; Pusey, 2:705B.

have wished to suffer."[46] The divine will that the human race be freed from death overrode Christ's human instinct for self-preservation.

Christ's mastery of the passions did not entail simply the suppression of the emotion but also entailed its transformation into a virtue. One passage in the Gospel where this motif is played out, according to Cyril, is John 12:27. At the time of his final entry into Jerusalem, Jesus confesses to the disciples, "Now is my soul troubled. And what should I say, 'Father save me from this hour'? No, it is for this purpose that I have come to this hour." Here Jesus's words are not at all shocking to Cyril, but they express the very ambivalence of a man possessed of both a vulnerable and frightened human nature and at the same time the divine nature ever committed to fulfilling the purposes of the plan of salvation. Cyril observes,

> Notice here again how easy it is to produce confusion and fear in human nature, whereas by contrast the divine and ineffable power is in all respects indestructible and invulnerable and oriented only towards the courage that befits it. For the thought of death has slipped in attempts to agitate Jesus, while the power of the divinity at once masters the emotion that has been aroused and immediately *transforms* that which has been conquered by fear into an incomparable courage.[47]

This passage will become significant for Cyril in his later dispute with Nestorius because it illustrates for Cyril how Christ is human and divine, simultaneously experiencing the drives and impulses of both natures. Unlike Nestorius's schizophrenic Jesus, Cyril's Christ of the hypostatic union does not speak at times from his humanity, and then in other passages proclaim the thoughts of the Word who speaks the divine message.[48] Cyril says of John's presentation of Jesus in the Fourth Gospel that he "elegantly preserv[es] for us in every way [Jesus's] dual character so that we see him who is by nature truly both God and man speaking as such at one and the same time, brilliantly combining the humble element of the humanity with the glory of the ineffable divine nature, and maintaining a proportionality of expression."[49] Here the point for Cyril is that Christ is a single person who feels the emotional pull of his human desire to flee death. In this single person possessing both divine

46. Cyril, *Commentary on John* 4.1, trans. Russell, 112; Pusey, 1:331B.

47. Cyril, *Commentary on John* 8, trans. Russell, 120; Pusey, 2:703D.

48. This is Cyril's characterization of Nestorius's position. "And he has the Word of God dwelling in Christ by participation as in an ordinary man, and he divides up the sayings in the Gospels, assigning them sometimes exclusively to the Word alone and sometimes exclusively to the man born from a woman." See Cyril, *Against Nestorius* 2, Proem, trans. Russell, 142; ACO 1.1:6.33.

49. Cyril, *Commentary on John* 11.9, trans. Russell, 126; Pusey, 2:970C–D.

and human natures, the Word experiences this impulse. Yet Christ, whose will is decisively set by his divine nature, checks his fear. For Cyril, Jesus's words, "No, for this purpose I have come to this hour," reflect the divine will forcefully reining in the timidity of his human nature. Moreover Christ controls his fear by stirring within himself a new emotion, resolute courage that transforms his emotional state by displacing his fear altogether with a virtuous emotion.

The Word's transformation of Christ's disordered emotion of fear into virtue is significant soteriologically; for here we see the sanctifying power of the Word upon the man Jesus. Christ suffers impassibly in the sense that the divinity of the Word is unchanged by the suffering, and also in the sense that though he suffers the emotions of fear and dread he is not swept away by the passions. He suffers impassibly precisely because his adherence to the Father's will is not changed by the passionate impulses of his flesh. Thus Christ's impassible suffering is a capacity not of the divine nature alone but also of divinized humanity. This is why in the first passage we examined from *On the Right Faith*, Cyril's suggestion that Christ suffered human things impassibly is immediately followed by his comment: "Thus, these events became an example for us in a human fashion, as I said to begin with, so that we might follow in his footsteps."[50] Christ's impassible suffering serves as an archetype revealing the character and power of human nature sanctified by the indwelling of Christ's Spirit and thereby giving an example for those who would take up his cross for themselves.

Impassible Suffering: An Example of Sanctification

One of the central themes of *On the Right Faith* is that Christ's suffering gives his disciples an example of impassible suffering, thereby enabling them to master their own passions in moments of temptation. The key text for Cyril is Hebrews 2:18, "For because he himself has suffered and been tempted, he is able to help those who are tempted" (RSV). Commenting on this verse, Cyril asserts that Jesus, far from withering under temptation, actually became stronger as a result of his wrestlings with Satan in the wilderness and then on the cross. The strength that Christ gained as a result of his temptation and suffering served a clear purpose for Cyril, "so that through his own flesh he might help those who are weary in their temptations."[51] He carries the argument of Hebrews to its full conclusion: Christ was perfected as a result of his

---

50. Cyril, *Ad reginas de recta fide oratio altera* 163, trans. Greer, 33; PG 76:1393B.
51. Cyril, *Ad reginas de recta fide oratio altera* 11, trans. Greer, 8; PG 76:1349A.

sufferings. This claim illustrates the degree to which Cyril is forced to defend the fully integrative character of the hypostatic union. Cyril takes issue with Nestorius's interpretation of Hebrews 2:10, which held that Hebrews speaks of the man born of woman being perfected and not the Word who assumes the man. The Word cannot be distinguished from the man, Cyril asserts; therefore, the pioneer of our salvation who is perfected through sufferings is "the Son made man." To this he adds the explanation, "For 'he endured the cross, despising the shame' entirely by the good pleasure of God the Father so that he might make us bold, taken by the hand to follow in his steps."[52] The whole person of Jesus Christ is perfected, not just his humanity. The divine Son is perfected in that he fulfills that purpose of the incarnation, sanctifying humanity so that we might follow in his perfection. Such perfection means imitating his manner of suffering, an impassible suffering at the hands of persecutors. In his circumstances, Cyril equated the persecutors with the enemies of christological orthodoxy. Christ's suffering emboldens his followers for their day of persecution. He writes, "Since they [Christ's disciples] were going to have affliction in the world and be persecuted by their enemies, . . . and since they were going to establish virtue well and truly by sweat and toil, he does not allow them to be unmanned by cowardice, but makes them fully courageous, since he himself ran his course through suffering."[53] Here Cyril is clear that Christ does not simply give his disciples an example so that they may see the good in order to do the good. Rather, his example of enduring suffering impassibly creates in their souls the necessary virtue, that is, courage, in order to endure their own persecutions and sufferings for the faith. This boldness enables them to imitate the unflinching faithfulness to the good that is the character of Christ's impassible suffering.

Christ's example provides his followers with courage and inspires their imitation because it reveals to them the glory that is the end of their suffering. Commenting on 1 Peter 2:20–21, Cyril tells Pulcheria and Eudocia that the Lord's suffering had two objectives. The first aim was to show them "how they ought to approach the assaults of temptation" and the demeanor they should show toward those who persecute his followers. Once again he reiterates the theme of Christ as our example. But immediately Cyril declares emphatically, "Still more than this, his purpose is to show how honorable the end of the obedience is, so that we may be found excellent and wise imitators of what was done by him in accord with the saving plan, and so that by zealously following in his steps we might truly be preserved in a life of

52. Cyril, *Ad reginas de recta fide oratio altera* 30, trans. Greer, 22; PG 76:1373C–D.
53. Cyril, *Ad reginas de recta fide oratio altera* 30, trans. Greer, 22; PG 76:1373D.

glory."[54] In other words, his disciples see not only Christ's suffering but also the glory that is conferred upon him as a result of the suffering, by virtue of which he is exalted above the angels (Heb. 1:3–4). The glory that is conferred upon Christ on account of his suffering strengthens his disciples' resolve and fortitude because they now set their minds upon the prize of glory that awaits those who endure. The vision of this glory strengthens the disciples because its splendor relativizes their present suffering.[55]

Christ's impassible suffering is able to serve as an example for his disciples to imitate because it exhibits the new and sanctified humanity produced by the hypostatic union. One of Cyril's favorite ways of speaking of Christ as sanctified humanity is Christ as the "new Adam," who summed up our common humanity, bringing it to perfection. The transformation of the human race effected in the incarnation enables us to be conformed to Christ's likeness—to bear the image of the last Adam, who is the man from heaven. Contrasting the "man of dust" with the "man from heaven" (1 Cor. 15:45–49), Cyril asks, "And what is the image of the heavenly man? It is *not to be conquered by passions* in any way; it is to be ignorant of transgression and free from subjection to death and decay; it is holiness, righteousness, and whatever is brother to these and like them."[56] As creatures sharing Christ's humanity, his followers will naturally enough experience suffering and all the accompanying passions. Yet as people possessing the image of the man from heaven, they are not to be subject to the passions' dominion, even as Christ himself was not.

This transformation of human nature is nothing short of moral divinization. Cyril writes, "The human qualities were active in Christ in a profitable way, not that having been set in motion they should prevail and develop further, as is the case with us, but that having been set in motion they should be brought up short by the power of the Word, since nature was first transformed in Christ into a better and more divine state. For it was in this way and in no other that the mode of healing passed over into ourselves too."[57] Here "the mode of healing" refers to Christ's suffering, but not only to his suffering on the cross. In this context, the mode of healing refers to his victory over the passions of fear and timidity that were stirred within him as he prayed in Gethsemane. Though he suffered the passions proper to human

54. Cyril, *Ad reginas de recta fide oratio altera* 39, trans. Greer, 31; PG 76:1389A–B.

55. This is certainly the sense of the passage when read in the context of the other passages in which Cyril speaks of Christ's suffering, giving his followers courage. Moreover, it is a motif present in the most famous martyrdom literature (see Ignatius, *To the Romans* 7.2–3; *Martyrdom of Polycarp* 2.3–4; Origen, *Exhortation to Martyrdom* 1.5; 11.15).

56. Cyril, *Against Nestorius* 111.2, trans. Russell, 163; ACO 1.1:6.60, emphasis added.

57. Cyril, *Commentary on John* 8, trans. Russell, 120; Pusey, 2:703E–4A.

weakness, he suffered them impassibly in the sense that he did not yield to the impulse of fear. They did not "prevail and develop further, as is the case with us," meaning that they did not cause him to retreat from death as we might be tempted to do. Instead, the passions were "brought up short," and his humanity was transformed into "a better and more divine state." That is to say, our human nature, which is inclined to succumb to the passions, was sanctified or divinized, meaning that human nature comes to share in God's impassibility. In his *Commentary on Isaiah*, Cyril explains that the phrase "rod of Jesse" is suggestive of a king's scepter and is thus symbolic of Christ's royal power, which "controls all things, and maintains them in well-being, and enables what is weak to stand up, that is to say human nature, which is drunk with the passions and all but brought down by them."[58]

The rectitude produced by the Word extends beyond the single instance of Jesus to include all of Adam's race. In the hypostatic union our common humanity was made rich in the sense that it was given the powers from the divine nature that grant us the capacity for joy and glory as well as freedom from bodily corruption. When the divine was united to a single human being, the whole of the human race was raised to his status. This, however, is no vicarious participation or union with God. Rather, Cyril says, "Therefore 'in Christ' that which is enslaved is liberated in a *real sense* and ascends to a mystical union with him who put on the form of a servant, while 'in us' it is liberated by an imitation of the union with the one [Christ] through our kinship in the flesh."[59] When Cyril speaks of our nature being in a mystical union by "an imitation of the union with the one through our kinship according to the flesh," he is referring to the hypostatic union. In other words, by virtue of the union of human and divine in the incarnation, the divine is united analogously to all humanity, thereby giving us the same capacity for joy and glory and incorruption that we witness in Jesus. Arguably, the effect of the indwelling of the divine in us is our sanctification, which is accomplished in a dialectic between purgation and illumination. Describing the effects of Christ's union with us, Cyril writes, "For when Christ has come to be within us, he lulls to sleep the law that rages in the members of the flesh. He rekindles our reverence toward God, while simultaneously causing the passions to atrophy."[60] As the soul is reoriented toward God in due reverence, the passions cease to have a hold upon us. We gain control over our warring members, the impulses of our animal nature. Indeed, this mastery over the

---

58. Cyril, *Commentary on Isaiah* 2.4, trans. Russell, 81; PG 70:312A.
59. Cyril, *Commentary on John* 1.9, trans. Russell, 107; Pusey, 1:96E.
60. Cyril, *Commentary on John* 4.2, trans. Russell, 119; Pusey, 1:365E–66A.

passions is precisely the effect we see of the Word's union with passible human flesh in the incarnation.

Christ's mastery over the passions of the flesh during his passion—a mastery achieved by the sanctifying power of the Word's divine nature—is paradigmatic for the sanctifying work of the Spirit dwelling in Christ's followers. For Christ sanctifies his disciples through the gift of his Spirit,[61] through whom God acts immediately in the lives of his creatures.[62] In the fall, humanity subjected its mind to the passions of the flesh[63] such that the Spirit who rested upon Adam and Eve in the beginning could no longer dwell in them.[64] With the union of the divine to all of humanity in Christ, the new Adam, Cyril says, the Spirit may once again rest upon those who are a new creation in Christ.[65] Since the Spirit is consubstantial with the Father and the Son, those in whom the Spirit dwells are partakers of the divine nature and so are "born of God." Thus in his *Commentary on John*, Cyril says that we are temples of God, whose Spirit dwells within us.[66] Although the indwelling of the Spirit in Christ's followers is not identical with the hypostatic union, Cyril here uses the same metaphor he employs to speak of the indwelling Word of Christ to describe the relation of the believer to the Spirit. Even as in the incarnation the human and the divine natures remained distinct though united, so too the Spirit does not change our creaturely nature into divinity. But the Spirit illuminates the

61. "Truly God the Father's glory is to do away with death through his own Begotten one. Therefore, his perfection through suffering supplies us with what is lacking from our birth. For what is in Christ is a new creation. . . . Thus the Son sanctifies, since he is God by nature. And *we* are sanctified by him through the Spirit." Cyril, *Ad reginas de recta fide oratio altera* 32, trans. Greer, 23; PG 76:1376D, emphasis added.

62. Brian Daley observes, "The distinctive role of the Spirit is to be even more intimately present in the experience of the creatures God calls to salvation than is the Father or the Son: to be precisely the point of contact between God and the creature, the active means by which the whole Trinity dwells in us." See Brian Daley, "The Fullness of the Saving God: Cyril of Alexandria on the Holy Spirit," in *The Theology of St. Cyril of Alexandria: A Critical Appreciation*, edited by Thomas Weinandy and Daniel A. Keating (Edinburgh: T&T Clark, 2003), 132.

63. Cyril, *Ad reginas de recta fide oratio altera* 9, trans. Greer, 6; PG 76:1345D.

64. Cyril explains that humans as creatures do not possess incorruptibility and immortality by nature and therefore have to be equipped with such capacities surpassing our own nature by being sealed with "the spirit of life." But with the fall, humanity was "stripped of the grace. The breath of life, that is, the Spirit who says, 'I am the Life,' departed from the earthly flesh, and the living being succumbed to death through the flesh alone, since the soul is preserved in its immortality." Cyril, *Commentary on John* 1.9, trans. Russell, 104; Pusey, 1:94E–95A.

65. Cyril, *Commentary on Isaiah* 2.4, PG 70:313C. Wilken, *Judaism and the Early Christian Mind*, 107, suggests that Cyril's most significant contribution to the development of the Adam-Christ typology is that he links it to the new creation.

66. "We are called gods [cf. Ps. 82:6], not simply by grace because we are winging our way towards the glory that transcends us, but because we already have God dwelling and abiding in us." See Cyril, *Commentary on John* 1.9, trans. Russell, 103; Pusey, 1:93C–E.

souls of the saints with the divine beauty and imprints the spiritual likeness of the Son upon us, transforming us into that which belongs to Christ.[67] Since Christ's impassible suffering is now understood to mean that even in suffering the weaknesses and passions of our human nature he did not deviate from his unshakable adherence to the good, in a similar way, Cyril insists, Christ's Spirit empowers Christians for the impassible endurance of temptation and suffering. This point Cyril illustrates in his discussion of the anointing of Christ by the Holy Spirit at his baptism.

Christ's baptism and his subsequent battle with Satan were, according to Cyril, the necessary triumph of Jesus as the new Adam for the redemption of the human race. Christ, he says, restored to humanity "robust spiritual health," eliminating the bodily and spiritual ailments that we have suffered since Adam's fall. This healing was accomplished because Christ in his incarnation took on our nature, which is vulnerable to the temptation of Satan, but his human nature empowered by the immutable sanctity of his divine nature rejected temptation, thereby repelling Satan's assault.[68] But Cyril goes on to make the point that Christ's entry into temptation in the wilderness and ultimate victory over Satan came *only after* his baptism, when he was anointed by the Holy Spirit. This could be a problem for Cyril since it might suggest that Christ's triumph through his sanctified humanity was the work of the Spirit, who empowered Jesus's humanity, and not of the Word, to whom his humanity was hypostatically united. Luke's comment that Jesus was "led" by the Holy Spirit does not mean, Cyril argues, that he was "taken off" against his will. Rather, he was "led" in the same sense that a good citizen leads himself blamelessly. In Christ's temptation in the wilderness, Cyril says, we see both his divine and his human natures. In his humanity, he hungered as a result of his fasting. Yet "by power suitable to God [he] had kept the flesh uncorrupted in the absence of drink and food, [and] he barely admits what is proper to it to suffer."[69] Here again we hear Cyril speak of suffering in a sense other than the physical pain of the cross, but without experiencing the physiological change one might expect in someone who has refrained from eating or drinking for an extended time. The divine power from the Holy Spirit strengthens his body beyond its natural capacity, preserving it from such change.

67. Cyril, *Against Nestorius* 3.2, ACO 1.1:6.60.
68. "Therefore, he enters the battle for us as man, and he conquers in a divine fashion. He is tempted, since Satan assaulted him as one like us and thought that the weakness of the flesh would join battle with him against the one who was tempted. But Satan withdrew, defeated by the nature of man which was renewed in Christ." Cyril, *Ad reginas de recta fide oratio altera* 36, trans. Greer, 27; PG 76:1384A.
69. Cyril, *Ad reginas de recta fide oratio altera* 36, trans. Greer, 27–28; PG 76:1384A.

Cyril goes on to call Pulcheria and Eudocia's attention to the key detail that Christ was not tempted in the wilderness prior to his baptism and the descent of the Holy Spirit. The reason for this timing was not that the power of the Word needed to be augmented by power from the Spirit but rather to give us an example of what is necessary in order to face temptation and possible martyrdom. In the power natural to human nature, Christ's followers are not strong enough "to endure manfully" Satan's assaults. It is only after baptism that the believer, "strengthened by sharing in the Holy Spirit and sealed by the grace from on high for robust health, namely, spiritual health, . . . shall be unassailable by Satan and . . . shall be preserved in life by the power of the Spirit."[70] Here Cyril almost verbatim repeats his earlier description of Christ's giving to his human nature and ours strength and health as a result of his victory over Satan. However, his description of Christ's disciples as becoming unassailable by Satan does not imply that we are immune to temptations or that we do not feel the impulses of our animal nature. Rather, by the indwelling of the Spirit the disciple does not yield to the temptations but stands as Christ did, resolutely faithful to the good and defiant of Satan. Through the Holy Spirit, Christ's followers are empowered for resistance to evil in the way that Christ Jesus resisted. Moreover, because the Holy Spirit came upon Christ, empowering him for his struggle with temptation, his followers see Christ's resistance to temptation through the power of the Spirit and recognize therein the effects of the very power now at work in them through the presence of the same Spirit. Christ's plea in Matthew 26, "Let this cup pass from me," Cyril says, illustrates the weakness of human nature unaided by the Holy Spirit when confronted with imminent suffering. "Do you see how weak human nature is, even in Christ himself, when it relies on its own power?" he asks. But immediately Cyril proceeds to explain that in the hypostatic union, Christ's disciples are shown how the divine empowers us to adhere to the divine will. "Through the Word that is united with it [i.e., the human nature], the flesh is brought back to a courage befitting God and is retrained in order to have a more valiant spirit, so as not to rely upon what seems right to its own will, but rather to follow the aim of the divine will and eagerly to run towards anything to which the Law of the Creator calls us."[71]

The weakness of Christ's flesh in the face of death serves as an example to us of our own vulnerability and impotence to fulfill God's will if we try to act within the reaches of our natural powers. At the same time, it demonstrates the degree to which our humanity, like Christ's, can be strengthened for the

70. Cyril, *Ad reginas de recta fide oratio altera* 36, trans. Greer, 28; PG 76:1384D.
71. Cyril, *Commentary on John* 4.1, trans. Russell, 113; Pusey, 1:332A.

purpose of fulfilling even God's most demanding callings. Thus the presence of the Spirit in Christ after his baptism gives his disciples hope of receiving the same power from the Spirit and so achieving victory over temptation and timidity. Cyril concludes this discussion by remarking, "For just as through his resurrection from the dead we have become stronger than corruption, so through his victory in temptation we have again received power."[72]

This is the soteriological context in which we must read Cyril's comment that Christ's impassible suffering serves as an example for his followers. The Christ of the hypostatic union reveals a new humanity, a divinized humanity summed up in the new Adam. Thus our nature possesses capacities not found in "the old man." Such capacities become actualized through the indwelling of Christ's Holy Spirit, whom Christians receive at baptism. The empowering Spirit does not free the disciple from suffering; rather, the Spirit enables disciples to remain unmoved with respect to the good even in the midst of suffering. This graceful and faithful endurance of suffering is the essence of Christ's impassible suffering, in which his disciples can now share.

Conclusion

Impassible suffering is significant for Cyril's explanation of the "great exchange" of the incarnation between the immutable Word and our impoverished humanity. *Pathoi apathōs* affirms that the Word took upon himself the suffering proper to weak humanity but without being corrupted by it. At the same time, it signifies that our humanity, ever prone to the temptations of the passions, received the moral rectitude of divine holiness as well as the divine incorruptibility that frees us from death. Impassible suffering is a paradox that arouses the curiosity of the intellect and drives it to explore the salvific work of the incarnation.

---

72. Cyril, *Ad reginas de recta fide oratio altera* 36, trans. Greer, 28; PG 76:1384D.

15

"THE IMPASSIBLE SUFFERS"

KALLISTOS WARE, METROPOLITAN OF DIOKLEIA

The Immortal dies, the Impassible suffers, the Invisible is seen.

Origen, *Homilies on Leviticus*

Only the suffering God can help.

Dietrich Bonhoeffer, *Letters
and Papers from Prison*

"O God, If It Were True!"

Some sixty years ago, there appeared a short article titled "Does God Suffer?," which provides in my opinion the best answer that has so far been given to this question from an Orthodox viewpoint. The article was written by the French priest Archimandrite Lev Gillet (1893–1980), better known by his *nom de plume* "A Monk of the Eastern Church," and it appeared in *Sobornost*, the journal of the Anglo-Orthodox Fellowship of St. Alban and St. Sergius.[1] Father

1. Lev Gillet, "Does God Suffer?" *Sobornost*, series 3, no. 15 (1954): 112–20. For a good discussion of the suffering of God, see in particular the works of three authors, respectively Orthodox, Roman Catholic, and Protestant: Paul L. Gavrilyuk, *The Suffering of the Impassible*

Lev begins by referring to an incident at the end of Helen Waddell's novel *Peter Abelard*, describing an imaginary conversation between a disgraced Abelard and his disciple Thibault.[2] The two of them, walking through the countryside, hear from a nearby wood "a thin cry, of . . . intolerable anguish." It comes from a rabbit, caught in a trap. They release it, but almost at once it dies.

"Thibault," says Abelard, "do you think there is a God at all? Whatever has come to me, I earned it. But what did this one do?"

"I know," Thibault replies. "Only—I think God is in it too."

Abelard responds by asking why, in that case, God does not stop the suffering.

"I don't know," says Thibault. "But all the time God suffers. More than we do."

"Do you mean Calvary?" asks Abelard.

Thibault replies, "That was only a piece of it—the piece that we saw—in time." And when Abelard speaks of the cross of Christ, Thibault answers, "God's cross. . . . And it goes on."

Abelard murmurs, "The Patripassian heresy," yet he then continues: "But, O God, if it were true. Thibault, it must be. At least there is something at the back of it that is true. And if we could find it—it would bring back the whole world."

"God's Cross—and it goes on." Developing this line of thought, Fr. Lev employs the phrase "the tears of God," recalling the words written by Victor Hugo at the foot of a crucifix: "You who weep, come to this God, for he also weeps."[3] So Fr. Lev poses the fundamental challenge: "Have we the right to say to the man or woman who is suffering: 'God himself, *at this very moment*, is suffering what you suffer, and is overcoming it'? ('Oh God, if it were true!')."[4] We notice Fr. Lev's words "and is overcoming it." What we ask from God is not simply compassion but also redemption and healing. A suffering God is not necessarily a helpless God.

In approaching the burning question "Does God suffer?" there is certainly a particular need for apophatic reticence. Here we may apply some words written by Evagrius of Pontus (d. 399) in a somewhat different context: "To

---

God: The Dialectics of Patristic Thought (Oxford: Oxford University Press, 2004); Thomas G. Weinandy, *Does God Suffer?* (Notre Dame, IN: University of Notre Dame Press, 2000); Paul S. Fiddes, *The Creative Suffering of God* (Oxford: Clarendon, 1988); compare also the more recent treatment by Fiddes, *Participating in God: A Pastoral Doctrine of the Trinity* (London: Darton, Longman & Todd, 2000), 152–90, "The Vulnerable God and the Problem of Suffering." For further bibliography, consult Gavrilyuk, *Suffering of the Impassible God*, 180–96.

2. See Helen Waddell, *Peter Abelard: A Novel* (New York: Holt, 1933), 263–65.

3. Gillet, "Does God Suffer?," 116.

4. Ibid., 112, emphasis original.

this question there is no answer; but in the *eschaton* the question itself will disappear."[5] Yet even though our question is for the time being unanswerable, nonetheless it is a question that we cannot avoid asking. As we speculate, however, let us at least take as our mentor the Angel of Good Silence (*Blagoe Molchanie*), depicted in Russian icons with a finger on his lips.

In matters such as this, there is always a danger of trying to say too much. So, whatever it be that we seek to assert, let it be said in the spirit of Origen (ca. 185–ca. 254), as he approached the theme of the final end or consummation: "We speak on these subjects with great fear and caution, discussing and investigating rather than laying down fixed and certain conclusions. . . . We are dealing, as best we can, with subjects that call for debate rather than for definition."[6] If only Origen's critics—persons of powerful intellect but narrow sympathies, such as Jerome and Justinian—had displayed the same humility as Origen himself! Apophatic reticence, in the manner of the Angel of Good Silence, means at least this: if we venture to attribute suffering to the transcendent Deity, let us recognize that suffering in his case is profoundly different from the suffering that we humans know. Different, yes, but not totally dissimilar.

Here, then, is our question. How far, according to the Bible and the tradition of the church, is God not only a transcendent but also an *involved* God, who suffers with and in his creatures, taking responsibility totally and unreservedly for all the consequences of his act of creation? Admittedly, as humans we are endowed with free will, and so God cannot be directly blamed for the human decisions that give rise to our sufferings. As Plato puts it in the myth of Er at the conclusion of the *Republic*, "He who chooses is to blame; God is blameless."[7] Yet surely there is more to be said about the matter than that.

"I Am the Holy One in Your Midst"

At the outset, let us attempt to clarify the meaning of the term "impassible." The English language has no exact equivalent for the Greek word *pathos*. Usually translated "passion," it signifies both suffering and, in a more positive sense, emotion, strong feeling, and sexual attraction. Linked to the verb *paschein*, "to suffer," *pathos* signifies basically a passive state, as contrasted with *dynamis*, an act of power. It denotes, then, something that overwhelms

---

5. Evagrius, *Gnostic Chapters* 3.70, ed. Antoine Guillaumont, PO 28.1 (1959): 127.
6. Origen, *First Principles* 1.6.1.
7. Plato, *Republic* 10.617E.

a person or object, to which that person or object is subjected, which to some extent is outside the person or object's control, an event or experience that is endured and undergone passively. Thus sleep and death are termed *pathos* by Clement of Alexandria (ca. 150–ca. 215),[8] and Gregory of Nazianzus (329–89) describes the phases of the moon as *pathē*.[9] Applied to the inner life of humans, *pathos* thus commonly has the sense of a violent feeling dominating the soul without its consent.[10]

If such is the meaning of *pathos*, then at first sight the answer to our question seems obvious: God cannot be subject to *pathos*. If God is, as Aristotle held and as traditional Christian theology has maintained, the "Unmoved Mover," "pure actuality," in whom there is no potentiality, no imperfection, no mutability, then the very idea of God excludes all suffering or *pathos* in the sense just indicated. God cannot be passible, for he cannot be controlled by something outside of himself. In the words of Thomas Aquinas (ca. 1225–74), "He cannot be conquered or suffer violence, for these things belong only to the one who can be moved."[11]

Yet must *pathos* be understood exclusively in this passive sense? If *pathos* indicates emotion or strong feeling, then should not love be regarded as a *pathos*? In that case *pathos*, so far from invariably denoting weakness or subjection, may sometimes be active, potent, and creative. This is a vital point, to which we shall in due course return. As a God of love, the Christian God is passible, yet not passive; vulnerable, yet not inert.

Such at any rate is the understanding of God that is found in Scripture. It is significant that the adjective *apathēs*, "impassible," and the noun *apatheia*, "impassibility," are nowhere used in the Septuagint or the New Testament, whether applied to God or to anything else. In the Old Testament, Yahweh is not an impassive or detached spectator but in the fullest sense an involved and indeed a passionate God, who cares for his chosen people, who suffers with them in their sufferings, who is filled with distress by their waywardness, who even repents of what he has done. So it is said, "The LORD was sorry that he had made humankind on the earth, and it grieved him to his heart" (Gen. 6:6);[12] "He could no longer bear to see Israel suffer" (Judg. 10:16). The covenant relationship between God and Israel means that God shares the

---

8. Clement of Alexandria, *Protrepticus* 10, ed. Otto Stählin and Ursula Treu, 3rd ed., GCS (Berlin: Akademie Verlag, 1972), 73, lines 28–29.

9. Gregory of Nazianzus, *Oration* 28, 30; PG 36:69B.

10. See Kallistos T. Ware, "The Meaning of 'Pathos' in Abba Isaias and Theodoret of Cyrus," StPatr 20 (1989): 315–22, esp. 315.

11. Thomas Aquinas, *Summa contra Gentiles* 2.25 (1016), cited by Gillet, "Does God Suffer?," 115.

12. For God's repentance, cf. Exod. 32:12, 14; 1 Sam. 15:11.

sufferings of his people in Egypt, and he hears their cries and groaning in their bondage (Exod. 2:23–25; 3:7–8).[13]

The prophets go so far as to place in God's mouth words of anguish and heartfelt reproach:

> When Israel was a child, I loved him. . . .
> It was I who taught Ephraim to walk,
>   I took him up in my arms. . . .
> How can I give you up, O Ephraim?
>   How can I hand you over, O Israel? . . .
> My heart recoils within me,
>   My compassion grows warm and tender.
>   (Hosea 11:1, 3, 8)

> Is not Ephraim my dear son,
>   The child in whom I delight?
> Though I often speak against him,
>   I still remember him.
> Therefore my heart yearns for him;
>   I have great compassion for him.
>   (Jer. 31:20 NIV)

In this way God is viewed throughout the Old Testament as our companion and defender whenever we are assailed by desolation and despair. He is with us when we "walk through the valley of the shadow of death" (Ps. 22:4 LXX [= 23:4 KJV]); he is present with us even in Sheol (Ps. 138:8 [139:8]). Nor is this all. Our unfaithfulness arouses not only his compassion but also his anger (Gen. 18:30, 32; Num. 25:3–4; Deut. 1:34, 37; 29:20; 4 Kingdoms 24:20 LXX [2 Kings 24:20]; Isa. 30:27; Jer. 4:8; etc.). He is wearied and roused to indignation by the hardness of our hearts (Ps. 94 [95]:8–11). The Hebrew view of God can thus be summed up in the phrase "I am the Holy One in your midst" (Hosea 11: 9; cf. Isa. 12:6). As the "Holy One," God is raised far above humankind—"I am God and no mortal" (Hosea 11:9)—yet this transcendent God is also "in our midst," intimately involved in all our concerns, afflicted with our afflictions, the fellow sufferer who understands. Full scope is to be given to both the otherness and the nearness of the Eternal.

Sometimes this vivid language applied to God in the Old Testament is explained away by modern critics as reflecting a "primitive" and "anthropomorphic" understanding of the Deity. Indeed, as Paul Gavrilyuk points out,

---

13. See also Isa. 63:9 (KJV, RSV), "In all their affliction he was afflicted" (but there is some doubt about this Hebrew text).

long before the era of modern criticism the Septuagint's translators of the Hebrew Scriptures felt it necessary to tone down several of the statements that we have just cited.[14] Now admittedly, when God is said to repent, to grieve, or to be angry, these things are not to be ascribed to him in exactly the same way as they are to humans. Even so, however much such language is to be interpreted in apophatic terms, it cannot be simply dismissed. There is a genuine analogy between the human and the divine; otherwise such language could not be used at all. The same applies, of course, to our references to the love of God. Divine love infinitely surpasses all that we humans understand by love; nevertheless our human experience of love is a true reflection of the love that exists in the heart of God.

"Grieve Not the Holy Spirit of God"

Turning from the Old Testament to the New, we find that, beyond any shadow of doubt, Jesus as incarnate Son of God is directly associated with our pain and suffering and with the full range of our human emotions, both in his body and in his human soul. As the Epistle to the Hebrews insists, "We do not have a high priest who is unable to sympathize with our weaknesses, but one who in every respect has been tested as we are, yet without sin[ning]" (4:15). Jesus was weary (John 4:6), hungry (Mark 11:12), thirsty (John 19:28), and angry (Mark 3:5). In Gethsemane he felt "horror and anguish" and even "sorrow to the point of death" (Mark 14:33–34, my trans.). On the cross he endured isolation and despair, entering into our human sense of the loss and absence of God: "My God, my God, why have you forsaken me?" (Mark 15:34).

Yet beyond the sufferings of Jesus Christ as God incarnate, does the New Testament authorize us to say that God undergoes suffering, not only as incarnate but also in himself as God? There are only a few explicit statements about this in the New Testament, but what is said agrees with the conception of an involved God as expressed in the Old Testament. Thus Christ affirms that not a single sparrow "is forgotten before God" (Luke 12:6 RSV); the heavenly Father (not just the incarnate Christ) is affected by the death of each and every one of these tiny birds (Matt. 10:29). In Hebrews 3:10–11 the words of the psalmist about God's anger at our hardness of heart (Ps. 94:8 LXX [95:8]) are quoted and endorsed. Most striking of all, the apostle Paul speaks of the "grief" of God's Spirit: "Do not grieve the Holy Spirit of God"

14. Gavrilyuk, *Suffering of the Impassible God*, 39–41.

(Eph. 4:30). This text has inspired "The Temple," one of George Herbert's most beautiful poems:

> And art thou grieved, sweet and sacred Dove,
>> When I am sowre [sour],
>> And crosse thy love?
> Grieved for me? the God of strength and power
> Griev'd for a worm? . . .
>
> Then weep mine eyes, the God of love doth grieve:
>> Weep foolish heart,
>> And weeping live. . . .
>
> Almightie God doth grieve, he puts on sense:
>> I sinne not to my grief alone,
>> But to my God's too; he doth grone [groan].[15]

"The Son of God Suffered in the Flesh"

While the term "impassibility" is absent from the pages of Scripture, as soon as we advance from the New Testament to the apostolic fathers, at once we encounter the language of *apatheia*. Ignatius of Antioch (ca. 35–ca. 107) makes use of the adjective *apathēs*: "The Timeless and Invisible has become visible for our sakes; the Impalpable and Impassible [*apathēs*] has for our sakes become passible."[16] Jesus Christ, who is "God in man," was "first passible and then impassible."[17] Similar statements recur in the apologists. God, states Justin Martyr (ca. 100–ca. 165), is "unbegotten and impassible."[18] According to Athenagoras (floruit ca. 177), God is "uncreated, impassible, and indivisible."[19]

Thereafter such language becomes a commonplace. God, says Clement of Alexandria, is "impassible and changeless."[20] "When we hear it said of a man that he is a father," writes Basil the Great (ca. 330–79), "then this includes the idea of passion [*pathos*]; but when it is said that God is Father, then we think of him as the impassible cause."[21] Although reaching out to

---

15. Francis E. Hutchinson, ed., *The Works of George Herbert* (Oxford: Clarendon, 1941), 135–36.

16. Ignatius, *To Polycarp* 3.2.

17. Ignatius, *To the Ephesians* 7.2.

18. Justin, *First Apology* 25.2.

19. Athenagoras, *Legation* 8.3.

20. Clement of Alexandria, *Eclogae propheticae* 52.2, ed. Otto Stählin and Ludwig Früchtel, 2nd ed., GCS (Berlin: Akademie Verlag, 1970), 151, line 24.

21. Basil the Great, *Against Eunomius* 2.23, PG 29:621B.

humankind in love, states Gregory of Nyssa (ca. 330–ca. 395), "God abides in impassibility"; the incarnation does not signify any change in God's inner being.[22] John Climacus (ca. 570–ca. 649) ends his chapter on *apatheia* in *The Ladder of Divine Ascent* by putting words into God's mouth: "Be still and know that I am God and I am impassibility."[23] This patristic emphasis upon divine impassibility and immutability is often attributed to the influence of Plato and Aristotle. No doubt there is truth in this, but such an explanation should not be pressed too far. While indebted to Hellenic philosophy, the fathers were often critical of it and did not automatically endorse the opinions of their non-Christian predecessors. In this particular instance, when the fathers insist that God is without passion or change, such language is used from a desire to safeguard divine transcendence; and this concern for divine transcendence is a marked feature not only of Hellenic philosophy but also of Judaism (even though the authors of the Old Testament also stress God's involvement in human affairs).

While thus maintaining that God as such does not and cannot suffer, the fathers qualified this by affirming that, in the person of Jesus Christ, the incarnate Son of God, God can and does suffer, as in the epigrammatic phrase of Origen: "The Impassible suffers."[24] This theopaschite approach, ascribing suffering to God within the context of the incarnation, is already implicit in Paul's affirmation: "They . . . crucified the Lord of glory" (1 Cor. 2:8). Christ is crucified, but he remains the divine Lord; he dies, yet he is still the transcendent King of glory. More explicitly, Ignatius of Antioch writes, "Permit me to be an imitator of the suffering [*pathos*] of my God."[25] Speaking with specific reference to Christ, Gregory of Nazianzus refers to the "sufferings of him who is impassible"[26] and goes so far as to assert: "We had need of a God who took flesh and was put to death."[27]

This standpoint—that God in himself does not suffer, but God incarnate can and does suffer—was given greater precision by the Third, Fourth, and Fifth Ecumenical Councils (Ephesus, 431; Chalcedon, 451; Constantinople II, 553). Ephesus, following the teaching of Cyril of Alexandria (d. 444), affirmed that the sole and unique personal subject in the incarnate Christ is the divine Logos; everything performed, spoken, or suffered by Christ in his earthly

22. Gregory of Nyssa, *Catechetical Oration* 15, GNO 3.4:44, line 5.

23. John Climacus, *Ladder* 29, PG 88:1152B; cf. Ps. 45:10 LXX (46:10 English).

24. Origen, *Homilies on Leviticus* 3.1, ed. W. A. Baehrens, GCS (Leipzig: Hinrichs, 1920), 300, lines 17–18.

25. Ignatius, *To the Romans* 6.3.

26. Gregory of Nazianzus, *Oration* 30.5, PG 36:109B.

27. Gregory of Nazianzus, *Oration* 45.28, PG 36:661C.

life is performed, spoken, or suffered by the Second Person of the Trinity. Accordingly, the Virgin Mary is to be called *Theotokos*, "Bearer of God"; in this context it is legitimate to say, "God was born."[28] Chalcedon gave greater precision to this by clearly distinguishing between the two natures of Christ: some things are performed or spoken by Christ in his divine nature; other things are spoken or suffered by him in his human nature. When Christ suffered, this was not in his divine but in his human nature.[29] Constantinople II supplemented the teaching of Ephesus by stating that, if God was born, then it is equally correct to state that God died; in the words of the council, "Jesus Christ, who was crucified in the flesh, is true God and Lord of glory and one of the Holy Trinity."[30]

Such, then, is the basic conciliar and patristic teaching: in the incarnate Christ are two natures but only a single person. Christ suffers in his human nature; yet since there is in the incarnate Christ only one subject of attribution, the divine Logos, it can be truly said that in Christ, God suffers. A distinction is to be made between the levels of person and nature; the Second *Person* of the Trinity suffers, but the divine *nature* remains impassible.

Accordingly, Cyril of Alexandria writes:

> In a similar way we say that he suffered and rose again, not that the Word of God suffered blows or piercing with nails or any other wound in his own nature (for the divine, being without a body, is incapable of suffering); but because the body which became his own suffered these things, he is said to have suffered them for us. For he was without suffering, while his body suffered. Something similar is true of his dying.[31]

In this context Cyril employs one of his key theological concepts, that of *oikeiōsis*, or "appropriation." The Logos, although in his divine nature impassible, "appropriated" or "made his own" the sufferings of his human nature:

> The only begotten Son born of God the Father, although according to his own nature he was not subject to suffering, suffered in the flesh for us according to the Scriptures, and was in his crucified body, and without himself suffering *made his own* the sufferings of his own flesh.[32]

28. See Cyril of Alexandria, *Third Letter to Nestorius*, Anathema 1, in Norman P. Tanner, *Decrees of the Ecumenical Councils*, 2 vols. (London: Sheed & Ward, 1990), 1:59, lines 10–15; cf. the *Formula of Union* (in 433), 1:70, lines 13–19.

29. See the Chalcedonian *Definition of Faith*, in Tanner, *Decrees*, 1:86, lines 14–43 (although this does not refer explicitly to the sufferings of Christ but refers only to his birth from Mary).

30. See Anathema 10, in Tanner, *Decrees*, 1:118, lines 37–40, alt.

31. Cyril, *Second Letter to Nestorius*, in Tanner, *Decrees*, 1:42, lines 20–31.

32. Cyril, *Third Letter to Nestorius*, in Tanner, *Decrees*, 1:53, lines 33–39, emphasis added.

Although in the two passages just quoted, Cyril refers only to the "body" or the "flesh" of the incarnate Christ, he makes it clear that by these terms he means to include also the human soul that Christ took at his incarnation.[33] Thus when he asserts that Christ "suffered in the flesh," this means that he suffered both physically and mentally. Summing up his teaching on the suffering of Christ, Cyril says: "He suffers humanly in the flesh as man, he is impassible divinely as God."[34] Yet more succinctly, he states: "He suffered impassibly."[35]

The same teaching on the suffering of Christ can be found in the *Tome* of Leo the Great (d. 461), although he lays greater emphasis than does Cyril upon the contrast between Godhead and manhood in Christ. "So the proper character of both natures was maintained and came together in a single person," writes Leo. "He could both on the one hand die and on the other hand be incapable of death."[36] Stressing the distinction of natures, Leo states: "Each form [i.e., nature] performs what is proper to it in communion with the other: that is, the Word performs what is proper to the Word, and the flesh accomplishes what belongs to the flesh."[37] But then Leo at once adds, in full agreement with Cyril, that while each of the two "forms" functions according to its specific character, both "forms" belong to a single personal subject, the divine Logos incarnate: "We must say this again and again: one and the same is truly Son of God and truly Son of Man."[38]

Three Questions

Thus far, from the viewpoint of traditional Christian teaching, we have been treading on secure ground: the incarnate Logos suffered in his human nature yet remained impassible in his divine nature. Let us attempt, however, to go somewhat further than this, venturing into contested territory, and let us ask three questions that are more speculative in character:

1. The divine Logos, we have said, suffered in his earthly life. But did he suffer *before* the incarnation? And does he continue to suffer *after* his resurrection and ascension into heaven?

33. The human soul of Christ is mentioned explicitly by Cyril, *Second Letter to Nestorius,* in Tanner, *Decrees,* 1:41, lines 26–29.

34. Cyril, *Scholia on the Incarnation* 36, ed. Philip E. Pusey, *Sancti patris nostri Cyrilli, archiepiscopi Alexandrini* (Oxford: Parker, 1875), 6:568, lines 29–30.

35. Cyril, *To Pulcheria and Eudocia* 26, ed. Philip E. Pusey, *Sancti patris nostri Cyrilli* (Oxford: Parker, 1877), 7:310, lines 25–26.

36. Leo, *To Flavian* 3, in Tanner, *Decrees,* 1:78, col. 2, lines 7–18.

37. Leo, *To Flavian* 4, in Tanner, *Decrees,* 1:79, col. 2, lines 3–7, alt.

38. Leo, *To Flavian* 4, in Tanner, *Decrees,* 1:79, col. 2, lines 12–15.

2. Father, Son, and Holy Spirit are one in essence (*homoousios*); between the three members of the Trinity there is *perichōrēsis*, mutual indwelling or coinherence. Can it therefore be said that, by virtue of this *perichōrēsis*, or *circumincessio*, the Father and the Spirit share in the suffering of the Son at his crucifixion? Can we speak of their cocrucifixion with Christ?

3. Outside the context of the incarnation of the Logos, can we assert that God as such suffers in his innate divinity? Was any early Christian writer, passing beyond the normal understanding of divine impassibility, prepared to claim that even God the Father is capable of suffering?

Below we treat each of these questions in turn.

Preincarnate and Postresurrection Suffering

Regarding the first of our three questions, several biblical texts do hint at the possibility of suffering on the part of the preincarnate Logos. Most striking is the enigmatic phrase in the Apocalypse, "the Lamb [that was] slain from the foundation of the world" (Rev. 13:8 KJV). The deeper significance of these words is emphasized by the Russian theologian Fr. Sergius Bulgakov (1871–1944) in his christological treatise *The Lamb of God*, perhaps the most original and creative work of Orthodox theology produced in the twentieth century. The crucifixion, viewed in a strictly historical perspective, is of course an event that occurred at a particular moment in time. Yet the crucifixion was also foreknown by God before the creation of the world. In creating the world God took upon himself full responsibility for its salvation; and this means that, in the very act of creating the world, God also decreed the death of his own Son for the world's salvation.[39] In Bulgakov's words: "The Son, the Lamb of God, is pre-eternally 'sacrificed' in the creation of the world. . . . This pre-eternal sacrifice is the foundation of the cross of Golgotha."[40]

This involvement of the preincarnate Christ in the suffering of the world is, at first sight, strikingly confirmed by the story of the three holy children in the book of Daniel. Gazing into the burning fiery furnace, Nebuchadnezzar exclaimed: "I see four men loose, and walking in the midst of the fire, and the appearance of the fourth is like the Son of God" (Dan. 3:25 [92] LXX). Such

---

39. This point is graphically emphasized in the autobiography of Archpriest Avvakum (1620–82): see *The Life Written by Himself*, ed. Kenneth N. Bostrom, Michigan Slavic Translations 4 (Ann Arbor: University of Michigan, 1979), 42.

40. Sergius Bulgakov, *The Lamb of God* (Grand Rapids: Eerdmans, 2008), 129, 338.

is the translation by Sir Lancelot Lee Brenton. The Septuagint text, however, may also be translated "a son of God"; indeed, an alternative manuscript reads "an angel of God," while the Hebrew can be rendered "a son of the gods" (see, e.g., RSV and NIV). So not too much weight should be placed upon this text, taken in isolation. It need not necessarily be understood as a reference to Christ.

Be that as it may, in his homily *On Pascha*, Melito of Sardis (d. ca. 190) certainly sees the preincarnate Logos as suffering in and with the suffering of the righteous in the Old Testament:

> It is he who in many endured many things:
> it is he that was murdered in Abel,
>> and bound in Isaac,
>> and exiled in Jacob,
>> and sold in Joseph,
>> and exposed in Moses,
>> and slain in the lamb,
>> and persecuted in David,
>> and dishonored in the prophets.[41]

Here Melito does not simply speak of the suffering of the righteous in the Old Testament as prefiguring or foreshadowing the suffering of Christ, but he asserts much more definitely that Christ actually participated in their sufferings. He sees the suffering of the Logos, in the words of Gavrilyuk, "as transcending the temporal boundaries of the incarnation and extending out into the whole of salvation history."[42]

The phrase "extending out into the whole of salvation history" brings us to a further issue: Can it also be said that Christ continues to suffer after his resurrection? Can we say (to paraphrase Fr. Lev), "Christ himself, *at this very moment*, suffers what we suffer, sharing in our pain and sorrow?" Such certainly was the conviction of Blaise Pascal (1623–62): "Jesus will be in agony until the end of the world."[43] William Temple (1881–1944) saw this belief in Christ's continued suffering confirmed by his first action when he appeared to his disciples on the evening of Easter Sunday, passing through closed doors: he showed them the wounds on his hands and in his side (John 20:20). Doubtless this was done for purposes of recognition, to assure the disciples that he was

41. Melito of Sardis, *On Pascha* 69, ed. Stuart George Hall (Oxford: Clarendon, 1979), 36.
42. Gavrilyuk, *Suffering of the Impassible God*, 74.
43. Blaise Pascal, "The Mystery of Jesus," in his *Pensées*, trans. A. J. Krailsheimer (Harmondsworth: Penguin, 1966), 313.

truly present among them, in that selfsame body in which they had seen him suffer and die on the cross. But on a deeper level, was it not also an indication that, even in his risen and glorified state, Christ continues to share in the sufferings of the world? "The wounds of Christ are his credentials to the suffering race of men," writes Temple. "Only a God in whose perfect Being pain has its place can win and hold our worship."[44]

It is noteworthy that the Gospel of Matthew ends with an assurance from the risen Christ of his continuing presence in the world: "Lo, I am with you always, to the close of the age" (Matt. 28:20 RSV). Although his visible appearance was withdrawn when he ascended into heaven, this did not in any way mean that he was no longer present and active on earth; for the ascension was an apparent separation that in reality was no separation at all. Now this promise of his continuing presence must surely mean, among other things, that he continues to share in our pain and distress. Ever present among us through the Holy Spirit, the glorified Savior has not for a single moment ceased to suffer with us and in us. He governs the world not by remote control but by rendering himself entirely vulnerable. "Surely he has borne our griefs and carried our sorrows" (Isa. 53:4 RSV). That still continues to be the case here and now. Jesus will be the suffering servant without any interruption until his second coming.

Accordingly, in the story of the sheep and the goats at the judgment of the nations (Matt. 25:31–46, emphasis added), Christ says, "*I* was hungry; . . . *I* was thirsty; . . . *I* was a stranger; . . . *I* was naked; . . . *I* was sick." In the case of everyone who is suffering and in need, Christ says "I." He himself is suffering within them.

Such was exactly the standpoint of the early Christians. When, at the beginning of the third century, the future martyr Felicitas was asked how she would be able to endure the suffering of her violent death in the arena, she replied: "There will be Another in me who will suffer for me."[45] As Origen insists, "It is inconceivable that Paul should grieve over sinners and weep over those who fall away, while my own Lord Jesus should be dry-eyed as he approaches his Father, stands before the altar, and offers propitiation for us. . . . He still tastes the bitterness of our sins."[46] Augustine of Hippo (354–430) maintains, "What we suffer, he too suffers with us," even though "he is now

---

44. William Temple, *Readings in St. John's Gospel,* 2nd series, *Chapters xiii–xxi* (London: Macmillan, 1940), 384–85.

45. *The Martyrdom of Saints Perpetua and Felicitas* 15, in *The Acts of the Christian Martyrs,* ed. Herbert Musurillo (Oxford: Clarendon, 1972), 122–24.

46. Origen, *Homilies on Leviticus* 7.2, ed. Baehrens, 375, line 29, to 376, line 4; quoted in Weinandy, *Does God Suffer?,* 257.

ascended into heaven and is seated at the right hand of the Father."[47] In the same spirit Julian of Norwich (ca. 1342–after 1416) states:

> Insofar as Christ is our head, he is glorious and impassible; but with respect to his body, to which all his members are joined, he is not yet fully glorified or wholly impassible. Therefore he still has that same thirst which he had upon the Cross, which desire, longing, and thirst, as I see it, were in him from without beginning; and he will have this until the time that the last soul which will be saved has come up into his bliss. . . . The ghostly thirst will persist in him so long as we are in need, and will draw us up to his bliss.[48]

It is significant that Julian, referring here to the "ghostly [spiritual] thirst" felt by Christ, states that this "was in him from without beginning." Evidently Julian believes that our human suffering, experienced by the incarnate Christ in his earthly life, was also experienced by him in his preincarnate state, as it is likewise experienced by him at this present moment in his glorified state in heaven. His "thirst" extends through the whole of salvation history.

It is surely this continuing solidarity of Christ with a suffering world that the apostle Paul has in view when he writes, "In my flesh I am completing what is lacking in Christ's afflictions for the sake of his body, that is, the church" (Col. 1:24). In common with Fr. Thomas Weinandy, I take this to mean, not that Paul's sufferings accomplish something that Christ has left incomplete, for Christ's sacrifice upon the cross is perfect and all-sufficient, but rather that Paul's sufferings are united with those of Christ himself. When Paul suffers as one of the members of Christ's body, then Christ who is the head of the body is suffering also. In Fr. Weinandy's words, "It is the present afflictions of Christ and not past sufferings that Paul was completing. . . . Paul's present suffering was truly Christ's present affliction."[49]

Here, then, in the words of Fr. Pierre Descouvement is "an enormous paradox." Risen from the dead, ascended into heaven, seated in glory at the right hand of the Father, Christ dwells in the infinite joy and bliss of the divine realm. Yet at the same time he continues to share unreservedly in our pain and anguish. There coexists in the glorified Christ "an indescribable suffering together with an unfailing joy."[50]

47. Augustine, On the Psalms 62.2, PL 36:749; quoted in Weinandy, Does God Suffer?, 253.
48. Julian of Norwich, Revelations of Divine Love 31L, trans. Edmund Colledge and James Walsh, Julian of Norwich: Showings, CWS (New York: Paulist Press, 1978), 230–31, alt.; quoted in Weinandy, Does God Suffer?, 257.
49. Weinandy, Does God Suffer?, 255.
50. Pierre Descouvemont, Dieu souffre-t-il? (Paris: Editions de l'Emmanuel, 2008), 25.

Such, then, is my answer to the double question: Did Christ suffer before the incarnation? Does he suffer now? In both cases I wish to respond with an emphatic *Yes*. Yet at the same time it is wise to speak with apophatic caution. Here we are raising an issue of deep complexity, nothing less than the nature of time and its relation to eternity. The crucifixion is an event in historical time, yet it is also supratemporal, finding its source and its fulfillment in transcendent eternity. "Jesus Christ is the same yesterday and today and forever" (Heb. 13:8).

The Suffering of the Trinity

Coming now to our second question, we ask: Can it be claimed that, when the Second Person of the Trinity suffers, the First and the Third Persons also suffer with him? The message of the Fifth Ecumenical Council has been summed up in the phrase, "One of the Trinity suffered in the flesh." Can we go beyond this and say that *all* of the Trinity suffered, and still continues to suffer? Only the Second Person of the Trinity became incarnate, and therefore it was he alone who died upon the cross. But were not the other two persons associated with him in his life-creating death?

Bulgakov in *The Lamb of God* clearly affirms that the suffering of Christ as God-man also involves the suffering of God the Trinity. "A real perichoresis occurs . . . in the passion on the cross," he writes. "The human nature makes the divine nature a coparticipant in its destiny and in its passion." With appropriate caution, Bulgakov at once adds, "This relation, clear in its principle, cannot be elucidated in its details, for it surpasses human understanding."[51]

Here Bulgakov goes beyond Cyril of Alexandria, who states (as we have seen) that Christ suffered only in his human and not in his divine nature. Yet according to the definition of faith endorsed by the Council of Chalcedon, the two natures of Christ are united "without division and without separation." This means, Bulgakov argues, that the suffering of Christ in his human nature must inevitably have implications also for his divine nature:

Can that which occurs with one of the natures have no effect on and no relation to the other nature? Does this not separate the inseparable natures in the divine-humanity? Does this not introduce into the life of the divine hypostasis itself a certain duality in virtue of which the God-Man's life is no longer one life but a dual life? Can it be the case that, being impassible in one life, He suffers in the other? . . . In virtue of the perichoresis, the human nature puts its imprint on the life of the divine nature, in a manner unfathomable to us.[52]

51. Bulgakov, *Lamb of God*, 258.
52. Ibid., 259.

If in this way, so Bulgakov continues, the human nature of the incarnate Christ "puts its imprint" on the divine nature, then it follows that the sufferings of Christ also affect the Father and the Spirit; for the divine nature, shared by all three persons of the Trinity, is altogether one and indivisible, and Father, Son, and Spirit are *homoousios*, "one in essence." It will not do, states Bulgakov, to maintain that since Christ suffers in his hypostasis but not in his divine nature, therefore the Father and the Spirit are not implicated in the Son's suffering; for this is to make an unacceptable severance between the hypostasis of Christ and his divine nature. That which is proper to the hypostasis, the experience of suffering, cannot be totally alien to the divine nature. The divine nature in Christ cosuffers with the human nature; and the Father and the Spirit, who share this indivisible divine nature, are also participants in this cosuffering.

Out of love for the world, Bulgakov affirms, the Father *sends* the Son into the world (see John 3:16–17); and this act of sending, which Bulgakov describes as an "act of sacrificial love," means that the Father cannot be indifferent to what happens in the incarnate life of his beloved Son:

> The Golgotha mystery is accomplished in its special sense in heaven as well [as on earth], in the Father's heart, which is the Holy Spirit. This is sometimes attested iconographically by representations of the sorrowing and suffering Father leaning from on high over the crucified Son, with the sun darkened and the earth trembling. The wisdom of the iconographer's vision is more profound here than scholastic theology.[53]

Such, then, is Bulgakov's conclusion:

> The Church confesses that only the Son, the God-Man Jesus, suffered in the flesh, was crucified on the cross, and tasted death—in virtue of His assumption of the human essence; and in *this* sense neither the hypostasis of the Father nor the hypostasis of the Spirit suffers with Him.[54] However, the nonparticipation of these hypostases in the work of redemption directly contradicts the Church dogma of the Incarnation. . . . When we speak of the spiritual "co-crucifixion" of the Father and the Holy Spirit with the Son, we only express the Church doctrine of their participation in the work of the redemption. God in His eternity, as the "immanent Trinity," is above the world; but the same Holy Trinity, as the Creator, finds itself in an "economic" interrelation with the world.[55]

53. Ibid., 260.

54. Here Bulgakov clearly repudiates the Patripassian heresy, which fuses the persons of the Father and Son, whereas Bulgakov carefully distinguishes them, while insisting also on their coworking.

55. Bulgakov, *Lamb of God*, 372, emphasis original.

Two generations before Bulgakov, Philaret (Drozdov), Metropolitan of Moscow (1782–1867), likewise emphasized the "cosuffering" of the Father and Spirit in the sacrifice of the Son:

"God so loved the world" (John 3:16). See! There is nothing here except the holy and blessed love of the Father, the Son, and the Holy Spirit towards a sinful and despairing mankind:

The love of the Father—in [the act of] the crucifying;
The love of the Son—[who is] the crucified;
The love of the Spirit—triumphing by the power of the cross.[56]

In answer, then, to our second question, Fr. Sergius and Philaret of Moscow reply—and I fully agree with them—that the Father and the Spirit participate in the redemptive "economy" of the Son, and therefore they do indeed "cosuffer" with him.

Ipse Pater non est impassibilis

This brings us to our third question. We have just seen how a modern Orthodox theologian such as Sergius Bulgakov is not afraid to speak of the "cocrucifixion" of the Father and the Spirit, in union with the crucifixion of the Son. Is there any parallel to this in the works of early Christian writers? More generally, was any early Christian writer willing to affirm that God the Father himself is subject to *pathos*?

The answer is that at least one author from the patristic era goes so far as to make such an affirmation; and that one author is no less a theologian than Origen. As a rule Origen upholds the normal patristic view concerning divine immutability and impassibility. "God is not subject to change," he writes.[57] "God is entirely without passion and destitute of all [human] emotions."[58] Biblical passages that speak of God as being angry are to be understood not literally but *tropikōs*, in a "spiritual" or allegorical sense.[59] In one text,

---

56. Philaret (Drozdov), quoted in Georges Florovsky, *Ways of Russian Theology*, part 1, Collected Works 5 (Belmont, MA: Nordland, 1979), 217, alt. When Philaret speaks of the Father as participating in "the act of the crucifying," presumably he means that the Father consented to the crucifixion of the Son, not that he caused or imposed it.

57. Origen, *Against Celsus* 4.14.

58. Origen, *First Principles* 2.4.4.

59. See Origen, *Commentary on John*, fragment 51, ed. Erwin Preuschen, GCS 10 (Leipzig: Hinrichs, 1903), 526, citing Exod. 15:7; Rom. 2:5; and 1 Thess. 2:16; Origen, *Homilies on Numbers* 23.2, ed. W. A. Baehrens, GCS 30 (Leipzig: Hinrichs, 1921), 212–14; Origen, *Against Celsus* 4.72.

however, Origen departs from this approach and explores with greater daring the possibility that God does indeed suffer. In a passage from the *Homilies on Ezekiel*, surviving only in Latin,[60] he goes so far as to assert, "The Father himself is not impassible" (*ipse Pater non est impassibilis*). When he uses here the word *passio*, translating the Greek *pathos*, we need to keep in mind the many-sided significance of the word, as we have indicated earlier: it means "suffering" but also "emotion," "feeling," "affection." Because there is no exact English equivalent, it is probably best to retain the Greek word *pathos* when translating this passage.

Origen begins this passage by taking the example of interpersonal relationships on the human level:

> When I speak to someone and entreat him on some account to have pity on me, if he is a person without pity, he is quite unaffected by the things that I say. But if he is a person of gentle spirit, and no callousness of heart has grown hard in him, he hears me and has pity upon me; his feelings are softened by my prayer.

On the human level, then, someone who is kindly and tenderhearted is affected by the feelings and suffering of others; not to share in the suffering of others indicates hardness of heart and a fundamental lack of love. If this is true of us humans, then it should also be attributed to Christ:

> I ask you to imagine something along the same lines with regard to the Savior. He came down to earth in pity for the human race. He was affected by our *pathē*, even before he underwent the sufferings of the cross and condescended to take our flesh upon him. If he had not shared in our sufferings, he would not have entered into full participation with our human life. First he was affected by our *pathē*, and then he came down and was made manifest.

Here we recall what was said above in answer to our second question. Origen clearly traces back Christ's solidarity with us in our *pathē*—in our feelings, emotions, and suffering—to the period before the incarnation. This solidarity existed also in the preincarnate life of the Logos. Indeed, it was precisely this compassion that formed the motive for the incarnation. Even before he became man, Christ was moved by our distress and participated in our pain and sorrow. If he had not been so moved, he would not have become incarnate. What Origen is telling us is that it is not enough to say that Christ shares in our suffering as a *result* of the incarnation. His participation in our *pathē* is

---

60. Origen, *Homilies on Ezekiel* 6.6, ed. W. A. Baehrens, GCS 33 (Leipzig: Hinrichs, 1925), 384, line 16, to 385, line 3. In what follows I use the translation of R. B. Tollinton, *Selections from the Commentaries and Homilies of Origen* (London: SPCK, 1929), 15–16, alt.

precisely the *cause* of the incarnation. Origen goes on to specify the precise character of this *pathos* that led the Logos to become incarnate: "What is this *pathos* by which he is affected on our account? It is the *pathos* of love."

At this point in his argument Origen takes a further step, applying what he says about the *pathos* of love not only to God the Son—whether incarnate or preincarnate—but also to God the Father:

> The Father himself, too, the God of the universe, long-suffering and of great compassion, full of pity, is not he also in some way liable to *pathos*? Do you not realize that, when he orders human affairs, he is subject to human *pathē*? "The Lord your God bears with you in your ways, just as a man bears with his own son" [see Deut. 1:31]. God then bears with our ways, just as the Son of God bears our *pathē*. The Father himself is not impassible. If we pray to him, he feels pity and grieves with us. He experiences the *pathos* of love. He concerns himself with things in which, according to the majesty of his nature, he can have no concern, and for our sakes he undergoes human *pathē*.

Central to the argument in this interesting passage—which, to the best of my knowledge, has no exact parallel elsewhere in the writings of Origen—is the connection that he establishes between *pathos* and the experience of love. To love another is to render oneself vulnerable, so that we are affected by what the other undergoes, making their joy or sorrow our own. The one who loves suffers with and for the other. If nothing that happens to the other has any effect upon our own inner life, then surely we cannot be said to love the other in any real sense. Love is mutuality of feeling; to love is to be changed by what the loved one does. All this, in Origen's view, applies also to God. Because God is a God of love—and this is true not only of the Son but also of the Father—then he is affected by all that we experience and suffer. Just as we can say of God, "His life is mine,"[61] so God also says to us, "*Your* life is mine: when you are in the midst of the fiery furnace, when you journey through the valley of the shadow of death, there am I with you; whatever your burden, I am carrying it with you. You are never alone; and I your faithful companion am divine."

God's power, then, is the power of suffering love; "omnipotent" thus means all-loving, all-suffering. It is this emphasis upon love that gives particular force to Origen's understanding of a suffering God. By speaking of the *pathos* of love, he has moved decisively away from the idea that suffering is merely passive. Suffering that is inflicted upon us contrary to our own will, that

---

61. Compare the title of the well-known book of Archimandrite Sophrony (Sakharov), *His Life Is Mine* (London: Mowbrays, 1977).

we reject with resentment and against which we protest with bitterness of heart, may prove to be entirely negative in its effect, crushing and destroying us. But suffering that we accept and embrace out of love, even though it too may sometimes seem to crush and destroy us, proves in the end to be creative and transfiguring. Indeed, there is no passivity in God; when he suffers out of love, he is not passive but supremely active. In the words of Hans Küng, "He does not suffer, as a philosopher might presume, because of a lack or a need for fulfillment. Then he would not be God. He suffers out of an abundance, that is to say, an abundance of love."[62] As Fr. Lev puts it, "God's suffering is divine love *freely creating* its own burden."[63]

With due deference, then, to the Angel of Good Silence, I venture to conclude: Yes, indeed, I believe in a suffering God. The Impassible suffers. Only the suffering God can help. Yet in reaching this conclusion, I would not have us forget some of the closely related truths that I have been seeking to emphasize. Suffering (*pathos*), I have insisted, is not merely passive, since love also is a *pathos*, and love is the strongest thing in the universe. Thus precisely because God's suffering is the immediate consequence of his love, this suffering is active and creative, an expression not of weakness but of power, not of subjection but of victory. The suffering God is at the same time the undefeated God. And this undefeated God offers us, not just companionship *in* suffering, but a way *through* suffering. As Fr. Lev puts it, God not only suffers what we are suffering, but through his cosuffering he enables us to overcome our own suffering.

Suppose that you are sinking into quicksand. It will not help you if I leap into the quicksand beside you, crying out, "You are not alone; I feel your pain." You might legitimately respond, "I do not ask for your sympathy; I want you to pull me out." And that I can do only if, as well as extending my hand to you, I also have my feet planted firmly upon a rock. So it is with the suffering of God. He shares our pain and sorrow, but—specifically because he is God—he also stands upon a rock, and so he has the ability to rescue us from the quicksand and to pull us out. He does not merely suffer with us, but he also lifts us out of suffering. He offers us not only sympathy but also new life, not only solidarity but also redemption and restoration.

When we think of the suffering of God, and more particularly of the suffering of God in Christ, we think at once of the crucifixion. But the cross of

62. Hans Küng, *Menschwerdung Gottes: Ein Einführung in Hegels theologisches Denken als Prolegomena zu einer künftiger Christologie* (Freiburg-im-Breisgan: Herder, 1970), 540, cited in Thomas G. Weinandy, *Does God Change? The Word's Becoming in the Incarnation* (Still River, MA: St. Bede's, 1985), 157.
63. Gillet, "Does God Suffer?," 118, emphasis original.

Christ is never to be isolated from that which came before it and that which came after: the transfiguration on Mount Tabor and the resurrection on the third day. The One who suffers with us is none other than the One who shines with uncreated glory and who has broken the bonds of death. His suffering brings us hope because it is the suffering of him who, by dying, has defeated death. So we enlarge Bonhoeffer's affirmation: "Only the suffering God, *risen from the dead*, can help." In the words of the homily attributed to John Chrysostom that is read in the Orthodox Church at the Paschal midnight service:

> Let none fear death, for the death of the Savior has set us free.
> He has destroyed death by undergoing death.
> He has despoiled hell by descending into hell. . . .
> Christ is risen and life reigns in freedom.[64]

---

64. For the full text, see Vladimir Lossky, *The Mystical Theology of the Eastern Church* (London: James Clarke, 1957), 247–49.

ABBREVIATIONS

ACO   *Acta Conciliorum Oecumenicorum*. Edited by Eduard Schwartz. Berlin: de Gruyter, 1924–40. New ed., J. Staub, 1971.

ACW   Ancient Christian Writers. New York: Newman, 1946–. More recently, Paulist Press.

ANF   *Ante-Nicene Fathers*. Edited by A. Roberts and J. Donaldson. Buffalo: Christian Literature, 1885–96. Reprint, Grand Rapids: Eerdmans, 1951–56.

CCSG   Corpus Christianorum: Series Graeca. Turnhout: Brepols, 1977–.

CCSL   Corpus Christianorum: Series Latina. Turnhout: Brepols, 1953–.

CSCO   Corpus Scriptorum Christianorum Orientalium. Louvain: Peeters, 1903–.

CSEL   Corpus Scriptorum Ecclesiasticorum Latinorum. Vienna: Geroldi, 1866–.

CWS   Classics of Western Spirituality. Edited by R. J. Payne et al. New York: Paulist Press, in progress.

FC   The Fathers of the Church. Washington, DC: Catholic University of America Press, 1947–.

GCS   Die griechischen christlichen Schriftsteller der ersten [drei] Jahrhunderte. Berlin: Akademie Verlag, 1897–.

GNO   *Gregorii Nysseni Opera*. Edited by W. Jaeger. Leiden: Brill, 1952–.

LCC   Library of Christian Classics. Edited by J. Baillie et al. Philadelphia: Westminster, 1953–66.

LCL   Loeb Classical Library. Cambridge, MA: Harvard University Press, 1912–.

NPNF[1]   *A Select Library of Nicene and Post-Nicene Fathers of the Christian Church*. Edited by Philip Schaff. 1st series. 14 vols. New York: Christian Literature, 1886–90. Reprint, Grand Rapids: Eerdmans, 1956.

NPNF[2]   *A Select Library of Nicene and Post-Nicene Fathers of the Christian Church*. Edited by Philip Schaff and Henry Wace. 2nd series. 14 vols. New York: Christian Literature, 1890–1900. Reprint, Grand Rapids: Eerdmans, 1952.

PG   Patrologia Graeca [= Patrologiae Cursus Completus: Series Graeca]. Edited by J.-P.
         Migne. 162 volumes. Paris, 1857–86.

PL   Patrologia Latina [= Patrologiae Cursus Completus: Series Latina]. Edited by J.-P.
         Migne. 217 vols. Paris, 1844–64.

PO   Patrologia Orientalis. Paris: Firmin-Didot, 1903–.

PTS   Patristische Texte und Studien. Berlin: de Gruyter, 1963–.

SC   Sources chrétiennes. Edited by H. de Lubac, J. Daniélou, et al. Paris: Cerf, 1942–.

StPatr   Studia Patristica. Louvain: Peeters, 1904–.

BIBLIOGRAPHY

Abrams, Judith Z. *Judaism and Disability: Portrayals in Ancient Texts from the Tanach through the Bavli*. Washington, DC: Gallaudet University Press, 1988.

Aeschylus. *Agamemnon*. In *Oresteia*, translated by Peter Meineck, 3–67. Indianapolis: Hackett, 1998.

Aland, Kurt, et al. *The Greek New Testament*. 2nd ed. New York: United Bible Society, 1968.

Anatolios, Khaled. *Athanasius: The Coherence of His Thought*. London: Routledge, 1998.

———. "The Body as Instrument: A Reevaluation of Athanasius' Logos-Sarx Christology." *Coptic Church Review* 18 (1977) 78–84.

———. "The Influence of Irenaeus on Athanasius." StPatr 36 (2001): 463–76.

Anderson, Gary A. "From Israel's Burden to Israel's Debt: Towards a Theology of Sin in Biblical and Early Second Temple Sources." In *Reworking the Bible: Apocryphal and Related Texts at Qumran*, edited by Esther G. Chazon et al., 1–30. Leiden: Brill, 2005.

———. "Garments of Skin in Apocryphal Narrative and Biblical Commentary." In *Studies in Ancient Midrash*, edited by James L. Kugel, 101–43. Cambridge, MA: Harvard University Press, 2001.

———. "The Resurrection of Adam and Eve." In *In Dominico Eloquio—In Lordly Eloquence: Essays on Patristic Exegesis in Honor of Robert Louis Wilken*, edited by Paul M. Blowers et al., 3–34. Grand Rapids: Eerdmans, 2002.

Assemani, Giuseppe Simone, trans. and ed. *Bibliotheca orientalis Clementino-Vaticana*. 3 vols. Rome: Typis Sacrae Congregationis de Propaganda Fide, 1719–28.

Attridge, Harold W. "The Philosophical Critique of Religion under the Early Empire." In *Aufstieg und Niedergang der römischen Welt*, edited by Hildegard Temporini and Wolfgang Haase, part 2, *Principat*, 16.1:45–78. Berlin: de Gruyter, 1978.

Auf der Maur, Ivo, OSB. *Mönchtum und Glaubensverkündigung in den Schriften des Hl. Johannes Chrysostomus*. Paradosis 14. Freiburg, Switzerland: Universitätsverlag Freiburg Schweiz, 1959.

Augustine of Hippo. *The City of God against the Pagans*. Translated by R. W. Dyson. Cambridge Texts in the History of Political Thought. Cambridge: Cambridge University Press, 1998.

———. *Concerning the City of God*. Translated by Henry Bettenson. London: Penguin, 1984.

———. *Confessions*. Translated by Henry Chadwick. Oxford World Classics. Oxford: Oxford University Press, 1991.

———. *De natura boni*. In *Augustine: Earlier Writings*, translated by John H. S. Burleigh, 326–48. LCC 6. Philadelphia: Westminster, 1953.

———. "Divine Providence and the Problem of Evil." In *The Writings of Saint Augustine*, translated by Robert P. Russell, 1:227–332. FC 2. New York: CIMA, 1948.

———. *The Enchiridion on Faith, Hope and Love*. Translated by J. F. Shaw. Washington, DC: Regnery, 1996.

———. *The Literal Meaning of Genesis*. Translated by John Hammond Taylor, SJ. ACW 42. New York: Newman, 1982.

———. *On Free Choice of the Will*. Translated by Anna S. Benjamin and L. H. Hackstaff. Library of Liberal Arts. New York: Macmillan, 1964.

———. *The Problem of Free Choice*. Translated by Mark Pontifex. ACW 22. Westminster, MD: Newman, 1955.

———. *Selected Writings*. Translated by Mary T Clark. CWS. New York: Paulist Press, 1984.

Aulén, Gustav. *Christus Victor: An Historical Study of the Three Main Types of the Idea of the Atonement*. New York: MacMillan, 1969. Swedish ed., 1930.

Avvakum Petrovich, Protopope. *Archpriest Avvakum, the Life Written by Himself*. Edited by Kenneth N. Bostrom. Michigan Slavic Translations 4. Ann Arbor: University of Michigan, 1979.

Ayres, Lewis. *The Faith of Nicaea*. Oxford: Oxford University Press, 2004.

Bacq, Philippe. *De l'ancienne à la nouvelle alliance selon S. Irénée: Unité du livre IV de l'Adversus haereses*. Paris: Lethielleux, Presses Universitaires de Namur, 1978.

Baker, Julia Watts. "Reading Talmudic Bodies: Disability, Narrative, and the Gaze in Rabbinic Judaism." In *Disability in Judaism, Christianity, and Islam: Sacred Texts, Historical Traditions, and Social Analysis*, edited by Darla Schumm and Michael Stoltzfus, 5–27. New York: Palgrave Macmillan, 2011.

Balthasar, Hans Urs von. *The Glory of the Lord: A Theological Aesthetics*. Vol. 2. Edinburgh: T&T Clark, 1984.

Bardy, Gustave. "'Philosophie' et 'Philosophe' dans le vocabulaire chrétien des premiers siècles." *Revue d'ascétique et de mystique* 25 (April–December 1949): 97–108.

Barnes, Timothy D. *Constantine and Eusebius*. Cambridge, MA: Harvard University Press, 1981.

Barr, James. *The Garden of Eden and the Hope of Immortality*. Minneapolis: Fortress, 1993.

Bartelink, G. J. M. "'Philosophie' et 'Philosophe' dans quelques oeuvres de Jean Chrysostome." *Revue d'ascetique et de mystique* 36 (October–December 1960): 487–92.

Behr, John. *Asceticism and Anthropology in Irenaeus and Clement*. Oxford Early Christian Studies. Oxford: Oxford University Press, 2000.

———. *Becoming Human: Meditations on Christian Anthropology in Word and Image*. Crestwood, NY: St. Vladimir's Seminary Press, 2013.

———. *Irenaeus of Lyons: Identifying Christianity*. Christian Theology in Context. Oxford: Oxford University Press, 2013.

———. *The Mystery of Christ: Life in Death*. Crestwood, NY: St. Vladimir's Seminary Press, 2006.

———. *The Nicene Faith*. Crestwood, NY: St. Vladimir's Seminary Press, 2004.

Bemporad, Jack. "Soul: Jewish Concept." In *Encyclopedia of Religion*, edited by Lindsay Jones, 12:8556–61. 2nd ed. Farmington Hills, MI: Macmillan Reference, 2005.

Berthouzoz, Roger. *Liberté et grace suivant la théologie d'Irénée de Lyon: Le debat avec la gnose aux origines de la theologie chretienne*. Fribourg, Switzerland: Éditions Universitaires; Paris: Cerf, 1980.

Bonner, Gerald. "Libido and Concupiscentia in Augustine." *StPatr* 6 (1972): 303–14.

Brock, Sebastian. "Clothing Metaphors as a Means of Theological Expression in Syriac Tradition." In *Typus, Symbol, Allegorie bei den östlichen Vätern und ihren Parallelen im Mittelalter*, edited by M. Schmidt and C. Geyer, 11–37. Regensburg: Friedrich Pustet, 1982.

Brown, Peter. *The Body and Society: Men, Women, and Sexual Renunciation in Early Christianity*. Lectures on the History of Religions, new series, 13. New York: Columbia University Press, 1988.

———. *The Making of Late Antiquity*. Cambridge, MA: Harvard University Press, 1978.

———. *Power and Persuasion in Late Antiquity: Towards a Christian Empire*. Madison: University of Wisconsin Press, 1992.

Bulgakov, Sergius. *The Lamb of God*. Grand Rapids: Eerdmans, 2008.

Burns, J. Patout. "Augustine on the Origin and Progress of Evil." In *The Ethics of St. Augustine*, edited by William S. Babcock, 67–85. JRE Studies in Religious Ethics 3. Atlanta: Scholars Press, 1991.

Cavadini, John. "Ambrose and Augustine *De bono mortis*." In *The Limits of Ancient Christianity: Essays on Late Antique Thought and Culture in Honor of R. A. Markus*, edited by William E. Klingshirn and Mark Vessey, 232–49. Ann Arbor: University of Michigan Press, 1999.

Cherniss, Harold. "The Sources of Evil according to Plato." *Proceedings of the American Philosophical Society* 98 (1954): 23–30.

Clark, Elizabeth A. "'Adam's Only Companion': Augustine and the Early Christian Debate on Marriage." *Recherches Augustiniennes* 21 (1986): 139–62.

———. "Heresy, Asceticism, Adam, and Eve: Interpretations of Genesis 1–3 in the Later Latin Fathers." In *Ascetic Piety and Women's Faith: Essays on Late Ancient Christianity*, 353–85. Lewiston, NY: Edwin Mellen, 1986.

———. "Holy Women, Holy Words: Early Christian Women, Social History, and the 'Linguistic Turn.'" *Journal of Early Christian Studies* 6, no. 3 (1998): 413–30.

———. "The Lady Vanishes: Dilemmas of a Feminist Historian after the 'Linguistic Turn.'" *Church History* 67, no. 1 (March 1998): 1–31.

———. *Women in the Early Church*. Message of the Fathers of the Church 13. Wilmington, DE: Michael Glazier, 1983.

Clement of Alexandria. *Eclogae propheticae*. Edited by Otto Stählin and Ludwig Früchtel. 2nd ed. GCS. Berlin: Akademie Verlag, 1970.

———. *Protrepticus*. Edited by Otto Stählin and Ursula Treu. 3rd ed. GCS. Berlin: Akademie Verlag, 1972.

Colish, Marcia. *The Stoic Tradition from Antiquity to the Early Middle Ages*. 2nd ed. 2 vols. Leiden: Brill, 1990.

Conzelmann, Hans. *Theology of St. Luke*. Philadelphia: Fortress, 1961.

Cooper, John M., and D. S. Hutchinson, eds. *Plato: Complete Works*. Indianapolis: Hackett, 1997.

Cooper, Kate. *The Virgin and the Bride: Idealized Womanhood in Late Antiquity*. Cambridge, MA: Harvard University Press, 1996.

Costello, Edward B. "Is Plotinus Inconsistent on the Nature of Evil?" *International Philosophical Quarterly* 7 (1967): 483–97.

Coxe, A. Cleveland, ed. *Fathers of the Third and Fourth Centuries*. ANF 7.

Cyril of Alexandria. *Cyrilli archiepiscopi Alexandrini Opera*. Edited by Philip E. Pusey. Reprint, Brussels: Culture & Civilisation, 1965.

———. *Five Tomes against Nestorius* [etc.]. Translated by Philip E. Pusey. Oxford: Parker, 1881.

———. *Sancti Patris nostri Cyrilli archiepiscopi Alexandrini: De recta fide ad Imperatorem, De incarnatione unigeniti dialogus, De recta fide ad Principessas, De recta fide ad Augustas, Quod unus Christus dialogus, Apologeticus ad Imperatorem*. Edited by Philip E. Pusey. Oxford: Parker, 1877.

———. *Sancti Patris nostri Cyrilli archiepiscopi Alexandrini: Epistolae tres oecumenicae, Libri quinque contra Nestorium, XII capitum explanatio, XII capitum defensio utraque, Scholia de incarnatione unigeniti*. Edited by Philip E. Pusey. Oxford: Parker, 1875.

———. *Sancti Patris nostri Cyrilli archiepiscopi Alexandrini in D. Ioannis Evangelium*. Edited by Philip E. Pusey. 3 vols. Oxford: Clarendon, 1872.

———. *Select Letters*. Translated and edited by Lionel R. Wickham. Oxford: Clarendon, 1983.

Daley, Brian. "The Fullness of the Saving God: Cyril of Alexandria on the Holy Spirit." In *The Theology of St. Cyril of Alexandria*, edited by Thomas G. Weinandy and Daniel A. Keating, 113–48. London: T&T Clark, 2003.

Deissmann, Adolf. *Light from the Ancient East*. New York: George H. Doran, 1927.

Descouvemont, Pierre. *Dieu souffre-t-il?* Paris: Éditions de l'Emmanuel, 2008.

Dewart, Joanne McWilliam. *The Theology of Grace of Theodore of Mopsuestia*. Washington, DC: Catholic University of America Press, 1971.

Dieu, Léon. "Le commentaire de Saint Jean Chrysostome sur Job." *Revue d'histoire ecclésiastique* 13 (1912): 650–68.

Digeser, Elizabeth DePalma. *The Making of a Christian Empire: Lactantius and Rome*. Ithaca, NY: Cornell University Press, 2000.

Drake, Harold A. *Constantine and the Bishops: The Politics of Intolerance*. Baltimore: Johns Hopkins University Press, 2000.

Elser, K. "Der heilige Chrysostomus und die Philosophie." *Theologische Quartalschrift* 76 (1894): 550–76.

Ephrem the Syrian. *Carmina Nisibena*. Translated and edited by Edmund Beck. 4 vols. CSCO 218–19, 240–41. Louvain: Secretariat du Corpus SCO, 1961–63.

———. *Hymnen De Nativitate*. Translated and edited by Edmund Beck. 2 vols. CSCO 186–87. Louvain: Secretariat du Corpus SCO, 1959.

Erickson, John H. *The Challenge of Our Past: Studies in Orthodox Canon Law and Church History*. Crestwood, NY: St. Vladimir's Seminary Press, 1991.

Evagrius of Pontus. *Gnostic Chapters*. Edited by Antoine Guillaumont. PO 28.1. Paris: Firmin-Didot, 1958.

Evans, Gillian R. *Augustine on Evil*. New York: Cambridge University Press, 2000.

Ferguson, Everett, ed. *Encyclopedia of Early Christianity*. 2nd ed. 2 vols. New York: Garland, 1997.

Fiddes, Paul S. *The Creative Suffering of God*. Oxford: Clarendon, 1988.

———. *Participating in God: A Pastoral Doctrine of the Trinity*. London: Darton, Longman & Todd, 2000.

Flannery, Austin, ed. *Vatican Council II*. Northport, NY: Costello, 1996.

Florovsky, Georges. *Ways of Russian Theology*. Part 1. Collected Works 5. Belmont, MA: Nordland, 1979.

Ford, David C. *Women and Men in the Early Church: The Full Views of St. John Chrysostom*. South Canaan, PA: St. Tikhon's Seminary Press, 1996.

Frankfurter, David. *Evil Incarnate: Rumors of Divine Conspiracy and Satanic Abuse in History*. Princeton: Princeton University Press, 2006.

Frend, William H. C. *The Rise of the Monophysite Movement*. Cambridge: Cambridge University Press, 1972.

Garland, Robert. *The Eye of the Beholder: Deformity and Disability in the Graeco-Roman World*. Ithaca, NY: Cornell University Press, 1995.

Garnsey, Peter. "Lactantius and Augustine." In *Representations of Empire: Rome and the Mediterranean World*, edited by Alan K. Bowman et al., 153–79. Oxford: Oxford University Press, 2002.

Gavrilyuk, Paul L. *The Suffering of the Impassible God: The Dialectics of Patristic Thought*. Oxford: Oxford University Press, 2004.

———. "*Theopathei*: Nestorius's Main Charge against Cyril of Alexandria." *Scottish Journal of Theology* 56, no. 2 (2003): 190–207.

Gillet, Lev. "Does God Suffer?" *Sobornost* 3, no. 15 (1954): 112–20.

Gray, Patrick. *The Defense of Chalcedon in the East (451–553)*. Leiden: Brill, 1979.

Greene, William Chase. *Moira: Fate, Good, and Evil in Greek Thought*. Cambridge, MA: Harvard University Press, 1944.

Greer, Rowan A. *The Captain of Our Salvation: A Study in the Patristic Exegesis of Hebrews*. Tübingen: Mohr, 1973.

———, trans. "Cyril of Alexandria, *Ad Reginas de Recta Fide Oratio Altera*." Unpublished.

Gregg, Robert C. *Consolation Philosophy: Greek and Christian* Paideia *in Basil and the Two Gregories*. Patristic Monograph Series 3. Cambridge, MA: Philadelphia Patristic Foundation, 1975.

Gregory of Nazianzus. *Briefe*. Edited by Paul Gallay. GCS 53. Berlin: Akademie Verlag, 1969.

———. *Poemata Arcana*. Translated and edited by Claudio Moreschini and D. A. Sykes. Oxford: Oxford University Press, 1997.

Gregory of Nyssa. *Ascetical Works*. Translated by Virginia Woods Callahan. FC 58. Washington: Catholic University of America Press, 1967.

———. *De pauperibus amandis orationes duo*. Edited by Arie van Heck. Leiden: Brill, 1964.

———. *The Life of Saint Macrina*. Translated by Kevin Corrigan. Peregrina Translations Series 10; Matrologia Graeca. Toronto: Peregrina, 1987.

———. *On the Soul and the Resurrection*. Translated by Catharine P. Roth. Crestwood, NY: St. Vladimir's Seminary Press, 1993.

———. *Vie de sainte Macrine*. Translated and edited by Pierre Maraval. SC 178. Paris: Cerf, 1971.

Griffin, David Ray. "Augustine and the Denial of Genuine Evil." In *The Problem of Evil: Select Readings*, edited by Michael L. Peterson, 197–214. Notre Dame, IN: University of Notre Dame Press, 1992.

Grillmeier, Aloys. *Christ in Christian Tradition.* 2nd ed. 2 vols. Translated by John Bowden. Atlanta: John Knox, 1975, 1985; Louisville: Westminster John Knox, 1994.

Guillaume, Denis, trans. *Paraclitique ou Grand Octoèque.* 2 vols. Rome: Diaconie Apostolique, 1979.

Gunton, Colin. *The Actuality of Atonement: A Study of Metaphor, Rationality, and the Christian Tradition.* Grand Rapids: Eerdmans, 1989.

Hallman, Joseph M. "The Seeds of Fire: Divine Suffering in the Christology of Cyril of Alexandria and Nestorius of Constantinople." *Journal of Early Christian Studies* 5, no. 3 (1997): 369–91.

Hanson, Paul D. "Rebellion in Heaven, Azazel, and the Euhemeristic Heroes in *1 Enoch* 6–11." *Journal of Biblical Literature* 96, no. 2 (1977): 195–233.

Hanson, R. P. C. *The Search for the Christian Doctrine of God.* Edinburgh: T&T Clark, 1988.

Hardy, E. R., ed. *Christology of the Later Fathers.* Philadelphia: Westminster, 1954.

Harrison, Nonna Verna. *God's Many-Splendored Image.* Grand Rapids: Baker Academic, 2010.

———. "Women and the Image of God according to St. John Chrysostom." In *Dominico Eloquio—In Lordly Eloquence: Essays on Patristic Exegesis in Honor of Robert Louis Wilken,* edited by Paul M. Blowers et al., 259–79. Grand Rapids: Eerdmans, 2002.

———. "Women, Human Identity, and the Image of God: Antiochene Interpretations." *Journal of Early Christian Studies* 9, no. 2 (2001): 205–49.

Harrison, Peter. "Laws of Nature, Moral Order, and the Intelligibility of the Cosmos." In *The Astronomy Revolution: 400 Years of Exploring the Cosmos,* edited by Donald G. York, Owen Gingerich, and Shuang-Nan Zhang, 375–86. Boca Raton, FL: CRC, 2011.

Harrison, Verna E. F. [Nonna Verna]. "Male and Female in Cappadocian Theology." *Journal of Theological Studies* 41 (1990): 441–71.

Hart, David Bentley. "A Gift Exceeding Every Debt: An Eastern Orthodox Appreciation of Anselm's *Cur Deus Homo.*" *Pro Ecclesia* 7 (1998): 333–48.

Hatlie, Peter. "The Politics of Salvation: Theodore of Stoudios on Martyrdom (*Martyrion*) and on Speaking Out (*Parrhesia*)." *Dumbarton Oaks Papers* 50 (1996): 263–87.

Hill, Robert C. "Chrysostom as Old Testament Commentator." *Estudios bíblicos* 46, no. 1 (1988): 61–77.

———. "Chrysostom on the Obscurity of the Old Testament." *Orientalia christiana periodica* 67, no. 2 (2001): 371–83.

———. *Reading the Old Testament in Antioch.* Bible in Ancient Christianity 5. Leiden: Brill, 2005.

———. "St. John Chrysostom: Preacher on the Old Testament." *Greek Orthodox Theological Review* 46, nos. 3–4 (2001): 267–86.

Hobbes, Thomas. *Leviathan*. Edited by Richard Tuck. Rev. student ed. Cambridge: Cambridge University Press, 1996.

Holman, Susan R. *The Hungry Are Dying: Beggars and Bishops in Roman Cappadocia*. Oxford: Oxford University Press, 2001.

Holsinger-Friesen, Thomas. *Irenaeus and Genesis: A Study of Competition in Early Christian Hermeneutics*. Journal of Theological Interpretation Supplements 1. Winona Lake, IN: Eisenbrauns, 2009.

Hutchinson, Francis E., ed. *The Works of George Herbert*. Oxford: Clarendon, 1941.

Irenaeus of Lyons. *Against the Heresies*. Translated and edited by A. Rousseau. SC 263–64, 293–94, 310–11, 100, 152–53 (sequence reflects order of work's main divisions). Paris: Cerf, 1979, 1982, 1974, 1965, 1969 (sequenced by order of work's main divisions).

———. *Against the Heresies*. Translated by D. J. Unger. Revised by J. J. Dillon and M. C. Steenberg. ACW 55, 64, 65. New York: Paulist Press, 1992, 2012, 2012.

———. *Demonstration of the Apostolic Preaching*. Translated by John Behr. Popular Patristics Series. Crestwood, NY: St. Vladimir's Seminary Press, 1997.

Isaac the Syrian. *Ascetical Discourses*. Boston: Holy Transfiguration Monastery, 1984.

Jacob of Sarug. *Homiliae selectae Mar-Jacobi Sarugensis*. Edited by Paul Bedjan. 5 vols. Paris: Harrassowitz, 1905–10. Rev. ed. as *Homilies of Mar Jacob of Sarug*. Edited by Paul Bedjan. With additional material by Sebastian P. Brock. 6 vols. Piscataway, NJ: Gorgias, 2006.

———. *Six homélies festales en prose*. Edited by Frédéric Rilliet. PO 43.3. Turnhout: Brepols, 1986.

John Chrysostom. *Baptismal Instructions*. Translated by Paul W. Harkins. ACW 31. New York: Paulist Press, 1963.

———. *Commentaire sur Job*. Translated and edited by Henri Sorlin and Louis Neyrand, SJ. SC 346, 348. Paris: Cerf, 1988.

———. *Commentary on Saint John the Apostle and Evangelist, Homilies 48–88*. Translated by Sr. Thomas Aquinas Goggin. FC 41. Washington, DC: Catholic University of America Press, 1959.

———. *The Cult of the Saints*. Translated by Wendy Mayer. Crestwood, NY: St. Vladimir's Seminary Press, 2006.

———. *Homilies on the Acts of the Apostles and the Epistle to the Romans*. NPNF¹ 11.

———. *Homilies on the Obscurity of the Old Testament*. Vol. 3 of *Old Testament Homilies*, translated by Robert C. Hill. Brookline, MA: Holy Cross Orthodox Press, 2003.

———. *Kommentar zu Hiob*. Translated by Ursula Hagedorn and Dieter Hagedorn. PTS 35. Berlin: de Gruyter, 1990.

———. *Omelie sull'oscurità delle profezie*. Translated and edited by Sergio Zincone. Verba Seniorum 12. Rome: Edizioni Studium, 1998.

————. *On Marriage and Family Life*. Translated by Catharine P. Roth and David Anderson. Crestwood, NY: St. Vladimir's Seminary Press, 1986.

————. *Six Books on the Priesthood*. Translated by Graham Neville. Crestwood, NY: St. Vladimir's Seminary Press, 2002.

————. *Sur le sacerdoce*. Translated and edited by Anne-Marie Malingrey. SC 272. Paris: Cerf, 1980.

————. *La virginité*. Edited by Herbert Musurillo, SJ. Translated by Bernard Grillet. SC 125. Paris: Cerf, 1966.

John Climacus. *The Ladder of Divine Ascent*. Translated by Colm Luibheid and Norman Russell. CWS. New York: Paulist Press, 1982.

Julian of Norwich. *Julian of Norwich: Showings*. Translated by Edmund Colledge and James Walsh. CWS. New York: Paulist Press, 1978.

Karras, Valerie. "Male Domination of Women in the Writings of St. John Chrysostom." *Greek Orthodox Theological Review* 36 (1991): 131–39.

Kartsonis, Anna D. *Anastasis: The Making of an Image*. Princeton: Princeton University Press, 1986.

Kazhdan, Alexander P. "Hagiographical Notes." *Byzantion* 56 (1986): 148–70.

Kesich, Veselin. "The Antiochenes and the Temptation Story." StPatr 7 (1966): 496–502.

Koch, Günter. *Die Heilsverwirklichung bei Theodor von Mopsuestia*. Münchener theologische Studien 31. Munich: Hueber, 1965.

————. *Structuren und Geschichte des Heils in der Theologie des Theodoret von Kyros*. Frankfurter theologische Studien 17. Frankfurt: Knecht, 1974.

Koen, Lars. *The Saving Passion: Incarnational and Soteriological Thought in Cyril of Alexandria's Commentary on the Gospel according to St. John*. Studia doctrinae Christianae Upsaliensia 31. Stockholm: Almqvist & Wiksell, 1991.

Köppen, Klaus-Peter. *Die Auslegung der Versuchungsgeschichte unter besonderer Berücksichtigung der Alten Kirche: Ein Beitrag zur Geschichte der Schriftauslegung*. Tübingen: Mohr Siebeck, 1961.

Kotzampassi, S. "To martyrio tōn saranta dyo martyrōn tou Amoriou: Hagiologika kai hymnologika keimena." *Epistēmonikē Epetēris tēs Philosophikēs Scholēs Aristotēleiou Panepistēmiou Thessaonikēs* 2 (1992): 109–53.

Küng, Hans. *Menschwerdung Gottes: Eine Einführung in Hegels theologisches Denken als Prolegomena zu einer künftigen Christologie*. Freiburg-im-Breisgau: Herder, 1970.

Lactantius. *De mortibus persecutorum*. Translated and edited by J. L. Creed. Oxford: Clarendon, 1984.

————. *De mortibus persecutorum*. Edited by S. Brandt. CSEL 27.2. Vienna: F. Tempsky, 1893.

————. *Divinae institutiones*. Edited by S. Brandt. CSEL 19.1–2. Vienna: F. Tempsky, 1890.

————. *Divine Institutes*. Translated by Anthony Bowen and Peter Garnsey. Liverpool: Liverpool University Press, 2003.

Lake, Kirsopp, trans. and ed. *Apostolic Fathers*. Vol. 1. LCL. 1913. Reprint, Cambridge, MA: Harvard University Press, 1976.

Layton, Richard A. *Didymus the Blind and His Circle in Late Antique Alexandria.* Urbana: University of Illinois Press, 2004.

Leduc, Francis. "Penthos et larmes dans l'oeuvre de Saint Jean Chrysostome." *Proche-Orient chrétien* 41, no. 1 (1991): 220–57.

Leemans, Johan, et al. *"Let Us Die That We May Live": Greek Homilies on Christian Martyrs from Asia Minor, Palestine and Syria (c. A.D. 350–A.D. 450)*. London: Routledge, 2003.

Limberis, Vasiliki. *Architects of Piety: The Cappadocian Fathers and the Cult of the Martyrs*. Oxford: Oxford University Press, 2011.

Long, Anthony A. "The Stoic Concept of Evil." *Philosophical Quarterly* 18 (1968): 329–43.

Lossky, Vladimir. *The Mystical Theology of the Eastern Church*. London: James Clarke, 1957.

Madec, Goulven. *Introduction aux "Révisions" et à la lecture des oeuvres de saint Augustin*. Paris: Institut d'Études Augustiniennes, 1996.

Malingrey, Anne-Marie. *"Philosophia": Étude d'un groupe de mots dans la littérature grecque, des Présocratiques au IVᵉ siècle après J.-C*. Études et Commentaires 40. Paris: Librairie C. Klincksieck, 1961.

Marcus, Joel. *Mark 1–8*. Anchor Bible 27. New York: Doubleday, 2000.

Markus, Robert A. *Conversion and Disenchantment in Augustine's Spiritual Career*. The Saint Augustine Lecture 1984. Villanova, PA: Villanova University Press, 1989.

————. "*De civitate Dei*: Pride and the Common Good." In *Proceedings of the PMR [Patristic, Medieval, and Renaissance] Conference 12/13* (Villanova, PA: Augustinian Historical Institute, Villanova University, 1987–88), 1–18.

Martens, John W. *The End of the World: The Apocalyptic Imagination in Film and Television*. Winnipeg: Shillingford, 2003.

Mateo-Seco, Lucas F., and Juan L. Bastero, eds. *El "Contra Eunomium I" en la producción literaria de Gregorio de Nisa: VI Coloquio Internacional sobre Gregorio de Nisa*. Pamplona, Spain: Ediciones Universidad de Navarra, 1988.

Maximus the Confessor. *On the Cosmic Mystery of Jesus Christ: Selected Writings from St Maximus the Confessor*. Translated by Paul M. Blowers and Robert Louis Wilken. Crestwood, NY: St. Vladimir's Seminary Press, 2003.

McGuckin, John A. *Cyril of Alexandria: The Christological Controversy; Its History, Theology, and Texts*. Leiden: Brill, 1994. Reprint, Crestwood, NY: St. Vladimir's Seminary Press, 2004.

————, ed. *The Westminster Handbook to Origen*. Louisville: Westminster John Knox, 2004.

McIntyre, John. *St. Anselm and His Critics*. London: Oliver & Boyd, 1954.

McKinion, Steven A. *Words, Imagery, and the Mystery of Christ: A Reconstruction of Cyril of Alexandria's Christology*. Leiden: Brill, 2000.

McLeod, Frederick G. *The Roles of Christ's Humanity in Salvation: Insights from Theodore of Mopsuestia*. Washington, DC: Catholic University of America Press, 2005.

Melito of Sardis. *On Pascha*. Edited by Stuart George Hall. Oxford: Clarendon, 1979.

Meyer, Ben F. "Election-Historical Thinking in Romans 9–11, and Ourselves." *Logos* 7, no. 4 (2004): 171–81.

Miles, Margaret R. *Augustine on the Body*. AAR Dissertation Series 31. Missoula, MT: Scholars Press, 1979.

Minns, Denis. *Irenaeus*. London: Geoffrey Chapman, 1994.

Mirkin, Mosheh Aryeh, ed. *Midrash Rabbah: Be-Midbar Rabbah*. Tel Aviv: Yavneh, 1987.

Mitchell, Margaret M. *The Heavenly Trumpet: John Chrysostom and the Art of Pauline Interpretation*. Hermeneutische Untersuchungen zur Theologie 40. Tübingen: Mohr Siebeck, 2000.

Momigliano, Arnaldo. "The Life of St. Macrina by Gregory of Nyssa." In *On Pagans, Jews, and Christians*, 206–21. Middletown, CT: Wesleyan University Press, 1987. Also in *The Craft of the Ancient Historian: Essays in Honor of Chester G. Starr*, edited by John W. Eadie and Josiah Ober, 443–58. Lanham, MD: University Press of America, 1985.

Morris, J. B., and W. H. Simcox. *Saint Chrysostom: Homilies on the Acts of the Apostles and the Epistle to the Romans*. NPNF[1] 11.

Moule, C. F. D. *The Epistles of Paul the Apostle to the Colossians and to Philemon*. Cambridge: Cambridge University Press, 1957.

Muffs, Yochanan. *Studies in the Aramaic Legal Papyri from Elephantine*. Reprint, Leiden: Brill, 2003.

Musurillo, Herbert, ed. *The Martyrdom of Saints Perpetua and Felicitas*. In *The Acts of the Christian Martyrs*, 107–31. Oxford: Clarendon, 1972.

Narsai. "Narsai's Metrical Homilies on the Nativity, Epiphany, Passion, Resurrection and Ascension." Edited by Frederick G. McLeod. PO 40.1 (1979): 1–193.

Nellas, Panayiotis. *Deification in Christ*. Crestwood, NY: St. Vladimir's Seminary Press, 1987.

Neuner, Josef, and Jacques Dupuis, trans. *The Christian Faith in the Doctrinal Documents of the Catholic Church*. New York: Alba House, 1982.

Norris, Richard A. *Manhood and Christ*. Oxford: Clarendon, 1963.

————. "Toward a Contemporary Interpretation of the Chalcedonian Definition." In *Lux in Lumine*, edited by Richard A. Norris, 62–79. New York: Seabury, 1966.

O'Brien, Denis. *Théodicée plotinienne, théodicée gnostique.* Leiden: Brill, 1993.

O'Connell, Robert J. *St. Augustine's Early Theory of Man, A.D. 386–391.* Cambridge, MA: Belknap Press of Harvard University Press, 1968.

O'Donovan, Oliver. *The Problem of Self-Love in Augustine.* New Haven: Yale University Press, 1980.

O'Keefe, John J. "Impassible Suffering? Divine Passion and Fifth-Century Christology." *Theological Studies* 58 (1997): 39–60.

Origen. "An Exhortation to Martyrdom." In *Origen*, translated by Rowan A. Greer, 41–79. CWS. New York: Paulist Press, 1979.

———. *Homilies on Leviticus.* Edited by W. A. Baehrens. GCS. Leipzig: Hinrichs, 1920.

———. *On First Principles.* Translated by G. W. Butterworth. New York: Harper & Row, 1973.

Paffenroth, Kim. "The Young Augustine: Lover of Sorrow." *Downside Review* 118, no. 412 (July 2000): 221–30.

Pascal, Blaise. *Pensées.* Translated by A. J. Krailsheimer. Harmondsworth: Penguin, 1966.

Perkins, Judith. "The 'Self' as Sufferer." *Harvard Theological Review* 85, no. 3 (1992): 245–72.

Petterson, Alvyn. *Athanasius.* London: Geoffrey Chapman, 1995.

———. *Athanasius and the Human Body.* Bristol: Bristol Press, 1990.

Plato. *The Collected Dialogues of Plato, Including the Letters.* Edited by Edith Hamilton and Huntington Cairns. Princeton: Princeton University Press, 1982.

———. *Complete Works.* Edited by John M. Cooper and D. S. Hutchinson. Indianapolis: Hackett, 1997.

Quantin, Jean-Louis. "A propos de la traduction de *philosophia* dans l'*Adversus oppugnatores vitae monasticae* de Saint Jean Chrysostome." *Revue des sciences religieuses* 61, no. 4 (October 1987): 187–97.

Ranke-Heinemann, Ute. *Eunuchs for the Kingdom of Heaven: Women, Sexuality, and the Catholic Church.* New York: Doubleday, 1990.

Rebillard, Éric. *In hora mortis: Évolution de la pastorale chrétienne de la mort au IVe et Ve siècles dans l'Occident latin.* Rome: École française de Rome, Palais Farnèse, 1994.

Reed, Annette Yoshiko. *Fallen Angels and the History of Judaism and Christianity: The Reception of Enochic Literature.* New York: Cambridge University Press, 2005.

Ricoeur, Paul. *The Symbolism of Evil.* Boston: Beacon, 1967.

Rist, John M. "Beyond Stoic and Platonist: A Sample of Origen's Treatment of Philosophy (*Contra Celsum* 4.62–70)." In *Platonismus und Christentum: Festschrift für Heinrich Dörrie*, edited by Horst-Dieter Blume and Friedhelm Mann, 228–38. Münster: Aschendorff, 1983.

———. "Plotinus on Matter and Evil." *Phronesis* 6 (1961): 154–66.

Robinson, Maurice A., and William C. Pierpont, ed. *The New Testament in the Original Greek: Byzantine Textform 2005*. Southborough, MA: Chilton, 2005.

Russell, Norman, trans. *Cyril of Alexandria*. London: Routledge, 2000.

Rylaarsdam, David M. *John Chrysostom on Divine Pedagogy: The Coherence of His Theology and Preaching*. Oxford: Oxford University Press, 2014.

Sakharov, Archimandrite Sophrony. *His Life Is Mine*. London: Mowbrays, 1977.

Schneweis, Emil. *Angels and Demons according to Lactantius*. Washington, DC: Catholic University of America Press, 1944.

Schwartz, Hans. *Evil: A Historical and Theological Perspective*. Minneapolis: Fortress, 1995.

The Services of Holy and Great Week. Columbia, MO: Newrome, 2012.

Skedros, James C. "The Cappadocian Fathers on the Veneration of the Martyrs." StPatr 37 (2001): 294–300.

Smith, J. Warren. "A Just and Reasonable Grief: The Death and Function of a Holy Woman in Gregory of Nyssa's *Life of Macrina*." *Journal of Early Christian Studies* 12, no. 1 (2004): 57–84.

———. *Passion and Paradise: Human and Divine Emotion in the Thought of Gregory of Nyssa*. New York: Crossroad, 2004.

Stark, Rodney. *The Rise of Christianity*. San Francisco: HarperSanFrancisco, 1997.

Steel, Carlos. "Proclus on the Existence of Evil." In *Proceedings of the Boston Area Colloquium in Ancient Philosophy*, edited by John J. Cleary and Gary M. Gurtler, 83–102. Leiden: Brill, 1999.

Steiner, Martin. *La tentation de Jésus dans l'interprétation patristique de Saint Justin à Origène*. Paris: Gabalda, 1962.

Stevenson, J., ed. *A New Eusebius*. London: SPCK, 1987.

Strack, Hermann L., and Paul Billerbeck. *Kommentar zum Neuen Testament aus Talmud und Midrasch*. 6 vols. Munich: Beck, 1922–61.

Sullivan, Francis A. *The Christology of Theodore of Mopsuestia*. Rome: Universitatis Gregoriana, 1956.

Symeon the New Theologian. *The Discourses*. Translated by C. J. deCatanzaro. CWS. New York: Paulist Press, 1980.

———. *On the Mystical Life: The Ethical Discourses*. Translated by Alexander Golitzin. 3 vols. Crestwood, NY: St. Vladimir's Seminary Press, 1995–97.

Tanner, Norman P., ed. *Decrees of the Ecumenical Councils*. 2 vols. London: Sheed & Ward, 1990.

Temple, William. *Readings in St. John's Gospel*. 2nd series, *Chapters xiii–xxi*. London: Macmillan, 1940.

Theodore of Mopsuestia. *Le commentaire sur les Psaumes (I–LXXX)*. Edited by Robert Devreesse. Vatican City: Biblioteca Apostolica Vaticana, 1939.

———. *The Commentaries on the Minor Epistles of Paul.* Translated by Rowan Greer. Atlanta: Society of Biblical Literature, 2010.

———. *Commentary on Psalms 1–81.* Translated by Robert C. Hill. Atlanta: Society of Biblical Literature, 2006.

———. *Commentary on the Twelve Prophets.* Translated and edited by Robert C. Hill. FC 108. Washington, DC: Catholic University of America Press, 2004.

———. *Theodori episcopi Mopsuesteni in epistolas B. Pauli commentarii.* Edited by H. B. Swete. 2 vols. Cambridge: Cambridge University Press, 1880–82.

———. *Theodori Mopsuesteni Expositionis in Psalmos.* Edited by Lucas de Coninck and Maria Josepha d'Hont. CCSL 88A. Turnhout: Brepols, 1977.

Theophilus of Antioch. *Ad Autolycum.* Translated and edited by Robert M. Grant. Oxford Early Christian Texts. Oxford: Clarendon, 1970.

Tollinton, Richard B. *Selections from the Commentaries and Homilies of Origen.* New York: Macmillan, 1929.

Vasilievskij, Vatroslav G., and P. Nikitin. *Skazanija o 42 amorijskich mucenikack.* St. Petersburg, 1905.

Waddell, Helen. *Peter Abelard: A Novel.* New York: Holt, 1933.

Ware, Kallistos T. "The Meaning of 'Pathos' in Abba Isaias and Theodoret of Cyrus." StPatr 20 (1989): 315–22.

Weinandy, Thomas G. *Does God Change? The Word's Becoming in the Incarnation.* Still River, MA: St. Bede's, 1985.

———. *Does God Suffer?* Notre Dame, IN: University of Notre Dame Press, 2000.

Weinandy, Thomas, and Daniel A. Keating, eds. *The Theology of St. Cyril of Alexandria: A Critical Appreciation.* Edinburgh: T&T Clark, 2003.

Werpehowski, William. "Weeping at the Death of Dido: Sorrow, Virtue, and Augustine's *Confessions.*" *Journal of Religious Ethics* 19 (Spring 1991): 175–91.

Wilken, Robert L. *Judaism and the Early Christian Mind: A Study of Cyril of Alexandria's Exegesis and Theology.* New Haven: Yale University Press, 1971.

Williams, Rowan. *Arius: Heresy and Tradition.* Rev. ed. Grand Rapids: Eerdmans, 2002.

———. "Macrina's Deathbed Revisited: Gregory of Nyssa on Mind and Passion." In *Christian Faith and Greek Philosophy in Late Antiquity: Essays in Tribute to George Christopher Stead*, edited by Lionel R. Wickham and Caroline P. Bammel, 227–46. Supplements to Vigiliae Christianae 19. Leiden: Brill, 1993.

Wills, Garry. *Saint Augustine: A Penguin Life.* New York: Penguin, 1999.

Wingren, Gustaf. *Man and the Incarnation: A Study in the Biblical Theology of Irenaeus.* London: Oliver & Boyd, 1959.

Wolfson, Harry A. *Philo.* LCL. Cambridge, MA: Harvard University Press, 1948.

List of Contributors

Gary A. Anderson is the Hesburgh Professor of Catholic Theology at the University of Notre Dame, specializing in Judaism and Christianity in antiquity. He is the author of *Sin: A History* (2009) and *Charity: The Place of the Poor in the Biblical Tradition* (2013), and editor of *New Approaches to the Study of Biblical Interpretation in Judaism of the Second Temple Period and in Early Christianity* (2013).

Fr. John Behr is dean and professor of patristics at St. Vladimir's Orthodox Theological Seminary. He is the author of *The Mystery of Christ: Life in Death* (2006), *Irenaeus of Lyons: Identifying Christianity* (2013), and *Becoming Human: Meditations on Christian Anthropology in Word and Image* (2013).

Brian E. Daley, SJ, is the Catherine F. Huisking Professor of Theology at the University of Notre Dame. His recent publications include *Light on the Mountain: Greek Patristic and Byzantine Homilies on the Transfiguration of the Lord* (2013), *Gregory of Nazianzus* (2006), and *The Hope of the Early Church* (1991).

Douglas Finn is assistant professor of theology at Boston College, specializing in patristics.

Paul L. Gavrilyuk is the Aquinas Chair of Theology and Philosophy at the University of St. Thomas. He is the author of *The Suffering of the Impassible God* (2004) and *Georges Florovsky and the Russian Religious Renaissance* (2014), and coeditor with Sarah Coakley of *The Spiritual Senses: Perceiving God in Western Christianity* (2012).

Nonna Verna Harrison formerly taught at Saint Paul School of Theology, specializing in patristics and church history. She is the author of *St. Basil the Great on the Human Condition* (2005), *St. Gregory of Nazianzus: Festal Orations* (2008), and *God's Many-Splendored Image* (2010).

David G. Hunter is the Cottrill-Rolfes Professor of Catholic Studies at the University of Kentucky, specializing in early Christianity and patristics. He is the author of *Marriage, Celibacy, and Heresy in Ancient Christianity: The Jovinianist Controversy* (2007) and coeditor of *The Oxford Handbook of Early Christian Studies* (2008).

John W. Martens is an associate professor at the University of St. Thomas, specializing in biblical studies. He is the author of *The End of the World: The Apocalyptic Imagination in Film and Television* (2003) and *"Let the Little Ones Come to Me": Children and Childhood in Early Christianity* (2007).

Eric Phillips has a doctorate in medieval and early Christian studies from the Catholic University of America and is a pastor at Ebenezer Lutheran Church in Nashville, Tennessee.

Dennis P. Quinn is associate professor of interdisciplinary general education and interim associate dean of the College of Education and Integrative Studies, California State Polytechnic University, Pomona, specializing in the Christianization of the Latin Roman World.

James C. Skedros is interim dean and professor of early Christianity and Byzantine history at Holy Cross Greek Orthodox School of Theology. He is the author of *St. Demetrios of Thessaloniki: Civic Patron and Divine Protector (4th–7th c. CE)* (1999).

J. Warren Smith is associate professor of historical theology at Duke Divinity School. He is the author of *Passion and Paradise: Human and Divine Emotion in the Thought of Gregory of Nyssa* (2004) and *Christian Grace and Pagan Virtue: The Theological Foundation of Ambrose's Ethics* (2010).

Regina L. Walton received a doctorate in religion and literature from Boston University and is pastor and rector of Grace Episcopal Church in Newton, Massachusetts. Her essays on George Herbert and seventeenth-century religious literature have appeared in *Studia Liturgica* and the volumes *Preaching and the Theological Imagination* (2015) and *George Herbert, Beauty, and*

Truth: New Essays on Herbert's Christian Aesthetic (forthcoming). Her poems have appeared in *Poetry East*, *Scintilla*, and other journals.

Bishop Kallistos Ware is Metropolitan of Diokleia and lecturer emeritus at the University of Oxford. He is the author of *The Orthodox Church*, new ed. (1993), *The Orthodox Way* (1995), and *The Inner Kingdom* (2000), plus other books and numerous essays.

Subject Index

history 5, 6
  human 12, 187
  universal 9, 168
sanctification 205, 208–9
Sarah (biblical) 102n22, 157n42
Satan 7, 9, 12–14, 57, 64, 66–70, 72–74, 76–79,
    100, 108, 117, 205, 210–11
Saul. *See* Paul (apostle)
Savior 43, 156, 178
science fiction 15
Scripture 34–36, 41, 115–16, 122, 128, 179, 182
Scythians 85
Semi-Pelagians 143
Sennacherib 165
sensuality 148
Septuagint 94, 224
  translators of 218
Sergius of Constantinople, Patriach 185, 186
serpent 44
sex 150–51, 154
sexual desire 154–55
sexuality 152
Sheol 78–80
Siloam 122–24
Simplician 132, 144
Simplicianus. *See* Simplician
sin 9–12, 14, 15, 27, 43–44, 61, 93, 111, 113,
    121–22, 128, 148–55, 157–60, 178
  angelic origin of 8
  human 8
  human origin of 8
  metaphor for 58, 61
  original 154
  origin of 11
  powers of 58
sinfulness 6
sinner 59
slavery 89
Smyrna 198
social class 89
social justice 86
Socrates 133–34
Son 179
  image of 37–38
Sophia 3
Sorlin, Henri 99
sorrow 10
soteriology 194, 205, 212
soul 148–150, 152, 154, 156, 158–59, 203
  pride of 149

Spirit, Holy 26, 45–46, 176, 211, 223, 225
Stagirius 106
Stoicism 97, 110, 160n53
Stoic moral theory 2
Stoics 1, 81–83, 98n2, 139
substance 186
suffering 1, 10, 11, 12, 14–15, 18–22, 25–26,
    28–29, 33, 47, 97–98, 107, 111–12, 114, 117,
    119, 148, 161, 163, 193–94, 197–99, 212,
    231–32
  human 182
  pedagogical 161, 163
  redemptive 26, 28, 32
Symeon the New Theologian 25n24
sympatheia 103
sympathy 109, 11, 113, 119
synalgein 103
Syriac fathers 64
Syriac (language) 63

Talmud 122, 128–29
Targum Onqelos 60
Taurians 85
temple, Jerusalem 121
Temple, William 224–25
Tertullian 3, 5n20, 63
Tetrarchy, Roman 55
Thalassius 187n41
theodicy 3, 5, 6, 12
  early Christian 3
Theodore (friend of Augustine) 132
Theodore of Mopsuestia 94n34, 161–70,
    181–82
Theodore the Recruit 30
Theodore the Studite 18–20
Theodoret of Cyrrhus 94n34, 181
Theodoret of Cyrus. *See* Theodoret of Cyrrhus
Theodoret of Tarsus 182
Theodorus of Mopsuestia. *See* Theodore of
    Mopsuestia
Theodosius II 191
Theophilus of Antioch 43
Theotokos. See Mary: Theotokos
Theotokos controversy 191
Thomas (apostle) 127
Thomas Aquinas 216
Tigris (river) 18
Tobit 79
tradition 34
tragic poets 1

MODERN AUTHORS INDEX

Scripture Index

Old Testament

Genesis

1 89, 95
1:26 39, 89
1:26–27a 94
1:26–27 41
1:27 89
1:28 152
1:31 33
2 94, 95
2:7 33, 123, 124
2:17 170n19
3 5
3:5 39
3:22 39
3:22–24 43n17
4:10 21
6 5
6:1–4 8
15:8 62
15:13 62
18:30 217
18:32 217
22 64
36:6 61, 62
45:5 46
50:15–17a 60
50:17 60

Exodus

2:23–25 217
3:7–8 217
6:7 162

7:5 162
15:7 229n59
32:12 216n12
32:14 216n12

Leviticus

5:1 59, 60
16:20–22 58

Numbers

20:14–15 62
25:3–4 217

Deuteronomy

1:34 217
1:37 217
29:20 217

Judges

10:16 216

1 Samuel

15:11 216n12

2 Kings

18:17–35 165n6
24:20 LXX 217

2 Chronicles

32:1–22 165n6

Job

1:1a 100
1:1b 100
1:20a 107
1:21 110, 110n72, 112
3:1–3 108
3:13–15 109
3:25 109
6:21a 111
9:2b 112
16:3–5 111

Psalms

7:9 LXX 163n3
9:21 LXX 163n2
13:5 LXX 165n7
22:4 LXX 217
46:2–3 LXX 168n14
75:12b–13 LXX 166n9
76:11 166
82:6 209n66
93:19 Vulgate 139n37
94:8 LXX 218
94:8–11 LXX 217
103:12 59
111:6 LXX 23
122:3a LXX 162n1
134 166
134:8 LXX 166n8
138:8 LXX 217

Ecclesiastes

2:7 89
5:29 149

269